Social Network Analysis

Interdisciplinary Approaches and Case Studies

Social Network Analysis

Interdisciplinary Approaches and Case Studies

Edited by
Xiaoming Fu · Jar-Der Luo · Margarete Boos

CRC Press
Taylor & Francis Group
Boca Raton   London   New York

CRC Press is an imprint of the
Taylor & Francis Group, an **informa** business

CRC Press
Taylor & Francis Group
6000 Broken Sound Parkway NW, Suite 300
Boca Raton, FL 33487-2742

© 2017 by Taylor & Francis Group, LLC

CRC Press is an imprint of Taylor & Francis Group, an Informa business

No claim to original U.S. Government works

Printed on acid-free paper

International Standard Book Number-13: 978-1-4987-3664-8 (Hardback)

Visit the Taylor & Francis Web site at
http://www.taylorandfrancis.com

and the CRC Press Web site at
http://www.crcpress.com

Contents

v

Foreword

Social network analysis has had a rich history as an intellectual enterprise. Since its inception in the 1930s and 1940s, it has made significant methodological and theoretical contributions to the analysis of social relations from microscopic relations to macroscopic systems of social networks. Initially employed to study dyadic relations and small social groups and communities, the scope of analysis and the participation of scholars have expanded significantly since the 1960s and 1970s as computers emerged as tools for analyzing larger social systems. Now, participating scholars come from a variety of disciplines, ranging from sociology, social psychology, anthropology, political science, business and management sciences, and other social and behavioral sciences to computer science, complex systems, statistics, and information and communication sciences. Interdisciplinary exchanges have become possible in many national, regional, and international meetings (e.g., most notably the annual meetings of the International Network for Social Network Analysis) and in the publications in journals (e.g., *Social Networks)* and in books and monographs.

Yet, most of the presentations, papers, and books have continued to be authored by scholars in a single discipline or at most two to three allied disciplines (e.g., sociology, management science, and social psychology). What have been lacking are truly collaborative efforts where skills and knowledge across disciplines, especially crossing the social science–computer science boundary, are brought together in advancing the methodology and theory.

The impetus for such collaborations gains momentum with the recent development and availability of Big Data, which begin to yield relationships in the cyberspace, hitherto undetected. As more computer scientists join in to mine such data, the realization of the need for substantive and strategic analyses propels more interest in dialogues between computer scientists and social and behavioral scientists. Such collaborations go beyond disciplinary boundaries, as typically scholars are bounded in their normative communities and media of presentation and publications. It would require extraordinary efforts on the part of scientists to cross such boundaries to bring such collaborations to fruition. It would also require the participation of outstanding scholars from their respective fields to advance knowledge in such collaborations.

It is, therefore, truly extraordinary to see such efforts and opportunities to have taken place when computer scientist, Xiaoming Fu, who has developed his distinguished career cross and beyond national boundaries of China and Germany, has sought and found collaborators in social sciences in China, Jar-der Luo, a sociologist, and in Germany, Margarete Boos, a social psychologist. They have brought their distinguished scholarships together, along with their colleagues, to create a book that demonstrates the utility of such collaborations in advancing the methodologies and in bringing about a deeper understanding of social structures, network behaviors, networks as complex systems, and collaborations and information dissemination in social networks. The book illustrates exemplary efforts and fruition in truly integrative collaborations between computer scientists and social and behavioral scientists. It has set a high benchmark for all such cross-disciplinary collaborations to come and has brought social network analysis to new heights.

Nan Lin
Professor of Sociology
Duke University
Durham, North Carolina

Preface

The roots of this book depict the genesis of a successful interdisciplinary, East–West academia cooperation. The book project sprung from an ongoing effort among a handful of scientists in China and Germany, following leaders of Nanjing University and the University of Göttingen having visited their respective cities in 2009. One of the originating authors, who had been involved in these visits and was shortly later appointed as a visiting chair professor at Tsinghua University, had the idea of an interdisciplinary collaboration on social network analysis between the countries' universities. To find the right sociologist in China interested in social network analysis, the coauthor phoned the university president's office of Tsinghua University and then Tsinghua University's research department head, dean of the School of Humanities and Social Sciences, and chair of the Sociology Department—who organized an introduction to an interested sociologist and eventually a contributing author to this book. At that time, yet another of the book's collaborators, who was from Nanjing University's Computer Science Department, was visiting the originating author's group at the University of Göttingen for a collaboration on the topic of mobile social networks with researchers within the university's Department of Social and Communication Psychology. As a result, the head of the said department, together with other scientists and leaders at the University of Göttingen, Nanjing University, and Tsinghua University, entered into discussions that developed into an organized Sino–German interdisciplinary collaboration on the broader domain of social networks. This intercultural, interdisciplinary collaboration took the form of several lectures, seminars, and annual workshops as well as several jointly supervised bachelor's degree, master's degree, and PhD students at Tsinghua University, Nanjing University, and the University of Göttingen.

A member of CRC Press eventually approached these collaborators for a possible book on some of the Sino–German interdisciplinary collaborations on social network analysis. We were given the freedom to organize the book's content, style, and format. In addition to solicitations for authoring book chapters from the three universities, a couple of international authors from the United Kingdom and the United States were invited and contributed several interesting chapters.

People are linked in social networks when they interact with their families, friends, colleagues, and other individuals and groups who share common interests and goals. Links in social networks are based on various reasons, which can range from family ties to the need for technical or business information transfer or other sorts of interdependencies. Today, social networks are highly dynamic entities, as they are fueled by open access to modern information and communication technologies and high geographic mobility, resulting in ever-increasing interpersonal and interdisciplinary interactions and collaborations.

This book will interest readers looking to learn more about new methods and techniques that are synthesized from the different research disciplines involved in the formation, analysis, and modeling of various traditional and digital social networks as well as their applications.

We have organized the book chapters into five clusters according to the following aspects:

- Methodologies for interdisciplinary social network research (Chapters 1 through 3)
- Social network structure (Chapters 4 through 7)
- Social network behaviors (Chapters 8 through 10)
- Social networks as complex systems and their applications (Chapters 11 and 12)
- Collaboration and information dissemination in social networks (Chapters 13 through 15)

We express our gratitude to the leaders of Nanjing University and Tsinghua University and especially to the University of Göttingen for ultimately making the publication of this book possible. We also thank the contributing authors who, as interdisciplinary collaborators often do, added the task of contributing to this collaboration to their already overextended schedule. We extend special thanks to Ruijun He at CRC Press and Taylor & Francis Group for his enduring patience as our editor and to the project coordinator, Amber Donley, in dealing with editorial matters such as layout and graphics, and a hearty thank-you to the support staff too numerous to mention. Without their help, this book edition would not have been possible.

Xiaoming Fu
Jar-Der Luo
Margarete Boos

Editors

Xiaoming Fu is a full professor of computer science and head of the Computer Networks Group at the Institute of Computer Science, University of Göttingen, Germany. He is also founding director of the Sino–German Institute of Social Computing, University of Göttingen. His research interests include Internet-based systems, protocols, and applications, including social networks. Professor Xiaoming holds a PhD in computer science from Tsinghua University, China. He is an IEEE distinguished lecturer and has served as secretary and then vice chair of the IEEE Communications Society Technical Committee on Computer Communications and chair of the Internet Technical Committee, the joint committee of the IEEE Communications Society and the Internet Society.

Jar-Der Luo is a professor at the Sociology Department, Tsinghua University in Beijing, China; he is also president of the Chinese Network for Social Network Studies and director of Tsinghua Social Network Research Center. He received his PhD in sociology from Stony Brook University in New York, supervised by Mark Granovetter. His researches cover numerous topics in social network studies, including social capital, trust, social network in Big Data, self-organization process, and Chinese indigenous management, such as guanxi, guanxi circle, and favor exchange.

Margarete Boos is a full professor of psychology and head of the Department of Social and Communication Psychology at the Institute for Psychology, University of Göttingen, Germany. Her research focuses on group psychology, especially coordination and leadership in teams, computer-mediated communication, and distributed teams, as well as methods for interaction and communication analysis. She holds a PhD in sociology. She applies her research methods and results to team diagnostics and team training and founded the start-up Malamut Team Catalyst GmbH together with colleagues in 2010. She developed the Göttingen Civil Courage Training and puts it into practice as a train-the-trainer concept in many institutions.

Contributors

Margarete Boos
Institute of Psychology

and

Sino-German Institute of Social
Computing
University of Göttingen
Göttingen, Germany

Julie Brownlie
School of Social and Political Sciences
University of Edinburgh
Edinburgh, United Kingdom

Ronald Burt
Booth School of Business

and

Department of Sociology
University of Chicago
Chicago, Illinois

Xiao Chen
Department of Computer Science
Texas State University
San Marcos, Texas

Meng-Yu Cheng
Department of Business
Administration
Feng-Chia University
Taichung, Taiwan, China

Lianghao Dai
Institute of Psychology
University of Göttingen
Göttingen, Germany

Patrick M. De Boer
Department of Computer Science
University of Zurich
Zürich, Switzerland

Fangda Fan
Department of Biostatistics
University of Illinois at Chicago
Chicago, Illinois

Tim Friede
Department of Medical Statistics
University of Göttingen
Göttingen, Germany

Xiaoming Fu
Institute of Computer Science

and

Sino-German Institute of Social
Computing
University of Göttingen
Göttingen, Germany

Hauke Fuehres
Galaxyadvisors AG
Aarau, Switzerland

Peter A. Gloor
Center for Collective Intelligence
Sloan School of Management
Massachusetts Institute of Technology
Cambridge, Massachusetts

Jens Grabowski
Institute of Computer Science
and
Sino-German Institute of Social
    Computing
University of Göttingen
Göttingen, Germany

Xiao Han
Business School
Shanghai University of Finance and
    Economics
Shanghai, China

Steffen Herbold
Institute of Computer Science
University of Göttingen
Göttingen, Germany

Wolfgang Himmel
Department of General Practice
University Medical Center
University of Göttingen
Göttingen, Germany

Daniel Honsel
Institute of Computer Science
University of Göttingen
Göttingen, Germany

Verena Herbold
Institute of Computer Science
University of Göttingen
Göttingen, Germany

Hong Huang
Institute of Computer Science
University of Göttingen
Göttingen, Germany

Yongfeng Huang
Department of Electronic Engineering
Tsinghua University
Beijing, China

Pan Hui
Department of Computer Science and
    Engineering
Hong Kong University of Science and
    Technology
Clear Water Bay, Hong Kong

Dmytro Karamshuk
Department of Informatics
King's College London
London, United Kingdom

Janka Koschack
Department of General Practice
University Medical Center
University of Göttingen
Göttingen, Germany

Ruiqi Li
School of Systems Science
Beijing Normal University
Beijing, China

Wenzhong Li
State Key Laboratory for Novel
    Software Technology
Department of Computer Science and
    Technology
and
Sino-German Institute of Social
    Computing
Nanjing University
Nanjing, Jiangsu, China

Lu Liu
TangoMe Inc.
Mountain View, California

Wei Lo
Department of Computer Science
Zhejiang University
Hangzhou, Zhejiang, China

Sanglu Lu
State Key Laboratory for Novel
    Software Technology
Department of Computer Science and
    Technology
and
Sino-German Institutes of Social
    Computing
Nanjing University
Nanjing, Jiangsu, China

Jar-Der Luo
Department of Sociology
and
Center for Social Network Research
Tsinghua University
Beijing, China

Philip Makedonski
Institute of Computer Sciences
University of Göttingen
Göttingen, Germany

Joao Marcos
Galaxyadvisors AG
Aarau, Switzerland

Jan Nagler
Computational Physics for Engineering
    Materials, IfB
ETH Zurich
Zurich, Switzerland
and
MPI for Dynamics and
    Self-Organization
Göttingen, Germany

Keiichi Nemoto
Fuji Xerox Co., Ltd.
Yokohama-shi, Kanagawa, Japan

Johannes Pritz
Courant Research Centre Evolution of
    Social Behaviour
University of Göttingen
Göttingen, Germany

Mladen Pupavac
School of Politics and International
    Relations
University of Nottingham
Nottingham, United Kingdom

Vanessa Pupavac
School of Politics and International
    Relations
University of Nottingham
Nottingham, United Kingdom

Nishanth Sastry
Department of Informatics
King's College London
London, United Kingdom

Frances Shaw
School of Social and Political Sciences
University of Edinburgh
Edinburgh, United Kingdom

Jie Tang
Department of Computer Science and
    Technology
and
Center for Social Network Research
Tsinghua University
Beijing, China

Stephan Waack
Institute of Computer Science
University of Göttingen
Göttingen, Germany

Zhiyuan Wang
School of Computer
National University of Defense
  Technology
Changsha, Hunan, China

Tongfeng Weng
Department of Computer Science and
  Engineering
Hong Kong University of Science and
  Technology
Clear Water Bay, Hong Kong

Fangzhao Wu
Department of Electronic Engineering
Tsinghua University
Beijing, China

Yaofeng Zhang
Department of Computer Science and
  Engineering
Hong Kong University of Science and
  Technology
Clear Water Bay, Hong Kong

Chaowen Zhou
Department of Sociology
Tsinghua University
Beijing, China

Yun Zhou
School of Computer
National University of Defense
  Technology
Changsha, Hunan, China

Konglin Zhu
School of Information and
  Communication Engineering
Beijing University of Posts and
  Telecommunications
Beijing, China

and

Sino-German Institute of Social
  Computing
University of Göttingen
Göttingen, Germany

METHODOLOGIES FOR INTERDISCIPLINARY SOCIAL NETWORK RESEARCH

I

Chapter 1

Methods for Interdisciplinary Social Network Studies

Xiaoming Fu, Jar-Der Luo, and Margarete Boos

Contents

1.1 Introduction

People participate in social networks when they interact with their families, friends, colleagues, and other individuals or groups. Social networks link people together via a common interest and/or other kinds of interdependencies. Today, the dynamics of social networks are often fueled by access to modern online platforms and high geographic/spatial mobility, resulting in greater interpersonal interaction. For example, Facebook, the most widely used online social networking service as of this writing, reported 1.79 billion (including 1.66 billion mobile) monthly active users as of September 30, 2016 (Facebook, n.d.). China's Tencent, one of the largest Internet companies in the world whose subsidiaries provide, among other services, instant messaging (Tencent QQ) and the mobile chat service WeChat, reported 1.1 billion registered WeChat users as of January 22, 2015, and 570 million daily active WeChat users as of November 5, 2015 (DMR, n.d.). Social networks—whether they be online or real world—are of vital importance to modern societies in that they influence daily work, contacts, and leisure activities. Social networks enable interactions for collaborating, learning, and information dissemination within physical (i.e., real world) or virtual (e.g., online) social networks.

A social network is composed of individual nodes (persons, teams, or organizations) and the ties (also called relationships, connections, edges, or links) between these individual nodes. Together these form a graph-based structure that is often complex (see e.g., Barabasi, 2003). Given the widespread presence of online social networks and also real-world networks, it is interesting to understand how a tie is created; how the network functions; what its structure looks like; and how it evolves, stabilizes, adapts, and changes. For practical cases and applications, we need to know how these features can be leveraged, such as how to bring together the strengths of diverse technical or scientific disciplines in creative collaboration, to make business or political decisions, and to develop risk-reducing measures to mitigate or control risk, for instance, in epidemics or stock markets, or even to curtail rumors/spam. This book intends to present new methods and techniques that are synthesized from different research disciplines involved in the formation, analysis, and modeling of various social networks as well as their applications.

Most existing studies on social networks (e.g., Milgram, 1967; Freeman, 2004) either study the network as a whole regarding its structure with specific relationships in the defined population, or the network from an individual perspective (so-called egocentered networks). Many have also studied the consequences for individuals who are embedded in social relations and networks, focusing, for example, on the effects in terms of receiving social support or finding a job (e.g., Granovetter, 1973). Physicists; social, behavioral, and epidemic researchers; and practitioners have developed and collected a large body of hypotheses, models, and empirical findings on the structure, processes, and consequences of social networks, both real word and online. In the last decade, online social networks have gained particular importance in everyday life due to their facilitation of the intercommunication (i.e., social networking) among a rising share of the population in modern societies. Indeed, the new forms of online social networks open up vast opportunities for studying social networks. Most networks that were studied in the social science domain were targeted at small groups, due to financial and practical limitations in accessing the data (Gjoka et al., 2010). Barriers that once made physical social networks inaccessible have now been overcome as a result of the emergence of big data storage, processing and traffic-managing capacities, and numerous social media and other online platforms. However, existing work among the so-called nodes of social networks—persons, teams, and organizations—does not yet take full advantage of the opportunities provided through interdisciplinary studies, which remains generally confined to specific fields. The result is a more intra- than interdisciplinary focus with limited advances. Interdisciplinary cooperation between social, behavioral, and epidemiological research, on one hand, and physics and computer science, on the other hand, holds the promise of enormous advances in the analysis of the potential of online social networks, and that of large-scale social networks in general.

We are pleased to witness a handful of researchers working with people from different disciplines, developing and employing various methodical approaches for studying complex social networks. A subset of such efforts is included in this book. These projects have been carried out in the form of close interdisciplinary collaborations by researchers with backgrounds in complex systems, statistics, and computer sciences, together with medical, management, behavioral, and social sciences, who continue to develop methods for data mining, network analysis, theory building, and more generally the interdisciplinary social network analysis methodologies.

By interlinking the expertise from divergent disciplines, new results and considerable progress are achievable in social network studies, as evidenced by the results reported in this book. Although a small set of chapters were written by scientists from the same discipline, knowledge and experiences from other disciplines were adopted and exploited in these chapters, constituting a broader sense of hybrid intra- and interdisciplinarity.

1.2 Methodology for Combining Big Data Mining and Qualitative Studies in Theory Building

This section will begin with a methodology developed during several case studies (e.g., see Chapters 4 through 7). In short, this methodology starts with quantitative studies, mining sample data with selected hypotheses (based on preliminary knowledge gained from a literature review), followed by qualitative analysis (e.g., through sociological interviews and questionnaires) towards ground truthing; based on this, predictions about certain network properties, patterns, or indicators can be made.

By iterating this process, which integrates qualitative and quantitative studies, several times, hypotheses can be tested and new models may be established or existing models refined.

Before going into details about the methodology, we briefly explain several terms that are frequently used in this book:

- *Big data*: data collected from the online world or other digitalized sources that are too complex or of a too huge volume to be analyzed by traditional data processing tools
- *Small data*: structured data collected from quantitative surveys performed in the real world or extracted from big data
- *Complex system*: a system consisting of elements plus the interactions between these elements
- *Data mining*: the process of finding predictors for a social phenomenon with little or no guidance of theories; in other words, extracting potentially useful (but yet-to-be-empirically-validated) patterns from data sources, for example, databases, texts, the web, images, etc.
- *Ground truth*: level of accuracy of the training set reflecting or approximating the real world or population under investigation
- *Ground truthing*: the process of garnering sufficiently representative data that reflects/approximates the real case
- *Hypothesis testing*: the process of designing an empirical study apt to falsify a hypothesis derived from theory
- *Machine learning*: similar to how humans learn from past experience, a computer (i.e., machine) system learns from data that represent some "past experiences" of the applied domain
- *Qualitative approach*: includes typical sociological methods such as interviewing, field observations, open questions' surveys, case studies, etc., which offer a way for hypothesis testing
- *Quantitative approach*: includes data mining and hypothesis testing based on structured and/or big data
- *Real-world social networks*: physical networks (e.g., families, teams, and organizations)
- *Online and other virtual social networks*: social networks that are media based (Internet, satellite, cell, Wi-Fi, computer, etc.)
- *Supervised learning*: method of labeling prior available example data (so-called training sets composed of observations, measurements, etc.) with predefined classes, which are used to train a model or algorithm to classify new data/instances into ones of the predefined classes
- *Theoretical model*: a theoretical mechanism that explains how explanatory variables influence the target social phenomenon
- *Modeling*: a process of developing a theoretical model for testing against quantitative data

- *Theory developing/building*: a process that begins with intuitions or interpretations (articulated as hypotheses), for example, on data mining results, then gives the reasoning behind the intuitions or interpretations, building a model based on said reasoning, defining the variables in the model, and collecting data from the real world to test the model in order to test the theory
- *Survey*: a method for collecting quantitative information about items in a population (Creswell, 2013)
- *Interview*: a conversation between two or more people where questions are asked by the interviewer to elicit facts or statements from the interviewee (Creswell, 2013)
- *Sampling*: selection of observations to acquire some knowledge of a statistical population (Creswell, 2013)
- *Sampling bias*: a bias in which a sample is collected in such a way that some members of the intended population are less likely to be included than others (Creswell, 2013)

The methodology of a research cycle in social network research often begins with mining of online data, with the expectation that some interesting social phenomena will be identified. We then interpret these findings by way of either a comparison with existing theories and/or by creating our own preliminary theory. Using preexisting theories and/or our own preliminary theory as a guide, various qualitative methods, such as interviews, field observations, open questions surveys, case studies, etc., can be used. Qualitative studies provide us with an understanding of ground truth, which can be used to test the findings and interpretations derived from data mining. Through the combination of ground truth, existing theories, and/or our preliminary theory, a base for theory building and hypothesis development is established. Then a model based on the operative theory is built in order to predict new facts, and more sets of data are collected for testing the theoretical model. Oftentimes, there are ground truths checked by surveys in the real world that do not jibe with our interpretation of the results of data mining, and/or further examination of initial qualitative studies reveals further observations not accessible through the findings and interpretations gained from the first-stage data mining. This will lead to a second run of data mining and qualitative studies. This process is illustrated in Figure 1.1.

The whole process of theory development concerning a social phenomenon includes several runs of data mining, interpretation, qualitative studies, and model building. Online big data opens up a new world for mining social science data upon which to build theories and for testing hypotheses to confirm theories. However, without checking the ground truth of online-mined data against real-world qualitative studies and quantitative surveys, the mining of online data remains invalidated and therefore largely useless.

Taking Chapter 7 as an example, where data about cooperation networks in the Chinese venture capital (VC) industry (based on the SiMuTon database) are

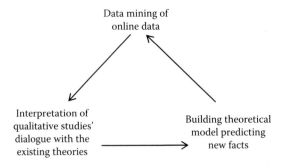

Figure 1.1 **A cycle of the dialogue between data mining and theory development.**

explored, the authors try to understand the relational circle of leading companies in this industry. Just like a Dunbar circle (Dunbar, 1992), an industry leader has several layers of partners in his/her egocentered network, differentiated by the frequency of their cooperation. A high cooperation frequency indicates a strong tie between two partners. Analyses of this industrial network using the exponential random graph model (ERGM) (Frank and Strauss, 1986; Wasserman and Pattison, 1996) show that different layers of partnership are separated by the following frequencies of cooperation: 2, 4, and 7 or 8. This result poses the following questions: Is this finding true? What is the meaning of the thresholds that separate cooperation ties of different strengths? For example, what makes cooperating once different from cooperating twice? Qualitative studies allow us to answer these questions by providing detailed information concerning a VC firm's behavior and motivations, while quantitative studies provide an overall picture of an industry and the average behaviors of different types of VC firms. Both of them are important for investigating a VC firm's syndication network and the motivation behind the networking behaviors.

The mixed approach through the dialogue between (1) big data mining, (2) qualitative studies and ground truth, and (3) theoretical modeling has been found to be very productive in many fields of social network studies, especially for modeling dynamic networks (Luo, 2011; Small, 2011; Creswell, 2013). While data mining is useful for generating some preliminarily quantitative indicators or discovering some patterns regarding certain social phenomenon, mixed methods show their utility through their strong ability to validate preliminary findings. Chapter 4 provides another example case to illustrate this. The authors try to uncover the guanxi circle of a department leader in a Chinese organizational setting. A guanxi circle, also like a Dunbar circle, has three layers of followers collected around an egocentered network. This poses a research question: Which methods can be used to quantitatively measure a leader's guanxi circle? By collecting quantitative network data, the authors devised several computing methods to answer this question.

At the same time, they employed three qualitative methods: field observations, interviews with key personnel, and reports written by leaders themselves. These methods are used to approximate ground truth, which allows us to validate various computing methods and select the best one.

1.3 A Tour of Interdisciplinary Approaches and Case Studies Presented in this Book

The methodological approach presented in Section 1.2 is not unique; many other studies have followed the same or similar (either extended or simplified) method, as described in the chapters of this book. We have organized these chapters into five clusters according to the following aspects:

1. Methodologies for interdisciplinary social network research (Chapters 1 through 3)
2. Social network structure (Chapters 4 through 7)
3. Social network behaviors (Chapters 8 and 9)
4. Social networks as complex systems and their applications (Chapters 10 through 12)
5. Collaboration and information dissemination in social networks (Chapters 13 through 15)

An overview of these chapters is as follows:

Title of the Chapter	Involved Disciplines	Applied Methodological Approaches
1. Methods for Interdisciplinary Social Network Studies	Computer science Sociology Social psychology	Synthesis from some specific cases, modeling, ground truthing combining quantitative and qualitative studies
2. Reflections on Initial Experiences with Transdisciplinary Engagement between Computer Science and the Social Sciences	Computer science International relations Sociology	Quantitative, qualitative, case studies

(Continued)

Title of the Chapter	Involved Disciplines	Applied Methodological Approaches
3. How Much Sharing Is Enough? Cognitive Patterns in Interdisciplinary Collaborations	Social psychology Sociology Computer science Physics	Survey, interview, modeling, theory building combining quantitative and qualitative studies
4. The Measurement of Guanxi Circles—Using Qualitative Study to Modify Quantitative Measurement	Sociology Computer science Management	Survey, interview, modeling, multiple runs of quantitative—qualitative iteration, validation
5. Analysis and Prediction of Triadic Closure in Online Social Networks	Computer science Sociology	Data mining, modeling, machine learning, validation
6. The Prediction of Venture Capital Co-Investment Based on Structural Balance Theory	Computer science Sociology Management	Data mining, machine learning, theory building, new hypothesis
7. Repeated Cooperation Matters—An Analysis of Syndication in the Chinese VC Industry by ERGM Model	Sociology Computer science Management	Hypothesis testing, data mining, machine learning, theory building
8. Patterns of Group Movement on a Virtual Playfield—Empirical and Simulation Approaches	Social psychology Computer science	Hypothesis testing, data mining, simulation, validation
9. Social Spammer and Spam Message Detection in an Online Social Network—A Co-Detection Approach via Exploiting Social Contexts	Computer science	Hypothesis testing, data mining, validation
10. Cultural Anthropology through the Lens of *Wikipedia*	Management science Computer science Anthropology	Data mining, modeling, intercultural comparison studies

(Continued)

Title of the Chapter	Involved Disciplines	Applied Methodological Approaches
11. From Social Networks to Time Series: Methods and Applications	Computer science Physics/complex systems	Modeling, data mining, and validation
12. How Do Online Social Networks Grow?	Computer science Physics/complex systems	Modeling, data mining, and validation
13. Information Dissemination in Social-Featured Opportunistic Networks	Computer science Physics/complex systems	Modeling, data mining, and validation
14. Sources of Information and Behavioral Patterns in Health Online Fora	Medical science (medical statistics and general practice) Computer science	Hypothesis, data mining, validation, qualitative and quantitative studies
15. Mining Big Data for Analyzing and Simulating Collaboration Factors Influencing Software Development Decisions	Theoretical computer science Practical computer science (software engineering)	Data mining, simulation, model building, and validation

1.3.1 Part I: Methodologies for Interdisciplinary Social Network Research

The first cluster of chapters focuses on interdisciplinary methodological aspects, starting with this chapter (Chapter 1), which presents general concepts, a methodological framework, and examples for interdisciplinary social network research, followed by an overview of the whole book.

The authors of Chapter 2 study the transdisciplinary collaboration between computer scientists, who take a primarily quantitative approach, and qualitative researchers in sociology and international relations from different universities. The chapter aims to understand how online platforms support or hinder the sharing of empathy and trust among people in extreme and vulnerable circumstances, through analyzing the human interactions in two exemplary topics: Digital Outreach and Emotional Distress, and Trust and Empathy Online in Disasters and Humanitarian Crises. It offers an iterative process model of research, starting with a qualitative approach, developing a classification schema and sampled coding of social media posts (expertise of social scientists), employing scaling mechanisms such as some customized machine learning framework to extrapolate the results of sampled coding to the data sets of a significantly larger scale quantitatively (expertise of computer scientists), then formulating qualitative cross-sectional analysis and interpretations of the data to understand what happened (requiring knowledge of both computer science and social science).

In Chapter 3, the authors present an investigative combination of two contemporary topics in scientific research: interdisciplinary collaborations and social networking—specifically Facebook. Exemplified by three actual case studies, either data initiated (computer scientists and physicists) or theory initiated (sociology and social psychology), the authors demonstrate that social networking goes far beyond its obvious use as a resource for bringing different disciplines together and that online social networking can be applied as a research platform to support such collaborations. After a review of how interdisciplinary collaboration is advancing today's empirical projects, the chapter focuses on the following three points that appear to dictate the success or failure of an interdisciplinary collaboration: (1) participants' acceptance of the differences in their methodological approaches, (2) importance of mutual benefit from the collaboration, and (3) willingness to combine strengths of disparate disciplines to actualize participants' mutually beneficial collaboration goals. The authors further elaborate on how these points can be quantified and qualified using the so-called "cognitive mapping" method to measure the quality and extent of sharing required for a successful interdisciplinary collaboration.

1.3.2 Part II: Social Network Structure

The second cluster applies interdisciplinary approaches to the analysis and applications for several typical social network structures, namely, dyad, triad, and quad.

Understanding guanxi networks (Fei, 1948/1992; Lin, 2001) inside Chinese organizations—usually considered as a dyadic structure (Figure 1.2)—is the topic of Chapter 4. As qualitative measures of guanxi have rarely been reported, the authors propose an approach for measuring and quantifying guanxi circles in a Chinese organization. The authors employ a typical, computational sociological method to collect egocentric relationship data for each member and conduct in-depth interviews to approximate the ground truth for testing the accuracy of the calculation of quantitative indicators of guanxi circles. After several runs of experiments, the guanxi circles with the highest accuracy rate are identified.

Figure 1.2 **A group of two nodes form the smallest social group: a dyad. The relationship between two nodes can be asymmetric or symmetric and can be based on family relation, common interests, work, trust, a joint action, etc.**

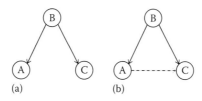

Figure 1.3 A group of three nodes form a social group called a triad. A triad can be **(a)** open or **(b)** closed. Triadic closure is a typical means for people to make connections in social networks.

In Chapter 5, the authors applied data mining on one month of Weibo (the "Chinese Tweeter") data. They were able to show that patterns of triads (Figure 1.3) in online social networks can be characterized into several key factors influencing triadic closure: user demographics (location, gender, and verified status), network structure, and social perspectives (popularity, structure hole, gregariousness, and status). The authors proposed a probabilistic machine learning model that incorporates the key factors observed from their small data analysis, then they used the mined big data to train the model parameters for predicting the closure with new data. Experiments involving the big data data sets showed that the proposed model achieved over 90% accuracy (2%–4% point higher than existing methods) for predicting triadic closure. Due to the weakness of data being entirely based on an online social network platform, the ground truth of such data is difficult to confirm, which will be validated with real-world qualitative studies and surveys.

In Chapter 6, the authors present some interesting findings from data mining that map well with the structural balance theory (see illustrated VC structures in Figure 1.4). The structural balance theory explains that a social system will incline to structure-balanced status (Figure 1.4b and d). The authors used the theory to identify what they propose are the top 10 factors influencing relationship building among Chinese VC investors. The list development was based on the structure of

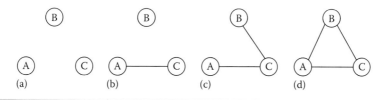

Figure 1.4 Illustration of VC configurations according to structural balance theory. Each node represents a VC, and VCs connected by a line are called co-investors. The structural balance theory implies an inclination toward two nodes joined as one VC co-investor pair **(b)** or all three pairs of VCs joined as co-investors **(d)**. **(a)** No joint investment; **(b)** A and B joint invest; **(c)** C joint invests with A and B; **(d)** each pair joint invests.

VC joint investment decisions, building on the triads of the structural balance theory (see Chapter 4) and a combination of quantitative (data mining) and qualitative (interpretation) processes. As in previous chapters, the interdisciplinary method played an important role in the "qualitative–quantitative–qualitative" iterative process.

The authors' findings suggest that common friends substantially increase the possibility of co-investment between the open ends in an open triad, leading to an important question: who are the friends—or, more precisely, trustworthy partners—for a VC co-investor? How many iterations of co-investment can indicate such friendship?

To answer this question, the authors of Chapter 7 model the decisions of joint VC investments as a quadratic network structure and its closure problem and employ the guanxi circle theory to assist in the analysis of such a network evolution process.

In a two-mode network of VCs and invested companies, as shown in Figure 1.5, the basic analytical element for two VCs is an open quadrangle (Figure 1.5a). There is an open quadrangle between two VCs, VC1 and VC2; as per Figure 1.5a, VC1 had initially invested in $Firm_1$ and $Firm_2$ and VC2 had initially invested in $Firm_1$. But when VC2 decided to also invest in $Firm_2$, the quadrangle then became closed (Figure 1.5b). The density of closeness represents the strength of the syndication tie between the two VCs. From the methodological perspective, the run of dialogues between qualitative and quantitative studies performed here functions as follows. First, some preliminary qualitative interviews and surveys are conducted for developing the theory. In the quadrangle model (Figure 1.5), the guanxi circle theory (mentioned in Chapter 4) assumes that open quadrangles can induce the formation of closed quadrangles, and a syndication tie with more joint investments formed between any pair of VCs will have higher probability in closing their open quadrangles. Second, by employing a statistical learning-based ERGM, the authors mine the borderlines between different types of friends to investigate the effects of syndication tie strength on the formation of closed quadrangles. As mentioned earlier, the more joint investments between two VCs, with open quadrangles and other network features as controls, the stronger the tie is between two VCs. A new run of

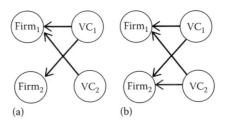

(a)   (b)

Figure 1.5   A group of four nodes forms a social group called quad or quadrangle, which is useful for more complex network study. An open quad can become closed by adding new links. (a) An open quadrangle; (b) A closed quadrangle.

a qualitative study will be performed, which is expected to modify the guanxi circle theory as it applies to this study.

1.3.3 Part III: Social Network Behaviors

In Chapter 8, the authors start with a brief description of why humans and other primate animals have evolved to live in groups, then they go on to describe phenomena such as swarming and flocking among larger groups. The authors establish that these group movement patterns are an expression of locally transmitted movement information occurring among the groups' members rather than transmitted centrally from the group leader. The chapter introduces the ground-breaking HoneyComb virtual playground, a research platform developed and applied to test whether and to what extent such evolutionary swarming movement patterns are expressed by humans. The described empirical studies that use this platform include manipulations to test whether the said patterns in humans can be compromised by motivators that benefit the individual rather than the group. The results produced by this interdisciplinary collaboration between social researchers, on one hand, and computer scientists, on the other hand, are an example of the promise of such collaborations when methodological differences are overcome.

The rich number of microblogging websites attracts many social spammers, who post massive social spam messages containing noisy and even dangerous content. It is therefore important to detect these social spammers and spam messages. In Chapter 9, the authors leverage three social contexts related to microblogs: (1) the friend and follower relationships between users, (2) the posting relations between users and messages, and (3) the connections between messages for detecting social spammers and spam messages in microblogging simultaneously. Experiments on a real-world microblog data set show that the proposed method can achieve an accuracy of over 86% for spammer detection (about 3%–4% point higher than alternative approaches) and over 92% (about 2% point higher than alternative approaches) for spam message detection. Although this chapter is technically not interdisciplinary in nature, the authors, who are computer scientists, propose a hypothesis that incorporates behavior science (here, assumptions for the spamming behavior detection mechanisms), conduct further data analysis, and find that the attribution of user-related social contexts (1 and 2) is effective for predicting spammers while the message-related contexts (2 and 3) provide good indicators for predicting messages, verifying the authors' hypothesis.

1.3.4 Part IV: Social Networks as Complex Systems and Their Applications

This cluster of chapters addresses several issues related to the analysis of complex social networks and their applications. Complex systems (systems in which the whole is the sum of its parts plus the interactions between those parts) and network science are a way to characterize various social networks, real world and online. However, depicting social networks with topological structures alone and without considering temporal and dynamic aspects may not fully capture the underlying mechanisms of complex systems. Several studies in this book attempt to address this issue.

Cultural and intercultural studies on traditional anthropological fieldwork is based on literature and textbooks, as well as storytelling from real-world individuals, but is limited due to the large amount of unstructured information in the books and the rather small number of individuals a research group can survey or interview. The emergence of *Wikipedia* articles in different languages offers a new means to study different cultures. The treatment of native speakers of different *Wikipedia* articles can be used as input for statistical analysis to understand the corresponding cultures and their differences. In Chapter 10, the authors introduce their own "Wikihistory," what they describe as a dynamic temporal map of the most influential people of all times in four different languages in *Wikipedia* (English, German, Chinese, and Japanese), which reflects a complex anthropological network structure. The authors also examine the different distributions of gender in English, Portuguese, Spanish, and German *Wikipedia*. Their comparison of these cultures focuses on gender equality, as well as sentiment and emotionality in Wikinews, the manually edited news page, which is a part of the Wikipedia Foundation.

Transforming social network structure into time series would help in understanding the mechanisms governing seemingly different social networks. In Chapter 11, the authors investigated a deterministic transformation method and a finite-memory, random-walk-based method for defining a network as a stochastic dynamical system. The former depicts the relationship between periodicity of time series and randomness of network structure analytically, but it is only applicable for the small-world network (Milgram, 1967) as it does not provide a unique way of assigning the temporal information. The latter leverages the long-range correlations of transformed time series, which can reflect the mixing pattern of online social networks. Specifically, the long-range correlation shows an assortative mixing pattern, while anticorrelation corresponds to a disassortative one. This interdisciplinary collaboration between computer scientists and physicists finds that these relationships are consistent across various social networks.

Understanding the user population growth of online social networks spatially and temporally would help describe the network dynamics and evolution, as well as city planning and resource allocation. In Chapter 12, the authors used the data from three online social network sites and applied statistical methods to fit into previously reported patterns of other systems, finding that the population growth in these networks was significantly determined neither by population size nor by spatial factors. These findings deviate from Gibrat's law (the proportional rate of growth of an organization is independent of its absolute size), as previously found in many social and economic systems. The findings of this interdisciplinary collaboration between computer scientists and physicists described in this chapter are not yet conclusive, as the reason why some data sets exhibit different patterns has not been fully revealed. Further analysis, experiments on other data sets, and possibly dialogues with social science knowledge and models are needed.

1.3.5 Part V: Collaboration and Information Dissemination in Social Networks

Information dissemination and collaborations are common uses of social networks, both real-world and virtual. One application of virtual social networks is to improve the efficiency of information dissemination in opportunistic networks using social network properties. A so-called opportunistic mobile social network exploits the mobile phone users' social characteristics, such as similarities, daily routines, mobility patterns, and interests to perform message routing and data sharing. The users of mobile phone nodes are able to form on-the-fly social networks through their phones working in ad hoc mode and by communicating with each other only when they move into their ad hoc network's communication range. This allows people to communicate without the Internet's network infrastructure. In order for these mobile devices to exchange information only when humans come into contact, opportunistic mobile social networks are tightly coupled with human social networks. In Chapter 13, the authors study how social features such as users' social profiles, social relationships, and network structures can be better exploited to build even more efficient information dissemination schemes. In this work, an opportunistic communication network is described as a complex network with social features where social profiles can be addressed to study the encounter opportunities of human beings. According to the principle of homophily, people tend to be associated with similar others regarding age, gender, class, and organizational role. The authors propose the concept of *social profile similarity*, which quantifies the degree of homophily between users in the opportunistic network and is intended to be used by the authors as an indicator to infer the future communication opportunities between individuals. This interdisciplinary project attempts to leverage the social network structure to achieve efficiency of the information dissemination process, more specifically the community structure. Community structure in opportunistic social networks occurs due to the regional characteristics of human movement and the local and remote contact patterns of individuals. To reveal this community structure, the authors design distributed community detection algorithms to eventually be used for improving the efficiency of information dissemination for intracommunity and intercommunity communications. As in Chapter 12, with the data-driven collaboration between computer scientists and physicists, further quantitative study would be desirable to understand why and how the different determining factors of such differentiating mechanisms alter the behavior of these opportunistic networks.

In Chapter 14, the authors study the emergence and evolution of online health information platforms and how online forums and social media have transformed the historically passive stance of a medical patient into what is today known as the "expert patient." The main variables that complicate this phenomenon—access to pseudoscientific information without the background to judge its soundness, and as of yet the lack of a comprehensive understanding of the information flows of health information in the scientific and lay communities—are harnessed by focusing on a single health malady. The authors then probe the "Pandora's box" of information available about this malady by developing and applying a six-task quantifying and qualifying analysis method to better understand the who, how, what, and why issues that affect the handling and "expert patient" understanding of this malady.

In Chapter 15, the authors first conduct a series of data mining to explore some collaboration characteristics in software development, such as how many developers are in an artifact, how work loading is distributed among them, how many direct and indirect collaborators are involved in the work of a certain software developer, etc. The authors then developed an explanatory model for assessment based on two hypotheses, which are supported by the existing arguments of network theory. The first assumes that if two developers are familiar with each other from working together in the past, they will achieve a better result than a collaboration of two strangers, since familiar partners have built mutual trust and a tacit understanding of each other. The second assumes that a collaboration project between two developers embedded in a dense network will decrease the likelihood of defects, since both of them are well acquainted with the behavioral patterns and norms in this dense network. Based on the dialogue with the existing network theory, the assessment model is further transformed into a defect prediction model—a model for simulating a software development process and predicting its outcomes. This project is meant to represent an example of a completed cycle from data mining to a dialogue with the existing theory in order to build a dynamic model for predicting future outcomes.

References

Barabasi, A.-L. (2003). *Linked: How Everything Is Connected to Everything Else and What It Means*, New York: Plume.

Burt, R.S. (1992). *Structural Holes: The Social Structure of Competition*, Cambridge, MA: Harvard University Press.

Creswell, J.R. (2013). *Research Design: Qualitative, Quantitative, and Mixed Methods Approaches* (4th edn.), Los Angeles, CA: SAGE Publications.

DMR (n.d.). 83 amazing WeChat statistics (November 2016). DMR Digital Report. http://expandedramblings.com/index.php/wechat-statistics/, retrieved on December 8, 2016.

Dunbar, R.I.M. (1992). Neocortex size as a constraint on group size in primates. *Journal of Human Evolution*, 22(6): 469–493.

Facebook (n.d.). Facebook company information. http://newsroom.fb.com/company-info/, retrieved on December 8, 2016.

Fei, X.T. (1948/1992). *From the Soil, the Foundations of Chinese Society*, Berkeley, CA: University of California Press. (Translated by G. Hamilton and Z. Wang. Xiangtu Zhongguo. Shanghai, China: Observer).

Frank, O. and Strauss, D. (1986). Markov graphs. *Journal of the American Statistical Association*, 81: 832–842.

Freeman, L.C. (2004). *The Development of Social Network Analysis: A Study in the Sociology of Science*. Vancouver, British Columbia, Canada: Booksurge Publishing.

Gjoka, M., Kurant, M., Butts, C.T., and Markopoulou, A.P. (2010). Walking in Facebook: A case study of uniform sampling of OSNs. *IEEE INFOCOM 2010*, San Diego, CA.

Granovetter, M. (1973). The strength of weak ties. *The American Journal of Sociology*, 78(6): 1360–1380.

Lin, N. (2001). Guanxi: A conceptual analysis. In: So, A.Y., Lin, N., and Poston, D. (eds.) *The Chinese Triangle of Mainland China, Taiwan, and Hong Kong. Comparative Institutional Analysis*. Westport, CT: Praeger.

Luo, J.-D. (2011). When social networks meet complex networks. *Keynote Speech in the Seventh National Complexity Science Annual Conference*, Chengdu, China, October 21–23, 2011.

Milgram, S. (1967). The small world problem. *Psychology Today*, 2: 60–67.

Small, M.L. (2011). How to conduct a mixed methods study: Recent trends in a rapidly growing literature. *Annual Review of Sociology*, 37(1): 57–86.

Wasserman, S. and Pattison, P.E. (1996). Logit models and logistic regression for social networks: I. An introduction to Markov graphs and p∗. *Psychometrika*, 61: 401–425.

Chapter 2

Towards Transdisciplinary Collaboration between Computer and Social Scientists: Initial Experiences and Reflections

Dmytro Karamshuk, Mladen Pupavac, Frances Shaw, Julie Brownlie, Vanessa Pupavac, and Nishanth Sastry

Contents

2.1 Introduction

The aim of this chapter is to explore a collaboration between computer scientists (NS and DK), who take a primarily quantitative approach, and qualitative researchers in sociology (JB and FS) and international relations (VP and MP). This computational social science collaboration is taking place within a large project, the "Space for Sharing" study, which aims to investigate how online platforms support or hinder the sharing of empathy and trust among people in extreme and vulnerable circumstances. The collaboration between JB, FS, DK, and NS is discussed in the section "Digital Outreach and Emotional Distress," and the collaboration between MP, VP, DK, and NS is discussed in the section "Trust and Empathy Online during Disasters and Humanitarian Crises." Although the two collaborations are reasonably independent of each other, there are fundamental commonalities that we hope will provide some food for thought on the nature of interactions between computer and social scientists.

In the following, we introduce the benefits of such interdisciplinary work within the emerging field of computational social science and describe the overall context for our collaborations. Following this, we report on our two collaborative efforts (Sections 2.2 and 2.3) and draw conclusions and lessons from our experience (Section 2.4).

2.1.1 Reflections on Computational Social Science

The Internet is transforming human relations and how we study them. Direct communication about how we feel, think, and behave is increasingly giving way to interactions that are mediated by Internet-based software such as online social networks or instant messaging platforms. Every interaction we make on such platforms can potentially be recorded, resulting in an extensive trace of our online actions and communications—a trace that sometimes can tell us more about people than they intend to reveal themselves.

Many studies have made use of data constituted through such online communications. A prominent example of the transformation that the Internet brings in studying human relations is the so-called "small-world" experiment (Travers and Milgram 1969), which showed experimentally that people are all connected within an average of *six degrees of separation*. The original experiment involved randomly selected subjects in Kansas and Nebraska, USA, who were asked to send a letter to a recipient in Massachusetts (if they knew him or her directly) or forward it to someone they knew *on a first name basis*, who, in their opinion, might be in a better position to forward the letter to the final recipient using the same rules. In the early years of this century, a team of physicists at Columbia University confirmed the six-degree-of-separation hypothesis on a considerably larger scale—a data set of e-mail conversations from 60k users (Dodds et al. 2003). Around the same time, computer scientist Jon Kleinberg analyzed the small-world phenomenon from an algorithmic perspective (Kleinberg 2000, 2001) and was one of the first to demonstrate that not only people are connected by very short paths but also they tend to be very good at finding those paths. The work of Kleinberg, Dodds et al., and many others since then has contributed to a proliferation of digital approaches to the study of human relations and transformed what once was the prerogative of social scientists into a truly interdisciplinary field, one that has been termed "computational social science" (Lazer et al. 2009).

The emerging computational social science literature has also cleverly used web data to test hypotheses and theories in various other areas of social science. For instance, De Choudhury et al. (2013) analyzed depression among Twitter users by measuring behavioral attributes relating to social engagement, emotion, language and linguistic styles, ego networks, and mentions of antidepressant medications. The authors identified significant indicators of depression in social media including a decrease in social activity, raised negative affect, and highly clustered ego networks. Althoff et al. (2014), by analyzing at scale an online community devoted to giving away free pizza to strangers that ask for one, attest how sociological concepts of *status and similarity* and linguistic characteristics of *politeness, sentiment, and reciprocity* lead to requests for favors being met. In Garcia et al. (2014), the authors conducted a large-scale evaluation of the *Bechdel Test*, which measures male bias in films. Experiments conducted on two large online social networks suggested that Twitter conversations have a clear male bias, which is not observed in Myspace discussions.

Given the increasing number of researchers employing such methods, few would disagree that *digitalization of social science* has the potential to significantly transform our understanding of human relationships. However, large-scale analysis of digital human traces also risks the loss of direct communication with *real people*—a core feature of traditional social science. While the task of revealing and understanding complex patterns of interactions between hundreds of millions of users can hardly be done via traditional interviews and surveys, it is also true that there are limits to what can be understood about individual users' perceptions and experience without direct communication with them. Computational social scientists working within rigorous mathematical norms may avoid making qualitative judgments, yet in traditional social sciences, such interpretation often yields the deepest insights.

One approach to tackling these limitations in computational science and combining the best of two worlds involves the creation of environments for interdisciplinary collaboration where social scientists can work with scientists from other disciplines on a common research agenda. Indeed, various initiatives including *interdisciplinary conferences* on social science (e.g., AAAI ICWSM, IEEE SocialCom, IC²S²), *interdisciplinary research centers* (e.g., MediaLab Amsterdam, Oxford Internet Institute), and *funding schemes* that encourage interdisciplinary research have been recently introduced.

2.1.2 Context: "Space for Sharing" ESRC Project

The authors of this chapter were awarded, with other colleagues, funding of a £1.3M study, by the UK Economic and Social Research Council (ESRC). The project was commissioned in the scope of a larger funding call "to develop a greater understanding of how empathy and trust are developed, maintained, transformed, and lost in social media interactions." Combining the research efforts of investigators from six different universities in the United Kingdom, the team comprises researchers from computer science, medical informatics, sociology, international relations, and philosophy and media theory. Transdisciplinary research across these disciplines is an explicit and fundamental goal of the "Space for Sharing" project* and we return to what we mean by this later in this chapter.

In "Space for Sharing," we are working toward a joint understanding of trust and empathy among users in various extreme circumstances including disasters and humanitarian crisis and emotional distress. People in these circumstances can be extremely vulnerable, and some of them may be seeking help that could make the difference between life and death. It may be necessary to establish trust and empathy very quickly to make that difference. In such extreme situations, people may end up oversharing information, or they may be disadvantaged by not sharing enough. At the same time, others in the online community need to know when they are responding to genuine distress.

To understand how empathy and trust mediate sharing practices in these circumstances, we have analyzed not only a wide range of data sources including public spaces for sharing (such as Twitter), but also more intimate communication channels (such as e-mails). The knowledge acquired through this analysis may transform how resources and aid are distributed on a local and global basis but also could enhance individual and community resilience. In the next two sections, we explore how computer and social scientists can work together to investigate these themes in relation to two different spheres: emotional distress and humanitarian and disaster-linked crises.

---

* A Shared Space & A Space for Sharing—http://www.space4sharingstudy.org/.

2.2 Digital Outreach and Emotional Distress

The sub-project, 'Digital Outreach and Emotional Distress', is shaped by the sociology of emotions and personal relationships (JB) on the one hand and Internet and social media studies (FS) on the other. It seeks to understand how empathy and trust play out in social interactions around emotional distress in online spaces. How do the spaces in which interactions take place shape response, and what is different about emotional support through social media compared with other online and offline contexts?

The project partner in this collaboration is *Samaritans UK*. Samaritans is a large voluntary organization that offers support to people in emotional distress through a variety of channels, including e-mail. As part of its effort to engage in other forms of digital outreach, the organization recently attempted to develop and launch a tool to help others provide support to people in emotional distress through Twitter.* For these reasons, the spaces of e-mail and Twitter emerged as topical and organizationally relevant sites for the study of the digital sharing of emotions and of empathy and trust online.

The aim is to find out about experiences of emotional support via e-mail (and to some extent via Samaritans' text messaging service) compared with other nondigital methods that the organization has employed—particularly phone, but also face-to-face. But we also want to find out how the move toward digital outreach fits or not with the organization's history, its nature of service, and philosophical approach to emotional support. Against this backdrop, we have been working with our computer science colleagues to explore and talk about emotional distress on Twitter. Key considerations have included the questions we can most usefully ask about such talk: how best can we go about collecting and analyzing relevant Twitter data and what are the ethics of doing so? Some of these are questions we are still trying to answer, but we explore the following three emergent aspects that might help shed light on interdisciplinary approaches to social media and big data research.

2.2.1 Balancing What Is Possible with What Is Meaningful

There is a seductive quality in working with big data: the larger the data set, the greater the possibility for developing models that are robust enough to be applied to other data sets. From a computer science perspective, this is a worthwhile aim in and of itself, though from within computing science there is also a growing awareness that this aim would be enriched by social-science-informed hypotheses (Lazer et al. 2009). While there are reservations about the assumptions embedded in datafication (van Dijck 2014), unease around big data analysis is writ larger when what the data involved are assumed to provide a measure of "emotions" and "relationships."

---

* Samaritans Radar, a Twitter app that was designed to alert users to tweets that people they follow had made that might signal some form of emotional distress. The application proved controversial and was taken down 8 days after launch due to a number of concerns.

Sociological research has aimed to develop a more nuanced understanding of emotions—framing these as fluid, as relational, and as not always expressible or even recognizable by self (e.g., see Brownlie 2014; Burkitt 2014). The messiness of emotions—how they are felt, expressed, and made sense of—sits uneasily with an approach that makes use of *sentiment analysis*, which attempts to quantify positivity and negativity. There are well-recognized limits of the computational understanding of the context of word use (e.g., figurative language and sarcasm), but from a sociological perspective, there are also epistemological and ontological problems with measuring emotions and reducing their complexity to fixed categories. Unease with the quantification of emotion is not new, but what is new is the scale and predictive drive of the analysis of big data. Part of working across disciplines in this context, then, involves being aware of how we are constituting and conceptualizing emotions through our research, and acknowledging these constructions might be at best in tension and at worst contradictory.

2.2.2 Small Data in Big Data

One part of our work with our computer science colleagues involves using a typology to examine tweets that are public responses to highly publicised deaths by suicide (whether the deaths of public figures or people who have become well known posthumously). This combines domain expert–led coding of social media posts with a machine learning–driven analysis of the phenomena on large-scale data sets. The expertise of social scientists is drawn on not only in the initial stages of the analysis to develop a coding schema for classifying social media posts, but also in the later stages when large-scale quantitative measurements are conducted. An actual labeling step might be outsourced to crowdsourcing platforms, for example, Amazon Mechanical Turk, ClickWorker, Cloud Crowd, and Micro Task. The expertise required from the computer scientists lies in providing scaling mechanisms to extrapolate the results of sampled coding to the data sets of a significantly larger scale. The scaling mechanism requires a custom machine learning framework designed to recognize a labeled class from a statistical distribution and linguistic characteristics of the words that appear in the posts. It is worth noting that a similar approach has been previously used to analyze politeness in social networks (Danescu-Niculescu-Mizil et al. 2013), community response to gun shootings in the United States (Glasgow et al. 2014), and understanding loneliness among Twitter users (Kivran-Swaine et al. 2014).

The approach mentioned earlier is consistent with a qualitatively driven approach to mixed method research (Mason 2006) as here qualitative analysis is being used as a way of improving key word searches in big data sets. However, there are limits to the depth of the qualitative work that can take place in relation to particular tweets. For example, tweets could appear to do the work of blaming or scapegoating a particular person or organization for a person's death by suicide, but without additional qualitative analysis, we cannot understand what arguments were used to make such claims or even who or what was blamed and how particular groups or individuals articulated these claims over time in the data.

For this reason, an iterative and complementary approach to quantitative and qualitative analysis of data has been most fruitful in our project design:

1. Qualitative methods provide the typology.
2. Computational methods process the data into categories.
3. Quantitative methods help us to find patterns in the data.
4. Qualitative analysis enables us to take a cross section of those data and understand what happened in that moment.

In the process of creating a typology, we look for emergent themes through qualitative coding. This involves zooming in on a sample of a thousand or so tweets among hundreds of thousands or even millions of tweets in the full data set. However, there is a problem with this approach, as it is time-consuming and cannot be understood in the context of the full data set. For example, we might know that some participants called for political activism in the Twitter discussion that followed a particular death by suicide, but we do not know how widespread this was or when it began to emerge unless we attempted to code a very large subset of tweets. This is too time-consuming and difficult a task for qualitative coders to undertake over a data set that might have millions of tweets. Computational methods then become useful because they can process the data automatically into different categories, which can then be tracked across time using quantitative methods. We could then identify a moment in time when calls for political activism increased. However, quantitative and computational methods cannot tell us *why*, *by whom*, or *how* these social practices were enacted, so we then need to return to qualitative analysis to understand how participants were behaving and explaining their behavior at that moment in time. In this final stage of the analysis, we can find out who is advocating political activism, what that activism involves, and how participants articulated the need for this activism to others. These are the *small data in the big data*, and an interdisciplinary approach is appropriate for seeking it out.

This movement between qualitative and quantitative research reminds us that even when making data "big," the small data through which it is constituted can point to narratives that counter the big picture. This iterative approach surfaces the ways big data are constituted and helps to challenge the idea of such data as raw, objective data (boyd and Crawford 2012), but at the same time, it recognizes that the work of processing big data allows us to find and systematically explore the small.

2.2.3 Finding the Everyday

Lev Manovich argued that digital media provide us with extremely rich data for the study of everyday lives and practices:

> For the first time, we can follow [the] imaginations, opinions, ideas, and feelings of hundreds of millions of people. We can see the images and the videos they create and comment on, monitor the conversations they are engaged in, read their blog posts and tweets, navigate their maps, listen to their track lists, and follow their trajectories in physical space. (Manovich 2012 in Burgess and Bruns 2012)

What, though, can we *meaningfully* understand about the way that people use digital media to express difficult feelings in the everyday, within the confines of the Twitter API and the methods that our computer science team has made available to them to collect people's everyday ideas and feelings?

The everyday is a core sociological interest and of increasing interest to those doing Twitter analysis, but for computer scientists, there are key difficulties in retrieving such data. As noted, part of our research in response to suicide has addressed public responses to well-publicized death by suicide. However, a second part of the Twitter project is concerned with another kind of response: *interpersonal in-platform response* (Twitter replies) at times when a person (famous or not) has expressed emotional distress on Twitter. These are very small, very specific moments, at odds with the majority of big data research, which tends to focus on the big event or campaigns delimited by a hashtag. This has been a challenge for our team. The computer scientists in the team have devised a simple tool that finds replies to an initial data set achieved through key word searching. This enables focusing on small, fleeting moments of empathy (a key concept in our project) through the collection of replies and provides an illustration of how a computational solution can be found to a sociological question, which in this case is how empathy happens (or not) in the everyday. We shall see some practical examples of this analysis in Section 2.4.

2.3 Trust and Empathy Online during Disasters and Humanitarian Crisis

Our second collaborative effort is looking at disasters and humanitarian crises through the lens of social media data. Big data are becoming a key theme in *international relations* and *international security* studies. Digital humanitarianism or the role of communications technology in humanitarian crisis situations is a new important area of study. There is excitement about the possibilities offered by big data available through social media and other communications technology in mapping emerging phenomena in real time, thereby facilitating rapid understanding of and responses to crisis situations, not just for governments but for communities. The collaboration between MP, VP, DK, and NS is exploring the role of social media in building or undermining empathy and trust in conflict or disaster situations, a core area of study in international relations.

Identifying the potential and limits of social media research is important for international researchers and policymakers in the context of situations where access on the ground and traditional field analysis may be difficult. Humanitarian innovation in the area of social media and big data is a theme of the planned first *World Humanitarian Summit* to be held in Istanbul in May 2016 (UN Secretary-General 2015). Teaming up with computer science specialists will allow international relations researchers to explore the theoretical, practical, and ethical role of social media more systematically in conflict or disaster situations. One central emerging ethical concern is over big data as a tool of enablement or *surveillance and containment* of populations.

We have chosen two case studies:

1. *Balkan floods 2014.* Social media and flood disaster responses among post-conflict ethnically divided communities in Bosnian/Croatian/Serbian and English languages.
2. *Ukraine conflict 2013 onward.* Social media and responses to the Ukraine conflict in Ukrainian, Russian, and English languages.

The conflict situation in Ukraine and the postconflict disaster situation in the Balkans have certain parallels in their local and international dynamics, in so far as its participants used to be citizens of the same country, many of them know their adversaries personally, and they can communicate in a language they all understand, where the concerns of divided communities have also become internationalized and become international security issues.

Our two case studies involve conflict and postconflict situations, in which the challenges of the postconflict Balkans have parallels and potential lessons for the Ukraine conflict. The Balkans have now experienced a quarter of a century of international intervention seeking to build regional peace and security. Yet the long-term international interventions have failed to achieve economic security or genuine reconciliation between the former warring parties. The Balkans experienced some initial postwar reconstruction and the successful revival of tourism in a few areas, but overall we see faltering economies, characterized by deindustrialization, rising long-term unemployment and underemployment, state and personal indebtedness, and depopulation, where wartime ethnic population displacements are being followed by peacetime economic migration abroad. Against this malaise, the negative wartime stereotypes are perpetuated in politics and the mainstream media. We see this in the recent series of divided twentieth anniversary war commemorations held across the region reaffirming nationalist perspectives. Nevertheless, the worst floods to hit the Western Balkans in a century in 2014 witnessed the galvanizing of assistance in communities and expressions of solidarity between the wartime adversaries supported through social media.

2.3.1 Role of Social Media

The development of social media over the last decade offers a new communicative tool for individuals in crisis situations and bridges of communication across frontlines. In the Yugoslav conflict in the 1990s, there was no social media but there were specialized lists, mainly journalists, academics, diplomats, and aid workers. In the Ukraine conflict, the role of social media is evident. Much of the population is taking part. To what extent are social media reflecting or influencing the mainstream media? And to what extent do social media therefore reinforce social mistrust or alternatively maintain or rebuild trust and empathy across divided communities against negative stereotypes?

Knowledge of the local political–socioeconomic context in which social media interactions are taking place is critically important in conducting social network analyses. Without such knowledge, it is nearly impossible to identify and map key actors (nodes) and their interactions (edges). Recognizing patterns of interaction among participants in a social network is extremely important because the trust that is usually developed in the process tends to last longer than the particular event that triggered it in the first place.

There are preliminary indications that the 2014 floods in the Balkans have brought divided communities together in their suffering, and that this has been facilitated through social media; but also that responses in the conflict in Ukraine that broke out in 2014 have become more polarized through social media.

2.3.2 Measuring Empathy and Trust

The challenge we face is demonstrating whether social media is reinforcing the mistrust created by the fighting or is helping to bridge the gap between the estranged communities. Sentiment analysis is a notorious challenge in Internet data research. The Balkans area specialism and language knowledge, combined with international relations expertise on the one hand and computer science expertise combined with fortuitous Ukrainian and Russian language and area knowledge on the other hand, has facilitated our research planning.

One way into identifying trust and empathy has been to compile a list of terms or hashtags as potential indicators of positive feelings or interethnic solidarity in Bosnian/Croatian/Serbian. This helps to narrow down the search criteria for data collection, which otherwise would be practically unfeasible. Another way is to explore the language communities of social media and whether specific online language networks express particular solidarities and are manifested in particular events being the focus of attention, in addition to how they are represented—in particular whether the use of Ukrainian, Russian, or English reflects or transcends political affiliations. To analyze this phenomenon quantitatively, we rely on several data mining techniques. On the one hand, we look at the temporal dynamics of Twitter activity during the political crisis in Ukraine and automatically identify various episodes of the conflict during which the volumes of posts diverge in different language communities. On the other hand, we measure the public empathy in response to those episodes by analyzing the sentiment of the posts in English-, Ukrainian-, and Russian-speaking Twittersphere. This analysis conducted on the data set of dozens of millions of social media posts can help us not only to understand the differences in public perception of the conflict in various language communities, but also to identify and analyze key triggers (e.g., events, persons), which mobilize public opinion during political crises and social unrests.

Furthermore, through the interdisciplinary research, we may identify how apolitical technological tools may have *unintentional political consequences*. For instance, it is known that search and news feed algorithms tend to reinforce people into their divided social media communities and compound their estrangement (Pariser 2011).

2.4 Social Network Analysis and Sentiment Exchange

Based on the considerations of the two collaborative scenarios mentioned earlier, in this section we demonstrate how the requirements and needs of social science research can be met with a practical application of social network analysis to study the patterns of empathy propagation in Twitter. We present *Sentiment Exchange Cascades*—a novel methodology to analyze exchange of sentiments in Twitter conversations—and demonstrate its applicability to analyze the dynamics of social conversation in Twitter for the two different use case scenarios presented in this chapter.

2.4.1 Data Collection

We consider two data sets of tweets for our analysis. The first one was collected during the Euromaidan protests in Ukraine in winter 2013–2014 and is composed of English tweets that contain the #euromaidan hashtag and/or mention Ukraine or the Kyiv city where the main protests took place. The second data set is collected in fall 2015 for around dozen key words that indicate depression in Twitter posts and that have been carefully devised by our social scientist partners, for example, feel + empty, if + kill + myself, and not + good + enough. For each tweet in both data sets—which were collected using Twitter streaming API—we also collected threads of reply messages from which we reconstructed the cascades of interactions between individuals (e.g., see Figure 2.1). We have used the following notation to represent the sentiment exchange in cascades of user interactions:

- ■ The node colors represent different Twitter users.
- ■ The size of the node represents the sentiment of the tweet as measured by SentiStrength library (Thelwall et al. 2010). Note that we only considered tweets written in English for this analysis. We also note that SentiStrength

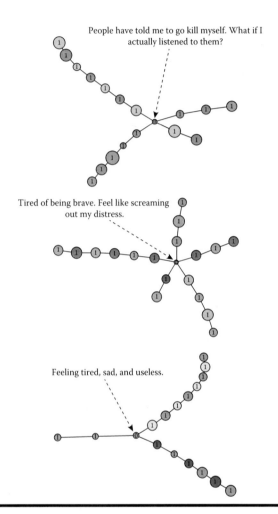

Figure 2.1 Sentiment Exchange Cascades in response to tweets that express emotional distress: The title of each figure is indicative of the words of the original tweet. (*Note:* This has been obfuscated, in accordance with ethical practice (Markham 2012), given that users may have placed the tweet in the public sphere but the tweet itself may or may not have been intended for public consumption.) Each node represents a tweet and an edge is drawn between two tweets if one is a reply to the other. Each individual user is represented by a different point on the gray scale. At the center is the original poster (pointed by the dotted arrow). Each reply thread originating from the first post is shown distinctly. The size of each node is proportional to the positiveness of the sentiment. The number in each node represents the number of people involved in the reply. Note how the sentiment of both the original posters and reposters becomes more and more positive as the reply threads evolve. Furthermore, most tweets involve just two parties and represent a more intimate conversation than seen in other scenarios (e.g., see Figure 2.2).

provides two scores to separately characterize the extent to which a tweet expresses positive (POS—an integer score between 0 and 5) and negative sentiments (NEG—an integer score between –5 and 0). For presentation, we compute the radius of the nodes with the following formula: $R = (5 + NEG + POS)^2$.

■ We used integer labels within the nodes to indicate the number of Twitter users mentioned in a post, for example, a tweet "Glad to meet @userA @userB @userC at this meeting today" mentions three different users.

The following sections show how this novel visualization of social network interactions allows us to develop a better understanding of what is happening in individual conversations and is leading to improved understanding from the social science side.

2.4.2 Friends in Need Are Friends Indeed: Effect of Social Network Interactions on Twitter Users in Emotional Distress

In Figure 2.1, we present several example cascades constructed from the first data set of depression-related tweets. The original tweets in the center of each cascade express emotional distress and, so, have a very negative sentiment (i.e., small radius). However, the positive sentiment tends to increase as the discussion deviates further from the original tweet. As indicated by the tweets with a larger radius (and so a more positive sentiment) located just next to central nodes, Twitter users try to "cheer up" their fellow Twitter users, for example, "you'll be ok!," "you are beautiful with an amazing twitter personality," "life needs you!," "sending you some love and support," and "stay strong." More interestingly, we also observe that the sentiment of consecutive tweets from the author of the original tweet (i.e., the tweets with the same color as the original tweet) is also amplified throughout the discussion suggesting that this public expression of distress changes the nature of the discourse: the user in need starts posting more positive tweets typically expressing thankfulness, for example, "thanks" and "I love you babe, thanks."

2.4.3 One-to-One Conversation versus Group Discussions

Next, we consider several sentiment exchange cascades for the tweets from the Ukraine protests (Figure 2.2). We observe several distinguishing features in comparison to our analysis of emotional distress in the previous section. We notice that the conversations with the longest cascades are mainly initiated by the famous figures, for example, politicians, journalists, or celebrities, who often do not follow up on replies from their followers. This is indicated by an observation that a single central node is colored in white. Nevertheless, we observe long threads of

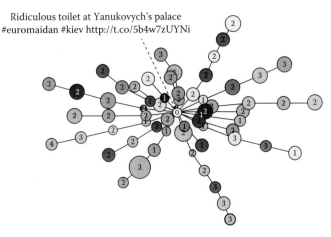

Ridiculous toilet at Yanukovych's palace
#euromaidan #kiev http://t.co/5b4w7zUYNi

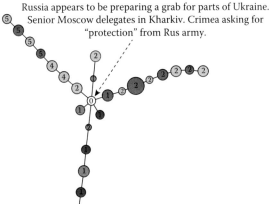

Russia appears to be preparing a grab for parts of Ukraine.
Senior Moscow delegates in Kharkiv. Crimea asking for
"protection" from Rus army.

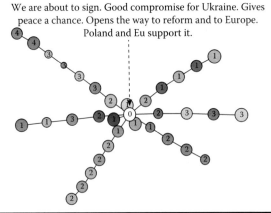

We are about to sign. Good compromise for Ukraine. Gives
peace a chance. Opens the way to reform and to Europe.
Poland and Eu support it.

Figure 2.2 Sentiment Exchange Cascades for Euromaidan tweets: The visualization scheme is similar to Figure 2.1.

conversations among the original Twitter user's followers. More interestingly, we observe that many discussions tend to engage multiple users (up to 5 as indicated by the number of users mentioned in the tweet within the node). The very nature of Twitter, with its small character limit for each tweet, limits the number of users who can be mentioned in any tweet. This is in contrast to the results from the previous sections where all threads of cascades are predominantly one-to-one conversations (i.e., all nodes have a label "1" indicating a single person is mentioned in each tweet).

As far as the sentiment is concerned, politics-related discussions have a much more nuanced nature. In many cases, the sentiment of individual users does not change. For instance, we notice that information propagation threads of the discussion predominantly feature neutral sentiment across the majority of tweets in the discussion. In other cases, the sentiment of users increases, sometimes of both the parties involved in a reply thread. When we examine the threads themselves, however, we find many instances with jingoistic discussions with a vivid confrontation pattern, which tend to have much more polarized sentiments throughout the conversation thread. Looking through individual tweets, we also observed a difference between the very confrontational discussions—which were predominantly attributed to one-to-one discussions between two opposing sides—and more open-minded discussions between a large number (up to 5) of participants.

Overall, we believe that the cascades of sentiment exchange presented in this section can prove to be a useful tool in interdisciplinary analysis of dynamics of interactions between users in social networks. This technique can facilitate the interdisciplinary approaches discussed in the earlier sections in two respects. On the one hand, with this approach, we aimed to build a visualization tool for social scientists to be able to "zoom in" within the large data sets of tweets and analyze the patterns of sentiment exchange within small, individual conversations that are so crucial to obtain insights into the social sciences. On the other hand, we aimed to leverage the idea of sentiment cascades to study the emerging patterns from sentiment exchange on a significantly larger scale, that is, in conversations among millions of individuals.

2.5 Metadiscussion on the Nature of Collaboration between Computer and Social Sciences

Having reported on the two collaborative efforts we are undertaking and how social network analysis has allowed us to easily draw new nuggets of insight from the vast mountain of data facing us, we conclude by discussing two metaquestions about the broader nature of our collaboration across disciplines, which have been vexing us. The first is motivated by a respect for the rights of those whom we study. Haunting all of these are crucial questions about the ethics of trawling Twitter to extract data on emotional distress or other extreme situations and what we then do with these data. How may we attach meaning to data, in such a context? The second question is more reflexive: are we doing transdisciplinary research? This is not merely a navel-gazing query but rather a yardstick to measure our collaboration against and to ensure we remain reflexive about the nature of our joint working.

2.5.1 Attaching Meaning to Data and Attendant Ethical Concerns

2.5.1.1 Being Lost or Found in Big Data

In the emotional distress study by using word search terms rather than hashtags, we seek Twitter users who are using the platform in a way that is arguably less public and more ephemeral and whose expectations for privacy are likely to be different (and greater). By making ephemeral—if not private—data public through research, we potentially spotlight these users and could risk revealing highly sensitive personal information.

Leaving aside well-rehearsed arguments about whether or not Twitter data are technically public, disciplinary differences in how we come to visualize such data are important. For those working quantitatively, all cases are anonymized or blurred; no one case is visible. When we begin to analyze Twitter qualitatively, we surface or spotlight cases that up until then had been invisible. Regardless of whether this is quantitative or qualitative analysis, extracting Twitter information and turning it into data, and creating new databases of tweets through archiving of research data, raise a number of serious ethical questions that up to this point have been dealt with through specific disciplinary approaches. Over and above the issue of archiving, there are also important ethical questions to ask about using data for analysis (Crawford and Finn 2015). There are ways to mitigate the risks of using data qualitatively, including what Markham (2012) calls "fabrication as an ethical practice" or thematic analysis that refrains from using quotes. Our choices in the presentation of data for analysis mean acknowledging, if not completely reconciling, different disciplinary perspectives on ethics.

2.5.1.2 Systems Approaches Facilitating Interdisciplinary Research

One potential solution to the previous concern, and a potential bridge between computer and social scientists working on this project, is provided by systems approaches, which have influenced key international relations theorists such as Kenneth Waltz (1979) or the peace theorists Johan Galtung (1996) and Anatol Rapoport (1974).

Systems thinking spans the social and natural sciences because of the inclusive and nonanthropomorphic notion of a system and can be very useful here in facilitating the integration of different facets of knowledge coming from different disciplines—in this case, international relations and computer science or sociology and computer science. Systems thinking as a general framework for observing and explaining the world is particularly useful in dealing with the complex interface between human/social and technological phenomena such as social media. Indeed, the concept of resilience, now central to international disaster, development, and security management, originates from systems thinking. Technologies, such as the Internet, have likewise challenged sociologists to rethink how they conceptualize and research the social (e.g., Castells' (2010) work on the global network society and Law and Hassard (1999) on actor network theory [ANT]). Such theories, like the systems approach within international relations, raise questions of what should be included in analysis of the social and at what level(s) this analysis should take place. ANT, for instance, proposes that nonhuman actors should be included in understandings of the social.

What significance may we attach to what people say on Twitter or other social media? How do social media interactions relate to offline interactions? How consistent are people's online activities with their offline lives? The virtual world and the patterns of the virtual world have their reality, but they are not all of reality. The situations of conflict or disaster involving the risk of death, injury, or physical loss and expressions of suicidal intent on social media starkly surface the relationship between the virtual and offline worlds.

The systems approach, as a way of coordinating or integrating research efforts of multiple researchers coming from different disciplines, is aimed at building common frames of understanding the natural and social reality. Generally, it involves using a system as the basic unit of analysis. The hope is that this ontological assumption can address the duality of natural and social worlds, which often stifles fruitful interdisciplinary collaboration. In the context of our analysis of Twitter responses to the 2014 floods in the Balkans and the Ukraine conflict, this approach is intended to allow us to see regularities and patterns in the seeming deluge of millions of tweets. Our particular concern has been to find out whether political communities transcending and blurring the existing boundaries of social and political interaction in the Western Balkans and Ukraine are emerging from this deluge. There is a reason to believe, for instance, that the trust and empathy triggered by the 2014 floods may last beyond the disaster and increase the resilience of the affected communities faced with similar disaster situations in the future.

We need to consider the relation between individual and aggregate data and how to reconcile the principle of methodological individualism with emerging patterns at the aggregate level. While individual tweets can be attributed to individual Twitter users, the patterned tweets do not constitute per se a conscious collective entity or conscious collective action, even if the patterns of social interaction have social consequences. While social media offers new powers of communication between individuals bypassing official institutions or traditional media, big data analysis may be inclined to see human behavior as following conditioned social behaviors and minimize the possibility of individual agency and freedom. Here we return to the question of the human as against the system and to what we earlier referred to as the need to hold on to small data within the big.

2.5.2 Learning through Doing: The Nature of Social and Computer Science Collaboration

As noted in the introduction, the broader project that our study is a part of was set up as a transdisciplinary one and could be seen to fit in with a general move toward harnessing research to solve problems outside the university, for instance, for government or industry. This is a move that could lead to a blurring, if not the dissolution, of disciplinary distinctions and autonomy (Krishnan 2009a). It is an open question whether what we are doing is multi-, inter-, cross-, or transdisciplinary research. If the key distinction between these practices rests on whether or not disciplinarity disappears, then we would seem to fall short of genuine transdisciplinarity. Moreover, transdisciplinarity is associated with a much longer process of planning at the research design and initial management stage than a sandpit process facilitates (Hollaender et al. 2008, p. 387). Perhaps more important than the label, however, is what we learn through doing. Like the reaction of the family in the children's book *Going on a Bear Hunt* (Rosen and Oxenbury 1989) when they encounter obstacles like mud: "We can't go over it. We can't go under it. Oh no! We've got to go through it!." The computer and social scientists involved in this project are finding out what it means to work together as computer and social scientists through "going through it," and it is this process we have illustrated through the two projects outlined in this chapter. In thinking across these two projects, a more interesting question than whether or not we are doing transdisciplinary work might be what we believe is being blurred through the process of crossing disciplinary boundaries. What, as Krishnan (2009b) suggests, do we hold to be true about our own discipline?

Working with our computer (respectively, social) science colleagues has been as revealing of ourselves, what we do and believe as sociologists or political and computer scientists, as it has about the nature of other disciplines and our relationship to them. Through this work, we are grappling with the fundamental questions about the distinctiveness of the sciences and the humanities. Those who champion this process of grappling and who are wary of philosophies claiming absolute knowledge about humanity might turn out to be our most useful guides in this "journey":

> To bring men to liberty means to bring them to converse with one another. Mere opinion melts away in favor of well-founded judgment in the loving struggle with one's neighbors (Jaspers, 1953, p. 154).

Acknowledgment

ESRC. 2014. The "A Shared Space and A Space for Sharing" project (Grant No. ES/M00354X/1) is one of several funded through the EMoTICON network, which is funded through the following cross-council programs: Partnership for Conflict, Crime and Security Research (led by the Economic and Social Research Council (ESRC)), Connected Communities (led by the Arts & Humanities Research Council (AHRC)), Digital Economy (led by the Engineering and Physical Sciences Research Council (EPSRC)) in partnership with Defence Science and Technology Laboratory (Dstl), Centre for the Protection of National Infrastructure (CPNI).

References

Althoff, T., Danescu-Niculescu-Mizil, C., and Jurafsky, D. 2014. How to ask for a favor: A case study on the success of altruistic requests. *The International AAAI Conference on Weblogs and Social Media,* Ann Arbor, MI.

boyd, D. and Crawford, K. 2012. Critical questions for big data: Provocations for a cultural, technological, and scholarly phenomenon. *Information, Communication & Society*, 15(5), 662–679.

Brownlie, J. 2014. *Ordinary Relationships*. New York: Palgrave MacMillan.

Burgess, J. and Bruns, A. 2012. Twitter archives and the challenges of "Big Social Data" for media and communication research. *M/C Journal*, 15(5).

Burkitt, I. 2014. *Emotions and Social Relations*. London, U.K.: Sage.

Castells, M. 2010. *The Rise of the Network Society*. Malden, MA: Wiley-Blackwell.

Ceren, B., Sharad, G., and Rao, J.M. 2016. Fair and balanced? Quantifying media bias through crowdsourced content analysis, *Public Opinion Quarterly*, 80(S1), 250–271.

Crawford, K. and Finn, M. 2015. The limits of crisis data: Analytical and ethical challenges of using social and mobile data to understand disasters. *GeoJournal*, 80(4), 491–502.

Danescu-Niculescu-Mizil, C., Sudhof, M., Jurafsky, D., Leskovec, J., and Potts, C. 2013. A computational approach to politeness with application to social factors. *Annual Meeting of the Association for Computational Linguistics*, Sofia, Bulgaria.

De Choudhury, M., Gamon, M., Counts, S., and Horvitz, E. 2013. Predicting depression via social media. *The International Conference on Web and Social Media,* Cambridge, MA.

Dodds, P.S., Muhamad, R., and Watts, D.J. 2003. An experimental study of search in global social networks. *Science* 301(5634): 827–829.

Galtung, J. 1996. *Peace by Peaceful Means: Peace and Conflict, Development and Civilization*, Vol. 14. New York: Sage.

Garcia, D., Weber, I., and Garimella, V.R.K. 2014. Gender asymmetries in reality and fiction: The Bechdel test of social media. *The International Conference on Web and Social Media,* Oxford, U.K.

Glasgow, K., Fink, C., and Boyd-Graber, J. 2014. Our grief is unspeakable: Measuring the community impact of a tragedy. *The International Conference on Web and Social Media*, Oxford, U.K.

Hollaender, K., Loibl, M.C., and Wilts, A. 2008. Management. In Hadorn, G.H., Hoffmann-Riem, H., Biber-Klemm, S., Grossenbacher-Mansuy, W., Joye, D., Pohl, C. et al. (Eds.). *Handbook of Transdisciplinary Research* (pp. 385–397). Dordrecht, the Netherlands: Springer.

Jaspers, K. 1953. *The Origin and Goal of History*. London, U.K.: Routledge and Kegan Paul.

Kivran-Swaine, F., Ting, J., Brubaker, J.R., Teodoro, R., and Naaman, M. 2014. Understanding loneliness in social awareness streams: Expressions and responses. *The International Conference on Web and Social Media*, Oxford, U.K.

Kleinberg, J. 2000. The small-world phenomenon: An algorithmic perspective. *Proceedings of 32nd ACM Symposium on Theory of Computing*, Portland, OR.

Kleinberg, J. 2001. Small-world phenomena and the dynamics of information. *Advances in Neural Information Processing Systems (NIPS)* 14, Vancouver, BC.

Krishnan, A. 2009a. Disciplines and interdisciplinarity NCRM. Working Paper. University of Southampton, Southampton, U.K.

Krishnan, A. 2009b. Five strategies for practising interdisciplinarity. ESRC National Centre for Research Methods. NCRM Working Paper Series. University of Southampton, Southampton, U.K.

Law, J. and Hassard, J. 1999. *Actor Network Theory and After*. Oxford, U.K.: Blackwell.

Lazer, D., Pentland, A., Adamic, L., Aral, S., Barabasi, A.-L., Brewer, D. et al. 2009. Life in the network: The coming age of computational social science. *Science*, 323(5915), 721–723.

Markham, A. 2012. Fabrication as ethical practice: Qualitative inquiry in ambiguous internet contexts. *Information, Communication & Society*, 15(3), 334–353.

Mason, J. 2006. Mixing methods in a qualitatively driven way. *Qualitative Research*, 6(1), 9–25.

Pariser, E. 2011. *The Filter Bubble: What the Internet Is Hiding from You*. London, U.K.: Penguin.

Rapoport, A. 1974. *Fights, Games, and Debates*. Ann Arbor, MI: University of Michigan Press.

Rosen, M. and Oxenbury, H. 1989. *We're Going on a Bear Hunt*. London, U.K.: Walker Books.

Thelwall, M., Buckley, K., Paltoglou, G., Cai, D., and Kappas, A. 2010. Sentiment strength detection in short informal text. *Journal of the American Society for Information Science and Technology*, 61(12), 2544–2558.

Travers, J. and Milgram, S. 1969. An experimental study of the small world problem. *Sociometry*, 32(4), 425–443.

UN Secretary-General. 2015. Secretary-General's remarks to Member States briefing on the World Humanitarian Summit. New York: United Nations, April 20, 2015.

Van Dijck, J. 2014. Datafication, dataism and dataveillance: Big Data between scientific paradigm and ideology. *Surveillance & Society*, 12(2): 197–208.

Waltz, K. 1979. *Theory of International Politics*. Long Grove, IL: Waveland Press.

Chapter 3

How Much Sharing Is Enough? Cognitive Patterns in Building Interdisciplinary Collaborations

Lianghao Dai and Margarete Boos

Contents

3.1 Interdisciplinary Collaboration: A Dynamic Social Networking

A social network is made up of nodes and ties (Wasserman and Faust, 1994). The nodes can be individuals, teams, or organizations, while ties represent interpersonal or interorganizational relationships, like trust, friendships, and investments. Among various scientific research questions related to social network dynamics, one of the most crucial is how people build, maintain, or change ties between them. There exist numerous works in the literature to answer this question. For example, Katz et al. (2004) listed in their review the following five schools of theories that attempt to answer that question: theories of self-interest, theories of social exchange or dependency, theories of mutual or collective interest, cognitive theories, and theories of homophily. The cognitive theories that we focus on in this chapter discuss how people's cognitions of certain relationships, other people, objects, or processes influence their relationship building. By asking how much knowledge sharing is enough for building interdisciplinary collaborations (ICs), the goal of this chapter is to identify the cognitive-based reasons for people from various disciplines to share enough information to build their collaboration ties.

IC occurs when researchers, each with their discrete disciplinary perspectives, borrow or adapt ideas and approaches from one another (Maton et al., 2006) across academic methodological and epistemological boundaries (Tress et al., 2007) and work jointly for the solutions to scientific problems (Stokols et al., 2003). IC is therefore an important dynamic of social networking (Haythornthwaite, 2006; Haines et al., 2011). Aiming to find a joint project to work on, researchers discuss and exchange ideas, generate topics, and develop relationships over time. For example, the three small groups examined in this chapter stem from an IC group we have fictitiously named computer science-sociology-psychology (CSP) to protect the identities of its members. Group members are computer scientists, sociologists, social psychologists, physicists, and medical scientists. During the first 3 years, they did not go any further than build up their interpersonal relationships, after which they realized that they must better understand each other's topics and perspectives in order to overcome barriers to knowledge differences. After another half year of detailed discussions on concepts and theories of each discipline and with new members entering and leaving the group, two additional smaller groups emerged. Altogether 8 people out of around 20 CSP members successfully converged their knowledge and found common topics to jointly work on.

We employ the cognitive map approach (Axelrod, 1976; Boos et al., 1990; Boos, 1996), an approach that applies graph theory to the analysis of human cognitions in order to identify the ways in which two or more knowledge networks combine with each other. The nodes in our cognitive maps represent single scientific terms that include notions, concepts, methods, names of colleagues, equipment, relevant events, or data. Directed links between the nodes in our cognitive maps represent relationships between those scientific terms, such as belonging ("can be divided into"), examples ("is a kind of"), deduction ("lead to"), and comparison ("compare with"). Together, these nodes and links comprising a cognitive map illustrate an individual's academic knowledge system—a logical, scientific, and processing knowledge network.

The cognitive map approach extends traditional social network analysis (SNA) by applying it to a knowledge network. From the maps, we were able to identify the mental representations of the IC project in members' minds and to show how these knowledge networks interact dynamically during the IC process. Knowledge sharing was investigated via comparisons among the individuals' cognitive maps: If the maps shared certain nodes and links, these overlapping nodes and links were seen as shared knowledge. Moreover, if a certain structure of nodes and links was shared, which meant they overlapped not only single nodes and links but also sub-structures of their connections, these shared structures of nodes and links were seen as shared components of knowledge structure.

3.2 Research Question

IC is playing an increasingly important role in our current academic world. Benefits of IC include triggering new scientific questions and fields, providing new under-standing to academic questions that cannot be solved by a single discipline, and dealing with complex practical issues by an integration of perspectives from various disciplines (Derry and Schunn, 2005). IC has affected consequential influence, to the point that some institutions and universities in both Germany and the United States have been influenced to the point of breaking from their traditional disci-pline settings and establishing new departments in order to function in interdisci-plinary modes (Sa, 2006).

That said, there are important barriers to such collaborations. Tress et al. (2007) conducted an empirical study on barriers to IC in landscape projects. Using fac-tor analysis, they found that the top three barriers to IC (interdisciplinary and transdisciplinary) were (1) organizational barriers, including coping with different academic traditions, different hierarchy in research groups, and inconvenient geo-graphical locations; (2) external barriers, such as time and funding pressures and different starting points in the projects; and (3) differing epistemologies, the lack of common terminology, and in some cases the lack of an academic culture of knowl-edge sharing (awareness of, interest in, or experience with knowledge sharing), which often lead to interpersonal barriers such as negative relationships between participants and personal unwillingness to try different academic ways of thinking and/or something new, including knowledge sharing.

Controlling for the first and the second types of barriers, this chapter focuses on what leads to an absence of knowledge sharing—the research status in which researchers encounter difficulty connecting each other's knowledge. This barrier has been identified, widely discussed, and investigated empirically in many studies (Klein, 1990; Burkart, 2002; Jakobsen and McLaughlin, 2004; Cummings and Kiesler, 2005; Hunecke, 2006; Maton et al., 2006; Tress et al., 2007; Cummings and Kiesler, 2008; Godemann, 2008). As researchers from different disciplines differ in their knowledge bases in terms of research objects, theoretical concepts, methodical approaches, and types of data, it is not surprising that they have difficulties understanding each other. These built-in barriers to sharing knowledge can result in the failure of IC projects. For example, in Burkart's (2002) work to put forth a framework for interdisciplinary social sciences, information sharing (IS) processes among IC team members were studied. He reported that what a speaker in the inter-/transdisciplinary team means sometimes is quite different from what the listener understands. In the same vein, the IC case study conducted by Jakobsen et al. (2004) revealed that the difficulty of cross-discipline understandings is caused by different meanings of the same vocabulary and the unawareness that these differences exist—as in scientists of different disciplines agreeing or disagreeing when they actually do not completely understand what the other has said. Another form of this barrier is caused by the unique methodologies employed by different disciplines. Such differences, such as standard processes of doing research and "normal" ways of collecting and analyzing data, play a negative role in IC (Jakobsen et al., 2004). Similar phenomena of core process differences were found decades earlier in the IC analyses of barriers to knowledge integration during IC processes (Luszki, 1958; Frey, 1973).

On a more positive note, there are studies that have suggested various ways to overcome these barriers and to build a shared and integrated knowledge base between individual researchers. Some have argued for boundary objects between various disciplines or a common ground developed in an IC team as its initial team task, comprising a common frame of reference, shared understanding of basic concepts, and an agreement upon perception of the research object (Clark and Brennan, 1991; Selin and Chavez, 1995; Clark, 1996; Jakobsen et al., 2004; Tress et al., 2007). Klein (2008a, p. 407) pointed out that the ability for trans-/interdisciplinary collaboration means to "generate a synthesis, integrative framework, or more holistic understanding for a particular theme, question, or problem." To meet these requirements, factors like prior experience in IC, physical togetherness, and good interpersonal relationships have been found to help the process of knowledge sharing (Cummings and Kiesler, 2005, 2008). Other authors have designed procedures and guidelines that help researchers better communicate with each other, support an understanding of each other's approaches, and in turn build common goals (Klein, 1990; Bergmann et al., 2005; MacMynowski, 2007; Godemann, 2008).

Even if we accept the points of view mentioned earlier, the question that has not yet been adequately answered is the cognitive-based reasons for people from various disciplines to share enough information necessary for building IC. This is the main question of this chapter.

3.3 Typologies for IC and Knowledge Sharing Theories

As the range of knowledge sharing likely differs, depending on the type of IC in question and the disciplines involved (Defila and Di Giulio, 2015), this section will begin by introducing some of the approaches to classifying the different methods of IC and the knowledge sharing theories that developed from these classifications. We will then outline the problems encountered in knowledge sharing and afterward introduce models that have emerged to help ensure successful IC in teams. In the closing paragraph of this section, we will cover contemporary methods for investigating IC in scientific teams.

3.3.1 Types of IC

In their investigation of the role of social sciences in integrated rural development in developing countries, van Dusseldorp and Wigboldus (1994) discussed the typological division of "narrow interdisciplinarity" and "broad interdisciplinarity". They described narrow versus broad IC as being at opposite ends of four IC team characteristics: (1) paradigms and methods (those of narrow IC are the same but those of broad IC are different), (2) number of disciplines (narrow IC has few disciplines involved but broad IC has many disciplines involved), (3) originating organizations (team members making up narrow IC are from the same organizations and those of broad IC are from different organizations), and (4) cultures (narrow IC team members are from the same culture, while broad IC team members are from different cultures). What is clear by their characterization of these two IC categories is that it is the disparity among IC participants rather than the size of an IC team that defines it as a narrow or broad IC. In fact, they began their paper by stating that most discussions of IC have to do with the challenges posed by broad IC efforts, pointing out that the more disparate an IC team is in its paradigms and methods, its mixture of disciplines, the organizations its participants represent, and the cultural makeup of its participants, the greater the IC communication and agreement challenges will be.

The van Dusseldorp and Wigboldus (1994) categorizations described previously provide a general IC typology. The integration type analyzed in the van Dusseldorp and Wigboldus (1994) empirical case study can be characterized as delegation, one of the four interdisciplinary collaborative types summarized by Krott (1996) and discussed by Defila et al. (2006) and Defila and Di Giulio (2015). These four types of collaboration procedures are shown in Figure 3.1.

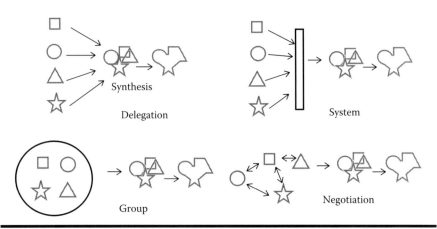

Figure 3.1 Typology for academic findings (represented by squares, triangles, stars, and circles) that converge into a synthesis. (Revised from Defila, R. and Di Giulio, A., *Futures*, 65, 123, 2015.) *Delegation* (integration by a leader/leadership group): sub-projects (or individuals) deliver findings separately and then one person or a small group of persons takes on the task of integrating them. *System* (modeling): findings are integrated into the framework of an existing (or specially developed) theory, model, catalogue of questions, scenario technique, or similar system. *Group* (common GL): the integration of findings is done by all members of the group involved, compiling a body of knowledge that they share as a group. *Negotiation* (negotiation among experts): individual projects (or persons) combine their findings with those of others, thus developing a partial synthesis before feeding it into the synthesis of the whole project.

3.3.2 Problems of Knowledge Sharing in IC

The typologies introduced earlier deal with methods in which findings from each discipline are integrated into group knowledge. What are not included in the summary earlier are the ways that each finding from each discipline is connected to another within the IC group. In SNA terminology, those typologies focus only on the functioning characteristics of the network structure as a whole but pay less attention to the characteristics of its nodes (differing cultures, languages, terminology, analysis processes), their ties (communication channels of their common social network), and how the ties between the social network nodes are established. For various reasons, these connections between disciplinary findings can be potentially quite different. We argue that the classification of collaborative patterns needs to be especially based on the nature of the specified disciplines and context, in terms of expertise knowledge (what people study) (Wesselink, 2009), methodology (how they acquire knowledge) (Maton et al., 2006), and epistemology (how they ensure the reliability and validity of knowledge) (Tress et al., 2007). Taken into context of the small IC groups/teams (around 3–10 participants) that we analyzed, this chapter asks what kinds of knowledge sharing patterns are employed between disciplines for their IC and how the differences between knowledge, methodology, and epistemology influence the IC patterns in order to share enough information necessary for building IC.

3.3.3 Models for Successful IC in Teams

Social psychology theories focusing on team/group cognition, such as shared mental models (SMM) (Cannon-Bowers et al., 1993), team mental models (TMM) (Klimoski and Mohammed, 1994), group learning (GL) (Argote et al., 1999), information sharing (IS) (Stasser and Titus, 1985), and transactive memory systems (TMS) (Wegner, 1987), provide rich inspiration for the investigation of interdisciplinary knowledge sharing. The basic premise of these theories is that, on the one hand, group/team members are assumed to provide highly specialized and unique knowledge to make the IC worthwhile but, on the other hand, members should cross expertise boundaries to work jointly and efficiently—a process that causes tension between uniqueness and sharedness (Lewis, 2003; Lewis and Herndon, 2011; Ren and Argote, 2011; Kotlarsky et al., 2015). The goal of these theories is to resolve this tension by creating the said system of knowledge sharing in order to improve team/group performance.

However, different understandings of "sharing" divide these theories into two categories: for theories such as TMS and IS, discrete knowledge is distributed among group/team members. For theories such as GL, SMM, and TMM, knowledge overlaps among team members. TMS professes that the discrete team member knowledge and expertise functions as external storage and ability. Rather than sharing details of each other's knowledge and expertise, they share a metaknowledge, a common group map of who knows what (Lewis, 2003). For knowledge overlap theories such as GL, SMM, and TMM, team members develop a common understanding of certain knowledge. It is assumed by SMM and TMM that the more common understandings of concepts and statements are shared by team members, the more efficiently and easily they fulfill collaboration goals (Mohammed and Dumville, 2001; Turner et al., 2014). These two understandings of knowledge sharing—distributed knowledge and knowledge overlaps—are not mutually exclusive. There are studies that consider both the development of TMS distribution and the overlapping of knowledge within the same teams (Wegner, 1987; Gupta and Hollingshead, 2010; Kotlarsky et al., 2015).

Regarding IC processes, these theories suggest two cognitive patterns of knowledge sharing that can occur within an IC effort. Even though TMS maintains that IC participants retain their own perspectives and methodologies as special expertise, they still need to understand exactly what they ask for from others and what others can provide to the team/group in order to build mission interfaces and assemble each single expertise into pipelines according to a shared metaknowledge expertise-provider map. Comparatively, the SMM and TMM knowledge overlap theories imply that the detailed perspectives of knowledge, including meanings of shared terms and statements of ideas, need to be discussed, understood, and combined as common ground. The IC can be seen as an integration process of specific concepts, objectives, methods, protocols, and knowledge for accomplishing the project task. In other words, the extent that the IC participants can collaborate depends greatly on the degree of overlapping of the specific disciplines' and their representatives' concepts, objectives, methods, protocols, and knowledge.

If we ask how one or the other of these two suggested cognitive patterns of knowledge sharing can be employed for people from disparate disciplines to share enough information to answer our question, "how much knowledge sharing is enough" in an IC, we may get quite different answers. Maybe both of these two patterns exist in IC but only fit for different conditions or certain sorts of IC teams. If this is so, which cognitive pattern is more suited for what kinds of IC situations and which cognitive pattern is more suited for what kinds of IC teams? To answer these questions, it is argued by related studies that it may mainly depend on efficiency and members' common understanding of the elements of the team's relevant environment (Mohammed and Dumville, 2001), similar beliefs, and understanding about common goals (Mohammed et al., 2010). This circles back to the van Dusseldorp and Wigboldus (1994) descriptions of narrow versus broad ICs and that an IC's communication challenges are based on the breadth of the disparity in methods, disciplines, organizations, and cultures between its participants. Guchait et al. (2015) suggest that successful IC depends not only on an understanding of common goals but also on the context/setting of the team, for instance, occupation of the participants and goal of the team. In their analyses of restaurant settings, which means their research target group included waiter and waitress, shared teamwork knowledge among the owner, waiters, cooks, kitchen help, bartenders, and hostesses is relatively more important than shared task work knowledge for team performance and team satisfaction. In their case studies, teamwork knowledge means knowledge about person-to-person work relationships in the team, as opposed to task knowledge, which is the knowledge about what each person does in the team. In a study on student teams, Mathieu et al. (2000) concluded that shared teamwork knowledge plays a more crucial role than shared task work knowledge for team performance and team satisfaction. However, Lim and Klein (2006), who analyzed IC data from military teams, came to the opposite conclusion. In line with the extant literature, this paper focuses on academic IC settings in which knowledge of academic task work is shared by participants from various disciplines in joint research projects.

3.3.4 Methods to Investigate IC in Scientific Teams

Compared with laboratory-based methods, which are mostly used in TMS studies (e.g., Liang et al., 1995; Moreland and Myaskovsky, 2000; Moreland et al., 2002) and workshop-based investigations employed by IC studies (see Heemskerk et al., 2003; Wesselink, 2009), we conducted an empirical case study based on actual sociological fieldwork to answer the study question of this chapter: What are the cognitive-based reasons for scientists from disparate disciplines to share enough information to build and benefit from an IC? The reason we posed this question using the approach of examining three small IC groups emerging voluntarily from a social network lies first in the conditions of our target group—professional academic professors and students were too busy to spend hours of their discretionary time to take part in any social psychology laboratory study. A 30 min interview was claimed to be excessive. Second, it is quite difficult to simulate mindsets and working logics because they have to be conducted among preset individuals in preset research conditions, which include already established collaborative relationships with colleagues using preset procedures of their preset IC study. This meant an external empirical study was required in order to go deep into their collaborative processes and observe what was taking place in their preset project. Third, it was not reasonable to expect an IC research project to be accomplished in a one-day workshop.

Instead, we employed approaches of both semistructured interviews and cognitive mapping methods to investigate three IC efforts of an extant social network IC group. The goal of the interviews was to learn the individual understandings of the participants of the project. Each interview lasted no more than 1.5 h. Six of the total eight people from the three IC projects agreed to be interviewed, and each of them was interviewed at least twice. The initial interview included questions about basic personal information, their IC project, how they were collaborating with each other, any barriers to their collaborations, and their own work and role in the IC project. From these interviews, we were able to analyze the development of their IC participation and basic ways of framing the interviewee's discipline in general. Moreover, we were better able to understand their research topic and research question, the role played by the interviewee in the project, and key problems of their IC process. We eventually were able to identify certain patterns that emerged from these understandings. All personal information, including name, age, gender, e-mail address, and name of department and university, was guaranteed to remain permanently confidential.

As described in the first section of this chapter, in order to understand how each IC participant shared their academic knowledge and their ways of doing research, graphic cognitive maps of each interviewee's knowledge network were created. By comparing the maps, we were able to identify shared nodes and links and by deduction were able to identify shared knowledge. Moreover, if a certain structure of nodes and links were shared, this meant they overlapped not only nodes and links but also certain ways of their connections, which can be seen as shared components of knowledge structure. To help ensure accuracy by eliminating gaps in knowledge sharing between ourselves and interviewees, we asked the interviewees to draw their own maps for us during the interviews. Because people's minds can change with time, we asked the interviewees to draw their maps in the same week and compare them in the same stage of interviews so that their cognitive maps were captured at the same or similar stage in their IC project. During the initial interview, we asked them to draw their cognitive maps. We then asked them to explain the meaning of each term and link. Following that request, we asked them to identify which elements of the map belonged to their work versus which elements belonged to which colleague with whom he/she was collaborating with. Finally, we asked them to describe how closely this map represented the working process of their research and how they were collaborating with each other in the IC project. Using this approach, we were able to analyze their general knowledge structure, their procedures of doing research, and the overlapping knowledge structure where they collaborated with each other. In this chapter, all illustrated maps from interviewees are encoded and drawn using UCINET software (https://sites.google.com/site/ucinetsoftware/home). All names used in this chapter are pseudonyms.

3.4 Case Studies on an IC Project: The CSP Project

The project fictitiously named CSP had a duration of about four and a half years, with new members joining and some exiting, its size hovered around 11 researchers from computer science, sociology, psychology, physics, and medical science—all from the same university during this period of time. This case study began after the target IC group had been trying to collaborate on interdisciplinary topics such as social networking for 3 years. After this period of time, the group still felt they were not clear enough about each other's expertise. As a result they spent a half-year semester to introduce each other's basic topics, disciplinary methodology, and theory. Then, after another half year's discussion about potential collaborative topics among each discipline, they finally developed joint projects and began collaborating.

We selected three out of several potential IC efforts in CSP. Among the three kinds of barriers to successful IC identified by the factor analysis mentioned earlier in this chapter (Tress et al., 2007), the control variables listed in the succeeding texts helped us select IC efforts that faced the same external and organizational environments. As a result, academic traditions—disciplinary knowledge, methodology, and epistemology—were compared in the studied cases. These controlled variables are as follows:

- Physical location and organization (Cummings and Kiesler, 2005, 2008). All participants in these three IC cases worked at the same university during the period of time they collaborated and under the same IC-related regulations of the university's administration (Maton et al., 2006).
- Gender and position title (Tress et al., 2007). Both male and female professors participated in each IC case.

▪ Group size (van Dusseldorp and Wigboldus, 1994). These three IC cases had similar group sizes—two of which had four participants; the other had five. Among these participants, there were two people who took part in two different groups.

▪ Participating time and personal relationships (Maton et al., 2006). Most of the key group members (except for one computer scientist in IC Case 3) were initiators of CSP, which meant they already knew each other personally and therefore did not need to spend time building interpersonal relationships.

▪ Language (van Dusseldorp and Wigboldus, 1994; Kotlarsky et al., 2015). Because the participants did not share a common native tongue, the working language in all three cases was English. This meant that even though there was a disparity in their birth cultures, they did not need to deal with problems of syntactical language translations.

▪ Participating disciplines (van Dusseldorp and Wigboldus, 1994). There were both natural scientists and social scientists involved in all three cases, which meant that along with not sharing an original birth culture, there was enough disparity among the participants' disciplines to classify all three projects as small-sized broad IC groups.

▪ Project budget (Tress et al., 2007). All of these three IC cases were self-funded.

3.4.1 Case 1: Sociology and Physics

The first IC case was a failed collaboration between Kate, a sociology professor, and Yann, a physicist, and his students, Albert and Chris. Albert and Chris were interested in the social networking habits of first-year university students. After their collection of data was completed, they realized that they could not build a reasonable mathematical model to simulate the dynamic process that included multidimensional information about personal attributes, such as nationality, gender, and departmental affiliation. In order to improve their research on social networking, they solicited help from their supervisor, Yann. Kate, a sociologist at the same university, was invited to join the IC by Yann, as Kate was considered the expert on "social laws" and therefore in a better position to provide the mechanics of freshmen's social networking habits. Kate was very interested in exploring high-end telecommunications technology in a large data analysis, which is outside the typical repertoire of a sociologist's analytical abilities. Their first and only meeting was held under an optimistic atmosphere but finally ended without any positive result.

We were not present at their meeting. In the interview we had with Yann and Kate, surprisingly, it was apparent that the central problem was about when and how to come up with a project hypothesis. Kate recalled that in that meeting she had asked Yann's team many times about the content of their hypothesis, which she contended was the first and essential step in sociological research. But according to Yann, the research hypothesis should not be addressed at the first stage of research. As a result, their project, according to Kate's point of view, had not been well designed.

Although Yann came to understand Kate's logic afterward, during the meeting he proposed implementing various mathematical tools in order to identify any potential interesting questions from the data, such as certain kinds of distributions, without proposing any hypothesis. Only after their first meeting were several hypotheses developed. On the methodological differences between Yann and Kate, Yann commented:

> We are not really meant to collaborate [with Kate] because of some language problems and stuff, which is quite disappointing. The whole 99% of the discussion was sort of nice, but in the end there was…some statements like "we do not understand your research questions, but we all like the data…". Maybe next time I will not speak my idea, but start with HYPOTHESIS, you know, even [if] I do not have one. Because people will not value your ideas if you do not follow their schedule, maybe next time I will try, if I really want something.

Yann realized that their conflictive attitude on hypotheses might have come from different procedures of doing research in their respective disciplines. He explained his procedure for researching physics as follows:

> The physics path is that you are just interested in something. But you don't have exact theories for this, you don't have exact hypotheses, you don't have specific questions. Sometimes you do, but not every time. Then for example you look at data, and you just look at data, and then you just analyze something, visualize the data, you try…you play around with some specific perspectives. And then you find something which you wouldn't have considered in the first place, which there was no way you could have formulated in the first place because it was like a surprise.
>
> And because of this, you get the idea what is the correct question, then you ask the correct question, then you have the hypothesis, and then you test with statistical methods from the data and hypotheses. And in addition, if you're lucky, you will come up with some sort of a model which links to causality. So you try to find a model and this model should explain if you have a basic mechanism or mechanisms for whatever the data.

His statement led to the conclusion that his physics procedure was data-initiated his work starts with data analysis and ends with a testable model. In this process, data will imply potential laws, inspire ideas, render hypotheses, and test a model.

Compared with Yann, Kate's description of quantitative sociological analysis was theory-initiated. Sociological research begins by generating hypotheses from theory and then collecting data to test the hypotheses. If the hypotheses cannot be disproved, this means that the data support the hypotheses. New theories then emerge from this process. Yann described what he had learned from his first meeting with Kate thusly:

> The main thing is before you do something, you just have a hypothesis. You have an idea what it might be about…what's the nature of something. So then from this you formulate your projection, and you formulate your question. Then you ask the question and you ask yourself what're the sort of experiments, what're the sorts of data I can go into. And then maybe you have already the data or you try to get the data yourself or do an experiment that somehow meets the two together. And then you check your hypothesis with whatever statistical measurement, with statistical means, and then you can probably throw away the hypothesis or maybe it cannot be rejected.

3.4.2 Case 2: Social Psychology and Computer Science

In the second case, which was successful, Marilyn, a professor of social psychology, and her bachelor student Dora collaborated with a computer scientist Powell, a professor, and his postdoc Landen. Together they studied opinion leadership on Facebook. Based on their first stage collaboration that took place a few years earlier, which was the cosupervision of Lucy's bachelor thesis, this time they further developed their Facebook questionnaires and theoretical ideas. In the total 4 months of their collaboration, they met twice for progress discussion of this project. During the remainder of this period, Dora received supervision from Marilyn, Landen, and Powell separately. Finally, she successfully completed her thesis as the result of this IC.

Introduced by Powell, the basic knowledge sharing in this project was centered on a set of online questionnaires. The knowledge sharing consisted of questionnaires inquiring about a representation of online opinion leadership, their distribution via Facebook, and the data analysis that resulted from it. Indeed, representatives from both disciplines involved in the collaboration—computer science and social psychology—agreed that they should focus on employing this questionnaire to understand online opinion leadership. In the interviews, both Marilyn and Powell drew their cognitive maps, from which this knowledge sharing is clearly illustrated.

Figures 3.2 and 3.3 show that their knowledge structures are quite similar. Their maps revealed total overlaps in the map's triangle structure of knowledge sharing: need to gather data on who are the opinion leaders, gather such data using questionnaires, and IC participants' specific knowledge on what to do with such data. That meant they all agreed that they should distribute the online questionnaire to identify the opinion leaders with certain expertise and that an IC sharing

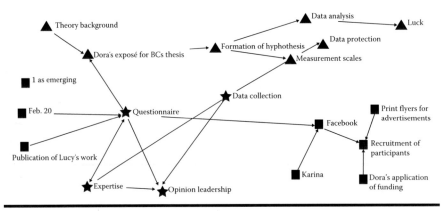

Figure 3.2   Marilyn's cognitive map (when she was collaborating with Powell). ▲ **represents logic and concepts of doing social psychology research,** ■ **shows her opinion about what the computer scientists will contribute to this project, and** ★ **signifies the overlapping elements between social psychology and computer science.**

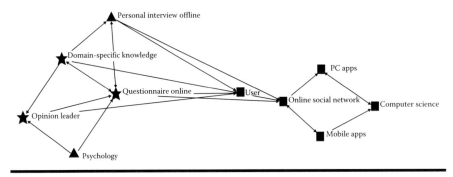

Figure 3.3   Powell's cognitive map (when he was collaborating with Marilyn). ■ **represents logic of doing computer science research,** ▲ **shows his opinion about what the social psychologist will contribute to this project, and** ★ **signifies the overlapped elements between social psychology and computer science.**

of specific knowledge on gathered data would be mutually beneficial. The interview with Powell highlighted this overlapping. He mentioned that the questionnaire design was the skill of social psychologists and that because social psychologists traditionally investigated the offline world, collaborating with computer scientists would facilitate the online distribution of the questionnaire, presenting the questions in a new and more far-reaching setting. The online questionnaire could garner more data and offer easier access to the data because people would not be so hesitant about being investigated due to the social psychologists' content design of the questionnaire guaranteeing anonymity.

In addition to the shared elements among their cognitive maps, they also had their unique nodes in each map. From the interviews, both Marilyn and Powell, revealed considerably different ways of constructing their research. Powell explained the following:

> The computer science is the tool to deliver online questionnaires and to design mobile applications…we only do the online part…Psychology deals with the question how to use questionnaires to determine opinion leadership…They provide something about ideas, interview skills, and how to measure specific knowledge systems. This is how we collaborate.

This description revealed that the computer scientists approach to the IC was data-initiated their role in the IC was to support the mechanics of collecting as much usable data as possible. The data collected about opinion leadership would in turn enrich their understanding about online user behavior and preferences as well as network theory, enabling them to build better online social network applications for both the PC and mobile phone:

> Opinion leadership is eventually implemented by the questionnaire handling knowledge of online social network users. Users are required to give feedback of online opinion leadership. Leadership is investigated by the questionnaire.
>
> Psychology has its methodology, while computer science has its domain knowledge about online social network and data processing, and also application design.

In contrast, Marilyn's cognitive map revealed her role in the IC was theory-initiated the social psychologists in the IC were to design the questionnaire in a way that supported a theory-initiated process; identify in turn theory background, hypotheses, and measurements; gather and analyze data; and decide whether analysis matched hypotheses:

> Now the questionnaire is nearly complete…the questionnaire is on opinion leadership and on expertise, and will be sent by Facebook… what we [social psychologists] do is to meet and to discuss an exposé for bachelor thesis, hypotheses, theory background…and measurement. And it will go back to the questionnaires, and to find scales to measure expertise and implement…and there are initial questions regarding data analysis….

Their different research procedures benefited their IC and empowered both sides: the social psychologists were able to analyze online opinion leadership behavior and expertise using their theory-initiated research process, and the computer scientists were able to gain a social psychology–enriched understanding of online social networking user's leadership behavior and the online social networking users' needs using their computer science data-initiated process.

Even though, like Case 1, the collaborators had different research procedures, in Case 2, their cognitive maps revealed they shared agreement on their initial research topic (online leadership) and data gathering tool (the questionnaire) upon which they could overlap their IC work of data processing and theory analysis and build upon these interfaces a mutually beneficial IC, which resulted in a joint publication.

3.4.3 Case 3: Social Psychology, Physics, and Computer Science

The third case was more complicated than the previous two because it involved three disciplines: social psychology (Marilyn), physics (Yann), and computer science (Weiss and Marilyn's former collaborator George). The collaboration was based on Marilyn's preliminary experiment, which was to examine relationships between followership and leadership. They met five times during the semester. They initially learned from Marilyn the concepts of leadership and followership, basic settings of the experimental paradigm, and visualization of the former experiment result. They then discussed new ideas about designing experiments that employed methods and factors in physics and computer science. They agreed that they could build a model by comparing results from Weiss' simulation with the existing experimental data. They worked jointly with the data, went deep into details of data collection and analytical tools such as source codes, movies as outcome of simulation, and models. Unfortunately, when the semester ended, Yann left for Switzerland and Weiss for China, which meant one controlled variable of their broad IC, the same physical location of participants, could no longer be maintained. However, their collaboration is still considered here because they worked together productively during that semester and eventually created a joint publication on the successful results of their project.

Marilyn described in the interview the way she designed the research question:

> In this project I have a certain concept of leadership in my mind that leadership and followership is an interactive phenomenon. So the two concepts define each other. And we have the movement data. What I think here comes to the idea generation. And Yann and computer scientist Weiss [optimization strategy, computing such strategies to empirical data]…do the data analysis. I hope from that [data analysis] we can get new ideas and be able to find new ideas and design for new experiments.

Weiss, like Marilyn, referred to theory-initiated methodology. In the interview, he mentioned that he already had relevant theories on human mobility. Through this collaboration, he wanted to understand human mobility by building a model in the experimental setting and perfect his model by comparing it with empirical data:

> They do experiments with the question about why is leadership of a group of people perceived as a goal. From my work on simulation I want to understand patterns or models of mobility. I want to try a model on how to maximize profits. So these are two different ways. For psychology way, they ask the question why, and I ask how they maximize profit, or optimization. I think something in common is that we need to compare my model with those real experiments to say how good my model can fit the experiment. Maybe my model gets more money than in experiment [which means maybe the team shows better group performance by following his model]. The model means I can find some patterns that can describe, I do not know, for example, like how many people can get the rewards. This means a model. A model means movement strategy and result of getting rewards.
>
> I am familiar with their experimental settings. We have the same formulation of the data, which can be used in both mobility analysis and leadership analysis.

Yann, whose research procedure was data-initiated figured out that Marilyn played a role as data provider and Weiss a role as builder of the model. Yann himself only dealt with the data analysis: first, he tried to understand Marilyn's definitions of leadership and followership and Weiss' definition of mobility and then tried to employ specific physics methods and variables to help analyze and measure his collaborators' concepts. In this way, he supported Weiss' model and Marilyn's theory.

Their shared knowledge can be identified from their cognitive maps (Figures 3.4 through 3.6).

Compared pairwise, Marilyn and Yann share nodes of existing data, leadership, and analysis. One can also see that Yann's physics methods such as convex hull and Arena support data analysis. Although Marilyn and Weiss built basic understandings about each other's work, in practical terms, they shared only experiment, data, and model nodes because Weiss informed us that the left part of his map was his work and that he did not participate in the right part. He said, "we are both interested in human mobility, but from different perspectives. For computer scientists, we want to have some model for human mobility. But for psychologists, they want to know why—what will lead to such kind of human mobility. (In their experiment) people want to follow the other to get more money from the movement. These are two different ways to do research." This meant that he and Marilyn kept their theory elements separate and collaborated only on methods and data. Weiss and Yann shared similar nodes—data, modeling, and type of diffusion/mobility pattern—as did Marilyn and Yann.

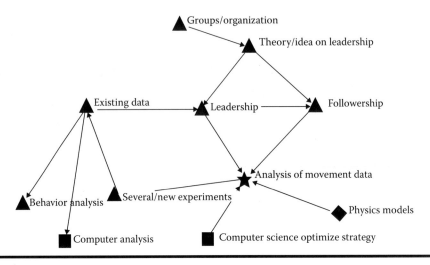

Figure 3.4 Marilyn's cognitive map (when she was collaborating with Weiss and Yann). ▲ represents logic and concepts of doing social psychology research, ■ shows her opinion about what the computer scientists will do in this project, ◆ shows her perception of physicist's work on this project, and ★ shows what she thinks are the overlapping elements of all group participants.

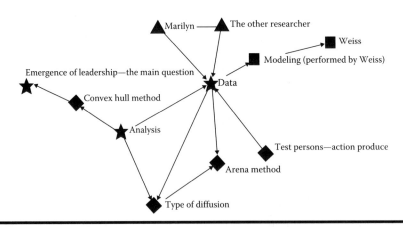

Figure 3.5 Yann's cognitive map (when he was collaborating with Weiss and Marilyn). ◆ represents logic and concepts of doing physics research, ■ shows his perception of what the computer scientists will do on this project, ▲ shows his perception of social psychologist's work on this project, and ★ shows what he thinks the overlapping elements of all the three participants are.

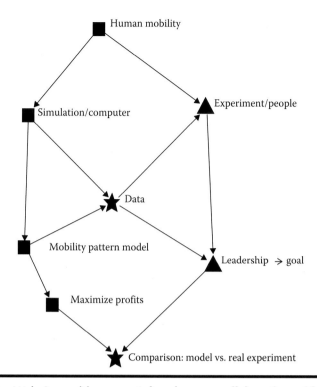

Figure 3.6 **Weiss' cognitive map (when he was collaborating with Yann and Marilyn).** ■ **shows his perception of what the computer scientists will do on this project,** ▲ **shows his perception of social psychologist's work on this project, and** ★ **shows what he thinks the overlapping elements of all three participants are.**

From the pairwise comparisons of participants' cognitive maps in this particular IC case, it appears that, on the one hand, the IC participants that shared the same research procedure mainly shared data-related knowledge. On the other hand, the participants that did not share the same research procedure shared the research topic and a more detailed understanding of what each of them could and could not provide, most likely because these understandings were acquired or thought about more overtly rather than assumed vis à vis a shared research procedure, resulting in a more concrete integrated structure of knowledge.

3.5 Differences between Two Kinds of IC Methodological Procedures

The interviews of participants in our three IC cases revealed a minimum of two disparate patterns of methodological procedures of doing research: data-initiated and theory-initiated.

If we compare successful Case 2 and Case 3 to unsuccessful Case 1, we can see that an important reason for a successful IC was the participants' acceptance of the differences in their methodological approaches, a disparity that can almost be assumed by the very nature of an IC. The other important reasons for their success were focusing on what can be mutually gained from the IC (data) and combining the strengths of their disparate disciplines' expertise to actualize their mutually beneficial data goals rather than insisting that the IC be conducted according to a certain methodological research approach—the downfall of Case 1. What we can also draw from comparisons of the Case 2 and Case 3 cognitive maps is that more overt patterns of knowledge sharing in IC occur when there are differences either in the methodological research procedures of the IC participants or in the research topics as goals of the IC.

Both the procedures of doing research are deeply rooted in certain disciplinary traditions. On the one hand, in physics, chemistry, and biology, the data-initiated procedure is sometimes employed as the methodological approach.

Comparing this to Yann's interview, we can see how his data-initiated research procedure meets the model depicted in Figure 3.7.

Make observations:

> The physics path is that you are just interested in something. But you don't have exact theories for this, you don't have exact hypothesis, you

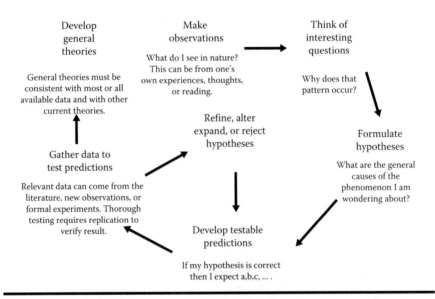

Figure 3.7 The scientific method as an ongoing process. (From Garland, Jr. T., "The_Scientific_Method_3", by Jr. T. Garland, Idea.Ucr.Edu. http://idea.ucr.edu/documents/flash/scientific_method/story.htm, retrieved October 21, 2016.)

don't have specific questions. Sometimes you do, but not every time. Then for example you look at data, and you just look at data. And then you just analyses something, visualize the data, you try…you play around some specific perspectives.

Think of questions:

And then you find something which you wouldn't have considered at the first place, which was no way you could have formulated at the first place because it was like a surprise. And because of this, you get the idea what is the correct question, then you ask the correct question.

Formulate hypotheses and develop testable predictions:

then you have the hypothesis.

Gather data to test predictions:

you test with statistic methods from the data and hypothesis.

General theories:

And in addition, if you're lucky, you will come up with sort of a model which link to causality. So you try to find a model and this model should explain if you have a basic mechanism and mechanisms whatever for the data.

One the other hand, the theory-initiated procedure can be found in methodology introductions in every textbook of social psychology (Franzoi, 2000) and sociology (Babble, 2010):

Step 1: Find a topic and literature review.
Step 2: Develop a theory and a hypothesis.
Step 3: Employ a scientific method and use it to design your research.
Step 4: Data collecting.
Step 5: Data analysis and hypothesis testing.
Step 6: Result publishing (Franzoi, 2000).

Both Kate and Marilyn followed this theory-initiated procedure. For example, we can see it from Marilyn's cognitive map (Figure 3.2):

Step 1: Theory background
Step 2: Dora's exposé and BSc thesis → formulation of hypothesis

Step 3: Measurement scales
Step 4: Data collection → opinion leadership → questionnaire
Step 5: Data analysis, expertise

It is important to note that we do not mean to imply that social sciences and humanities only employ the theory-initiated procedure and that natural sciences only employ the data-initiated procedure nor do we claim that each discipline fits for only one pattern. Our point is that research approaches must be carefully discussed in the context of observed field conditions.

3.6 Collaborative Patterns

What we learned from our investigation of three IC cases was that when interdisciplinary participants come together to collaborate with each other, at least two collaborative patterns can be employed.

One collaborative pattern is what the Maton et al. (2006) IC research investigation coined a technical collaborative pattern. IC participants that share the same research procedure only need to share details about individual points of knowledge, specific research techniques, objects of research, and so on, which may or may not be found at the same level of detail from their respective cognitive maps. For example, in Case 3, Marilyn and Weiss worked separately on their respective research topics. Their cognitive maps revealed that they only needed to collaboratively share data-related terms. Even though Weiss was aware of the experimental paradigm Marilyn used for studying leadership, Weiss was not required to work on that with her or to understand social psychology theories related to leadership. Yann's nodes of experiment and leadership in his cognitive map were only around labels of the data and model. Similarly, Marilyn's cognitive map revealed she did not know Weiss' idea about human mobility, which was related to several computational models. Weiss' contribution to the IC with Marilyn and Yann was his computer skills.

We can visualize this technical IC pattern by the procedures illustrated in Figure 3.7 and Franzoi's (2000) textbook. As both Marilyn and Weiss shared the same theory-initiated research procedure but not the same research topic, we take this procedure and their IC as an example.

From Figure 3.8, we can clearly see that the research topics discussed by Weiss and Marilyn differed from each other. But they shared the same process of data collection and data analysis, which each of them could use in their own findings publishing as well as their joint research results.

The second successful collaborative pattern that we observed from this case study is what we will call a theory-method IC pattern. Most of the researchers who mentioned mutual understandings (Clark and Brennan, 1991; Selin and Chavez, 1995; Clark, 1996; Jakobsen et al., 2004; Tress et al., 2007; Klein, 2008b) and

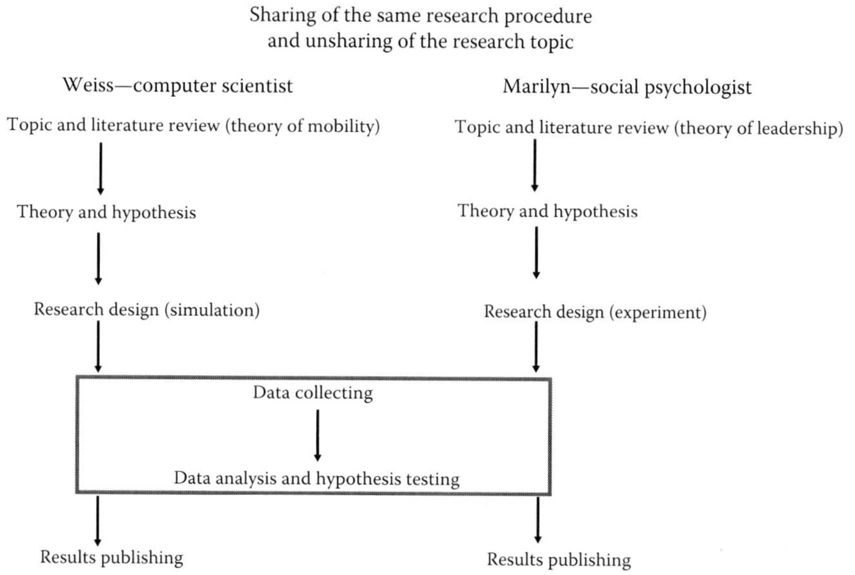

Sharing of the same research procedure
and unsharing of the research topic

Weiss—computer scientist   Marilyn—social psychologist

Topic and literature review (theory of mobility)   Topic and literature review (theory of leadership)

Theory and hypothesis   Theory and hypothesis

Research design (simulation)   Research design (experiment)

Data collecting

Data analysis and hypothesis testing

Results publishing   Results publishing

Figure 3.8   The technical IC pattern between Weiss and Marilyn in Case 3.

boundary objects (Hall et al., 2005; Wesselink, 2009) between disciplines were talking about this kind of IC pattern. The broad IC discussed by van Dusseldorp and Wigboldus (1994) shared the same requirement of scale of knowledge integration with this theory-method pattern, but van Dusseldorp and Wigboldus did not characterize IC by the difference of research procedures and topics as we are here.

This theory-method collaborative pattern was used in both Case 2 and Case 3. In both of these cases, the IC participants differed in their research procedures and therefore needed to share their research topic by exchanging much more information about each other's specialized knowledge and expertise than in a technical collaborative pattern. Each participant needed to fully understand what topic each other was working on, what each term in their respective cognitive map meant, what each participant's variables employed for data analysis presented, and how they could combine/contribute to each other's work. This IC offers an example of participants from one discipline providing theories and hypothesis, while participants from another discipline testing the common hypothesis with specialized methods of data collecting and analysis. That is why we inductively named it the theory-method IC pattern.

As shown in the cognitive maps, shared nodes among their respective maps were more complicated than the technical collaborative pattern. In analyzing Figure 3.4 (Marilyn's cognitive map), it can be seen that Yann's (the physicist) cognitive map (Figure 3.5) greatly enriched content to Marilyn's. The comparison between analysis feeding to convex hull method feeding to leadership in his cognitive map (Figure 3.5) and leadership feeding to analysis of movement data in Marilyn's cognitive map (Figure 3.4) shows that Yann provided the IC with a method to analyze both leadership and followership behavior in the experiment, based upon a detailed understanding of what his fellow collaborator—Marilyn, the social psychologist—needed.

Figure 3.9 illustrates the theory-method IC pattern between Marilyn/Weiss and Yann in Case 3 and portrays how they combined different research procedures into a joint working waterline. We can clearly see that Marilyn and Weiss constructed their data collecting work as an interface between each of them and Yann. The data collecting and analysis, which is shown in Marilyn/Weiss' procedure, played a role of input into Yann's observation step and his data collection step. Yann's whole data-initiated procedure ended with his general theories step, which is the result of Marilyn/Weiss' data analysis and hypothesis testing, which eventually feeds back to Marilyn/Weiss' result publishing. This combination between theory-initiated and data-initiated procedures is based on a well-discussed negotiation and mutual understandings upon what is needed from Marilyn/Weiss' data analysis and what Yann's data-initiated procedure can provide.

Case 2 showed similar theory-method IC findings as Case 3 discussed previously. In Case 2, Marilyn and the computer scientist, Powell, with whom she collaborated did not share the same research procedure but did share the same research topic. A comparison between Figures 3.2 and 3.3 shows that the star symbols representing overlapping elements of knowledge, which is questionnaire feeding to opinion leadership feeding to expertise in Figure 3.2 and questionnaire online feeding to opinion leader feeding to domain-specific knowledge in Figure 3.3, are

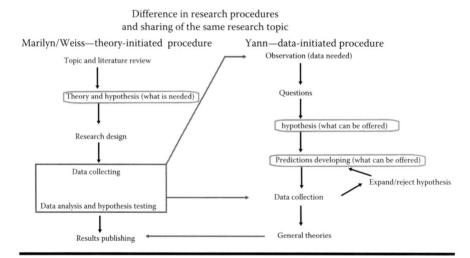

Figure 3.9 The theory-method IC pattern between Marilyn/Weiss and Yann in Case 3.

the shared process of data collection constructed by both computer online social network applications and the social psychology questionnaire approach. As in Case 3 discussed earlier, by this interface illustrated in the cognitive maps, the computer scientists successfully used their professional skills to help the social psychologists distribute their questionnaires via the online medium and provide online data analysis as outputs.

In sum, if we extract these two dimensions—research topic sharing and procedure sharing—a 2 × 2 table emerges.

Table 3.1 summarizes the two research patterns observed from the three IC case studies. In the cell where neither the research procedure nor the research topic is shared, as was true for Case 1, an IC cannot succeed. In the cell where there is a redundancy of participants' procedure and theory, they do not require an IC because there is nothing to collaborate upon.

Then how much sharing is enough for participants in each collaborative pattern to build a successful IC? From our analysis of the three IC cases, the cognitive maps of their respective participants, and the two patterns of IC used in the successful ICs, our observation is that the theory-method collaborative pattern needs an integrated, mutually beneficial knowledge structure (indicated by the cognitive maps) between each participant's different disciplines. This pattern meets the theoretical idea of SMM and TMM. In the technical collaborative pattern, though participants can share the same knowledge structures, the content (specific knowledge and skills) of their disparate disciplines remains different. This means that in order to come to a mutually benefiting exchange of disciplinary expertise, the participants need to share at least one of the several key nodes or labels in their respective cognitive maps. Compared with the theory-method collaborative pattern, the technical pattern fits the description of TMS: each of the participants needs to know who has certain expertise that is missing from their discipline and build an interface between each other. They do not need to integrate each other's discipline's perspectives or research approaches but simply make mutual beneficial use of them.

Table 3.1 Cognitive Patterns of Knowledge Sharing

	Share the Same Research Procedure	*Differences in Research Procedure*
Share the same research topic	Redundancy	Theory-method collaborative pattern (in Case 2, Marilyn and Powell; in Case 3, Marilyn/Weiss and Yann)
Differences in research topic	Technical collaborative pattern (in Case 3, Marilyn and Weiss)	Cannot fulfill IC (Case 1: Kate and Yann)

3.7 Discussion

In a comparison of the three IC cases, this chapter reveals that IC participants can exercise at least two different approaches to their research (data-initiated and theory-initiated). Considering this together with whether the research topic in an IC project is shared or not, we observed two kinds of cognitive patterns of knowledge sharing—a technical collaborative pattern and a theory-method collaborative pattern. By examining the cognitive-based reasons for people from various disciplines to share enough information to build and benefit from an IC, this chapter answers the question of how much knowledge sharing is enough for IC. In the technical pattern, IC participants need to share a requirement for at least one compelling knowledge set/skill of the other collaborators' disciplines; while in the theory-method pattern, IC participants need to share an integrated, mutually beneficial knowledge structure between each other's different disciplines. Compared with other IC studies, we feel the highlight of this study is demonstrating how IC participant–generated cognitive maps help the IC participants come to a clearer knowledge connection and, with that, an identification of what knowledge/skill set(s) the other disciplines have that they can benefit from. From this use of cognitive maps, we show that a small-sized broad IC (van Dusseldorp and Wigboldus, 1994) can overcome disparate collaborative patterns, topics, and even research procedures by employing one of the IC patterns mentioned earlier.

Moreover, we connect theories of SMM and TMS with these two interdisciplinary collaborative patterns. The reason for the connection of these two theories is not only to strengthen an understanding of the workings of IC interactions but also to offer a method for overcoming the disparities between the two models. In the technical collaborative pattern, skills, methods, and data play a role of outside memory that is available to project participants. The IC in this pattern is built upon the metaknowledge of who possesses which skills and methods and how can they be applied to the joint project that is mutually beneficial to all participants. Comparatively, in the theory-method collaborative pattern, participants not only overlap in their knowledge but also integrate their knowledge into a combined new structure that creates a mutually beneficial IC. This typology of collaborative patterns is based on the disparate nature of disciplines—especially disciplinary differences regarding research procedures.

There are obvious shortages in this chapter that we intend to address in future research. First, our observations are drawn from only three IC cases, which we intend to statistically test using data drawn from a larger sample in future research. Second, the technique of cognitive mapping needs to be improved in order to reveal even more detail about the connections between each IC participant. We intend to augment the participant-created cognitive maps during the interview processes in our next study. Third, by conducting a dynamic observation of the actual ongoing IC interactions between each participant's cognitive maps, we expect this to reveal more detail about the success of participants' collaborating processes and whether these projects lead to additional ICs. Finally, we intend to investigate how other social connecting factors of social networking, specifically interpersonal relationships, play a role in the mechanics of building collaborative connections. We want to empirically investigate whether the stronger the ties are, for example, scientists talking to each other more frequently (interpersonal relationship level), the higher the opportunities there are for those scientists to fulfill knowledge sharing (cognitive map level) and eventually realize an IC opportunity.

Acknowledgments

This study is funded by China Scholarship Council's award for outstanding self-financed students abroad. Yu Qiu from the University of Cambridge, Prof. Dr. Karin Kurz, Prof. Dr. Xiaoming Fu, Dr. Ezequiel Fernandez Castelao, and Yuhuan Huang from the University of Göttingen offered us great support and valuable suggestions. We want to express our highest appreciation to all of them as well as all IC participants for their selfless information about their IC studies. Margarita Neff-Heinrich proofread this chapter as an English-for-the-sciences specialist.

References

Argote, L., Gruenfeld, D., and Naquin, C. 1999. Group learning in organizations. In M.E. Turner (Ed.). *Groups at Work: Advances in Theory and Research* (pp. 369–411). Hillsdale, NJ: Lawrence Erlbaum Associates.

Axelrod, R. (Ed.). 1976. *Structure of Decision: The Cognitive Maps of Political Elites.* Princeton, NJ: Princeton University Press.

Babble, E. 2010. *Introduction to Social Research* (5th edn.). Andover, MA: Wadworth.

Bergmann, M., Brohmann, B., Hoffmann, E., Loibl, M.C., Rehaag, R., Schramm, E., and Voß, J.P. 2005. *Quality Criteria of Transdisciplinary Research. A Guide for the Formative Evaluation of Research Projects.* ISOE-Studientexte Nr. 13, Institute for Ecological Economy Research, Berlin, Germany.

Boos, M. 1996. Entscheidungsfindung in Gruppen. Eine Prozeßanalyse. Bern, Switzerland: Huber.

Boos, M., Morguet, M., Meier, F., and Fisch, R. 1990. Zeitreihenanalysen von Interaktionsprozessenbei der BearbeitungkomplexerProbleme in Expertengruppen. *Zeitschrift für Sozialpsychologie*, 21, 53–64.

Burkart, R. 2002. Kommunikationswissenschaft. Grundlagen und Problemfelder; Umrisse einer interdisziplinären Sozialwissenschaft. 4., überarb. und aktualisierteAufl [Communication science: Foundations and challenges. A framework for an interdisciplinary social science (4th edn.)]. Wien, Austria: Böhlau.

Cannon-Bowers, J.A., Salas, E., and Converse, S. 1993. Shared mental models in expert team decision making. In N.J. Castellan (Ed.). *Individual and Group Decision Making* (pp. 221–246). Hillsdale, NJ: Lawrence Erlbaum Associates.

Clark, H.H. 1996. *Using Language.* Cambridge, U.K.: Cambridge University Press.

Clark, H.H. and Brennan, S.E. 1991. Grounding in communication. In L.B. Resnick and J.M. Levine (Eds.). *Perspectives on Socially Shared Cognition* (pp. 127–149). Washington, DC: American Psychological Association.

Cummings, J.N. and Kiesler, S. 2005. Collaborative research across disciplinary and organizational boundaries. *Social Studies of Science*, 35(5), 703–722.

Cummings, J.N. and Kiesler, S. 2008. Who collaborates successfully? Prior experience reduces collaboration barriers in distributed interdisciplinary research. *CSCW'08*, San Diego, CA, November 8–12, 2008.

Defila, R. and Di Giulio, A. 2015. Integrating knowledge: Challenges raised by the "Inventory of Synthesis". *Futures*, 65, 123–135.

Defila, R., Di Giulio, A., and Scheuermann, M. 2006. Forschungsverbundmanagement. Handbuch für die Gestaltung inter- und transdisziplinärer Projekte. Zürich, Switzerland: vdf Hochschulverlag an der ETH Zürich.

Derry, S.J. and Schunn, C.D. 2005. Interdisciplinary: A beautiful but dangerous beast. In S.J. Derry, C.D. Schunn, and M.A. Gernsbacher (Eds.). *Interdisciplinary Collaboration: An Emerging Cognitive Science* (pp. xiii–xx). Mahwah, NJ: Lawrence Erlbaum Associates.

Franzoi, S. 2000. *Social Psychology*. Columbus, OH: McGraw-Hill.

Frey, G. 1973. Methodological problems of interdisciplinary discussions. *RATIO*, 15(2), 161–182.

Garland, T., Jr. (n.d.). The_Scientific_Method_3.Idea.Ucr.Edu. Retrieved October 21, 2016, from http://idea.ucr.edu/documents/flash/scientific_method/story.htm.

Godemann, J. 2008. Knowledge integration: A key challenge for transdisciplinary cooperation. *Environmental Education Research*, 14(6), 625–641.

Guchait, P., Lei, P., and Tews, M.J. 2015. Making teamwork work: Team knowledge for team effectiveness. *Journal of Psychology*, 150(3) 1–22.

Gupta, N. and Hollingshead, A.B. 2010. Differentiated versus integrated transactive memory effectiveness: It depends on the task. *Group Dynamics: Theory, Research, and Practice*, 14(4), 384.

Haines, V.A., Godley, J., and Hawe, P. 2011. Understanding interdisciplinary collaborations as social networks. *American Journal of Community Psychology*, 47(1–2), 1–11.

Hall, R., Stevens, R., and Torralba, T. 2005. Disrupting representational infrastructure in conversations across disciplines. In S.J. Derry, C.D. Schunn, and M.A. Gernsbacher (Eds.). *Interdisciplinary Collaboration: An Emerging Cognitive Science* (pp. xiii–xx). Mahwah, NJ: Lawrence Erlbaum Associates.

Haythornthwaite, C. 2006. Learning and knowledge networks in interdisciplinary collaborations. *Journal of the American Society for Information Science and Technology*, 57(8), 1079–1092.

Heemskerk, M., Wilson, K., and Pavao-Zuckerman, M. 2003. Conceptual models as tools for communication across disciplines. *Conservation Ecology*, 7(3): 8.

Hunecke, M. 2006. Eine forschungsmethodologische Heuristik zur Sozialen Ökologie [A research method heuristic for social ecology]. München, Germany: Oekom.

Jakobsen, C.H., Hels, T., and McLaughlin, W.J. 2004. Barriers and facilitators to integration among scientist in transdisciplinary landscape analysis: A cross-country comparison. *Forest Policy and Economics*, 6(1), 15–31.

Jakobsen, C.H. and McLaughlin, W.J. 2004. Communication in ecosystem management: A case study of cross-disciplinary integration in the assessment phase of the interior Columbia Basin ecosystem management project. *Environmental Management*, 33(5), 591–606.

Katz, N., Lazer, D., Arrow, H., and Contractor, N. 2004. Network theory and small groups. *Small Group Research*, 35(3), 307–332.

Klimoski, R. and Mohammed, S. 1994. Team mental model: Construct or metaphor? *Journal of Management*, 20(2), 403–437.

Klein, J.T. 1990. *Interdisciplinary: History, Theory and Practice.* Detroit, MI: Wayne State University Press.

Klein, J.T. 2008a. Education. In G.H. Hadorn, H. Hoffmann-Riem, and S. Biber-Klemm (Eds). *Handbook of Transdisciplinary Research* (pp. 399–410). Bern, Switzerland: Springer.

Klein, J.T. 2008b. Evaluation of interdisciplinary and transdisciplinary research: A literature review. *American Journal of Preventive Medicine*, 35(2), 116–123.

Kotlarsky, J., van den Hooff, B., and Houtman, L. 2015. Are we on the same page? Knowledge boundaries and transactive memory system development in cross-functional teams. *Communication Research*, 42(3), 319–344.

Krott, M. 1996. Interdisziplinarität im Netz der Disziplinen. In P. Balsiger, R. Defila, and A. Di Giulio (Eds.). Ökologie und Interdisziplinarität–eine Beziehung mit Zukunft? Wissenschaftsforschung zur Verbesserung der fachübergreifenden Zusammenarbeit [Ecology and interdisciplinarity—A relationship with future? Scientific research to improve multidisciplinary collaboration] (pp. 87–97). Basel, Switzerland: Birkhäuser.

Lewis, K. 2003. Measuring transactive memory systems in the field: Scale development and validation. *Journal of Applied Psychology*, 88(4), 587–604.

Lewis, K. and Herndon, B. 2011.Transactive memory systems: Current issues and future research directions. *Organization Science*, 22(5), 1254–1265.

Liang, D.W., Moreland, R., and Argote, L. 1995. Group versus individual training and individual performance: The mediating role of transactive memory. *Personality and Social Psychology Bulletin*, 21(4), 384–393.

Lim, B.C. and Klein, K. 2006. Team mental models and team performance: A field study of the effects of team mental model similarity and accuracy. *Journal of Organizational Behavior*, 27(4), 403–418.

Luszki, M.B. 1958. *Interdisciplinary Team Research Methods and Problems.* Washington, DC: Natural Training Laboratories.

MacMynowski, D.P. 2007. Pausing at the brink of interdisciplinary: Power and knowledge at the meeting of social and biophysical science. *Ecology and Society*, 12(1), 20.

Mathieu, J.E., Heffner, T.S., Goodwin, G.F., Salas, E., and Cannon-Bowers, J.A. 2000. The influence of shared mental models on team process and performance. *Journal of Applied Psychology*, 85(2), 273.

Maton, K.I., Perkins, D.D., and Saegert, S. 2006. Community psychology at the crossroads: Prospects for interdisciplinary research. *American Journal of Community Psychology*, 38(1–2), 9–21.

Mohammed, S. and Dumville, B.C. 2001. Team mental models in a team knowledge framework: Expanding theory and measurement across disciplinary boundaries. *Journal of Organizational Behavior*, 22(2), 89–106.

Mohammed, S., Ferzandi, L., and Hamilton, K. 2010. Metaphor no more: A 15-year review of the team mental model construct. *Journal of Management*. Advance online publication.

Moreland, R.L., Argote, L., and Krishnan, R. 2002. Training people to work in groups. In R.S. Tindale, J. Edwards, E.J. Posavac, F.B. Bryant, Y. Suarez-Balcazar, E. Henderson-King, and J. Myers (Eds.). *Theory and Research on Small Groups* (pp. 37–60). New York: Plenum Press.

Moreland, R.L. and Myaskovsky, L. 2000. Exploring the performance benefits of group training: Transactive memory or improved communication? *Organizational Behavior and Human Decision Processes*, 82(1), 117–133.

Ren, Y. and Argote, L. 2011. Transactive memory systems 1985–2010: An integrative framework of key dimensions, antecedents, and consequences. *Academy of Management Annals*, 5(1), 189–229.

Sa, C.M. 2006. Interdisciplinary strategies at research-intensive universities (Doctoral dissertation). Available from ProQuest Dissertation and theses database of Penn State (UMI No. 3334950). https://etda.libraries.psu.edu/catalog/7048.

Selin, S. and Chavez, D. 1995. Developing an evolutionary tourism partnership model. *Annals of Tourism Research*, 22(4), 844–856.

Stasser, G. and Titus, W. 1985. Pooling of unshared information in group decision making: Biased information sampling during discussion. *Journal of Personality and Social Psychology*, 48(6), 1467–1478.

Stokols, D., Fuqua, J., Gress, J., Harvery, R., Phillips, K., Baezconde-Garbanati, L., Unger, J. et al. 2003. Evaluating transdisciplinary science. *Nicotine and Tabacco Research*, 5(Suppl. 1), S21–S39.

Tress, G., Tress, B., and Fry, G. 2007. Analysis of the barriers to integration in landscape research projects. *Land Use Policy*, 24(2), 374–385.

Turner, J.R., Chen, Q., and Danks, S. 2014. Team shared cognitive constructs: A meta-analysis exploring the effects of shared cognitive constructs on team performance. *Performance Improvement Quarterly*, 27(1), 83–117.

van Dusseldorp, D. and Wigboldus, S. 1994. Interdisciplinary research for integrated rural development in developing countries: The role of social sciences. *Issues in Integrative Studies*, 12, 93–138.

Wasserman, S., and Faust, K. 1994. Social network analysis: Methods and applications (Vol. 8). Cambridge: Cambridge University Press.

Wegner, D.M. 1987. Transactive memory: A contemporary analysis of the group mind. In I.B. Mullen and G.R. Goethals (Eds.). *Theories of Group Behavior* (pp. 185–208). New York: Springer-Verlag.

Wesselink, A. 2009.The emergence of interdisciplinary knowledge in problem-focused research. *Area*, 41(4), 404–413.

SOCIAL NETWORK STRUCTURE

Chapter 4

Measurement of Guanxi Circles: Using Qualitative Study to Modify Quantitative Measurement*

Jar-Der Luo, Xiao Han, Ronald Burt, Chaowen Zhou, Meng-Yu Cheng, and Xiaoming Fu

Contents

---

* Part of this book chapter is adapted from the following two papers: Luo and Cheng (2015) and Luo and Yeh (2012). Luo, Jar-Der takes all responsibility for this paper. Ronald Burt provides this article with the computation methods of guanxi circle.

4.1   Introduction: Methodological and Theoretical Questions

We begin with a workplace phenomenon in which a supervisor categorizes his staff into in-group and out-group members, using different rules of social exchange with the different groups. This phenomenon is called leader–member exchange theory (in brief, LMX theory, Graen and Cashman, 1975; Graen, 1976; Sparrowe and Liden, 1997). However, differentiating between in-group and out-group members is a difficult methodological problem. Our methodological question is, "can we find a method to categorize in-group and out-group members?" Our theoretical question is as follows: "Are there only two types of subordinators in the mind of a supervisor? Or are there more than two categories?"

LMX theory argues that the strength of relationships increases over time (Graen, 1976). Relationships between supervisors and their subordinates foster different levels of interpersonal trust through tangible and intangible social exchanges (Dienesch and Liden, 1986). For example, subordinates actively repay and generously share resources with their supervisor in a high-quality exchange relationship, whereas a low-quality dyadic relationship involves only formal and in-role interactions (Blau, 1964). In-group members with strong relationships have not only cooperative working ties but also intimate and loyal relations with their supervisor, which results in higher job satisfaction and lower turnover rates than out-group members (Graen and Uhi-Bien, 1995). In addition, in-group members are more likely to receive emotional support, trust, and empowerment, which bring about better performance and higher evaluation, and in turn increase the quality of the relationship with the supervisor.

LMX indicators are composed of a series of attitude questions, such as "I like the personality of my supervisor," "It's very pleasant to work with my supervisor," and "I enjoy talking with my supervisor," which in general adopt Likert's seven-point scale for measurement (Dienesch and Liden, 1986; Graen and Uhl-Bien, 1995; Schriescheim et al., 1999). Each subordinate is assigned an LMX score, and this score determines their position in a continuum from the outer ring to the most intimate group of the supervisor of the organization. Thus, the methodological question becomes, "can we find a method to draw a line between the in-group and out-group in this continuum?"

We begin with three characteristics to distinguish leader–member relationships in China. As sociologist Fei (1992) called "the differential mode of association" (in Chinese, cha xu ge ju), a Chinese ego-centered network is composed by multiple layers of rings, in which different behavioral and moral standards are applied for each of these different layers of guanxi. At the core of the ego network, family ethics is the base for a Chinese person to build and maintain his or her guanxi (Liang, 1983; Bond and Hwang, 1986; Chua et al., 2008, 2009). Based on family ethics, the innermost ring of a Chinese ego-centered network is called a "family tie," which includes real- and pseudofamily ties (Yang, 1993; Luo, 2011). An important feature of Chinese guanxi is its moral requirement of obligation (Mao et al., 2012). Both sides of a family tie maintain complete and unbreakable responsibility to each other, just like "obligatory ties" defined by Zhang and Zhang (2006). On the contrary, a "reciprocal tie" requires both sides to take long-term but limited responsibilities.

Adjacent to the core, there is a special type of guanxi named after "familiar ties" (Yang, 1993; Luo, 2005), which form the most important part of a Chinese person's ego-centered social network. Familiar ties in Chinese society are a type of strong tie, since they involve not only reciprocal exchanges but also intimacy and emotional support. Similar to Yang's argument of family ethics, Bian (1997) and Bian et al. (2015) separated strong ties into two categories, family members and general strong ties, in studying guanxi favoritism.

In Chinese particularistic society, "the rule of favor exchange" (Hwang, 1987, 1988) that guides familiar ties introduces a kind of quasi-collective behavior not true of the outermost ring, the third category of relationships (stranger ties in Yang's categorization). However, such familiar ties are still in reality instrumental exchange relations, so self-interest and calculative rationality are central elements in this category. Conducting long-term favor exchanges is the basis of mutual interactions between "familiar ties" (Yang, 1993). Hwang (1987, 1988) also divided Chinese guanxi into three categories. The term "rule of need" is used to explain the exchange principle of "expressive ties." In long-term social exchanges, Chinese people often mix up expressive and instrumental motivation in "mixed ties" by following what Hwang called the "rule of favor exchange." The third category in Hwang's (1987) classification is "instrumental ties," which follow the "rule of equity." The outermost ring of guanxi is composed by purely instrumental ties. They could also be called "utilitarian ties" (Zhang and Zhang, 2006).

Since many Chinese social scientists argue that there are three categories in Chinese guanxi, we begin by looking for three layers in a supervisor's guanxi circle in the Chinese workplace.

4.2 What Is a Guanxi Circle in an Organization

Guanxi circles are actually pseudofamilies in a person's working life and at work usually develop from ego-centered social networks around one focal person. That is why a guanxi circle can be formed around a particular person, for example, a director's circle or president's circle. Power is the key to understanding a guanxi circle, since it is required to mobilize resources for carrying out a series of actions and exchanging favors among members. Most Chinese workers wish to build up their own guanxi circles, but only those with formal power or informal influence turn their ego-centered networks into circles that act as significant stakeholders in an organization.

The main guanxi circle in a workplace is generally centered on the supervisor at the highest level. Other circle leaders derive their power from the supervisor; their guanxi circles are thus subsets of the supervisor's. In other words, a guanxi circle of this sort has a treelike structure in which a large circle contains several smaller circles. Some circles are independent from the main circle but have bridging ties to maintain a connection with the latter. However, some are comparatively closed groups that do not overlap with the other circles. A whole network diagram of a workplace full of guanxi circles is shown in Figure 4.1. Guanxi circles often make a Chinese workplace a fragmented network structure.

In general, a guanxi circle is centered on a powerful formal or informal leader, with a network structure of differential modes of association (Fei, 1992). Several rings of social ties like ripples expanded from the center's family members to the

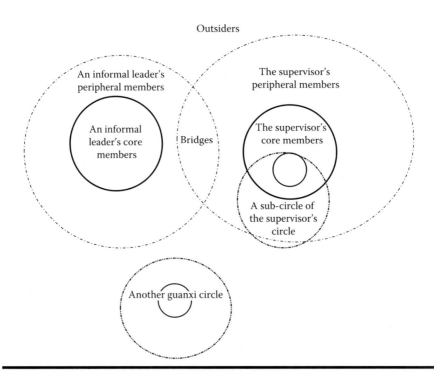

Figure 4.1 Guanxi circles and fragmented network structure in Chinese workplaces.

most intimate friends, then to familiar ties, and finally to weak ties. The nature of differential modes of association makes a Chinese leader categorize his or her staff into in-group and out-group members. He or she further divides the in-group members into circle core and peripheral members. Therefore, there is always an inner core surrounded with peripheral members in a guanxi circle.

The concept of guanxi circles is similar to action sets (Mayer, 1966) rather than a closed group or an association. A guanxi circle is not a closed group, because it is ego-centered and loosely organized without fixed membership. The concept of "set" refers to a group of people, all of who have ties with the focal person (Barnes, 1954). An action set comprises social connections intentionally mobilized by its focal person, who aims to carry out a series of actions for an individual or collective goal. That is, as a type of action set, guanxi circles are characterized as being groups that include only two types of strong ties in the Chinese cultural context: family ties, including family and pseudofamily members, and very good friends, or familiar ties in Yang's (1993) terms. Weak ties, as well as strangers, are excluded as outsiders. In addition, guanxi circles carry out a series of ongoing actions, such as finishing tasks, achieving the objectives of the circle or organization, competing for resources for one's own use, expanding its scale, and increasing its influence.

The ring of pseudofamily ties (Yang, 1993) makes up the core of a guanxi circle, which is characterized by loyal and intimate relationships, similar to those of family members. This core may be called the "basic team" (Chen, 1998) or "confidants" (Chi, 1996), since it is the basic force and most intimate relation for the person at the center.

Outside the core, peripheral circle members are mainly composed of long-term relations with limited liability in frequent social exchanges. These members follow the rule of familiar ties when exchanging favors (Hwang, 1987). This ring is the interface between the core and the outside world. Their guanxi practices are more flexible and open than the core's but much stronger in mobilizing resources than weak ties. Since the social ties of this sort can be suspended, broken up, and repaired, a circle leader has much more room for guanxi manipulation and he or she may move peripheral members out and put outsiders in, according to the situation.

Flexible guanxi operation usually makes a guanxi circle's boundary open. In this dynamic process, a guanxi circle may absorb outsiders into the inner group and also move trustworthy periphery members into the core. The boundaries within and outside a guanxi circle are not well defined, and thus, there are often overlapping areas among guanxi circles. In other words, there are bridges connecting various circles.

As stated earlier, a guanxi circle is composed of core and periphery members. However, there is another type of guanxi circle member who is in the overlapping area between two or more guanxi circles and connects these groups. We can call these guanxi circle members "bridges."

Since an organization supervisor generally has more power and resources, his or her guanxi circle members may enjoy better treatment during favor exchanges. Therefore, we distinguish these members of the supervisor's guanxi circle from core members in other informal leader's guanxi circles. Those who don't belong to any guanxi circle are "outsiders." Thus, as described in Figure 4.1, we categorize Chinese workers into five types:

1. Core members in a supervisor's guanxi circle
2. Periphery members in a supervisor's guanxi circle
3. Core members in an informal leader's guanxi circles
4. Bridges
5. Outsiders

Circle core member: Among guanxi circle members, a core is a comparatively closed clique of pseudofamily ties. Core members who have organizational supervisors as the center egos of their guanxi circle are coded as "supervisor's core" in the following sections. Those who do not are coded as core members in informal leaders' guanxi circles and are denoted as "informal leader's core."

Circle peripheral members: A guanxi circle is composed of a group of people who at least have familiar ties connecting them to the centered ego. As the theory states earlier, the boundary is not closed, so new members may be introduced into the guanxi circle by the centered ego or ego's intermediaries. Those members in a supervisor's circle who are excluded by cores are coded as "members in the supervisor's guanxi circles," who are denoted as "peripheral members."

Bridges and outsiders: Periphery members who are included in two or more guanxi circles are coded as "bridges." Those who are not included in any guanxi circle are coded as "outsiders."

This chapter presents a novel comprehensive methodology to quantify guanxi in workplaces, which incorporates both quantitative data and qualitative results in a complementary manner. It works as follows: First, upon the quantitative collection of data from all actors within an organization (or a department of the organization), we compute each actor's guanxi circle effect, which is the closeness of an actor to his or her supervisor. Then, by using each actor's guanxi circle effect, we will categorize all actors in a department into core members, peripheral members, and outsiders centered around the department supervisor. Therefore, informal leaders' circle members and bridges will not be included in this chapter.

In the following, we will use the methodology described in the "Introduction" of this book to address the questions raised at the beginning of this chapter. That is, we will use qualitative studies to find the "ground truth," which can be used to modify our quantitative methods of classifying in-group and out-group members. In the several stages of comparison between qualitative and quantitative studies, this chapter will illustrate the process of picking out the best indicator for measuring a supervisor's guanxi circle.

4.3 Qualitative Study

4.3.1 Data Collection

To study guanxi circles in a workplace, we choose a real-estate company in a business group as our research site. The business group has about 700 employees and 20 firms, which are split into three industries: chemistry, investment, and real estate. The real-estate company is a good site for our study, since it has a formal organizational structure with obvious boundaries and its organizational chart clearly defines each worker's position, reporting line, and function. In addition, the business group is owned by a single person, who assigned supervisor ZL as his agent in the real-estate company. Thus, the power structure of this firm is simple: With a clear-cut boundary around the firm, we can accurately survey the whole network of informal relations in this firm and we can easily identify the center of power and the guanxi rings around the center. In a complex organization with multiple centers of power, it will be more difficult for us to categorize each worker's relational proximity to the various centers. In this kind of exploratory research, a firm with a simple organizational structure, such as the real-estate company in the business group, is a good sample.

4.3.2 Qualitative Study

A qualitative study was conducted from the beginning of 2012 to the end of March 2012, as shown in Table 4.1. It includes four types of studies:

1. We collected and analyzed secondhand data, including employee information, organizational charts, various arrangements of formal institutions, job descriptions, and codes of behaviors.

Table 4.1 Time of Qualitative Studies

Stage	Date	Days	Location	Researches
First stage	January 9–13, 2012	5	The headquarter of B business group	The collection of secondhand data
Second stage	February 2–11, 2012	9	The real-estate company in business group B	Observation in the company
Third stage	March 2–30, 2012	29	The real-estate company in the business group B	Interview and survey

2. One research assistant, under the guise of an intern student, conducted observations in formal or informal arenas, such as formal business meetings, discussion forums, dinner banquets, lunch meetings, and off-duty social activities. A diary of everyday observations was recorded and is used as raw data for analysis.

3. This research assistant adopted a probing manner during conversations with his colleagues so that he could deeply understand the social activities, social relations, and network structure in the firm.

4. Two research assistants interviewed many employees with a semistructured questionnaire. Each interview lasted for 0.5–2.5 hours, and many interviewees were interviewed twice. Most of the interviews were allowed to be recorded, since we guaranteed the anonymity of interviewees. Overall, 31 out of 60 employees in this company were included in our interviews.

During this qualitative study, we used the following three methods to identify each actor's role in supervisor ZL's guanxi circle:

1. A senior researcher in the research team directly asked ZL to name people in his circle.

2. The research assistant interviewed some expert informants—those who have more precise knowledge about social relations in the firm, such as secretaries and people active in after-work social activities, and asked them to draw a picture of the network structure of the firm.

3. The research team analyzed the raw data from our observations and interviews to find out the structure of the guanxi circles, such as the people who have dinner with ZL, are involved in off-duty social activities with the supervisor, and get special jobs with ZL's trust.

From the qualitative studies as shown earlier, we eventually compiled a list of the guanxi circle roles of each actor. While some actors are easily categorized into the supervisor's "circle core" or "circle peripheral," others are not easily identified as a certain role. For example, some coded as "marginal members" of ZL's circle are probably outsiders; some supervisor's peripheral members are also core members in an informal leader's circle, and they are probably bridges. We thus need more information to help in identifying all actors' roles.

4.3.3 Quantitative Study

In the last week of March 2012, the whole research team entered the research site to conduct a series of interviews with high-ranking officers and do quantitative survey with all employees in the company. The questionnaire includes 18 whole network question items covering four dimensions: friendship ties, instrumental ties (Krackhardt, 1992), trust relations (Mishra, 1996), and mixed ties combining expressive and instrumental motivations (Hwang, 1987; Luo, 2011). Each question forms a network. In these 18 networks, only those friendship- and mixed-tie networks show a high association with guanxi circle measurement, since guanxi circle in theory is involved with expressive feelings. Ten theoretically relevant guanxi circle–specific questionnaire items are listed in Table 4.2.

We collected the data from all 60 employees in the firm, but 3 employees gave invalid data. So in total, we had 57 valid cases. Finally, UCINET was used to draw the pictures of the 10 whole networks. We found that no marginal members have direct symmetric ties to ZL and his core members but have some ties to his peripheral members. Four of them have a dense network with those circle members, while most of them have only one or two ties connected to ZL's circle. So the former have a strong indirect connection to the supervisor and can be classified as "circle peripheral members."

As shown in Table 4.3, there are two types of marginal members found in qualitative studies at the margin of the supervisor's circle. The first is people who are separated by three steps to the supervisor; they are "marginal members," as stated earlier. The second is marginal people embedded in a dense network connected to ZL, and they are classified as a peripheral member of ZL in this chapter. We further classify the other "marginal members" as "outsiders."

In another example, some core members in informal leaders' circles are also peripheral members in the supervisor's circle, such as LHZ and LL, and they are actually "bridges" between the two circles. They are categorized as "peripheral members" in this study.

Combining the qualitative research results and the supplementation from the pictures of network structure, we get a final classification of each actor's role in the supervisor's circle, as shown in Table 4.3. This list of roles can be taken as the "ground truth" in developing the quantitative measurement of guanxi circle.

The qualitative study has many merits: accuracy, rich information, detailed observations, good judgment of relevant informants, and grounded knowledge collected in the field. However, this method's limitations are also significant. One of the limitations is the lack of replicability in the field studies that makes the research results subjective. We thus use the quantitative data to remedy the insufficiencies in the qualitative research.

Another major deficiency of the qualitative study is its high cost. Taking our research as an example, one assistant spent most of his time in a 3-month period to get the research results from one company. We thus need a method with easy and standardized procedure to measure guanxi circles, which can collect data from many research sites in a relatively inexpensive fashion.

Table 4.2 Questions of Guanxi in Whole Network Survey

	Dept. 1				Dept. 2			...
	A1, A2	A1, A3	...	A32, A33	B1, B2	...	B26, B27	
The best five questions (according to the results of experiment 2)								
16. I am willing to share a new thought with him or her.								
15. I am willing to lend 1 month's salary or more to him or her.								
17. If he or she asks, I would like to help his or her friends.								
1. I am involved in social activities (like shopping, dining, etc.) with him or her after work.								
14. Whenever I learn new knowledge concerning jobs, I would like to teach him or her.								
The other five questions in the comparison								
3. I will keep contact with him or her even after I leave this job.								

(Continued)

Table 4.2 (*Continued*) Questions of Guanxi in Whole Network Survey

	Dept. 1				Dept. 2			...
	A1, A2	A1, A3	...	A32, A33	B1, B2	...	B26, B27	
4. With whom do you talk about your private affairs during your daily chats?								
5. Who can be listed among your best friends?								
9. I think that he or she is concerned about my well-being.								
18. I would like to introduce him or her to my friends.								

Table 4.3 Categorization of Each Actor's Role in Qualitative Studies

Qualitative Study Results	Classification in This Study	Name
Supervisor	Supervisor	ZL
Core member	Core member	XJY
Core member	Core member	YYL
Core member	Core member	HJ
Peripheral member	Peripheral member	MFY
Peripheral member	Peripheral member	WWD
Marginal member	Outsider	XDC
Marginal member	Outsider	HLC
Peripheral member	Peripheral member	YLL
Marginal member	Outsider	ZMH
Peripheral member	Peripheral member	FLF
Peripheral member	Peripheral member	LJI
Peripheral member	Peripheral member	LWF
Marginal member with dense networking	Peripheral member	LJ
Marginal member	Outsider	LYS
Marginal member with dense networking	Peripheral member	ZB
Peripheral member	Peripheral member	CB
Marginal member	Outsider	HZL
Marginal member	Outsider	WWS
Marginal member	Outsider	THC
Marginal member	Outsider	XHP
Marginal member with dense networking	Peripheral member	ZHM
Outsider	Outsider	YJP
Marginal member	Outsider	HL
Marginal member with dense networking	Peripheral member	JHJ

(Continued)

Table 4.3 (*Continued*) Categorization of Each Actor's Role in Qualitative Studies

Qualitative Study Results	Classification in This Study	Name
Outsider	Outsider	YS
Peripheral member	Peripheral member	ZZB
Marginal member	Outsider	HT
Marginal member	Outsider	ZH
Marginal member	Outsider	LYR
Outsider	Outsider	YXX
Outsider	Outsider	PYP
Outsider	Outsider	LY
Outsider	Outsider	LYL
Peripheral member	Peripheral member	HHQ
Outsider	Outsider	JJ
Marginal member	Outsider	XHR
Informal leaders' core or bridge	Peripheral member	LHZ
Outsider	Outsider	WHY
Outsider	Outsider	LYE
Informal leaders' core or bridge	Peripheral member	YL
Outsider	Outsider	LJJ
Outsider	Outsider	XJJ
Outsider	Outsider	LLJ
Informal leaders' core	Outsider	WNZ
Outsider	Outsider	WQ
Informal leaders' core	Outsider	XYQ
Informal leaders' core or bridge	Peripheral member	YTA
Informal leaders' core or bridge	Peripheral member	LL
Outsider	Outsider	WQJ

(*Continued*)

Table 4.3 (*Continued*) Categorization of Each Actor's Role in Qualitative Studies

Qualitative Study Results	Classification in This Study	Name
Marginal member	Outsider	DBQ
Peripheral member	Peripheral member	WXY
Outsider	Outsider	ZXH
Outsider	Outsider	ZBW
Informal leaders' core	Outsider	LQP
Outsider	Outsider	PFL
Outsider	Outsider	LAH
Outsider	Outsider	ZSJ
Outsider	Outsider	YHY
Outsider	Outsider	PLH

Notes: In this study, marginal members and informal leaders' core will be taken as outsiders. Those dense networking members and bridges will be taken as peripheral members.

4.4 Measurement of a Guanxi Circle

4.4.1 Guanxi Circle Effect

In this section, we propose a method to compute network proximity to the core of a guanxi circle, G_{ji}. Let variable Z_{ji} measure the strength of a connection between actor j and supervisor i: 0 for no connection, 1 for an asymmetric connection from j to i, 2 for an asymmetric tie from i to j, and 3 for reciprocal connections. The following index measures the proximity of person j and supervisor i:

$$G_{ji} = Z_{ji} + \sum_k Z_{jk} \times Z_{ki}, \quad \text{for all } k \neq i \text{ or } j.$$

The first term (Z_{ji}) measures the direct connection between j and i. The summed term measures connections from j with strong connections to colleagues k, who have strong connections to supervisor i. The combination, G_{ji}, measures the extent to which actor j is central in the guanxi circle around supervisor i. The stronger j's connection to i and the stronger j's connections with i's closest colleagues, the more central actor j is in the guanxi circle around supervisor i.

However, the indirect effect of a connection ranges from 12 to 46, for example, in Question 14, while the direct effect is between 0 and 3. So we propose three methods to reduce the impact of the exaggerated indirect effect in G_{ji}:

1. Divided by 9

$$G_{ji} = Z_{ji} + \left[\left(\sum_k Z_{jk} \times Z_{ki} \right) \Big/ 9, \quad \text{for all } k \neq i \text{ or } j. \right.$$

   Since the highest number of $Z_{jk} \times Z_{ki}$ is 9 (3 × 3), so the sum item is divided by 9. That means, the highest indirect effect via a good friend to connect the supervisor is 1. Thus, a person's total indirect effect is limited to 1.33–5.11, a little higher than the direct effect in general cases.

2. Divided by network size

$$G_{ji} = Z_{ji} + \left[\left(\sum_k Z_{jk} \times Z_{ki} \right) \Big/ 56, \quad \text{for all } k \neq i \text{ or } j. \right.$$

   Fifty-six is the effective network size excluding the supervisor, that is, 57–1. That means the indirect effect is divided by network size. The larger a network is, the higher the indirect effects of network members are. Thus, it is sufficient to cancel out the impact of network size, and the total indirect effect is limited from 0.21 to 0.82, much smaller than the direct effect.

3. Normalization

$$G_{ji} = Z_{ji} + 3 \times \left[\left(\sum_k Z_{jk} \times Z_{ki} \right) - \text{Min} \left(\sum_k Z_{jk} \times Z_{ki} \right) \right] \Big/ \left(\text{Max} \left(\sum_k Z_{jk} \times Z_{ki} \right) \right.$$

$$\left. - \text{Min} \left(\sum_k Z_{jk} \times Z_{ki} \right) \right), \quad \text{for all } k \neq i \text{ or } j.$$

   Using normalization, the indirect effect is reduced to between 0 and 3; the same as the range for direct effects.

4.4.2 First Experiment: Choice among Three Indicators

When ranking G_{ji}, a three-stage "hill" is often formed; there are two "cliffs," which divide all actors into three categories, as is shown in Figure 4.2. This is a picture of a normalized G_{ji} computed from Question 17. Those in the highest mountain can be classified as core members of ZL's guanxi circle, those in the next lower level are peripheral members, and those in the "valley" are outsiders. This helps us categorize various roles in the supervisor's guanxi circle.

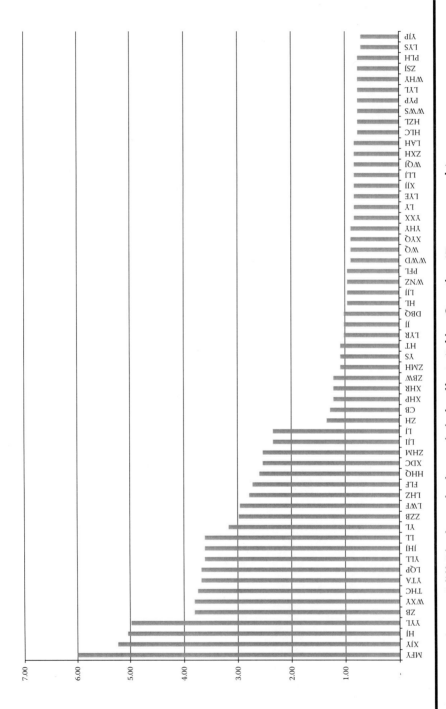

Figure 4.2 The two "cliffs" in the rank of guanxi circle effects (taking Question 17 as an example).

By using the five covering mixed ties, Questions 14 through 18, we computed the three measures of G_{ji} and averaged them to get a single index of each person's guanxi circle proximity. By finding the "cliffs," we categorized all actors into three types of guanxi roles and then compared them with the "ground truth" obtained from the qualitative study and pictures of network structure.

Table 4.4 shows the results of the comparison. There are two types of errors. Type I error is denoted by "type I" in a cell, that is, this person is categorized as "peripheral member" in qualitative studies, but the computation of G_{ji} doesn't find the same result. Type II error is denoted by "type II" in a cell, that is, G_{ji} classifies this actor as "peripheral" but the qualitative study doesn't support this conclusion. Those coded as "circle" or "core" in cells are correct results in the quantitative study. At the bottom of Table 4.4, the summary of a computing method is shown as "2.1.18/21," that is, "the number of type I error, the number of type II error, and the number of correct results/sum of the number of these three categories." Accuracy rate is computed by the number of correct results divided by the sum. We found that the three methods get very similar accuracy rates, but the normalized G_{ji} is a little better than the other two.

4.4.3 Second Experiment: Choice among 10 Questionnaire Items

In the next step, we use all 10 types of ties to compute their normalized G_{ji} and compare the results with the "ground truth." As shown in Table 4.5, the best item is Question 16, "I am willing to share a new idea with him or her," and its accuracy rate is 0.863. The two second-best questions are as follows: Question 15, "I am willing to lend my 1-month salary or more to him or her," and Question 17, "If he or she asks, I would like to help his or her friends." Following these three questionnaire items, Question 1, "I am involved in social activities (like shopping, dining) with him or her after work," and Question 14, "Whenever I learn new knowledge concerning jobs, I would like to teach him or her," can be included in the top five questions.

In the comparison between Tables 4.4 and 4.5, we find that the analytical results from multiple questions are better than those computed from a single questionnaire item. In Table 4.6, the first column illustrates the result from the best three questions stated earlier. If a person in two or more out of three questions is coded as a certain role in the supervisor's guanxi circle, then he or she will be taken as this role. The accuracy rate of this computing method is 0.869. The second column shows the analysis based on the five best questions. If a person in three or more out of five questions is classified in a certain ring around the supervisor, then he or she will be put into this certain category. The accurate rate is as high as 0.863. By using five questions, the accuracy rate is not improved.

Table 4.4 Comparison among the Three Computing Methods

Name	Divided by 9	Divided by Network Size	Normalized	Divided by 9	Divided by Network Size	Normalized
ZL	Supervisor	Supervisor	Supervisor			
XJY	Core	Core	Core	6.47	3.54	5.75
YYL	Core	Core	Core	5.84	3.44	5.34
HJ	Core	Core	Core	5.84	3.44	5.31
MFY	Circle	Circle	Circle	4.73	1.92	3.88
WWD	Type I	Type I	Type I	1.49	0.23	1.28
XDC				1.58	0.41	1.17
HLC				0.91	0.14	0.66
YLL	Circle	Circle	Circle	3.67	1.08	2.82
ZMH				1.11	0.17	0.76
FLF	Circle	Circle	Circle	2.80	1.11	2.26
LJI	Type I	Type I	Type I	2.09	0.66	1.63
LWF	Circle	Circle	Circle	3.47	1.72	3.13
LJ	Circle	Circle	Circle	2.56	1.07	2.14
LYS				0.80	0.12	0.56
ZB	Circle	Circle	Circle	3.69	1.08	2.82

(Continued)

The leftmost column also lists role descriptions for each name:

Name	Role
ZL	Supervisor
XJY	Core member
YYL	Core member
HJ	Core member
MFY	Peripheral member
WWD	Peripheral member
XDC	Outsider
HLC	Outsider
YLL	Peripheral member
ZMH	Outsider
FLF	Peripheral member
LJI	Peripheral member
LWF	Peripheral member
LJ	Peripheral member
LYS	Outsider
ZB	Peripheral member

Table 4.4 (Continued) Comparison among the Three Computing Methods

Name		Divided by 9	Divided by Network Size	Normalized	Divided by 9	Divided by Network Size	Normalized
CB	Peripheral member	Circle	Circle	Circle	3.51	1.05	2.84
HZL	Outsider				1.13	0.18	0.89
WWS	Outsider				0.98	0.15	0.69
THC	Outsider	Type II			2.42	0.71	1.82
XHP	Outsider				1.31	0.20	0.96
ZHM	Peripheral member	Circle	Circle	Circle	2.80	1.11	2.26
YJP	Outsider				0.84	0.13	0.60
HL	Outsider				1.22	0.19	0.89
JHJ	Peripheral member	Circle	Circle	Circle	3.73	1.26	2.84
YS	Outsider				1.20	0.19	0.84
ZZB	Peripheral member	Circle	Type I	Circle	2.91	0.96	2.40
HT	Outsider				1.22	0.19	0.92
ZH	Outsider				1.82	0.45	1.38
LYR	Outsider				1.29	0.20	0.97
YXX	Outsider				0.82	0.13	0.56
PYP	Outsider				1.18	0.18	0.90

(Continued)

Table 4.4 (Continued) Comparison among the Three Computing Methods

Name		Divided by 9	Divided by Network Size	Normalized	Divided by 9	Divided by Network Size	Normalized
LY	Outsider				0.91	0.14	0.65
LYL	Outsider				0.89	0.14	0.65
HHQ	Peripheral member	Circle	Circle	Circle	3.42	1.38	2.94
JJ	Outsider				1.42	0.22	1.09
XHR	Outsider				1.38	0.21	1.02
LHZ	Peripheral member	Circle	Circle	Circle	3.09	1.16	2.73
WHY	Outsider				0.87	0.13	0.61
LYE	Outsider				0.89	0.14	0.61
YL	Peripheral member	Circle	Circle	Circle	3.67	1.41	3.02
LJJ	Outsider				1.09	0.17	0.78
XJJ	Outsider				0.91	0.14	0.67
LLJ	Outsider				0.89	0.14	0.62
WNZ	Outsider				1.04	0.16	0.73
WQ	Outsider				1.02	0.16	0.74
XYQ	Outsider				1.02	0.16	0.72

(Continued)

Table 4.4 (Continued) Comparison among the Three Computing Methods

Name		Divided by 9	Divided by Network Size	Normalized	Divided by 9	Divided by Network Size	Normalized
YTA	Peripheral member	Circle	Circle	Circle	3.62	1.24	3.09
LL	Peripheral member	Circle	Circle	Circle	4.02	1.47	3.19
WQJ	Outsider				0.91	0.14	0.65
DBQ	Outsider				1.18	0.18	0.83
WXY	Peripheral member	Circle	Circle	Circle	4.58	1.56	3.81
ZXH	Outsider				0.87	0.13	0.60
ZBW	Outsider				1.62	0.42	1.26
LQP	Outsider	Type II	Type II	Type II	3.24	1.01	2.34
PFL	Outsider				1.09	0.17	0.77
LAH	Outsider				0.87	0.13	0.59
ZSJ	Outsider				0.89	0.14	0.61
YHY	Outsider				0.89	0.14	0.60
PLH	Outsider				0.82	0.13	0.56
		2.2.19/23	3.1.18/23	2.1.19/22			
		0.826	0.826	0.863			

Table 4.5 Comparison among the 10 Networks

Name	Question 1	Question 3	Question 4	Question 5	Question 9	Question 14	Question 15	Question 16	Question 17	Question 18
ZL Supervisor	Supervisor	Supervisor	Supervisor	Supervisor	Supervisor	Supervisor	Supervisor	Supervisor	Supervisor	Supervisor
XJY Core member	Core	Core	Core	Core	Core	Core	Core	Core	Core	Core
YYL Core member	Core	Core	Core	Core	Core	Core	Core	Core	Core	Core
HJ Core member	Core	Core	Type II	Core	Core	Core	Core	Core	Core	Core
MFY Peripheral member	Circle	Circle	Circle	Type I	Circle	Type I	Circle	Circle	Type I	Type I
WWD Peripheral member	Type I	Type I	Type I	Type I	Circle	Type I	Type I	Type I	Type I	Type I
XDC Outsider					Type II				Type II	
HLC Outsider										
YLL Peripheral member	Circle	Type I	Circle	Type I	Circle	Circle	Type I	Circle	Circle	Type I
ZMH Outsider										
FLF Peripheral member	Type I	Circle	Circle	Type I	Circle	Type I	Circle	Circle	Circle	Type I
LJI Peripheral member	Type I	Circle	Circle	Circle	Type I	Type I	Type I	Circle	Circle	Type I

(Continued)

Table 4.5 (Continued) Comparison among the 10 Networks

Name		Question 1	Question 3	Question 4	Question 5	Question 9	Question 14	Question 15	Question 16	Question 17	Question 18
LWF	Peripheral member	Type I	Circle	Circle	Circle	Circle	Circle	Circle	Circle	Circle	Circle
LJ	Peripheral member	Circle	Circle	Type I	Type I	Type I	Circle	Circle	Circle	Circle	Type I
LYS	Outsider										
ZB	Peripheral member	Circle	Circle	Type I	Circle	Circle	Circle	Type I	Circle	Circle	Type I
CB	Peripheral member	Circle	Type I	Circle	Type I	Circle	Circle	Circle	Circle	Type I	Type I
HZL	Outsider	Type II	Type II								
WWS	Outsider										
THC	Outsider							Type II		Type II	
XHP	Outsider										
ZHM	Peripheral member	Circle	Circle	Circle	Type I	Circle	Circle	Circle	Circle	Circle	Type I
YJP	Outsider					Type II					
HL	Outsider										
JHJ	Peripheral member	Type I	Type I	Type I	Circle	Circle	Circle	Circle	Circle	Circle	Type I

(Continued)

Table 4.5 (Continued) Comparison among the 10 Networks

Name		Question 1	Question 3	Question 4	Question 5	Question 9	Question 14	Question 15	Question 16	Question 17	Question 18
YS	Outsider										
ZZB	Peripheral member	Circle	Circle	Circle	Circle	Circle	Type I	Circle	Circle	Circle	Type I
HT	Outsider										
ZH	Outsider	Type II	Type II		Type II	Type II	Type II				
LYR	Outsider										
YXX	Outsider										
PYP	Outsider										
LY	Outsider					Type II					
LYL	Outsider										
HHQ	Peripheral member	Circle	Circle	Circle	Circle	Circle	Circle	Circle	Circle	Circle	Circle
JJ	Outsider										
XHR	Outsider					Type II					
LHZ	Peripheral member	Circle	Type I	Type I	Type I	Type I	Type I	Circle	Circle	Circle	Circle
WHY	Outsider										
LYE	Outsider										

(Continued)

Table 4.5 (*Continued*) Comparison among the 10 Networks

Name		Question 1	Question 3	Question 4	Question 5	Question 9	Question 14	Question 15	Question 16	Question 17	Question 18
YL	Peripheral member	Circle	Circle	Type I	Circle	Circle	Circle	Circle	Circle	Circle	Circle
LJJ	Outsider										
XJJ	Outsider										
LLJ	Outsider										
WNZ	Outsider		Type II								
WQ	Outsider										
XYQ	Outsider					Type II					
YTA	Peripheral member	Type I	Type I	Type I	Type I	Circle	Circle	Circle	Type I	Circle	Circle
LL	Peripheral member	Circle	Type I	Type I	Circle	Circle	Circle	Circle	Circle	Circle	Circle
WQJ	Outsider					Type II					
DBQ	Outsider			Type II							
WXY	Peripheral member	Circle	Circle	Type I	Circle	Circle	Circle	Circle	Circle	Circle	Circle
ZXH	Outsider										
ZBW	Outsider		Type II	Type II							

(*Continued*)

Table 4.5 (*Continued*)   Comparison among the 10 Networks

Name		Question 1	Question 3	Question 4	Question 5	Question 9	Question 14	Question 15	Question 16	Question 17	Question 18
LQP	Outsider					Type II	Type II		Type II	Type II	
PFL	Outsider										
LAH	Outsider										
ZSJ	Outsider										
YHY	Outsider										
PLH	Outsider										
		5.3.15/23	7.4.14/25	10.2.11/23	9.1.12/22	3.8.18/29	6.2.15/23	4.1.17/22	2.1.19/22	3.3.18/24	11.0.10/21
		0.652	0.56	0.478	0.55	0.620	0.652	0.772	0.863	0.75	0.476

Table 4.6 Comparison between the Combinations of Three and Five Questions

Name		Three Questions Combination	Five Questions Combination
ZL	Supervisor	Supervisor	Supervisor
XJY	Core member	Core	Core
YYL	Core member	Core	Core
HJ	Core member	Core	Core
MFY	Peripheral member	Circle	Circle
WWD	Peripheral member	Type I	Type I
XDC	Outsider		
HLC	Outsider		
YLL	Peripheral member	Circle	Circle
ZMH	Outsider		
FLF	Peripheral member	Circle	Circle
LJI	Peripheral member	Circle	Type I
LWF	Peripheral member	Circle	Circle
LJ	Peripheral member	Circle	Circle
LYS	Outsider		
ZB	Peripheral member	Circle	Circle
CB	Peripheral member	Circle	Circle
HZL	Outsider		
WWS	Outsider		
THC	Outsider	Type II	
XHP	Outsider		
ZHM	Peripheral member	Circle	Circle
YJP	Outsider		
HL	Outsider		

(Continued)

Table 4.6 (*Continued*) Comparison between the Combinations of Three and Five Questions

Name		Three Questions Combination	Five Questions Combination
JHJ	Peripheral member	Circle	Circle
YS	Outsider		
ZZB	Peripheral member	Circle	Circle
HT	Outsider		
ZH	Outsider		
LYR	Outsider		
YXX	Outsider		
PYP	Outsider		
LY	Outsider		
LYL	Outsider		
HHQ	Peripheral member	Circle	Circle
JJ	Outsider		
XHR	Outsider		
LHZ	Peripheral member	Circle	Circle
WHY	Outsider		
LYE	Outsider		
YL	Peripheral member	Circle	Circle
LJJ	Outsider		
XJJ	Outsider		
LLJ	Outsider		
WNZ	Outsider		
WQ	Outsider		
XYQ	Outsider		
YTA	Peripheral member	Circle	Circle
LL	Peripheral member	Circle	Circle

(Continued)

Table 4.6 (*Continued*)   Comparison between the Combinations of Three and Five Questions

Name		Three Questions Combination	Five Questions Combination
WQJ	Outsider		
DBQ	Outsider		
WXY	Peripheral member	Circle	Circle
ZXH	Outsider		
ZBW	Outsider		
LQP	Outsider	Type II	Type II
PFL	Outsider		
LAH	Outsider		
ZSJ	Outsider		
YHY	Outsider		
PLH	Outsider		
		1.2.20/23	2.1.19/22
		0.869	0.863

4.5 Conclusions and Discussions

To summarize the earlier stated computing methods and experiments, we conclude the following steps can be used to distinguish guanxi roles in the workplace:

Step 1: Collect whole network data by using Questions 16, 17, and 15, as shown in the first table of Table 4.3.
Step 2: Identify the supervisor as node i.
Step 3: Compute the normalized G_{ji} by using the following formula:

$$G_{ji} = Z_{ji} + 3 \times \left[\left(\sum_k Z_{jk} \times Z_{ki} \right) - \text{Min}\left(\sum_k Z_{jk} \times Z_{ki} \right) \right] \Big/ \left(\text{Max}\left(\sum_k Z_{jk} \times Z_{ki} \right) \right.$$

$$\left. - \text{Min}\left(\sum_k Z_{jk} \times Z_{ki} \right) \right), \quad \text{for all } k \neq i \text{ or } j.$$

Step 4: Identify the "cliffs" in the rank of normalized G_{ji} computed from the three networks.

Step 5: Categorize each actor into various roles in the supervisor's guanxi circle. By using the top three questions, Questions 15, 16, and 17, if a person is coded as a certain role in two or more out of the three networks, they will be taken as a certain role.

There are some flaws in this method of computation for measuring a guanxi circle. The most important one is the incorrect prediction of two people's roles: WWD and LQP. They are listed in type I or type II error in almost all questions and computation methods. WWD is recognized as a circle member by almost everyone but has a very low G_{ji}. He is a senior engineer with a strong technical background and is respected by almost everyone. Because of his age, seniority, expertise, and good reputation, ZL consults with him a lot and respects him very much. But he is totally inactive in social life. How to predict the role of this type of person requires more experiments in various ways to find a better computation method.

LQP is densely embedded in an informal leader's circle, and she has strong indirect connections to ZL through her guanxi network, so she gets a pretty high G_{ji} score and is classified as a circle peripheral member in the quantitative study. However, she is actually neither close to the supervisor nor important in function. So she is often recognized by others as an outsider in the qualitative study.

There are many cases like LQP in different networks, which is why G_{ji} computed from some questions has a large amount of type II error. As stated earlier, we didn't develop the method in this chapter to identify informal leaders' guanxi circles and check for overlapping areas among various circles, that is, bridges. It is probable that LQP is a bridge between the supervisor's circle and her own circle. In future studies, we need to develop methods to identify informal leader's circle members and bridges so that the whole picture of guanxi circles in a workplace's network structure will be clearer.

In this chapter, we add direct and indirect connections to measure proximity to the core of a guanxi circle. If we experiment with some other methods to integrate these two effects rather than simply adding them together, there may be better outcomes. How to better use the two guanxi circle effects to explore more social phenomena in workplaces is a challenge to be addressed in future studies.

This chapter again demonstrates the importance of integrating qualitative and quantitative studies together, as shown in the "Introduction" of this book. For finding a good quantitative indicator of a variable, data mining itself is not enough. Without being supplemented by qualitative studies, data mining cannot achieve "ground truth."

Acknowledgments

This is partially supported by the Center for Social Network Research, Tsinghua University; and the Sino-German Institute of Social Computing, University of

Göttingen; Tsinghua's research project "Trust and Guanxi Studies on the Internet," project number: 20121088015; Chinese Natural Science Foundation Project "Social Network in Big Data Analysis: A Case in Investment Network," project number: 71372053; National 863 project, project number: 20141860074; and the project "Simulation Center" sponsored by State Lower Saxony and Volkswagen Foundation, Germany.

References

Barnes, J. A. 1954. Class and committees in a Norwegian island parish. *Human Relations*, 7: 39–58.

Bian, Y. J. 1997. Bringing strong ties back in: Indirect ties, network bridges, and job searches in China. *American Sociological Review*, 62: 266–285.

Bian, Y. J., Huang, X., and Zhang, L. 2015. Information and favoritism: The network effect on wage income in China. *Social Networks*, 40: 129–138.

Blau, P. 1964. *Exchange and Power in Social Life*. New York: Wiley.

Bond, M. H. and Hwang, K. K. 1986. The social psychology of Chinese people. In: M. H. Bond (Ed.), *The Psychology of the Chinese People*. Hong Kong, China: Oxford University Press, pp. 213–266.

Chen, C. H. 1998. *Bandi and Laoban*. Taipei, Taiwan: Linking Books (in Chinese).

Chi, S. C. 1996. The empirical study in roles of leader's confidant. *Management Review*, 15(1): 37–59.

Chua, R., Ingram, P., and Morris, M. 2008. From the head and the heart: Locating cognition and affect-based trust in managers' professional networks. *Academy of Management Journal*, 51: 436–452.

Chua, R., Morris, M., and Ingram, P. 2009. Guanxi vs networking: Distinctive configurations of affect- and cognition-based trust in the networks of Chinese vs American managers. *Journal of International Business Studies*, 40: 490–508.

Dienesch, R. M. and Liden, R. C. 1986. Leader–member exchange model of leadership: A critique and further development. *Academy of Management Review*, 11(3): 618–634.

Fei, H. T. 1992. *From the Soil: The Foundations of Chinese Society*. Berkeley, CA: University of California Press.

Graen, G. B. 1976. Role-making processes within complex organizations. In: M. D. Dunnette (Ed.), *Handbook of Industrial and Organizational Psychology*. Chicago, IL: Rand McNally, pp. 201–245.

Graen, G. B. and Cashman, J. F. 1975. A role-making model of leadership in formal organizations: A developmental approach. In: J. G. Hunt and L. L. Larson (Eds.), *Leadership Frontiers*. Kent, OH: Kent State University Press, pp. 143–166.

Graen, G. B. and Uhl-Bien, M. 1995. Relationship-based approach to leadership: Development of leader–member exchange (LMX) theory of leadership over 25 years: Applying a multi-level multi-domain perspective. *The Leadership Quarterly*, 6(2): 219–247.

Hwang, K. K. 1987. Face and favor: The Chinese power game. *American Journal of Sociology*, 92: 944–974.

Hwang, K. K. 1988. *The Chinese Power Game*. Taipei, Taiwan: Linking Books (in Chinese).

Krackhardt, D. 1992. The strength of strong ties: The importance of philos in organizations. In: N. Nohria and R. G. Eccles (Eds.), *Networks and Organizations*. Boston, MA: Harvard Business School Press, pp. 216–240.

Liang, S. M. 1983. *The Comparison between Chinese and Western Cultures*. Taipei, Taiwan: Li-Ren Publishing House (In Chinese).

Luo, J. D. 2005. Particularistic trust and general trust—A network analysis in Chinese organizations. *Management and Organizational Review*, 3: 437–458.

Luo, J. D. 2011. Guanxi revisited—An exploratory study of familiar ties in a Chinese workplace. *Management and Organizational Review*, 7(2): 329–351.

Luo, J.-D. and Cheng, M.-Y. 2015. Guanxi circles' effect on organizational trust—Bringing power and vertical social exchanges into intra-organizational network analysis. *American Behavioral Scientist*, 59(8): 1024–1037.

Luo, J.-D. and Yeh, K. 2012. Neither collectivism nor individualism—Trust in Chinese guanxi circles. *Journal of Trust Research*, 2(1): 53–70.

Mao, Y., Peng, K. Z., and Wong, C. S. 2012. Indigenous research on Asia: In search of the emic components of guanxi. *Asia Pacific Journal of Management*, 29(4): 1143–1168.

Mayer, A. C. 1966. The significance of quasi-groups in the study of complex society. In: M. Banton (Ed.), *The Anthropology of Complex Societies*. New York: Frederick A Praeger Publishers, pp. 97–122.

Mishra, A. K. 1996. Organizational responses to crises: The centrality of trust in organizations. In: R. M. Kramer and T. R. Tyler (Eds.), *Trust in Organizations*. London, U.K.: Sage Publications, Inc., pp. 261–287.

Schriesheim, C. A., Castro, S. L., and Cogliser, C. C. 1999. Leader–member exchange (LMX) research: A comprehensive review of theory, measurement, and data-analytic practices. *Leadership Quarterly*, 10(1): 63–113.

Sparrowe, R. and Liden, R. C. 1997. Process and structure in leader–member exchange. *Academy of Management Review*, 22(2): 522–552.

Yang, G. 1993. Chinese social orientation: An integrative analysis. In: T. Y. Lin, W. S. Tseng, and Y. K. Yeh (Eds.), *Chinese Societies and Mental Health*. Hong Kong, China: Oxford University Press (in Chinese).

Zhang, Y. and Zhang, Z. 2006. Guanxi and organizational dynamics in China: A link between individual and organizational levels. *Journal of Business Ethics*, 67(4): 375–392.

Chapter 5

Analysis and Prediction of Triadic Closure in Online Social Networks

Hong Huang, Jie Tang, Lu Liu, Jar-Der Luo, and Xiaoming Fu

Contents

5.1 Introduction

Online social networks (OSNs) are becoming a bridge that connects our physical daily life with the online world. For example, as of July 2014, Facebook has 1.3 billion users, which makes Facebook the second biggest "country" in the world. Twitter has 0.65 billion users, who "tweet" 1 billion times every 5 days. These connections produce a huge volume of data, including not only the content of their communications but also user behavioral logs. The popularity of the social web and the availability of social data offer us opportunities to study interaction patterns among users and to understand the generative mechanisms of different networks, which were previously difficult to explore, due to the unavailability of data. A better understanding of user behavior and underlying network patterns could enable an OSN provider to attract and keep more users and thus increase its profits.

In social networks, group formation—the process by which people come together, seek new friends, and develop communities—is a central research issue in the social sciences. Examples of interesting groups include political movements and professional organizations [1].

A triad is a group of three people. It is one of the simplest human groups. Roughly speaking, there are two types of triads: *closed triads* and *open triads*. In a closed triad, for any two persons in the triad, there is a relationship between them. In an open triad, there are only two relationships, which means that two of the three people are not connected with each other.

One interesting question is how a closed triad develops from an open triad. The problem is referred to as the "triadic closure process." It is a fundamental mechanism in the formation and evolution of dynamic networks [6]. Understanding the mechanism of triadic closure can help in predicting the development of ties within a network, in showing the progression of connectivity and in gaining insight into decision-making behavior in global organizations [9,20].

The triadic closure process has been studied in many fields. Sociologists first used the triadic closure process to study human friendship choices—that is, whether people may choose new acquaintances who are the friends of friends [14]—and found that friends of friends tend to become friends themselves [14,40]. In computer science, empirical studies have shown that triads tend to aggregate, creating interest groups of widely varying size, but of small diameter. For example, these tightly knit groups indicated a common topic for hyperlinks [10] on the World Wide Web. Literature [11,20,35,45] proposed network generative models based on triadic closure principles. Milo et al. [28,29] defined the recurring significant patterns of interconnections as "network motifs" and emphasized their importance. But these studies focused only on uses of the triadic closure process, without clarifying the underlying principles of triadic closure.

Romero and Kleinberg [33] studied the problem of triadic closure process and developed a methodology based on preferential attachment, for studying how directed "feed-forward" triadic closure occurs. Moreover, Lou et al. [27] investigated how a reciprocal link is developed from a parasocial relationship and how the relationships develop into triadic closure in a Twitter dataset. However, these studies only examined some special cases of the triadic closure process. Many challenges are still open and require further methodological developments. First, how do user demographics, network characteristics, and social properties influence the formation of triadic closure? Moreover, how can we design a unified model for predicting the formation of triadic closure? In particular, how can we quantify correlation (similarity) between triads?

In this chapter, employing a dataset from a large microblogging network, Weibo,* as the basis of our study, we examine patterns in the triadic closure process in order to better understand factors that trigger the formation of groups among people. Our contributions are multifold:

- We first investigate the triadic closure patterns in the microblogging network from three aspects: user demographics, network characteristics, and social perspectives. We find some interesting phenomena; for example, men are more willing to form triadic closures than women; celebrities are more likely to form triadic closures (with a probability 421× as high) than ordinary users. Furthermore, we find that interactions like retweeting play an important role in the establishment of friendship and in triadic closure formation.
- Based on our observations, we tackle the issue of triadic closure prediction. We present a probabilistic triad factor graph model (TriadFG) combined with different kernel functions, which quantify the similarity between triads to

---

* Weibo.com, the most popular microblogging service in China, with more than 560 million users.

predict triadic closure. Compared with alternative methods based on support vector machine (SVM) and logistic regression, the presented model achieves significant improvement (+7.43%, $p \ll 0.01$) in triadic closure prediction.

■ We compare the observations obtained from the Weibo dataset with those from the Twitter dataset. Interestingly, although there are common patterns—for example, "the rich get richer"—underlying the dynamics of the two networks, some distinct patterns (and corresponding users' motivations) exist, potentially reflecting cultural differences of behaviors between Weibo and Twitter users.

■ One straightforward application of our findings is friend recommendation. We apply our proposed triadic closure prediction model to the Weibo data-set to evaluate the effectiveness of friend recommendation. The online A/B test demonstrates that our method can achieve an advantage of +10% over the existing recommendation algorithm. Other potential applications include group formation [1,33], social search, and user behavior modeling.

5.2 Problem Definition

Let $G = (V, E)$ denote a static network, where $V = \{v_1,\ldots,v_{|V|}\}$ is a set of users and $E \subset V \times V$ is a set of relationships connecting those users. Notation $e_{v_i v_j} \in E$ (or simply e_{ij}) denotes there is a relationship between users v_i and v_j. The network evolves over time. Let us denote the network at time t as G^t. To begin with, we give the definitions of *closed triad* and *open triad* in a static social network based on the "following" relationships:

Definition 5.1 [Closed triad] For three users $\Delta = (A,B,C)$, if there is a relationship between any two users—that is, $e_{AB}, e_{BC}, e_{AC} \in E$—then we say that Δ is a *closed triad*.

Definition 5.2 [Open triad] For three users $\Delta = \{A,B,C\}$, if we have only two relationships among them—for example, $e_{AB}, e_{BC} \in E \wedge e_{AC} \notin E$—then we call the triad Δ an *open triad*.

The triads are formed in a dynamic process. We use function $t(e_{AB}) \rightarrow 1,2,\ldots$ to define the timestamp at which the relationship e_{AB} was formed between A and B. For simplicity, we use t to denote the timestamp. In this chapter, we try to understand how an *open triad* becomes a *closed triad*. The problem exists in both directed and undirected networks. For example, in a coauthor network at time t, if B coauthored with A and C, respectively, but A and C did not coauthor, we say (A,B,C) is an open triad. If later, A and C also have a coauthorship, we say A, B, and C form a closed triad. In directed networks, the problem becomes more complicated. In some sense, the problem in undirected networks can be considered a special case of the problem in directed networks. In this chapter, we focus on directed networks like Twitter (i.e., follower networks) and Weibo (Chinese Twitter).

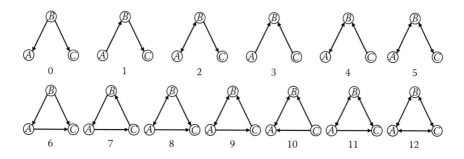

Figure 5.1 Open triads and closed triads. The number below is the index of each triad. Triad 0–Triad 5 are open triads and Triad 6–Triad 12 are closed triads. A, B, and C represent users.

Table 5.1 How Open Triad Forms Triadic Closure

Open $\xrightarrow{A\rightarrow C}$ Close	Open $\xrightarrow{A\leftarrow C}$ Close	Open $\xrightarrow{A\leftrightarrow C}$ Close
$0 \xrightarrow{A\rightarrow C} 6$	$0 \xrightarrow{A\leftarrow C} 6$	$0 \xrightarrow{A\leftrightarrow C} 10$
$1 \xrightarrow{A\rightarrow C} 6$	$1 \xrightarrow{A\leftarrow C} 7$	$1 \xrightarrow{A\leftrightarrow C} 9$
$2 \xrightarrow{A\rightarrow C} 8$	$2 \xrightarrow{A\leftarrow C} 9$	$2 \xrightarrow{A\leftrightarrow C} 11$
$3 \xrightarrow{A\rightarrow C} 6$	$3 \xrightarrow{A\leftarrow C} 6$	$3 \xrightarrow{A\leftrightarrow C} 8$
$4 \xrightarrow{A\rightarrow C} 9$	$4 \xrightarrow{A\leftarrow C} 10$	$4 \xrightarrow{A\leftrightarrow C} 11$
$5 \xrightarrow{A\rightarrow C} 11$	$5 \xrightarrow{A\leftarrow C} 11$	$5 \xrightarrow{A\leftrightarrow C} 12$

Figure 5.1 shows all the possible examples of open and closed triads in a directed network. Table 5.1 shows how these open triads become closed triads when a following action happens between A and C. For each entry in the table, left and right numbers indicate the index of triads in Figure 5.1. The expression above the arrow indicates the action that a new link between A and C is created. For example, $0 \xrightarrow{A\rightarrow C} 6$ means if at time t' A follows C, then open triad 0 becomes an isomorphous of closed triad 6.

The situation becomes more complex if we further consider the time when each relationship was formed in the (open/closed) triads. To simplify the following explanation, and without loss of generality, we assume that in an open triad $\Delta = (A,B,C)$, the relationship between B and C was established (at time t_2) after the establishment (at time t_1) of a relationship between A and B—that is, $t_2 > t_1$. Given this, our goal is to predict whether an open triad will become a closed triad at time $t_3(t_3 > t_2)$. Formally, we have the following problem definition:

Problem 5.1 Triadic closure prediction. Given a network $G^t = (V,E)$ at time t and historical information regarding all existing relationships, to every candidate open triad, we associate a hidden variable y^t. Our goal is to use the historical information to train a function f, so that we can predict whether an open triad in G^t will become a closed triad ($y^t = 1$) at some time $t'(t' > t)$ or not ($y^t = 0$)—that is,

$$f : (\{G^\alpha, Y^\alpha\}_{\alpha=1,\dots,t}) \rightarrow Y^{t'}$$

where $Y^t = \{y_i^t\}$ denotes the set of all values of the hidden variables at time t.

We also study how interaction between users can help the formation of triadic closure. We consider retweeting behavior in a microblogging network. In particular, for an open triad (A, B, C), if retweeting happens both between A and B and B and C, suppose the action between B and C happens after the action between A and B (which is called candidate relationship-interaction open triad [R-I open triad]), will this retweeting help A and C to build a relationship?

Please note that the interaction can be in different forms, for example, the retweeting mentioned earlier, "mention" ("@" in Twitter or Weibo), or "reply." To simplify the analysis, we focus on retweeting.

We could extend Problem 5.1 as follows: Given a network $G^t = (V, E)$ at time t, to every candidate R-I open triad, we associate a hidden variable y_{RI}^t. Our goal is to train a function f, so that we can predict whether an open triad in G^t will become a closed triad at time $t'(t' > t)$—that is,

$$f : (\{G^\alpha, Y_{RI}^\alpha\}_{\alpha=1,\dots,t}) \rightarrow Y_{RI}^{t'}$$

where Y_{RI}^t denotes all values of the hidden variables at time t.

5.3 Data and Observation

5.3.1 Data Collection

One objective of the study is to reveal the fundamental factors that influence triadic closure formation in social networks. We use Weibo data as the basis for our study. The triadic closure process is the formation of a directed triad (also referred to as directed closure process [26,33]). To obtain the dynamic information, we crawl a network with dynamic updates from Weibo. The dataset was crawled in the following ways. To begin with, 100 random users were selected; then, their followees and followees' followees were collected as seed users. The crawling process produced in total 1,776,950 users and 308,489,739 following links among them, with an average of 200 out-degree per user, 317,555 new links and 745,587 newly formed closed triads per day. We also crawled the profiles of all users, which contain name, gender, location, verified status, and posted microblogs. Finally, the resultant dynamic networks span a period from September 29, 2012, to October 29, 2012. Table 5.2 gives statistics of the dataset.

Table 5.2   Data Statistics of the Weibo Dataset

Item	Number
#Users	1,776,950
#Following-relationships	308,489,739
#Original-microblogs	300,000
#Retweets	23,755,810
#New links per day (average)	317,555
#New open triads per day (average)	6,203,842,388
#New closed triads per day (average)	745,587

We construct a network based on the following relationships, which is different from a coauthor network or friendship network. The former is a directed network, while the latter is an undirected network. The main difference between the two is the directed nature of a Weibo relationship, which is like a Twitter relationship. In a coauthor network or a message network, a link represents a mutual agreement by users, while on Weibo, a user is not obligated to reciprocate followers by following them. Thus, a path from one user to another may follow different hops or not exist in the reverse direction [18].

5.3.2 Observations

We view the network on the first day (September 28, 2012, denoted as T_0) as the initial network and then every 4 days* as a timestamp (denoted as $T_1, T_2, ..., T_7$). The number of newly formed links per timestamp period is shown in Figure 5.2a, and the number of newly formed open triads per timestamp period is shown in Figure 5.2b. In Figure 5.2c, we have the cumulative distribution function of newly formed triadic closures per day, from which we can see that within 8 days about 60% triadic closures are formed. In order to obtain fair and balanced observations among the limited samples, we only consider the triadic closures generated in 8 days† after

---

* We followed the work in [27], where they used 4 days as a timestamp period to study triadic closure patterns in Twitter.
† As shown in Figure 5.2c, about 60% open triads closed in 8 days and 80% open triads closed in 13 days. Since we only have 1 month's worth of observations, 8 days seems to be a better choice than 13 days: first, 8 days corresponds to two timestamp periods, which is easy for calculating; second, we can get more effective observations with 8 days if we choose all samples with the same observed time period. For example, if we select 12 days, triads in the last two timestamp periods can only be observed in two timestamp periods, so their observations are not complete. Thus, 8 days yields more observations than 12 days.

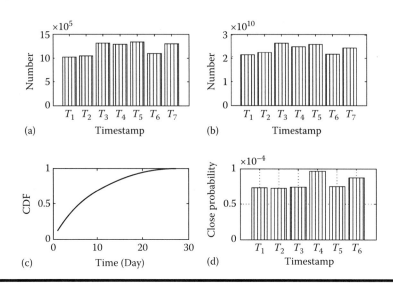

Figure 5.2 Overall observation. (a) *Y*-axis: the number of newly formed links in different timestamp periods. (b) *Y*-axis: the number of newly formed open triads in different timestamp periods. (c) *Y*-axis: cumulative distribution function of newly formed triadic closures per day. (d) *Y*-axis: probability that open triads form triadic closures.

the open triad formed. Figure 5.2d shows the triadic closure probability in different timestamp periods, from which we can see that time slightly affects the closure probability of T_1, T_2, T_3, and T_5 (i.e., $P_{T_1} \approx P_{T_2} \approx P_{T_3} \approx P_{T_5}$).

Exceptions occurred in timestamp periods T_4 (open triads formed from October 11 to October 14 and triadic closure formed from October 12 to October 20) and T_6 (open triads formed from October 22 to October 25 and triadic closures formed from October 23 to October 31). Coincidentally, on October 11, the news that Mo Yan (a Chinese writer) won a Nobel Prize in Literature in 2012 began to spread over Weibo. In the following days, an increasing number of people focused on this topic because Mo Yan was the first Chinese citizen to win the Nobel Prize in its 111-year history. Maybe it is partly the reason that the closure probability in timestamp period T_4 is much higher than that in other timestamp periods. For simplicity, we only show the overall observations in our later discussion without considering the status of each timestamp period.

Since we are interested in the major factors that contribute to triadic closure formation, we first investigate the impact of different factors from three aspects: user demographics, network characteristics, and social perspectives. For user demographics, we consider location, gender, and user's verified status. For network characteristics, we focus on the network structure before and after the triadic closure. For social perspectives, we focus on the popularity of the people within the triads, people who span "structural holes," the gregariousness of users, and status theory. We also consider the effects of social interaction.

5.3.2.1 User Demographics

Location From user profiles, we can obtain location information (province and city that the user comes from). We test whether a user's location will influence the closure of a triad. We can see from Figure 5.3a, if three users all come from the same province, the probability that the open triads will be closed is much larger (about four times as large) than the case for which all users are from different provinces. Even if two of the three users are from the same province, the probability is obviously greater than the *null* case, where all three users are from different provinces. If we consider city scale, the result is more definitive; the probability of closure for three persons from the same city is eight times as high as that of the *null* case. Although OSNs make distances between people smaller, location is still one important factor that influences the formation of triadic closure.

Gender We test whether or not gender homophily affects triadic closure formation. We use three-bit binary codes to indicate the gender status of a triad—that is, (XXX) $X = 0$ or 1, where 0 means female and 1 means male. As shown in Figure 5.3b, we can see that if the three users are all male, triadic closures is about six times more likely to form than the case in which all three users are female. We also notice that with more male users in a triad, the triad will have a higher probability to become closed. For example, for any case (such as 001) in Figure 5.3b, if we replace one female user of "0" with a male user ("1"), the probability that the triad will close will increase to 0.6–1 times higher.

Verified status In Weibo, users can choose to verify their real status, for example, organization, company, famous people, media, and active users. In some sense, a verified user could be regarded as a celebrity. Among the 1.7 million users in our sample, about 0.7 million users have verified their status. On the other hand, we have 21,622,013 closed triads, among which we have 7,608,598 closed triads with two verified users and 8,995,533 with three verified users.

Here we check whether verified status affects triadic closure formation. We use three-bit binary codes $(XXX)(X = 0$ or 1, where 0 means status is not verified and 1 means status is verified) to represent triad status. As shown in Figure 5.3c, we can see that if the middle user (i.e., user B) verified his or her status, it has negative influence on triadic closure $(P(X0X) > P(X1X))$, while if the other users verified their status, an open triad is more likely to become closed $(P(XX1) > P(XX0), P(1XX) > P(0XX))$. For example, if users A and C verified their status, the probability that an open triad will close is about 70 times higher than the case in which only user B verified his or her status.

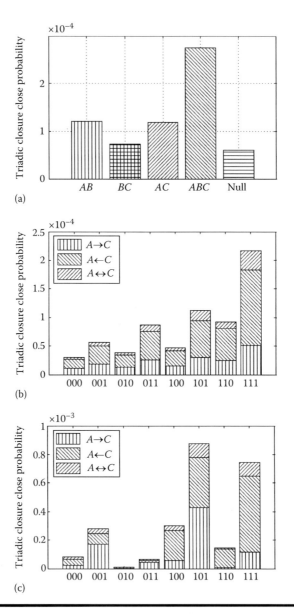

Figure 5.3   User demographics. *Y*-axis: probability of triadic closures. The status of the third link—the newly formed link is presented in a different color—for example, blue means the third link is accomplished by user *A*, who follows user *C*. (a) *X*-axis represents whether certain users are from the same province, for example, *AB* means that only *A* and *B* are in the same province. *Null* means users in a triad all come from different provinces. (b) *X*-axis represents genders in the triad; 0 means female and 1 means male. (c) *X*-axis represents the verified status of the triad; 0 means the user hasn't been verified and 1 means the user is verified.

5.3.2.2 Network Characteristics

We then check the correlation between characteristics of the microblogging network and the formation of triadic closure. In a directed network, there are 13 possible three-node subgraphs [29] as shown in Figure 5.1—if isomorphous subgraphs are only counted once—among which there are 6 open triads and 7 closed triads.

Among all the open triads, open triad 3 is the most frequent, which is around 95% of all open triads. The case corresponds to the tendency of users in Weibo to follow "superstars," such as a famous person or news media, to get information. Figure 5.4a shows the distribution of new triadic closures. We can see that triad 6 has the largest number among all the closed triads, while triad 7 has the smallest number.

Figure 5.4b shows the probability that each open triad forms triadic closure. We can see that open triad 5 has the highest probability of becoming closed, which means if there exist two two-way (reciprocal) relationships in an open triad, it is likely that the triad becomes closed. Meanwhile, open triad 3 is the least likely to form triadic closure, as there are large numbers of this kind of open triads (94.9%).

Figure 5.4c shows the probability for each type of open triad to change into each type of closed triad. We can see that a one-way relationship is much easier to build than a two-way relationship; for example, $P_{5\to11} > P_{5\to12}$.

5.3.2.3 Social Perspectives

We turn now to several social metrics, to check how they influence triadic closure formation. These include popularity, structural hole, gregariousness, status, and interaction.

5.3.2.3.1 Popularity

For popularity, we test this question: if one of the three users in an open triad is a popular user (e.g., an opinion leader, a celebrity), how likely is the open triad to become closed? Here we employ Pagerank [32] to estimate the users' popularity in the network, based on which the top-1%-ranked users* are defined as "popular" users, while the rest are viewed as ordinary ones. Among all the 21,622,013 closed triads, we have 5,918,130 with any popular users and 461,396 with three popular users.

We also test popularity using other metrics, like in-degree, and find similar patterns. We use three-bit binary codes $(XXX)(X = 0$ or $1)$ to represent a user's status: 0 for an ordinary user and 1 for a popular user. Figure 5.5a shows the correlation

---

* We follow the work [41], which has shown that less than 1% of Twitter users produce 50% of its content, and [27], which also uses the top-1%-ranked users to study triadic closure in Twitter.

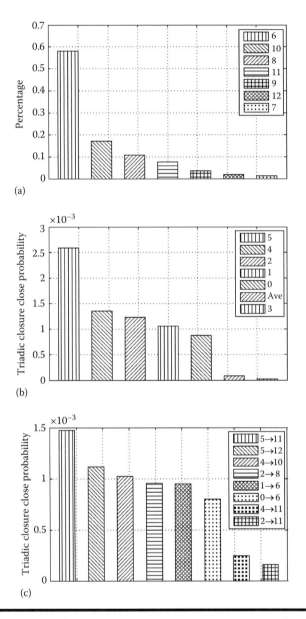

Figure 5.4 **Network characteristics.** (a) *Y*-axis: percentage of newly formed closed triads. (b) *Y*-axis: probability that each open triad becomes closed. The number by the color bars means the index of open triads. (c) *Y*-axis: probability for each type of open triad (i.e., triad 0) to change into each type of closed triad (i.e., triad 6). Expressions attached to color bars represent the probability that an open triad becomes a specific triadic closure, for example, 0 → 6 represents the probability that triad 0 forms triad 6.

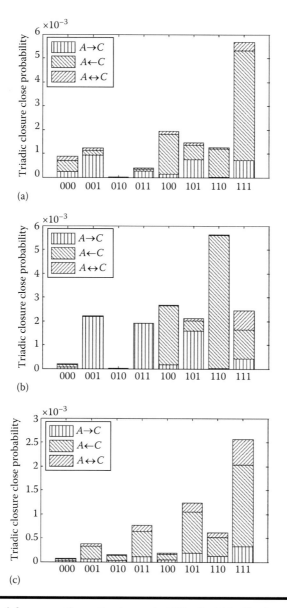

Figure 5.5 Social perspectives. *Y*-axis: probability that triadic closures form. The status of a newly formed link is presented in a different color; for example, blue represents the fact that a third link is accomplished by user *A*, who follows user *C*. (a) *X*-axis represents the popularity of the triad. 0 represents an ordinary user and 1 represents a popular user. (b) *X*-axis represents the structural hole spanner status of the triad. 0 means an ordinary user and 1 means a structural hole spanner. (c) *X*-axis represents the gregariousness of the triad. 0 indicates an ordinary user and 1 is used for a gregarious user.

between users' popularity and the proportion of triadic closures to total open triads. We can see that if the middle user—that is, user *B*—is a popular user, the probability to close the open triads is small. We explain this phenomenon thus: User *B* can be a superstar, a politician, or an official account, who has a lot of followers and relatively few followees and plays a more important role than ordinary users in the network; meanwhile, ordinary users, such as *A* and *C*, follow them but are unlikely to interact with each other, so the probability to close the open triads is small in these cases. But if the three users are all popular users, the probability that the open triads will close is high.

5.3.2.3.2 Social Structural Hole

The theory of structural holes [5] suggests that individuals would benefit from filling the holes (called "structural hole spanners") between people or groups that are otherwise disconnected [26]. We further test whether users who span structural holes will have different influences on the formation of closed triads. Again, we use three-bit binary codes $(XXX)(X = 0$ or $1)$ to represent triad status: 0 indicates an ordinary user and 1, a structural hole spanner. Figure 5.5b shows the correlation between users' social structural hole properties and the proportion of triadic closures to total open triads. We can see from this figure that if only user *B* is a structural hole spanner, the open triad is not likely to become closed. In another case, if *A* or *C* is a structural hole spanner, *A* and *C* are more willing to connect with each other to get more resource for themselves [31,34,36], so the open triads are more likely to become closed.

5.3.2.3.3 Gregariousness

Gregariousness represents the degree that a user is social and enjoys being in crowds. In sociology, gregariousness is often simply represented by out-degree; that is, a high out-degree reflects a strong desire to be socially active and accepted. Here we examine whether gregariousness will play some role in triadic closure formation. Similarly, we view the top-1%-ranked out-degree users as gregarious. Among all the 21,622,013 closed triads, we have 1,105,892 closed triads with two gregarious users and 109,030 with three gregarious users.

We still use three-bit binary codes $(XXX)(X = 0$ or $1)$ to represent the triad status: 0 refers to a common user and 1 refers to a gregarious user. Figure 5.5c shows the correlation between users' gregariousness and the ratio of triadic closures to the total open triads. We can see from this figure that if three users are all common users (000), open triads are less likely to become closed. On the other hand, if the three users are all gregarious (111), the open triads have a high probability of becoming closed—almost 39 times as high as that of case 000. We also notice that with more gregarious users in a triad, the triad will have a higher probability to become closed. For example, for any case (such as 001) in Figure 5.5c, if we replace one user of "0" with a gregarious user ("1"), the probability that the triad becomes closed will double or triple.

5.3.2.3.4 Transitivity

Transitivity [22,40] is an important concept that attaches many social theories to triadic structures. One social relation among three users A, B, and C is transitive if the relations $A \rightarrow B$, $B \rightarrow C$, and $A \rightarrow C$ are present. Extending this definition, a triad is said to be transitive if all the relations it contains are transitive, for example, where A's friends' friends are A's friends as well. In Weibo, it is more likely (98.8%) for users to be connected in a transitive way.

5.3.2.3.5 Social Interaction

We next consider the effects of interaction information upon the triads—say, retweet information. For each user, the crawler collected the 1000 most recent microblogs (including tweets and retweets). Since we focus on retweet behaviors in the microblogging network, we select 300,000 popular microblog diffusion episodes from the dataset. Each diffusion episode contains the original microblog and all its retweets. On average, each microblog has been retweeted about 80 times. The sampled dataset ensures that for each diffusion episode the active (retweet) status of followees in one τ-ego network* is completed. The dataset was previously used for studying social influence in the diffusion process [44]. With these retweeting data, we study how triadic closure formation has been influenced by retweeting behaviors.

First, let us define some notations: $t_{R_{BC}}$ denotes the time that a retweeting behavior happens between B and C; $t_{R_{AB}}$ denotes the time that a retweet happens between A and B. If there are several actions, $t_{R_{BC}}$, $t_{R_{AB}}$ denotes the time that the first action happens; $t_{L_{AC}}$ denotes the time that link AC is established. For retweeting behaviors, according to the time ordering of retweeting behaviors, we have the following four cases:

1. User B posted one tweet, and then users A and C retweeted it, respectively. Given that A retweeted it earlier than C, we have $t_{R_{BC}} > t_{R_{AB}}$.
2. Assume that A has retweeted some tweets posted by B and C has retweeted some tweets posted by B. Suppose A did it earlier than C, then we have $t_{R_{BC}} > t_{R_{AB}}$.

---

* A τ-ego network means a subnetwork formed by the user's τ-degree friends in the network; $\tau \geq 1$ is a tunable integer parameter that controls the scale of the ego network.

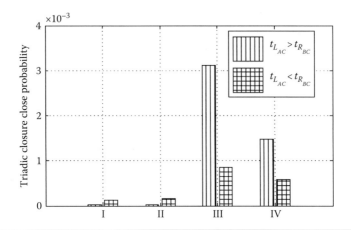

Figure 5.6 **Open triads that form triadic closures with social interaction information in different cases. X-axis: cases. Y-axis: probability that open triads form triadic closures.** $t_{L_{AC}}$ **means the time that link AC is established, and** $t_{R_{BC}}$ **means the time that a retweet happens between users B and C.**

3. User A posted one tweet, and then user B and C retweeted it, respectively. Given that B retweeted it earlier than C, we have $t_{R_{BC}} > t_{R_{AB}}$.
4. Assume that B has retweeted some tweets posted by A and C has retweeted some tweets posted by B. Suppose A did it earlier than C, and then we have $t_{R_{BC}} > t_{R_{AB}}$.

Our intent is to study whether one kind of retweeting will influence triadic closure formation. Figure 5.6 shows the probability of triadic closure in different cases. We see that if the connecting node B is the first to post a tweet (cases 1 and 2), regardless of whether others retweet the tweet or once retweeted his or her tweets, the retweeting behavior has little influence on triadic closure formation. However, if user A is the initial user who posts a tweet (cases 3 and 4), the open triads are more likely (about three times as probable) to become closed.

5.3.2.4 Summary

We summarize our observations as follows:

- ◼ Male users trigger triadic closure formation. The probability that three male users form a closed triad is 6× as high as that of three female users.
- ◼ Gregarious users help form closed triads. The probability that three gregarious users form a closed triad is 39× as high as that of three ordinary users.
- ◼ Celebrity users are more likely to form closed triads. Three users with high Pagerank scores are 421× as likely to form closed triads as three ordinary users. We also find similar patterns in the study for verified status users.

■ Structural hole spanners are eager to close an open triad for more social resources (>10× higher than that of three ordinary users). On the other hand, they are also reluctant to have two disconnected friends to be linked together.
■ Interaction among users plays an important role in forming closed triads. An open triad is 3× as likely to become closed if there is interaction among the users in certain cases than if there is none.
■ In general, the closing action is often done by the third user (Figures 5.3b and 5.5c); since the third user is the last "active" user, he or she is more willing than the other users to connect the link. However, if the user has some social position, like "celebrity" or "resource holder," then ordinary users are more likely to connect with them (Figures 5.3c and 5.5a and b) and close the triad.

5.4 Triadic Closure Prediction

Based on the observations in Section 5.3, we see that the closure of an open triad not only depends on the demographics of the users involved in the triad but also is influenced by the structural position and social position of the users within the triad in the network. Technically, the challenge in triadic closure prediction is how to integrate all relevant information in a unified model. In this chapter, we present a TriadFG model and its variations (TriadFG with binary function [TriadFG-BF], with kernel function [TriadFG-KF], with exponential kernel function [TriadFG-EKF]) for triadic closure prediction. A similar model has been studied in [26] for reciprocal relationship prediction.

5.4.1 Modeling

For a given network $G^t = \{V, E, X, Y\}$ at time t, we first extract all candidate open triads and define features for each triad. Here we use Tr to denote candidate open triads; X to denote features defined for candidate open triads—for example, the demographics of users as analyzed in Section 5.3; Y indicates whether open triads become closed or not. With this information, we can construct a TriadFG model.

For simplicity, we remove the superscript t if there is no ambiguity. Therefore, according to the Bayes theorem, we can get the posterior probability of $P(Y|\mathbf{X},G)$ as follows:

$$P(Y|\mathbf{X},G) = \frac{P(\mathbf{X},G|Y)P(Y)}{P(\mathbf{X},G)} \propto P(\mathbf{X}|Y) \cdot P(Y|G) \tag{5.1}$$

where
$P(Y|G)$ denotes the probability of labels, given the structure of the network
$P(\mathbf{X}|Y)$ denotes the probability of generating the attributes $\mathbf{X}$ associated with each triad Tr, given their label Y

Assuming that the generative probability of attributes, given the label of each triad, is conditionally independent, then

$$P(Y|\mathbf{X},G) \propto P(Y|G)\prod_i P(\mathbf{x}_i|y_i) \tag{5.2}$$

$$P(\mathbf{x}_i|y_i) = \prod_j F_j(x_{ij}, y_i) \tag{5.3}$$

where
$P(\mathbf{x}_i|y_i)$ is the probability of generating attributes $\mathbf{x}_i$ given the label y_i
$F_j(x_{ij}, y_i)$ is jth factor function defined for attribute x_i

The problem is how to instantiate the probabilities $P(Y|G)$ and $F_j(x_{ij}, y_i)$. In principle, they can be instantiated in different ways. In this work, we instantiate them in the following three ways.

5.4.1.1 TriadFG-BF

Straightforwardly, we model these factor functions in a Markov random field, and by the Hammersley–Clifford theorem [13], we have

$$F_j^{BF}(x_{ij}, y_i) = \frac{1}{Z_1}\exp\{\alpha_j f_j(x_{ij}, y_i)\} \tag{5.4}$$

$$P(Y|G) = \frac{1}{Z_2}\exp\left\{\sum_c\sum_d \mu_d h_d(Y_{Tr_c})\right\} \tag{5.5}$$

where Z_1 and Z_2 are normalization factors. Equation 5.4 indicates that we define a feature function $f_j(x_{ij}, y_i)$ for each attribute x_{ij} associated with each triad, where α_j is the weight of the jth attribute. Equation 5.5 represents that we define a set of correlation feature functions $\{h_d(Y_{Tr_c})\}_d$ over each triad Tr_c in the network, where μ_d is the weight of the dth correlation feature function and Y_{Tr_c} is the correlation attribute associated with triad Tr_c.

For factor functions $f_j(x_{ij}, y_i)$, and $h_d(Y_{Tr_c})$, it can be defined as a binary function. For example, if three users in one triad come from the same city, then a feature $f_j(x_{ij}, y_i)$ is specified as 1; otherwise, it is 0. Note that such a feature definition is often used in graphical models such as conditional random fields [19].

We call this approach TriadFG with binary function (TriadFG-BF).

5.4.1.2 TriadFG-KF

Generally speaking, the binary feature function can discriminate closed triads and open triads. However, it cannot accurately capture correlation between features. To this end, we propose a variant of the TriadFG model: TriadFG-KF. Given some attribute samples $\mathbf{X}$, we want to choose feature function F so that $(\mathbf{X},F)$ is as similar

$$
\begin{array}{ccc}
& A\ B\ C \\
\begin{matrix} A \\ B \\ C \end{matrix} &
\begin{bmatrix} 0 & 0 & 0 \\ 1 & 0 & 1 \\ 0 & 0 & 0 \end{bmatrix}
\end{array}
\quad
\begin{array}{ccc}
& A\ B\ C \\
\begin{matrix} A \\ B \\ C \end{matrix} &
\begin{bmatrix} 0 & 1 & 0 \\ 0 & 0 & 1 \\ 0 & 0 & 0 \end{bmatrix}
\end{array}
\quad
\begin{array}{ccc}
& A\ B\ C \\
\begin{matrix} A \\ B \\ C \end{matrix} &
\begin{bmatrix} 0 & 1 & 0 \\ 1 & 0 & 1 \\ 0 & 0 & 0 \end{bmatrix}
\end{array}
$$

Triad 0   Triad 1   Triad 2

$$
\begin{array}{ccc}
& A\ B\ C \\
\begin{matrix} A \\ B \\ C \end{matrix} &
\begin{bmatrix} 0 & 1 & 0 \\ 0 & 0 & 0 \\ 0 & 1 & 0 \end{bmatrix}
\end{array}
\quad
\begin{array}{ccc}
& A\ B\ C \\
\begin{matrix} A \\ B \\ C \end{matrix} &
\begin{bmatrix} 0 & 1 & 0 \\ 1 & 0 & 0 \\ 0 & 1 & 0 \end{bmatrix}
\end{array}
\quad
\begin{array}{ccc}
& A\ B\ C \\
\begin{matrix} A \\ B \\ C \end{matrix} &
\begin{bmatrix} 0 & 1 & 0 \\ 1 & 0 & 1 \\ 0 & 1 & 0 \end{bmatrix}
\end{array}
$$

Triad 3   Triad 4   Triad 5

Figure 5.7 **Matrix representation of open triads.**

as possible to the training samples. In this sense, we can use a kernel function as a similarity measure/weighting function to estimate variable density. Kernel methods like SVM have led to generalizations of algorithms in the machine learning field and to successful real-world applications [3,38,42]. In this chapter, we use kernel-density estimate (KDE) [39] to estimate the density functions of samples **X**.

To form a KDE, we need to place a kernel—a smooth, strongly peaked function—at the position of each data point and then add up the contributions from all kernels to obtain a smooth curve, which can be evaluated at any point along the *x*-axis. For instance, for a network structure feature, we have six open triads and we want to obtain some functions to see which kind of open triads is more likely to become closed. In order to use KDEs, we need to know the distance between the incoming samples. To this end, we define the distance metric based on the similarity of open triads.

We set a 3 × 3 matrix with rows and columns labeled by vertices for every open triad, with a 1 or a 0 in position (m_i, m_j), according to whether there is a link from m_i to m_j. So we have the matrix representations of open triads in Figure 5.7. Hence, we can define the similarity of triads using a Pearson's correlation coefficient as follows.

Definition 5.3 [Triad similarity] Suppose triad *i* has matrix representation *I* and triad *j*'s matrix representation is *J*, then the similarity $Sim(i, j)$ of triad *i* and triad *j* is

$$
Sim(i, j) = \frac{\sum_n (I_n - \bar{I})(J_n - \bar{J})}{\sqrt{\sum_n (I_n - \bar{I})^2}\sqrt{\sum_n (J_n - \bar{J})^2}}
\tag{5.6}
$$

where
n is the number of entries in the matrix
$$
\bar{I} = (1/n)\sum_n I_n
$$
$$
\bar{J} = (1/n)\sum_n J_n
$$

Since the distance function is required to satisfy the four conditions [37] (nonnegativity, identity of indiscernibles, symmetry, and triangle inequality), we define the triad similarity–based distance function as follows:

Definition 5.4 [Triad distance] Suppose the similarity between triad i and triad j is $Sim(i,j)$; we define the distance $Dis(i, j)$ between these two triads as

$$Dis(i, j) = \sqrt{1 - Sim(i, j)} \tag{5.7}$$

Suppose that the region that encloses the N examples is a hypercube with sides of length β centered at the estimation point x; then its volume is given by $V = \beta^D$, where D is the number of dimensions. We can use kernel function $k(\cdot)$ to find the number of examples that fall within this region. The total number of points inside the hypercube is then

$$Q = \sum_{n=1}^{N} k\left(\frac{x - x_n}{\beta}\right) \tag{5.8}$$

So the structure feature function can be rewritten as

$$F_j^{KF}(x_{ij}, y_i) = \sum_{i=1}^{N} \frac{1}{\beta} k\left(\frac{x - x_{ij}}{\beta}\right), \quad j = s \tag{5.9}$$

where
  $k(\cdot)$ is the kernel function—for example, Gaussian kernel $k(x) = \dfrac{1}{\sqrt{(2\pi)}} \exp\left(-\dfrac{1}{2}x^2\right)$
  β is the kernel bandwidth
  s represents the structure feature

The KDE of structure information using the Gaussian kernel is shown as a curve in Figure 5.8, and the histogram of the distance to open triad 3 is shown as bars in Figure 5.8.

For other factors, we model them similarly in TriadFG-BF. Thus, we have

$$F_j^{KF}(x_{ij}, y_i) = \begin{cases} \displaystyle\sum_{i=1}^{N} \frac{1}{\beta} k\left(\frac{x - x_{ij}}{\beta}\right), & j = s \\ \exp\{\alpha_j f_j(x_{ij}, y_i)\}, & j \neq s \end{cases} \tag{5.10}$$

We name this approach TriadFG with kernel function (TriadFG-KF).

5.4.1.3 TriadFG-EKF

With the discoveries regarding network structure, and taking TriadFG-BF into account, we can use the kernel function together with an exponential function to rewrite $F_j(x_{ij}, y_i)$ as follows:

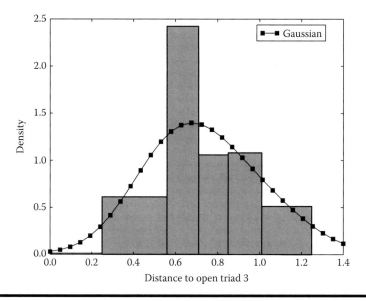

Figure 5.8 Kernel-density estimation for structure information.

$$F_j^{EKF}(x_{ij}, y_i) = \begin{cases} \exp\left\{\alpha_j \sum_{i=1}^{N} \frac{1}{\beta} k\left(\frac{x - x_{ij}}{\beta}\right)\right\}, & j = s \\ \exp\{\alpha_j f_j(x_{ij}, y_i)\}, & j \neq s \end{cases}$$ (5.11)

We call this approach TriadFG with exponential kernel function (TriadFG-EKF).

Objective function Based on the equations mentioned earlier, we can define the following log-likelihood objective function $\mathcal{O}(\theta) = \log P_\theta(Y|\mathbf{X}, G)$:

$$\mathcal{O} = \sum_{i}^{|Tr|}\left\{\sum_{j}^{|fe|}\alpha_j F_j(x_{ij}, y_i) + \sum_{c}\sum_{d}\mu_d h_d(Y_{Tr_c})\right\} - \log Z$$ (5.12)

where

Z is a normalization factor to guarantee that the result is a valid probability

$|Tr|$ denotes the number of candidate (open) triads in the network

$|fe|$ is the number of features defined for the triads (more details for feature definition are given in Section 5.4.2)

x_{ij} is the jth feature value of the ith triad

c corresponds to a correlation function

Tr_c indicates a set of all related triads in the correlation function

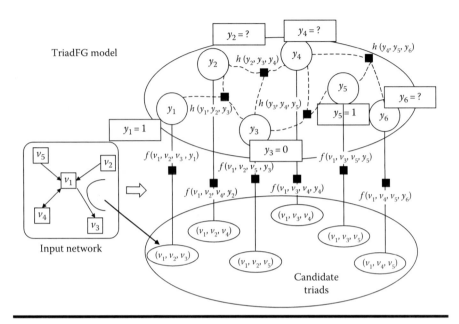

Figure 5.9 **Graphical representation of the TriadFG model. There are five users in the input network. Candidate open triads are illustrated as blue ellipses in the bottom right. White circles indicate hidden variables y_i. $f(v_1, v_2, v_3)$ represents the attribute factor function and $h(\cdot)$ the correlation function among triads.**

Example To provide a concrete understanding of the proposed model, we give a simple example of TriadFG in Figure 5.9. The left part is the input network, where we have five users and four kinds of following links among them. From the input network, we can derive six open triads—for example, (v_1, v_2, v_3) and (v_1, v_3, v_4). In the prediction task, we view each open triad as a candidate; thus, we have six candidates, which are illustrated as blue ellipses in the right-hand model. All features defined over open triads are denoted as such—that is, $f(v_1, v_2, v_3)$. In addition, we also consider social correlation. For example, the closure of (v_1, v_2, v_3) may imply a higher probability that (v_1, v_3, v_4) will also be closed at time $t + 1$. Given this, we build a correlation function $h(\cdot)$ among related triads. Based on all the considerations, we construct the TriadFG (as shown in Figure 5.9).

5.4.2 Feature Definitions

We now depict how we define the factor functions in our models. According to the observations in the previous section, we define 11 features of five categories: network structure (N), demographics (D), verified status (V), social information (S), and social interaction (I).

Network structure According to Figure 5.4b, we notice open triads 2, 4, and 5 are more likely to be closed than others, so for TriadFG-BF, we define one feature: whether the open triad is open triad 2, 4, or 5. For TriadFG-KF and TriadFG-EKF, we use a KDE to get the feature value.

Demographics Here we consider location and gender features. For location, we define one feature: whether the three users come from the same place; for gender, we define two features: whether all three users in one triad are female or male.

Verified status We define two features for verified status: whether the connecting user verified her status or not; other users have the opposite status (cases 010 and 101).

Social information We consider popularity, structural hole spanning, and gregariousness here. For popularity, we define one feature: whether all the three users in the triad are popular users. For structural hole spanning, we define one feature: whether user A and user B are structural hole spanners. For gregariousness, we define two features: whether all three users are gregarious users, and whether the three users follow the pattern: A and C are gregarious users, while user B isn't.

Social interaction For the problem of triadic closure prediction with interaction information, we define one feature for social interaction: whether a retweeting action happens among the three users in one triad.

5.4.3 Learning and Prediction

We then want to estimate a parameter configuration of the TriadFG model $\theta = (\{\alpha_j\}, \{\mu_d\})$ that maximizes the log-likelihood objective function, $\theta = \arg\max \mathcal{O}(\theta)$. We employ a gradient descent method for model learning. The basic idea is that each parameter—for example, μ_d—is assigned an initial value, and then the gradient of each μ_d with regard to the objective function is derived. Finally, the parameter with learning rate η is updated. The details of the learning algorithm can be found in [27].

With the estimated parameters θ, we can predict the labels of unknown variables $y_i = ?$ by finding a label configuration that maximizes the objective function—that is, $Y^\star = \arg\max \mathcal{O}(Y|X, G, \theta)$. To do this, we use the learned model to calculate the marginal distribution of each open triad with unknown variable $P(y_i|\mathbf{x}_i, G)$ and assign each open triad a label of the maximal probability.

5.5 Experiments and Discussions

5.5.1 Experiment Setup

We use the dataset described in Section 5.3 in our experiments. To quantitatively evaluate the effectiveness of the proposed model and the methods for comparison, we divide the network into seven timestamp periods, by viewing every 4 days as a timestamp period. For each timestamp period, we divide the network into two subsets by using the first two-thirds of the data as a training set and the rest as a test set. Our goal is to predict whether an open triad will become closed in the test set.

Comparison methods and evaluation measures We compare the proposed three approaches with two alternative baselines.

SVM It uses the same attributes associated with each triad as features to train a classification model and then uses the classification model to predict triadic closure in the test data.

Logistic Similar to the SVM method. The only difference is that it uses a logistic regression model as the classification model.

TriadFG-BF It represents the proposed TriadFG model with binary feature functions (Cf. Section 5.4.1.1).

TriadFG-KF It represents the proposed TriadFG model with kernel feature functions (Cf. Section 5.4.1.2).

TriadFG-EKF It represents the proposed TriadFG model with exponential kernel functions (Cf. Section 5.4.1.3).

For SVM and Logistic, we use Weka [12]. All the TriadFG models are implemented in C++, and all experiments are performed on a PC running Windows 7 with an AMD Opteron(TM) Processor 6276(2.3 GHz) and 4 GB memory. We evaluate the performance of different approaches in terms of accuracy, precision, recall, and F1-Measure.

5.5.2 Triadic Closure Prediction

5.5.2.1 Prediction Performance

We now list the performance results for different methods in Table 5.3. It can be seen that our proposed TriadFG-BF outperforms the other two comparison methods (SVM and Logistic), and TriadFG-EKF performs the best among all the methods. In terms of F1-Measure, TriadFG-BF achieves a +7.43% improvement over SVM and +7.85% over Logistic. TriadFG-KF achieves a +6.93% improvement

Table 5.3 Triadic Closure Prediction Performance

Algorithm	Accuracy	Precision	Recall	F1-Score
Logistic	0.7394	0.7657	0.7393	0.7316
SVM	0.7422	0.7683	0.742	0.7344
TriadFG-BF	0.7523	0.6989	0.9068	0.7890
TriadFG-KF	0.8426	0.8102	0.8613	0.8482
TriadFG-EKF	**0.8444**	**0.8360**	**0.9084**	**0.8564**

over TriadFG-BF, +14.88% over SVM, and +15.32% over Logistic. TriadFG-EKF achieves a +1.24% improvement over TriadFG-KF, +8.26% over TriadFG-BF, +16.31% over SVM, and +16.76% over Logistic. Our proposed algorithm is much better than SVM and Logistic in terms of F1-Measure. TriadFG-BF performs slightly better than they do because it uses binary feature functions that do not capture the similarities/correlations between different features. That is why we propose TriadFG-KF and TriadFG-EKF, which incorporate kernels to quantify the similarities. Meanwhile, the new proposed methods also do better on recall, which is partly because TriadFG can detect some cases by leveraging transitive correlation and homophily correlation.

5.5.2.2 Factor Contribution Analysis

For triadic closure prediction, we examine the contribution of four different factor functions: network structure (N), demographics (D), verified status (V), and social information (S). We first rank the individual factors by respectively each factor from our model and evaluate the decrease in prediction performance. Thus, a larger decrease means a higher predictive power for the removed factor. We thus rank these factors according to predictive power as follows: network structure (N) > verified status (V) > demographics (D) > social information (S).

We then remove them one by one in the reverse order of their prediction power. We denote TriadFG-S as removing social information and TriadFG-SD as removing demographics, finally removing verified status, denoted as TriadFG-SDV. As shown in Figure 5.10, we can observe a slight performance decrease when ignoring social information and demographics, which means these factors contribute significantly to predicting triadic closure.

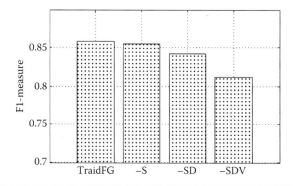

Figure 5.10 **Factor contribution analysis. −S denotes ignoring social information when we use TriadFG model, and −SD denotes ignoring social information and demographics, while −SDV denotes further ignoring verified status information.**

Table 5.4   Triadic Closure Prediction Performance of Each Open Triad

Triads	Accuracy	Precision	Recall	F1-Score
0	0.5479	0.5533	0.5478	0.5335
1	0.5320	0.5472	0.5322	0.4695
2	0.5894	0.6085	0.5895	0.5797
3	**0.6420**	**0.7058**	**0.6420**	**0.6097**
4	0.5988	0.6145	0.5990	0.5823
5	0.5551	0.5562	0.5552	0.5503

5.5.2.3 Prediction Performance on Triads

We now consider the prediction performance for each of the triads shown in Table 5.4. We can see that for triad 3, the prediction performance is much better than others, while for triad 1, the performance is the worst. This may be because triad 3, which corresponds to the case in which two fans follow one popular user, can be trained with a large number of features in our model, such as social information, which gives better prediction results than for other kinds of triads. However, the closure of triad 1, which has some transitive cases, cannot be easily predicted using our features and shows worse prediction performance than triad 3.

5.5.3 Triadic Closure Prediction with Interaction Information

5.5.3.1 Prediction Performance

Now we consider the triadic closure prediction problem with interaction information. Here, we consider retweeting behavior as interaction information.

Since TriadFG-EKF performs the best on Problem 5.1, we use TriadFG-EKF here to study this extended problem. The performance of TriadFG-EKF and TriadFG-EKF-I (with interaction information) is shown in Table 5.5. We can

Table 5.5   Triadic Closure Prediction Performance with Interaction Information

	Accuracy	Precision	Recall	F1-Score
TriadFG-EKF	0.6805	0.6834	0.7075	0.6953
TriadFG-EKF-I	**0.7276**	**0.7149**	**0.7838**	**0.7478**

see that our proposed TriadFG-EKF-I outperforms TriadFG-EKF. In terms of F1-Measure, TriadFG-EKF-I achieves a +7.55% improvement over TriadFG-EKF, which indicates that interaction information, such as retweeting behavior, plays an important role. We will further discuss how much it contributes to triadic closure prediction.

5.5.3.2 Factor Contribution Analysis

In this section, we again examine the contribution of five different factor functions, especially the retweeting function: network structure (N), demographics (D), verified status (V), social information (S), and interaction (I). According to predictive power of each factor, we rank these factors as follows: interaction (I) > network structure (N) > verified status (V) > social information (S) > demographics (D). We then remove them one by one in the reverse order of their prediction power. TriadFG-D denotes removing demographics, TriadFG-SD denotes removing social information from that set, TriadFG-SDV signifies removing verified status from that, and TriadFG-SDVN denotes removing network structure.

As shown in Figure 5.11, we observe a slight performance decrease when ignoring social information and demographics, but a large performance decrease when ignoring network structure—which means network structure information also contributes a lot to the prediction of triadic closure. However, interaction information has the strongest predictive power here, which indicates that interaction information is a good feature in this microblogging service and plays an important role in the establishment of friendship.

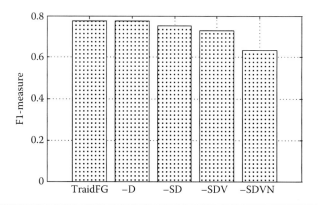

Figure 5.11 Factor contribution analysis. −D denotes ignoring demographics when we use the TriadFG model, and −SD denotes ignoring social information and demographics, while −SDV denotes also ignoring verified status information, and −SDVN denotes further ignoring network structure information.

5.5.4 Comparison with Twitter Observations

We compare the results with a similar study about popularity within triads on Twitter [15] and find the following:

- Both results demonstrate the phenomenon of "the rich get richer"—that is, $P(1XX) > P(0XX)$, which validates the mechanism of preferential attachment in both networks (Twitter and Weibo).
- In Twitter, popular users play an important role in forming closed triads— that is, $P(X1X)$ is about three times as high as $P(X0X)$, while in Weibo, the result is opposite. Possibly it is because Weibo provides more features to help users interact with each other, and ordinary users have more chances to connect with others. In China, Weibo is a combination of Twitter and Facebook and integrates the features of both.
- The probability $P(111)$ for popular users in Weibo is much higher than that in Twitter. In Twitter, $P(111)$ is twice as high as $P(000)$, while in Weibo, $P(111)$ is eight times as high, which implies that popular users in China have more closeness connections.

5.6 Related Work

In terms of related work, we identify two areas: triadic closure and link prediction in social networks. We will discuss them in detail as follows:

5.6.1 Triadic Closure Study

There are many studies on triadic closure study. They mainly focus on the following three aspects:

1. *Network evolution/formation.* One of the fundamental issues of social networks is to reveal the possible generic laws governing the formation/evolution of networks. Since it is unrealistic to get global information for preferential attachment processes to establish new social ties, the triadic closure principle, whose assumption is that a node's linking dynamics only rely on its neighbors or next neighbors, is relevant to social network formation. Klimek et al. [17] and Li et al. [25] both declared that triadic closure could be identified as one of the fundamental dynamic principles in social multiplex network formation/evolution. References 7, 8, and 20 also provided some triadic-closure-based network generation models.

2. *Network structure.* Milo et al. [28,29] defined recurring significant patterns of interconnections as "network motifs" and emphasized the importance of these patterns, which included six open triads and seven closed triads, which

we use in this chapter. Romero and Kleinberg [33] studied the problem of triadic closure and developed a methodology based on preferential attachment for studying the directed triadic closure process. Zhang et al. [43] use triadic structures to study link diffusion process.

3. *Triadic closure formation.* Lou et al. [26] investigated how a reciprocal link is developed from a parasocial relationship and how the relationships further develop into triadic closure, in a Twitter dataset. Zignani et al. [46] studied the triadic closure problem on undirected networks like Facebook and Renren.

However, none of these works systematically studied triadic closure formation and prediction in real large-scale directed networks.

5.6.2 Link Prediction

Our work is also related to the link prediction problem, which is one of the core tasks in social networks. Existing work on link prediction can be broadly grouped into two categories, based on the learning methods employed: unsupervised link prediction and supervised link prediction. Unsupervised link prediction usually assigns scores to potential links based on intuition—the more similar the pair of users are, the more likely they are to be linked. Various similarity measures of users are considered, such as preferential attachment [30] and the Katz measure [16]. Lichtenwalter et al. [24] presented a flow-based method for link prediction. A survey of unsupervised link prediction research can be found in [23].

There are also a number of works that employ supervised approaches to predict links in social networks, such as [2,21,24]. Backstrom and Leskovec proposed a supervised random walk algorithm to estimate the strength of social links. Leskovec et al. employed a logistic regression model to predict positive and negative links in OSNs.

However, unlike link prediction studies, we focus only on triadic closure, which means we only focus on the last "link" that constitutes the closed triad. Moreover, our model is dynamic and can learn from the evolution of the Weibo network. We also combine social theories into the semisupervised learning model.

5.7 Conclusions

In this chapter, we study an important phenomenon of triadic closure formation in dynamic social networks. Employing a large microblogging network (Weibo) as the source in our study, we formally define the problem and systematically study it. We propose a probabilistic factor model for modeling and predicting whether three persons in a social network will finally form a triad. Our experimental results on

Weibo show that the proposed model can more effectively predict triadic closure than alternative methods, in terms of F1 measurement.

Several among these findings are especially interesting in a sociological sense and deserve future studies. First, the findings about structural holes collaborate with the existing theory. According to Burt [4], a structural hole spanner as a mediator enjoys information and control benefits. Thus, exactly as the prediction of structural hole theory, B as the mediator in tweeting behavior doesn't want the open triad closed. On the contrary, if A or C is a hole spanner, then he or she would like to form triadic closure, so that B will not benefit from the disconnection between A and C. The collaboration between the existing theory and the finding from data mining allows us to arrive at the following hypothesis: An open triad with a structural hole spanner as the mediator is less likely to be closed than that with a structural hole spanner on the disconnected ends. We may infer this hypothesis to any type of OSN other than Weibo and collect different datasets to test it.

Another interesting finding is that celebrity users are more likely to form closed triads. Three users with high Pagerank scores are 421 times as likely to form closed triads as three ordinary users. This effect is much higher than the influence of other factors, such as gender, gregariousness, hole spanning, location, and retweeting interactions. One possible interpretation is that Weibo actually functions as personal broadcasting stations, on which each actor tries to broadcast his or her own speech or increase personal influence rather than making friends in OSNs. Thus, those celebrity users tend to retweet each other's tweets, which attract much more attention than an ordinary user's tweets. In Weibo, some celebrity users have tens of millions of followers, and many of ordinary users attract followers by retweeting celebrities tweets. Retweeting mostly occurs between a celebrity and an ordinary user rather than in the circles of friends. This interpretation leads us to investigate the motivations of users in using Weibo. Furthermore, it is an interesting question to compare tweeting and retweeting behaviors among different countries, and future studies may investigate the cultural influence on networking behaviors.

References

1. Backstrom L., D. Huttenlocher, J. Kleinberg, and X. Lan. Group formation in large social networks: Membership, growth, and evolution. In *KDD'06*, ACM, New York, pp. 44–54, 2006.
2. Backstrom L. and J. Leskovec. Supervised random walks: Predicting and recommending links in social networks. In *WSDM'11*, ACM, New York, pp. 635–644, 2011.
3. Ben-Hur A. and W.S. Noble. Kernel methods for predicting protein–protein interactions. *Bioinformatics*, 21(Suppl. 1):i38–i46, 2005.
4. Burt R.S. *Structural Hole*. Harvard Business School Press, Cambridge, MA, 1992.
5. Burt R.S. The social structure of competition. In Swedberg R. (ed.), *Explorations in Economic Sociology*, Russell Sage Foundation, New York, pp. 65–103, 1993.

6. Coleman J. *Foundations of Social Theory*. Harvard, Cambridge, MA, 1990.

7. Dong Y., J. Tang, S. Wu, J. Tian, N.V. Chawla, J. Rao, and H. Cao. Link prediction and recommendation across heterogeneous social networks. In *ICDM'12*, IEEE Computer Society Washington, DC, pp. 181–190, 2012.

8. Dong Y., Y. Yang, J. Tang, Y. Yang, and N.V. Chawla. Inferring user demographics and social strategies in mobile social networks. In *KDD'14*, ACM, New York, pp. 15–24, 2014.

9. Easley D. and J. Kleinberg. *Networks, Crowds, and Markets*. Cambridge University Press, New York, Vol. 6(1), p. 6-1, 2010.

10. Eckmann J.-P. and E. Moses. Curvature of co-links uncovers hidden thematic layers in the world wide web. *Proceedings of the National Academy of Sciences of the United States of America*, 99(9):5825–5829, 2002.

11. Gong N.Z., W. Xu, L. Huang, P. Mittal, E. Stefanov, V. Sekar, and D. Song. Evolution of social-attribute networks: Measurements, modeling, and implications using Google+. In *IMC'12*, ACM, New York, pp. 131–144, 2012.

12. Hall M., E. Frank, G. Holmes, B. Pfahringer, P. Reutemann, and I.H. Witten. The Weka data mining software: An update. *ACM SIGKDD Explorations Newsletter*, 11(1):10–18, 2009.

13. Hammersley J.M. and P. Clifford. Markov field on finite graphs and lattices. Unpublished manuscript, 1971.

14. Holland P.W. and S. Leinhardt. Transitivity in structural models of small groups. *Comparative Group Studies*, 2:107–124, 1971.

15. Hopcroft J., T. Lou, and J. Tang. Who will follow you back? Reciprocal relationship prediction. In *CIKM'11*, ACM, New York, pp. 1137–1146, 2011.

16. Katz L. A new status index derived from sociometric analysis. *Psychometrika*, 18(1):39–43, 1953.

17. Klimek P. and S. Thurner. Triadic closure dynamics drives scaling laws in social multiplex networks. *New Journal of Physics*, 15(6):063008, 2013.

18. Kwak H., C. Lee, H. Park, and S. Moon. What is twitter, a social network or a news media? In *WWW'10*, ACM, New York, pp. 591–600, 2010.

19. Lafferty J., A. McCallum, and F.C.N. Pereira. Conditional random fields: Probabilistic models for segmenting and labeling sequence data. In *ICML'01*, Morgan Kaufmann Publishers Inc., San Francisco, CA, pp. 282–289, 2001.

20. Leskovec J., L. Backstrom, R. Kumar, and A. Tomkins. Microscopic evolution of social networks. In *KDD'08*, ACM, New York, pp. 462–470, 2008.

21. Leskovec J., D. Huttenlocher, and J. Kleinberg. Predicting positive and negative links in online social networks. In *WWW'10*, ACM, New York, pp. 641–650, 2010.

22. Leskovec J., D. Huttenlocher, and J. Kleinberg. Signed networks in social media. In *CHI'10*, ACM, New York, pp. 1361–1370, 2010.

23. Liben-Nowell D. and J. Kleinberg. The link-prediction problem for social networks. *JASIST*, 58(7):1019–1031, 2007.

24. Lichtenwalter R.N., J.T. Lussier, and N.V. Chawla. New perspectives and methods in link prediction. In *KDD'10*, ACM, New York, pp. 243–252, 2010.

25. Li M., H. Zou, S. Guan, X. Gong, K. Li, Z. Di, and C.-H. Lai. A coevolving model based on preferential triadic closure for social media networks. *Scientific Reports*, 3:2512, 2013.

26. Lou T. and J. Tang. Mining structural hole spanners through information diffusion in social networks. In *WWW'13*, ACM, New York, pp. 837–848, 2013.

27. Lou T., J. Tang, J. Hopcroft, Z. Fang, and X. Ding. Learning to predict reciprocity and triadic closure in social networks. *ACM Transactions on Knowledge Discovery from Data (TKDD)*, 7(2):5, 2013.

28. Milo R., S. Itzkovitz, N. Kashtan, R. Levitt, S. Shen-Orr, I. Ayzenshtat, M. Sheffer, and U. Alon. Superfamilies of evolved and designed networks. *Science*, 303(5663):1538–1542, 2004.

29. Milo R., S. Shen-Orr, S. Itzkovitz, N. Kashtan, D. Chklovskii, and U. Alon. Network motifs: Simple building blocks of complex networks. *Science*, 298:824–827, 2002.

30. Newman M.E.J. Clustering and preferential attachment in growing networks. *Physical Review E*, 64(2):025102, 2001.

31. Obstfeld D. Social networks, the tertius iungens orientation, and involvement in innovation. *Administrative Science Quarterly*, 50(1):100–130, 2005.

32. Page L., Brin S., Motwani R., and Winograd T. The Pagerank citation ranking: Bringing order to the web. Stanford InfoLab, Stanford, CA, 1999.

33. Romero D.M. and J. Kleinberg. The directed closure process in hybrid social-information networks, with an analysis of link formation on Twitter. *Statistics*, 1050:12, 2010.

34. Burt R.S. Structural holes versus network closure as social capital. In Lin N., K. Cook, and R.S. Burt (eds.), *Social Capital: Theory and Research*, Aldine de Gruyter, New York, 2001.

35. Sala A., L. Cao, C. Wilson, R. Zablit, H. Zheng, and B.Y. Zhao. Measurement-calibrated graph models for social network experiments. In *WWW'10*, ACM, New York, pp. 861–870, 2010.

36. Sasovova Z., A. Mehra, S.P. Borgatti, and M.C. Schippers. Network churn: The effects of self-monitoring personality on brokerage dynamics. *Administrative Science Quarterly*, 55(4):639–670, 2010.

37. Schweizer B. and A. Sklar. *Probabilistic Metric Spaces*. Courier Dover Publications, Mineola, NY, 2011.

38. Shawe-Taylor J. and N. Cristianini. *Kernel Methods for Pattern Analysis*. Cambridge University Press, Cambridge, U.K., 2004.

39. Wasserman L. *All of Statistics: A Concise Course in Statistical Inference*. Springer, New York, 2004.

40. Wasserman S. *Social Network Analysis: Methods and Applications*, Vol. 8. Cambridge University Press, Cambridge, U.K., 1994.

41. Wu S., J.M. Hofman, W.A. Mason, and D.J. Watts. Who says what to whom on twitter. In *WWW'11*, ACM, New York, pp. 705–714, 2011.

42. Yang M.-H. Kernel eigenfaces vs. kernel fisherfaces: Face recognition using kernel methods. In *FG'02*, Washington, DC, pp. 0215–0220, 2002.

43. Zhang J., Z. Fang, W. Chen, and J. Tang. Diffusion of "following" links in microblogging networks. *IEEE Transactions on Knowledge and Data Engineering*, 27(8):2093–2106, 2015.

44. Zhang, J. B. Liu, J. Tang, T. Chen, and J. Li. Social influence locality for modeling retweeting behaviors. In *IJCAI'13*, AAAI Press, Palo Alto, CA, pp. 2761–2767, 2013.

45. Zheleva E., H. Sharara, and L. Getoor. Co-evolution of social and affiliation networks. In *KDD'09*, ACM, New York, pp. 1007–1016, 2009.

46. Zignani M., S. Gaito, G.P. Rossi, X. Zhao, H. Zheng, and B.Y. Zhao. Link and triadic closure delay: Temporal metrics for social network dynamics. In *ICWSM'14*, AAAI Press, Palo Alto, CA, pp. 564–573, 2014.

Chapter 6

Prediction of Venture Capital Coinvestment Based on Structural Balance Theory

Yun Zhou, Zhiyuan Wang, Jie Tang, and Jar-Der Luo

Contents

6.1 Introduction

Venture capital (VC) is financial capital provided to early-stage, high-potential growth start-up firms. VCs are unsung heroes behind high-tech firms, such as Google, PayPal, and Alibaba, especially when the firms are in their infancy. Without VC, high-tech start-ups will suffer from a shortage of funds and business directions, and so more and more importance has been given to VC in the era of information technology and network economy.

High-tech industry routinely acknowledges that communities knit together by networks of social relations are essential for the development of the industry and emphasizes that VCs hold central positions in these networks [1]. Based on the statistics on the free online CrunchBase dataset (cf. Section 6.3), 80.9% of VC investments are related to at least two investors; thus, coinvestment is an important phenomenon in the VC market. We cannot fully understand VC behavior without a detailed exploration of coinvestment.

In this chapter, we study the problem of predicting whether two VCs will coinvest or not in the near future, given the existing VC network. This research is also of great interest to practitioners in the field of investment. For instance, the study can help a VC manager to find coinvestors from a large number of candidates automatically. However, due to complexity and uncertainty of VC behavior, it's challenging to accurately predict future coinvestments, and we address the challenges as follows. First, what factors influence the formation of coinvestment relationships? Second, how do we select a small number of fundamental factors that best explain the formation without significant drop in performance? Third, how do we design a mechanism that incorporates social network theory affecting the formation of coinvestment relationships?

Coinvestment has been studied for many years in sociology and economics, such as [16,17,25,26,30]. Lerner [17] studied the principle of who will be a good coinvestor and when to reconstruct a coinvestment. Sorenson and Stuart [26] studied the effect of geographic spaces on coinvestment. Based on 45 years of VC data from the United States, Kogut et al. [16] found several features that might have influence on new coinvestments. Powell et al. [25] studied four kinds of effects on interorganizational collaboration. However, most of researches dealt with a small dataset with at most hundreds of VCs except [16], and they only explored a few features for coinvestment without detailed analysis of contribution of different kinds of features. In addition, few works predicted future coinvestment with a unified model and presented the performance of prediction.

6.1.1 Solution and Contribution

In this chapter, we formulate the problem of coinvestment prediction in the VC network and perform a series of observations of the data. Based on the observations and structural balance theory, we propose a structural balanced factor graph model named SBFG to predict the coinvestment at time $t + 1$, given coinvestment network of time span $\{1, t\}$. We develop an approximate algorithm using loopy belief propagation (LBP) to efficiently learn the proposed model. Experiment results demonstrate that the proposed model SBFG significantly (+9% in terms of accuracy) outperforms the baselines, that is, logistic regression (LR) and support vector machine (SVM).

We design a larger number of features from the perspective of both domain knowledge and social network, which cover most features that have been proposed in past literature, such as [16,17,25,26,30]. In order to gain both interpretability of features and high accuracy, we select prominent features by group least absolute shrinkage and selection operator (Lasso). It is shown that only the top 10 features selected by group Lasso can explain the formation of the VC network quite well (it drops by only 0.18% in terms of accuracy compared with a total of 81 features), for example, nationality, number of common neighbors, betweenness, shortest distance, investor type, number of invested fields, and Jaccard index of invested fields. We have some interesting findings by exploring the prominent features, which can be used to explain investment behavior in the VC market.

We introduce two new investment datasets for the academic community, which can be applied to the study of data mining or social network analysis.

6.1.2 Organization

Section 6.2 formulates the problem. Section 6.3 introduces the dataset. Section 6.4 describes feature design and feature selection by group Lasso. Section 6.5 presents observation of the prominent features selected by group Lasso. Section 6.6 proposes structural balance–based factor graph model and learning algorithm. Section 6.7 presents experiment results and detailed analysis. Section 6.8 further explores another dataset that focuses on the start-ups in China. Section 6.9 reviews the related work and Section 6.10 concludes the chapter.

6.2 Problem Formulation

In this section, we first give an illustration of investment and coinvestment, present the formal definition of coinvestment, and then propose a formal description of the problem. We formulate the problem in the context of VC to keep things concrete.

Figure 6.1 shows the investment and coinvestment in the capital market. In Figure 6.1a, the red person represents a VC, the blue box represents a start-up that gets funded, and a line between a VC and a start-up represents an investment. VCs and start-ups are in heterogeneous spaces, which are denoted by two plates in Figure 6.1b. To simplify the network, we consider the coinvestment of VCs by adding a link between two VCs that invest in a common start-up in the same year, as shown in Figure 6.1c. Given the VC network in the past, we'd like to predict

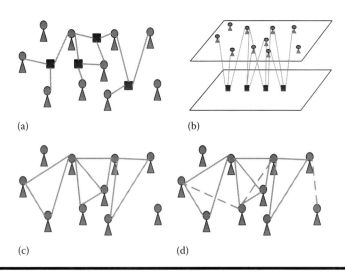

(a)   (b)

(c)   (d)

Figure 6.1   Investment and coinvestment. Each person represents a VC, and the rectangle box represents a start-up. The line in (a) and (b) indicates an investment. The solid (dashed) line in (c) and (d) indicates the past (future) coinvestment between VCs. (a) Investment; (b) two plates; (c) coinvestment; (d) new coinvestment.

whether two VCs will coinvest or not in the near future, and the dashed lines in Figure 6.1d are new coinvestments in the near future.

Definition 6.1 (Coinvestment). We say that two VCs coinvest in a given year, if they invest in the same start-up(s) in the year. Accordingly, they call each other coinvestor.

The number of investments increases over time, and the VC network $G^t = (V^t, E^t)$ is also evolving, where V^t is the set of accumulated VCs ($|V^t| = N$) and $E^t \subseteq V^t \times V^t$ is the set of accumulated coinvestment relationships between VCs until time t. We are concerned with the following problem.

Problem 6.1 Predict whether two VCs will coinvest or not in the next year. Let $G^t = (V^t, E^t)$ be the VC network in time span $\{1, t\}$; given two VCs, the task is to predict whether they will coinvest or not in time $t + 1$.

It bears pointing out that our problem is quite different from existing link prediction problems [2,12,19]. First, the VC network is intrinsically dynamic and multi-dimensional, which are not well treated in the traditional link prediction research. Second, it is not clear what are the fundamental factors that influence the formation of the VC network. Finally, one needs to incorporate the different factors (e.g., social theories, statistics, and our intuition) into a unified model to better explain the coinvestment relationship.

6.3 Data Description

The dataset (CRUNCH) comes from the free online CrunchBase [7], which is updated frequently. The dataset contains open investment events in the world from 1984 to 2014, and there are a total of 18,716 VCs, 25,327 start-ups, 90,280 investments, and 152,227 coinvestments. The original information and statistics of CRUNCH are summarized in Table 6.1.

In recent years, the VC investment developed very quickly. The distribution of investment over year is shown in Figure 6.2. In the first 15 years (1984–1998), the number of investments every year was less than 50 and it rose to 168 in 1999. After 6 years of steady increase (1999–2004), the number jumped to 4196 in 2005. From then on (2005–now), the number increases rapidly, with the exception of 2009, due to the economic depression.

The distribution of VC and start-up over country/area is shown in Figure 6.3, where the notation of three letters denotes the country, which is defined in ISO 3166-1 [15]. For instance, *USA* denotes the United States, and *GBR* denotes the United Kingdom. *OTH* denotes all other countries as a whole. Since VCs in the

Table 6.1   Information and Statistics of CRUNCH

Item	CRUNCH (1984–2014)
Investment information	VC, start-up, funded year, round, raised amount
VC information	Investor type, location, field
Start-up information	Field, location
#Investment	90,282
#VC	18,716
#Start-up	25,327

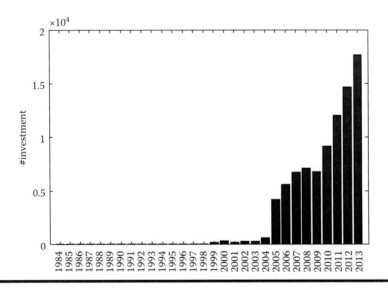

Figure 6.2   Distribution of investment over year. The number of investments increases rapidly from 2005.

United States account for more than half of total VCs in the world, the state of the United States is treated as an entity in the statistics, where *CA* denotes California, *NY* denotes New York, and so on. Note that the number of VCs in the state of California is even larger than that of any other country in the world, and this area dominates the VC market of the world. Figure 6.3a lists the top 15 countries/areas with the most VCs, and Figure 6.3b lists the top 15 countries/areas with the most start-ups.

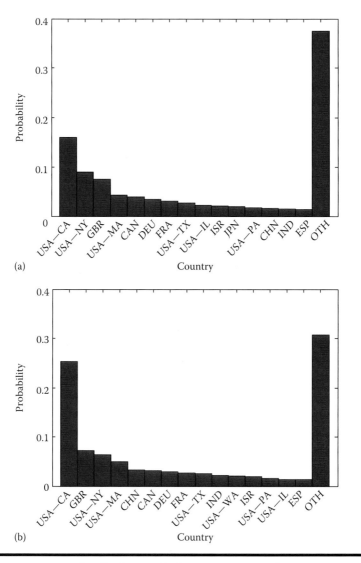

Figure 6.3 (a) VC distribution and (b) start-up distribution over country. California is the most active area of VC and start-up in the world.

The difference between the numbers of investments of different VCs is very large. The distribution of VC over the number of investments is shown in Figure 6.4, where the curve roughly obeys the power law. From 1984 to 2014, every VC has 4.8 investments on average. The five VCs with the most investments are Sequoia Capital (659 investments), Start-Up Chile (607), Intel Capital (571), New Enterprise Associates (536), and Y Combinator (533). The percentage of VCs that have only

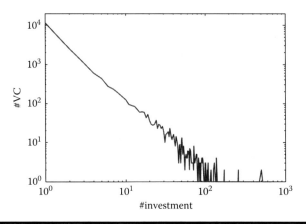

Figure 6.4 **Power-law distribution of VC over the number of investments (both *y*-axis and *x*-axis have logarithmic scale). The investments of 7.6% VC firms account for 64.7% of all investments.**

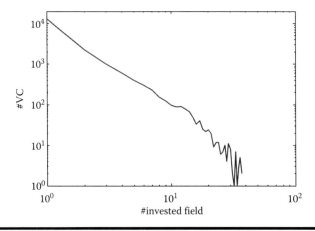

Figure 6.5 **Power-law distribution of VC over the number of invested fields (both *y*-axis and *x*-axis have logarithmic scale).**

one investment is 62.7%. The VCs with more than 10 investments account for 7.6% of all VCs, and they have 64.7% of all investments.

Usually, VCs invest in several different fields to avoid risks. The distribution of VC over the number of invested fields is shown in Figure 6.5, where the curve also roughly obeys power law. There are 44 fields in CRUNCH (cf. Figure 6.7). From 1984 to 2014, every VC invested in 2.2 fields on average. The VCs with the most invested fields are SV Angel, Start-Up Chile (37 invested fields), Kleiner Perkins

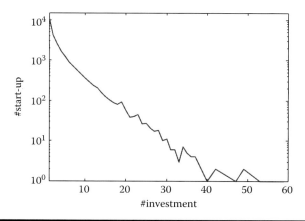

Figure 6.6 **Distribution of start-up over the number of investments (*y*-axis has a logarithmic scale).**

Caufield & Byers, Sequoia Capital, Y Combinator, New Enterprise Associates, and Techstars (36 invested fields).

The distribution of start-up over the number of investments is shown in Figure 6.6. Note that, different from Figures 6.4 and 6.5, in Figure 6.6, only the *y*-axis has a logarithmic scale. From 1984 to 2014, every start-up gets 3.6 investments on average. The five start-ups with the most investments are Fab (59 investments), ecomom (58), CardioDx (54), Practice Fusion (53), and Aperto Networks (49). 68.8% of start-ups are with less than or equal to 10 investments.

The distribution of start-up over the field is shown in Figure 6.7. There are 44 fields in CRUNCH, where the top 5 fields are software (13%), biotech (8.9%), mobile (7.4%), web (7.3%), and enterprise (7.2%).

6.4 Feature Design and Selection

6.4.1 Feature Design

We design a large number of features for coinvestment from the perspective of both domain knowledge and social network. According to the time characteristics, the features can be categorized into static features and dynamic features. The static feature does not change over time, such as nationality and investor type, but the dynamic feature changes over time, such as invested fields and betweenness on the VC network. Note that the static feature takes the same value for different years, while the dynamic pattern should be normalized within the year (cf. Section 6.5.2); otherwise, the values are not comparable between years. The dynamic features can

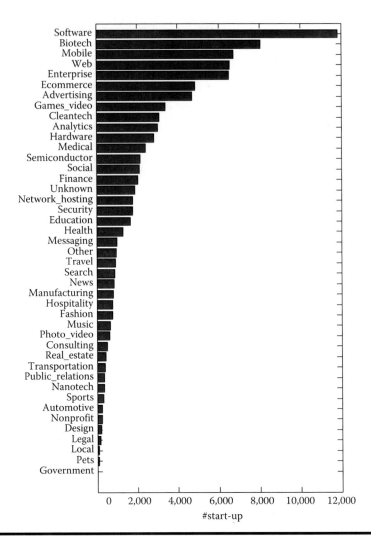

Figure 6.7 Distribution of start-up over field. Software, mobile web, and biotech are the most active fields for start-up.

be further divided into dynamic domain features and dynamic topology features. The former is related to domain knowledge of VC, and the latter is related to the evolving VC network.

All features for coinvestment are summarized in Table 6.2. The features are self-explained, and the fifth column shows a short description of the features. In Section 6.5, we shall explain the important features in detail.

Table 6.2 All Features for Coinvestment

Feature	No.	Ord.[a]	Name	Short Description
Static feature	01	43	latitudeMax	Larger value of latitude.
	02	34	latitudeMin	Smaller value of latitude.
	03	26	latitudeSingle	Single value of latitude.
	04	33	latitudeDiff	Difference of latitude.
	05	43	longitudeMax	Larger value of longitude.
	06	31	longitudeMin	Smaller value of longitude.
	07	16	longitudeSingle	Single value of longitude.
	08	23	longitudeDiff	Difference of longitude.
	09	20	absoluteDistance	Straight-line distance.
	10	17	timeZoneDiff	Difference of time zone.
	11	80	sameCity	Are two VCs in the same city?
	12	01	sameCountry	Are two VCs in the same country?
	13	14	ethnicitySim	Ethnicity similarity.[b]
	14	39	languageSim	Language similarity.[b]
	15	29	religionSim	Religion similarity.[b]
	16	06	investorCombination	Combination of investor type.
	17	36	sameCVCField	Are two company VCs of the same field?

(*Continued*)

Table 6.2 (*Continued*)   All Features for Coinvestment

Feature	No.	Ord.[a]	Name	Short Description
Dynamic domain feature	18	08	fieldsMax	Larger value of #field.
	19	07	fieldsMin	Smaller value of #field.
	20	09	fieldsSingle	Single value of #field.
	21	61	fieldsDiff	Difference of #field.
	22	77	fieldsSum	Sum of #field.
	23	10	fieldsJaccard	Jaccard similarity of fields.
	24	23	shortTrendMax	Larger value of short trend.[c]
	25	13	shortTrendMin	Smaller value of short trend.
	26	18	shortTrendSingle	Single value of short trend.
	27	23	longTrendMax	Larger value of long trend.
	28	39	longTrendMin	Smaller value of long trend.
	29	12	longTrendSingle	Single value of long trend.
	30	36	firstInvestYearMax	Larger value of first year of investment.
	31	20	firstInvestYearMin	Smaller value of first year of investment.
	32	81	firstInvestYearSingle	Single value of first year of investment.
	33	61	firstInvestYearDiff	Difference of first year of investment.

(Continued)

Table 6.2 (*Continued*)   All Features for Coinvestment

Feature	No.	Ord.[a]	Name	Short Description
Dynamic topology feature	34	04	distanceBefore	Shortest distance of two VCs.
	35	39	degreeMax	Larger value of degree.
	36	52	degreeMin	Smaller value of degree.
	37	20	degreeSingle	Single value of degree.
	38	47	degreeDiff	Difference of degree.
	39	69	degreeSum	Sum of degree.
	40	36	shConstraintMax	Larger value of structural hole constraint.[d]
	41	56	shConstraintMin	Smaller value of structural hole constraint.
	42	34	shConstraintSingle	Single value of structural hole constraint.
	43	73	shConstraintDiff	Difference of structural hole constraint.
	44	67	shConstraintSum	Sum of structural hole constraint.
	45	55	shConstraintMaxEgo	Larger value of structural hole constraint of ego net.
	46	52	shConstraintMinEgo	Smaller value of structural hole constraint of ego net.

(*Continued*)

Table 6.2 (*Continued*) **All Features for Coinvestment**

Feature	No.	Ord.[a]	Name	Short Description
	47	43	shConstraintSingleEgo	Single value of structural hole constraint of ego net.
	48	71	shConstraintDiffEgo	Difference of structural hole constraint of ego net.
	49	73	shConstraintSumEgo	Sum of structural hole constraint of ego net.
	50	03	betweennessMax	Larger value of betweenness.
	51	11	betweennessMin	Smaller value of betweenness.
	52	05	betweennessSingle	Single value of betweenness.
	53	76	betweennessDiff	Difference of betweenness.
	54	42	betweennessSum	Sum of betweenness.
	55	49	betweennessMaxEgo	Larger value of betweenness of ego net.
	56	19	betweennessMinEgo	Smaller value of betweenness of ego net.
	57	26	betweennessSingleEgo	Single value of betweenness of ego net.
	58	65	betweennessDiffEgo	Difference of betweenness of ego net.
	59	67	betweennessSumEgo	Sum of betweenness of ego net.
	60	30	densityMaxEgo	Larger value of ego density.

(Continued)

Table 6.2 (*Continued*)   All Features for Coinvestment

Feature	No.	Ord.[a]	Name	Short Description
	61	56	densityMinEgo	Smaller value of ego density.
	62	43	densitySingleEgo	Single value of ego density.
	63	78	densityDiffEgo	Difference of ego density.
	64	61	densitySumEgo	Sum of ego density.
	65	49	firstNeighborsMax	Larger value of #neighbor.
	66	56	firstNeighborsMin	Smaller value of #neighbor.
	67	26	firstNeighborsSingle	Single value of #neighbor.
	68	47	firstNeighborsDiff	Difference of #neighbor.
	69	72	firstNeighborsSum	Sum of #neighbor.
	70	02	firstCommonNeighbors	#common neighbor.
	71	65	secondNeighborsMax	Larger value of #secondary neighbor.
	72	52	secondNeighborsMin	Smaller value of #secondary neighbor.
	73	15	secondNeighborsSingle	Single value of #secondary neighbor.
	74	69	secondNeighborsDiff	Difference of #secondary neighbor.
	75	56	secondNeighborsSum	Sum of #secondary neighbor.

(Continued)

Table 6.2 (*Continued*)   All Features for Coinvestment

Feature	No.	Ord.[a]	Name	Short Description
	76	31	secondCommonNeighbors	#common secondary neighbor.
	77	51	clusterCoefficientMax	Larger value of clustering coefficient.
	78	73	clusterCoefficientMin	Smaller value of clustering coefficient.
	79	56	clusterCoefficientSingle	Single value of clustering coefficient.
	80	79	clusterCoefficientDiff	Difference of clustering coefficient.
	81	61	clusterCoefficientSum	Sum of clustering coefficient.

[a] Ord. denotes the reverse shrinking order of the feature in group Lasso, and the feature with a smaller Ord. is considered to be more important.
[b] Cf. [1] for calculation of similarity of ethnicity, language, and religion.
[c] Follow-the-trend indicates that VCs tend to match their choices with the dominant choices of others, cf. [25] for more details.
[d] Cf. [5] for structural hole theory.

6.4.2 Feature Selection with Group Lasso

As stated in the previous section, a large number of features have been taken into consideration. However, the relations among features are interdependent and nonlinear. In order to select the most important and interpretable features, we preselect the features by group Lasso with logistic loss.

Lasso [29] provides a way to gain the sparsity of the parameters by imposing a 1-norm regularization. The objective function to be minimized is defined as

$$Q(\theta) = \text{loss}(\theta) + \lambda \, \|\theta\|_1 \qquad (6.1)$$

where
  θ is the parameter vector in the model
  $\text{loss}(\theta)$ is the loss function
  $\|\cdot\|_1$ is the 1-norm

As λ is increased, the components of θ are gradually shrunk to zero so as to achieve sparsity. The feature whose weight is shrunk later is considered to be more important, and so the shrinking order can be used to select features.

However, the categorical variable in the model is usually coded via dummy variables, and so the dummy variables corresponding to one categorical variable may be set to zero in different time in Lasso, which makes the sparsity of Lasso less powerful. Thus, Yuan and Lin [35] proposed group Lasso to shrink the dummy variables of a group together for least-squared loss, and later, group Lasso was generalized to logistic loss [21]. The objective function is

$$Q(\theta) = \text{loss}(\theta) + \lambda \sum_{j=1}^{q} m_j \left\| \theta_{G_j} \right\|_2 \tag{6.2}$$

where all features are divided into j groups according to the coding of dummy variables, that is, $G_1, G_2, \dots, G_j$. The multiplier m_j serves for balancing cases where the groups are of different sizes, and $\|\cdot\|_2$ denotes the Euclidean norm.

We use a large number of categorical features, and group Lasso is employed to select features by group. Since the proposed SBFG (cf. Section 6.6) is a kind of generalized linear model, we choose the logistic loss for feature selection. We fit group Lasso for LR by the group descent algorithm in the R package "grpreg" [3,4]. Group Lasso only needs the labeled training data, and the data in 1984–2010 of CRUNCH are fed to Group Lasso for determining the reverse shrinking order of features, which is shown in the third column of Table 6.2. For instance, the No. 12 feature has order 01, which means that the weight of the No. 12 feature is the last to shrink to zero, and so it is regarded as the most important feature in the model.

6.5 Observation of Prominent Features

As mentioned in Section 6.4, the features are categorized into three kinds, that is, static features, dynamic domain features, and dynamic topology features, and we will describe the top 10 features selected by group Lasso in this order, since the handling of static features is different from the dynamic ones.

6.5.1 Static Features

Nationality: Figure 6.8 shows the distribution of VCs' nationality, where the orange bar denotes the positive instances (the existent coinvestments in the dataset, cf. Section 6.7) and the blue bar denotes the negative instances. It is clearly shown that the two VCs tend to coinvest when they are from the same country.

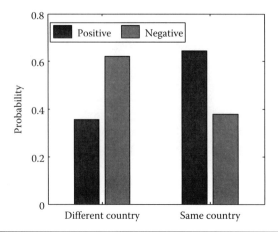

Figure 6.8 Nationality. *y*-axis: probability, conditioned on nationality. The orange bar denotes the positive instances in the dataset, while the blue bar denotes the negative instances. Two VCs tend to coinvest when they are from the same country.

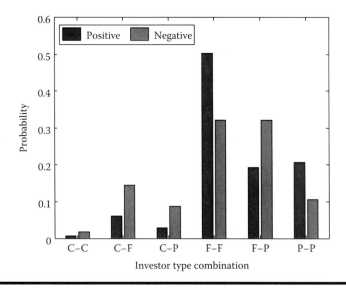

Figure 6.9 Investor-type combination. *y-axis*: probability, conditioned on investor-type combination. "C" indicates company venture capital, "F" indicates financial organization, and "P" indicates person investor.

Investor type: The investor types of VCs in CRUNCH are categorized into company VC (C), financial organization (F), and person investor (P). There are 2875 company VCs, 8038 financial organizations, and 7803 person investors in CRUNCH. Figure 6.9 shows that financial organization tends to coinvest with financial organization, person investor tends to coinvest with person investor, and other combinations are not very popular.

6.5.2 Dynamic Domain Features

Invested fields reflect investment interest and investment diversity of VC. Since #field (# indicates the number, the same hereinafter) is a measure that changes over time, the values of the feature in different years are not directly comparable, and we use the rank of #field in the given year instead of the original value of #field, as shown in Figure 6.10. We employ the "equal-frequency binning" technique to discretize #field of the same year into a small number of distinct ranges. #field in the bin with the largest value is ranked 1, #field in the bin with the second largest value is ranked 2, and so on. After discretization within the same year, the comparability of #field in different years is improved. This technique is also applied to some other dynamic features, for example, betweenness.

Since a potential coinvestment involves two VCs, there are two values of #field for a potential coinvestment. The larger one of the two values is shown in Figure 6.10a, the smaller one is shown in Figure 6.10b, and we find that VCs with large #field (small rank) tend to coinvest in both cases.

6.5.2.1 Jaccard Similarity of Invested Fields

Besides the number of invested fields, we calculate the Jaccard similarity of the invested fields (jacc for short) for a VC pair, that is, $(|IF_t(vc_1) \cap IF_t(vc_2)|)/(|IF_t(vc_1) \cup IF_t(vc_2)|)$, where $IF_t(vc_1)$ denotes the set of invested fields of vc_1 before time t. As shown in Figure 6.11, when jacc is smaller than 0.1, the VC pair does not tend to coinvest, probably due to a lack of common interests. When jacc is larger than 0.8, the VC pair does not tend to coinvest either, probably because they cannot complement each other very well. Thus, the VC pair with appropriate jacc tends to coinvest.

6.5.3 Dynamic Topology Features

Besides the features from domain knowledge, there are also features related to social network that are selected by group Lasso, which are explained as follows:

Common neighbors reflect the link homophily between two VCs. Since this feature is related to the evolving VC network, we use the *common neighbor ratio*

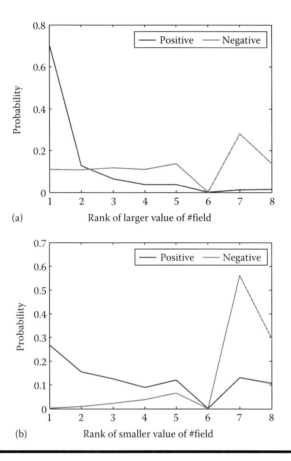

(a)   Rank of larger value of #field

(b)   Rank of smaller value of #field

Figure 6.10 **Invested fields.** *y-axis*: **probability, conditioned on rank of larger/ smaller value of #field. Smaller rank indicates larger #field. (a) Larger value; (b) smaller value.**

instead, which is defined as the ratio of the number of common neighbors to the sum of the number of neighbors of two VCs. Figure 6.12 shows the histogram of positive instances and negative instances, where the bar heights are normalized so the area for each bar represents the probability for the corresponding interval. Comparing the histogram for positive instances (Figure 6.12a) with the histogram for negative instances (Figure 6.12b), we find that VCs with a larger common neighbor ratio are more likely to coinvest with other VCs.

Betweenness is one of centrality measures of nodes in social network [8]. Although many centralities have been taken into consideration, such as degree, closeness, and structural hole (cf. Table 6.2), betweenness is identified as the prominent feature in the coinvestment prediction by group Lasso. Betweenness is a

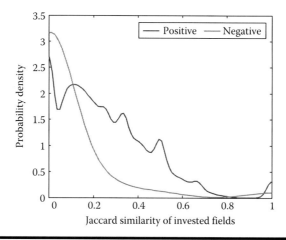

Figure 6.11 **Jaccard similarity of invested fields. The VC pair with appropriate (not too large and not too small) jacc tends to coinvest.**

measure of the evolving VC network and so we use the rank of betweenness in the given year instead of the original value, as shown in Figure 6.13. Since a potential coinvestment involves two VCs, there are two values of betweenness for a coinvestment. The larger one of the two values is shown in Figure 6.13a, the smaller one is shown in Figure 6.13b, and we find that VCs with large betweenness (small rank) tend to coinvest in both cases.

Shortest distance is considered to be one of the most important features in link prediction [12]. As shown in Figure 6.14, when two VCs that have invested before (i.e., the shortest distance is 1) or have a common neighbor (i.e., the shortest distance is 2), they are highly likely to coinvest. When the shortest distance is equal to or larger than 3, the likelihood of coinvestment decreases rapidly. When there is no path between two VCs in the network (the shortest distance is *inf* in Figure 6.14), that is, one or two candidate VC(s) of the potential coinvestment are not connected to the biggest component of the VC network, they are not likely to coinvest.

6.6 Model Framework

Basically, the binary classification problem (coinvest or not) can be solved by any classifier, such as LR and SVM. However, these models suffer from the same limitation that they cannot model the correlation between/among coinvestments, so we try to develop an integrated factor graph model to capture both feature and correlation.

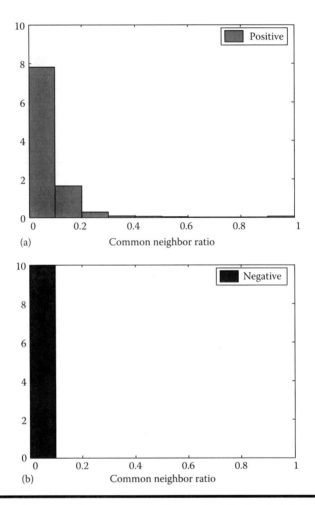

Figure 6.12 **Histogram of common neighbor ratio. The bar height is normalized so the area for each bar represents the probability for the corresponding interval. (a) Positive histogram; (b) negative histogram.**

6.6.1 Structural Balance Theory

We explore an important pattern in the VC network based on the structural balance theory [8], which will be the theoretical foundation of our proposed model. Figure 6.15 shows the triad relationships, where the line between two VCs indicates the coinvestment and the two VCs connected by the line are called coinvestors. For every group of three users (called triad), the structural balance theory implies that either all three pairs of these VCs are coinvestors or only one pair of them is a coinvestor. As shown in Figure 6.16, the number of balanced triads (those with three coinvestments or one coinvestment) is by far larger than that of unbalanced triads

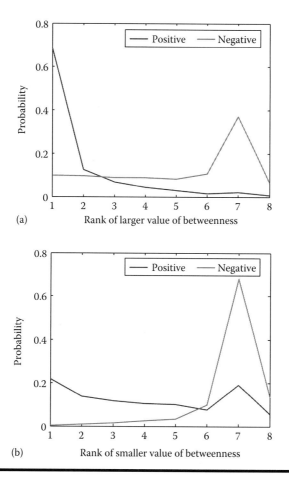

(a)

(b)

Figure 6.13 Betweenness. *y-axis*: probability, conditioned on rank of larger/ smaller value of betweenness. Smaller rank indicates larger betweenness. (a) Larger value; (b) smaller value.

(those with two coinvestments or zero coinvestment) in CRUNCH. Moreover, the connected triads (those with two coinvestments or three coinvestments) are of particular interest to us, since the fact that the number of closed triads (those with three coinvestments) is much larger than that of open triads (those with two coinvestments) reflects the prevalence of triadic closure in the VC network, that is, the coinvestor of my coinvestor is likely to be my coinvestor.

6.6.2 Proposed Model

The original VC network is built intuitively with VC as a node, but the goal of our research is to predict the coinvestment between VCs. In addition, it is hard

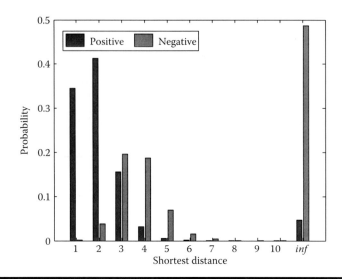

Figure 6.14 **Shortest distance on the VC network. VCs tend to coinvest when they have a short distance on the coinvestment network.**

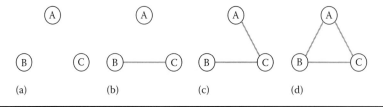

Figure 6.15 **Illustration of structural balance theory. The line between VCs indicates coinvestment, and the two VCs connected by the line are called coinvestors. The structural balance theory implies that either all three pairs of these VCs are coinvestors (d) or only one pair of them is a coinvestor (b). (a) No coinvestment, (b) only B and C have coinvestment, (c) B and C have coinvestment, A and C have coinvestment, and (d) A, B, and C have coinvestments each other.**

to model the correlation between/among coinvestments (e.g., the triad correlation mentioned earlier) if with VC as a node. Thus, we prefer to model the coinvestment as a node directly in the graphical model, and first, the original VC network with VC as a node is converted to a graph model with coinvestment as a node.

Our proposed model, that is, structural balance–based factor graph (SBFG) model, is inspired by the structural balance theory and observation in CRUNCH. The model is shown in Figure 6.17. The left figure shows the original VC network, where the edges with label 1/0 indicate whether two VCs coinvested or not in time span $\{1, t\}$, and the edges with label? are those that we try to predict in time $t+1$. The solid/dashed line indicates whether the edge exists or not in the ground truth.

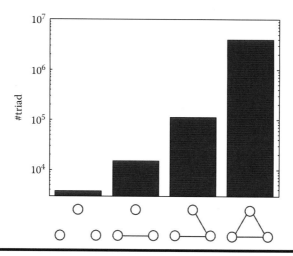

Figure 6.16 Structural balance in the VC network. The number of balanced triads (those with three coinvestments) is by far larger than that of unbalanced triads (those with two coinvestments).

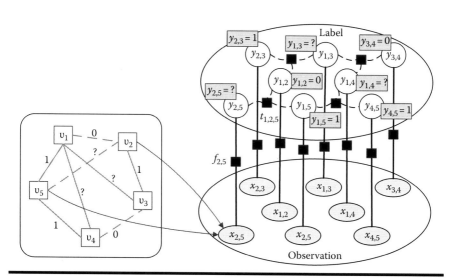

Figure 6.17 Graphical representation of SBFG model. The left figure shows the original VC network with VC as a node, where the edges with label 1/0 represent whether two VCs coinvest or not in time span {1,t}, and the edges with label? are those that we try to predict in time $t + 1$. The right figure is the SBFG model with coinvestment as a node. $y_{i,j}$ is the latent variable that indicates whether two VCs v_i,v_j coinvest, and $x_{i,j}$ is the observation of two VCs v_i,v_j. $f_{i,j}$ is the feature factor for a coinvestment, and $t_{i,j,k}$ is the triad factor for three possible coinvestments.

The right figure is the SBFG model derived from the original VC network. $y_{i,j}$ is the latent variable that indicates whether two VCs v_1, v_2 coinvest or not, and $x_{i,j}$ denotes the observation of two VCs v_i, v_j. The SBFG model expresses the joint distribution over all variables as a product of factors over subsets of those variables, and the edge between a factor and a variable in the SBFG model indicates that the variable is an argument of the factor function. We define two kinds of factors in the SBFG model. $f(x_{i,j}, y_{i,j})$ ($f_{i,j}$ for short) represents the feature factor defined for the coinvestment. $t(y_{i,j}, y_{i,k}, y_{j,k})$ ($t_{i,j,k}$ for short) represents the triad factor, which is used to capture the structural balance among three possible coinvestments $y_{i,j}$, $y_{i,k}$, $y_{j,k}$ sharing common VCs.

Y denotes the vector that contains all latent variables. Since we already know the coinvestments in time span $\{1, t\}$, the latent variable vector Y in the SBFG can be divided into labeled subset Y^L and unlabeled subset Y^U (to be predicted). We formalize the network with Markov random fields. According to the Hammersley–Clifford theorem [11], the probability of latent variable vector Y given observations X can be factorized as

$$p(Y \mid X) = \frac{1}{Z} \prod_{\text{possible } i,j} f_{i,j} \prod_{\text{possible } i,j,k} t_{i,j,k} \qquad (6.3)$$

where
  "possible *i,j*" means all possible values that i, j can take in the dataset
  "possible *i,j,k*" has similar meaning

Factors are defined as

$$f_{i,j} = \exp\left\{\alpha_{i,j}^T \mathbf{g}(x_{i,j}, y_{i,j})\right\} \qquad (6.4)$$

$$t_{i,j,k} = \exp\{\beta_{i,j,k} h(y_{i,j}, y_{i,k}, y_{j,k})\} \qquad (6.5)$$

where
  $\mathbf{g}(x_{i,j}, y_{i,j})$ is the function vector for the feature factor $f_{i,j}$
  $h(y_{i,j}, y_{i,k}, y_{j,k})$ is the function for the triad factor $t_{i,j,k}$
  $\alpha_{i,j}$, $\beta_{i,j,k}$ are corresponding weights

The component of $\mathbf{g}(x_{i,j}, y_{i,j})$ is defined as

$$g_m(x_{i,j}, y_{i,j}) = 1_{\{y_{i,j} = \tilde{y}_{i,j}\}} \cdot g_m(x_{i,j}) \qquad (6.6)$$

where $g_m(x_{i,j})$ is a certain feature for the observation $x_{i,j}$, as defined in Table 6.2. Each feature is nonzero only for a single label $\tilde{y}_{i,j}$. This particular form of function leads to a larger feature set, which is a common practice in feature engineering of Markov random fields, and can lead to better prediction accuracy since the final decision boundary can be more flexible [27]. The definition of $h(y_{i,j}, y_{i,k}, y_{j,k})$ is as follows:

$$h(y_{i,j}, y_{i,k}, y_{j,k}) = 1_{\{\#\text{positive co-investment} = a | a = 0,1,2,3\}} \tag{6.7}$$

That is to say, we use the number of positive coinvestments in the triangle as a feature,* and there are a total of four features for the triad factor (if using indicator function form, as in Equation 6.7). When the model is fitted to the training data, the number of balanced triads is much larger than that of unbalanced ones, and so the weight of the feature for balanced triad should be larger than the weight of the feature for unbalanced triad after training. Finally, the model will encourage the balanced triads when predicting the test data.

Furthermore, we pack all weights $\alpha_{i,j}$, $\beta_{i,j,k}$ into a long weighting vector θ and pack all features $\mathbf{g}(x_{i,j}, y_{i,j})$, $h(y_{i,j}, y_{i,k}, y_{j,k})$ into a long feature vector $\mathbf{s}$, regardless of the type of factors. Thus, the conditional probability, that is, Equation 6.3, is simplified to be

$$p(Y \mid X) = \frac{1}{Z} \exp\{\theta^T \mathbf{s}\} \tag{6.8}$$

Then, we try to get proper weighting vector θ in the learning phase.

6.6.3 Learning

The latent variables in time span $\{1, t\}$, that is, Y^L, are labeled, and our optimization goal is to minimize the loss function, which is defined as the negative log-likelihood:

$$
\begin{aligned}
-\text{loss}(\theta) &= O(\theta) \\
&= \log p(Y^L \mid X) = \log \sum_{Y^U} p(Y^L, Y^U \mid X) \\
&= \log \sum_{Y^U} p(Y \mid X) = \log \sum_{Y^U} \frac{1}{Z} \exp\{\theta^T \mathbf{s}\} \\
&= \log \sum_{Y^U} \exp\{\theta^T \mathbf{s}\} - \log Z \\
&= \log \sum_{Y^U} \exp\{\theta^T \mathbf{s}\} - \log \sum_{Y} \exp\{\theta^T \mathbf{s}\} \tag{6.9}
\end{aligned}
$$

---

* There is a slight abuse of the word "feature" here. The "feature" here represents the structure of a triad consisting of three coinvestments (called "triad feature" temporarily), instead of the feature for only one coinvestment as listed in Table 6.2 (called "node feature").

To minimize the loss function, we consider a gradient decent method, and the gradient is calculated as follows:

$$\frac{\partial O(\theta)}{\partial \theta} = E_{p(Y^U|Y^L,X)}[\mathbf{s}] - E_{p(Y^U,Y^L|X)}[\mathbf{s}] \tag{6.10}$$

where $E_{p(Y^U|Y^L,X)}[\mathbf{s}]$ and $E_{p(Y^U,Y^L|X)}[\mathbf{s}]$ are expectations of $\mathbf{s}$ on different distributions. The derivation of the two terms in the right part of Equation 6.10 is similar, and we only present the former for abbreviation:

$$\frac{\partial}{\partial \theta}\left[\log \sum_{Y^U} \exp\{\theta^T \mathbf{s}\}\right] = \frac{1}{\sum_{Y^U} \exp\{\theta^T \mathbf{s}\}} \sum_{Y^U} \exp\{\theta^T \mathbf{s}\} \cdot \mathbf{s}$$

$$= \sum_{Y^U} \frac{\exp\{\theta^T \mathbf{s}\}}{\sum_{Y^U} \exp\{\theta^T \mathbf{s}\}} \cdot \mathbf{s} = \sum_{Y^U} \frac{Z \cdot p(Y \mid X)}{\sum_{Y^U} Z \cdot p(Y \mid X)} \cdot \mathbf{s}$$

$$= \sum_{Y^U} \frac{p(Y^U, Y^L \mid X)}{p(Y^L \mid X)} \cdot \mathbf{s} = \sum_{Y^U} p(Y^U \mid Y^L, X) \cdot \mathbf{s}$$

$$= E_{p(Y^U|Y^L,X)}[\mathbf{s}] \tag{6.11}$$

The calculation of expectations in Equation 6.10 is converted to the calculation of the marginal probability $p(Y^U|Y^L,X)$ and $p(Y^U,Y^L|X)$ and is further converted to message passing along edges in the graph, which can be done by the standard belief propagation [23]. When applied to tree-structured graph, the belief propagation gives the exact result. However, the graphical structure of our proposed SBFG can be arbitrary and contains cycles, and it's not feasible to use exact inference. We can still employ belief propagation to approximate the marginal probability, and the algorithm is called loopy belief propagation (LBP) in this case [10]. Although the precise conditions of convergence of LBP are not well understood [22,31], it works well in our model. Note that we should perform LBP twice in each step, one for estimating marginal probability $p(Y^U,Y^L|X)$ and the other for $p(Y^U|Y^L,X)$. At the end of each step, we update the weighting vector θ with the gradient and a constant learning rate η. η is set to 0.001, which is determined by preliminary experiments on a subset of the training data.

Algorithm 6.1: SBFG Learning Algorithm

    Input: labeled variables Y^L, observations X, learning rate η
    Output: weighting vector θ
    Initialize θ;

While *not converged* **do**

Calculate $E_{p(Y^U|Y^L,X)}[\mathbf{s}]$ using LBP;

Calculate $E_{p(Y^U,Y^L|X)}[\mathbf{s}]$ using LBP;

Calculate the gradient $\dfrac{\partial O(\theta)}{\partial \theta}$ according to Equation 6.10;

Update θ with $\theta^{new} = \theta^{old} - \eta \cdot \dfrac{\partial O(\theta)}{\partial \theta}$

Return θ

The learning algorithm is shown in Algorithm 6.1, and the time complexity of the algorithm is mainly determined by the computation of marginal probability using LBP. Generally, the time complexity of LBP is $O(nES^C)$, where n represents the number of features, E is the number of edges, S is the number of labels, and C is the size of the maximal clique.* In our case, $E = 3T$, $S = 2$, $C = 3$, where T is the number of triads, and so the time complexity is $O(nT)$, which is a linear function of the number of features n and the number of triads T.

6.6.4 Prediction

Once we get the learned weight vector θ, we can predict the unlabeled Y^U by first computing the marginal probability of $p(Y^U|Y^L,X)$ and then select the value with the largest marginal probability as the label. Again, the marginal probability of $p(Y^U|Y^L,X)$ is calculated by running LBP, and the marginal probability is then taken as the prediction confidence.

6.7 Experiments and Analysis

6.7.1 Experiment Setup

CRUNCH contains 18,716 VCs and 152,227 coinvestment events from 1984 to 2014. The 152,227 coinvestments are positive instances in our experiments. There are no direct negative instances in the dataset, and then we consider all possible combinations of accumulated VCs until a given time point. However, the number of combinations is hundreds of times larger than the number of positive instances, which constitutes imbalanced data. There is a large amount of research on imbalanced data, and the methods include making the learning process active or cost-sensitive and treating the classifier score with different thresholds [6,13].

---

* Although there are other factors that affect the time complexity of LBP (e.g., the number of iterations of gradient decent), their order of magnitude usually does not change much, so they are not included in the formula to facilitate the analysis.

We employ random undersampling due to its effectiveness and ease of implementation. Specifically, we randomly sample the same number of negative instances as positive instances.

Our goal is to predict coinvestments in time $t + 1$ (test dataset), given data in time span $\{1, t\}$ (training dataset), and we construct four cases for CRUNCH. The first case is to predict coinvestments in 2011 given data in 1984–2010, the second is 2012 given data in 1984–2011, the third is 2013 given data in 1984–2012, and the fourth is the first 3 months in 2014 given data in 1984–2013.

6.7.2 Prediction Performance

We compare our proposed model with state-of-the-art supervised machine learning algorithms, and the results are shown in Table 6.3.

> *Measures*: For evaluating the prediction of coinvestment, four popular measures are used to evaluate the performance, that is, precision, recall, F1 measure, and accuracy. Let TP denote #true positive; FP, #false positive; FN, #false negative; and TN, #true negative.

$$\text{Precision} = TP/(TP + FP), \text{Recall} = TP/(TP + FN), F1 = \frac{2 * \text{Precision} * \text{Recall}}{\text{Precision} + \text{Recall}},$$

$$\text{and Accuracy} = \frac{TP + TN}{TP + FP + FN + TN}.$$

> *Baselines*: The coinvestment prediction is formulated as a binary classification problem in this chapter. There are a large number of classifiers, and SVM and LR are regarded as state-of-the-art general-purpose classifiers. The baselines are support vector classifier (SVC) with L2 regularization and LR with L2 regularization. These two algorithms are implemented in the LIBLINEAR software package [9]. All baselines use the top 10 features selected by group Lasso but not the structural balance factor, since the pointwise classifiers (SVC and LR) cannot model the correlation among coinvestments efficiently. SBFG employs both the top 10 features and the structural balance factor.

As shown in Table 6.3, SBFG significantly exceeds all state-of-the-art algorithms in all measures except precision. The prediction accuracy and F1 value of SBFG are above 0.9, which are satisfactory for coinvestment prediction.

6.7.3 Feature Contribution Analysis

We examine the contribution of different features by removing them one by one in the model for the case of 2014. As shown in Figure 6.18, SBFG stands for the

Table 6.3 Prediction Performance of Coinvestment with the Top 10 Features

Data	Alg.	Pre.	Rec.	F1	Acc.
2011	SVC	**0.8615**	0.7082	0.7773	0.8078
	LR	0.8601	0.7071	0.7761	0.8068
	SBFG	0.8236	**0.9939**	**0.9008**	**0.8963**
2012	SVC	**0.8770**	0.7059	0.7822	0.8129
	LR	0.8721	0.7095	0.7825	0.8122
	SBFG	0.8431	**0.9939**	**0.9123**	**0.9090**
2013	SVC	**0.8693**	0.7124	0.7831	0.8104
	LR	0.8664	0.7133	0.7825	0.8095
	SBFG	0.8395	**0.9920**	**0.9094**	**0.9050**
2014 (first 3 months)	SVC	0.9143	0.7210	0.8062	0.8287
	LR	0.9164	0.7240	0.8089	0.8309
	SBFG	**0.9308**	**0.9924**	**0.9606**	**0.9598**
Average	SVC	**0.8805**	0.7119	0.7872	0.8150
	LR	0.8788	0.7135	0.7875	0.8149
	SBFG	0.8593	**0.9931**	**0.9208**	**0.9175**

Measures: Pre. denotes precision, Rec. denotes recall, F1 denotes F1 value, and Acc. denotes accuracy. *Compared methods:* SVC denotes support vector classifier, LR denotes logistic regression, and SBFG denotes the proposed method in this chapter.

proposed method with top 10 features. The plus mark denotes additional features besides the top 10 features, and minus mark denotes features that are excluded from the top 10 features. N denotes remaining 71 features other than the top 10 features; S, the structural balance factor; C, common neighbors; B, betweenness; D, shortest distance; F, the number of invested fields; and J, the Jaccard similarity of invested fields.

When the 71 remaining features are excluded from the model, the accuracy drops by only 0.18% (from 96.16% to 95.98%), which shows that the top 10 features selected by group Lasso can explain the formation of the VC network quite well. Note that, if there is no feature selection mechanism like group Lasso, it is hard to say that betweenness centrality is more predictive than structural hole

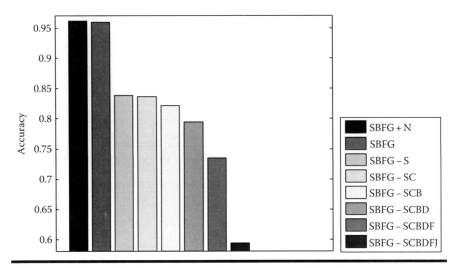

Figure 6.18 Feature contribution analysis for the case of 2014. SBFG stands for the proposed method with the top 10 features. The plus mark denotes additional features besides the top 10 features, and the minus mark denotes features that are excluded from the top 10 features.

constraint in coinvestment prediction. When the structural balance factor is removed from the model, the accuracy drops by 12.13% (from 95.98% to 83.85%), which demonstrates the prediction power of structural balance theory. When the features are excluded from the model one by one, the performance drops gradually. Finally, when all dynamic features SCBDFJ are excluded from the model, there are only two static features, that is, nationality and investor type, and the accuracy of the model is only 59.38%, which is slightly better than a random guess since the task is predicting the evolving link formation.

6.7.4 Country Analysis of Prediction

We analyze the prediction performance for the top 10 countries with the most VCs. We calculate accuracy for coinvestments that involve the given country, respectively, as shown in Figure 6.19. It is shown that the proposed method SBFG exceeds the baselines by a large margin for all 10 countries. The average accuracy of baselines for Asian countries (Japan, China, and India) is relatively low compared with other countries, while the average accuracy of SBFG for Asian countries is not low. Furthermore, China is the country with the lowest baselines accuracy and the highest SBFG accuracy. It probably suggests that VCs of Asian countries, especially of China, are more likely to have social relations due to their special economic culture, and they rely on the robustness of networks to avoid risks.

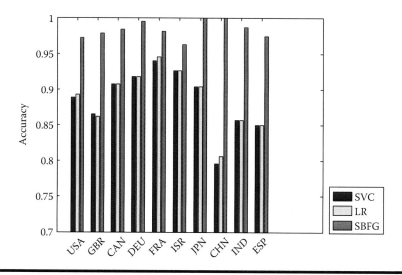

Figure 6.19 **Prediction performance of different countries. The performance gap between baseline method and SBFG of Asian countries is larger than other countries.**

6.7.5 Investor-Type Analysis of Prediction

We analyze the prediction performance for different investor types by calculating accuracy for coinvestments that involve the given investor type, as shown in Figure 6.20. *FinanOrg* denotes financial organization, *Company* denotes company investor, and *Person* denotes person investor. For the baseline algorithms (SVC and LR), the accuracy of person investor is by far lower than (–20%) that of financial organization and company investor. However, our proposed SBFG model can largely compensate for the performance gap for person investor (only 4% lower than financial organization), which demonstrates the power of structural balance in coinvestment prediction.

6.7.6 Case Study

Now we present a case study to demonstrate the effectiveness of the proposed model. In Figure 6.21, each node represents a VC. The node in the upper left corner is Draper Fisher Jurvetson (DFJ for short); upper right, Nexus Venture Partners (Nexus); lower left, Gray Ghost Ventures (Gray); and lower right, Garage Technology Ventures (Garage). The line between nodes denotes the coinvestment, and the mark on the line indicates that the algorithm makes a mistake. Our goal is to predict coinvestments in 2014 given data in 1984–2013. SVC and LR correctly predict the coinvestments of DFJ–Gray and Nexus–Garage, but they miss the other two ones. Besides DFJ–Gray and Nexus–Garage, our proposed SBFG successfully

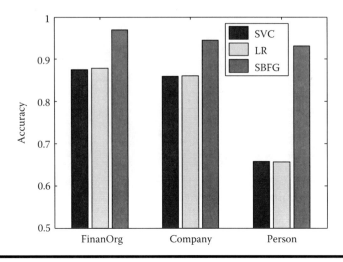

Figure 6.20 Investor-type analysis. *FinanOrg* denotes financial organization, *Company* denotes company investor, and *Person* denotes person investor.

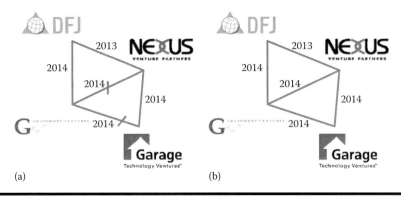

Figure 6.21 Case study. The goal is to predict coinvestments in 2014 given data in 1984–2013. SVC and LR miss two coinvestments, while SBFG successfully predicts them by incorporating structural balance theory. (a) SVC/LR; (b) SBFG.

predicts Gray–Nexus and Gray–Garage. After adding Gray–Nexus and Gray–Garage, both the upper left triangle and the lower left triangle become balanced.

6.8 Study on Another Dataset

Another investment dataset (CHN*), which focuses on investments to Chinese start-ups, is also explored to further verify the model and features mentioned earlier.

---

* We will publish this dataset on the publicly available website after being anonymized.

6.8.1 Data Description

It takes 2 years to collect and clean the data in CHN manually and then verify it by a questionnaire. CHN contains investments for Chinese start-up from 1995 to 2011, and there are a total of 1,541 VCs, 5,494 Chinese start-ups, 10,275 investments, and 5,856 coinvestments. The percentage of investments in CHN that are related to two or more investors is 50.8%, which is much lower than that of CRUNCH (80.9%). CHN is five times (in terms of the number of investments) larger than the subset of CRUNCH related to Chinese start-ups (denoted by CRUNCH-China), although the time range of CHN is only half that of CRUNCH-China. The information and statistics of CHN and CRUNCH-China are summarized in Table 6.4.

The different names of information between CHN and CRUNCH are italicized in Table 6.4. For example, CHN provides property right and year of establishment for VC firms. Besides the information of different names, the information with the same name could also be different between CHN and CRUNCH-China. For example, VCs of CHN are categorized into seven investor types, that is, angle, VC, private equity, company VC, strategic investor, bank/trust, and others, which are different from the categorization of the three investor types of CRUNCH. In addition, there are 20 coarse-grained fields and 205 fine-grained fields in CHN, which are also different from the categorization of 44 fields of CRUNCH. Although the genre, size, and information of CHN are different from those of CRUNCH, the structural balance phenomenon also holds in CHN (the pattern is quite similar to Figure 6.16 and so omitted).

6.8.2 Performance and Discussion

We employ the top 10 features in Table 6.2, plus the extra information provided by CHN, that is, property right, year of establishment, and features related to

Table 6.4 Information and Statistics of CHN and CRUNCH-China

Item	CHN (1995–2011)	CRUNCH-China (1984–2014)
Investment information	VC, start-up, funded year	VC, start-up, funded year, *round, raised amount*
VC information	Investor type, location, *property right, year of establishment*	Investor type, location, *field*
Start-up information	Field, location	Field, location
#Investment	10,275	1986
#VC	1,541	453
#Start-up	5,494	781

Table 6.5   Prediction Performance of Coinvestment in CHN

Data	Alg.	Pre.	Rec.	F1	Acc.
2008	SVC	0.7729	0.7015	0.7354	0.7565
	LR	0.7925	0.7363	0.7634	0.7797
	SBFG	**0.8627**	**0.9505**	**0.9045**	**0.9031**
2009	SVC	0.7791	0.7556	0.7672	0.7784
	LR	0.7869	0.7218	0.7529	0.7711
	SBFG	**0.9136**	**0.8741**	**0.8934**	**0.8992**
2010	SVC	0.8444	0.6609	0.7415	0.7764
	LR	0.8472	0.7093	0.7721	0.7968
	SBFG	**0.9212**	**0.9006**	**0.9108**	**0.9144**
2011	SVC	0.7944	0.7385	0.7654	0.7814
	LR	0.7920	0.7385	0.7643	0.7801
	SBFG	**0.8887**	**0.9203**	**0.9042**	**0.9059**
Average	SVC	0.7977	0.7141	0.7524	0.7732
	LR	0.8047	0.7265	0.7632	0.7819
	SBFG	**0.8966**	**0.9114**	**0.9032**	**0.9057**

fine-grained fields, to train the model and make predictions. We construct four datasets that are with settings similar to CRUNCH (cf. Section 6.7). The experiment results are shown in Table 6.5.

Due to the different genre, size, and information, the results of CHN and CRUNCH are not directly comparable. However, the accuracy of our proposed SBFG model is over 90% on CHN, and it outperforms SVC or LR significantly (+12% in accuracy), which further verifies the effectiveness of the proposed model and features.

6.9 Related Works

6.9.1 Coinvestment

In sociology and economics, the study of coinvestment dates back to Wilson's theory on syndication [32], and Lerner [17] studied the principle of who will be a good coinvestor and when to reconstruct a coinvestment. More recently, some scholars studied coinvestment/syndication from the perspective of link formation, such as [16] and [24] through [26]. Based on 45 years of VC data from the United States, Kogut et al. [16] found several features that might have influence on the new link. However, Kogut et al. [16] only used the node features and they did not make predictions. Powell et al. [25] studied four kinds of effects on interorganizational collaboration. The existing researches only explored a few features for coinvestment without detailed analysis of contribution of features.

6.9.2 Link Prediction

Our work is related to link prediction, and the existing works on link prediction can be broadly grouped into two categories based on the learning algorithms: unsupervised link prediction and supervised link prediction. The classic works of unsupervised prediction were surveyed in [19] and recently Lichtenwalter et al. [20] designed a flow-based method. There are many works on supervised link prediction, such as [2,14,18,28,33,34]. Hopcroft et al. [14] studied the extent to which the formation of a reciprocal relationship can be predicted in a dynamic network. Tang et al. [28] developed a framework for classifying the type of social relationships by learning across heterogeneous networks. The coinvestment network is intrinsically dynamic and multidimensional, and there is still nothing reported about the prediction of coinvestment as far as we are informed. In this work, we focus on studying the underlying patterns that influence the formation of coinvestment and propose a factor graph model to incorporate structural balance theory and the discovered patterns.

6.10 Conclusion and Future Work

In this chapter, we study the prediction of coinvestment of VCs. We present a series of observation analysis, design a large number of features, and then select prominent features for coinvestment by group Lasso. Then, we propose a factor graph model SBFG based on structural balance theory to formalize the observation into a unified model. For the model learning, we employ the LBP to obtain an approximate solution. Experiment results show that the proposed method can accurately (around 90% in terms of accuracy) predict the coinvestment in the near future with only 10 features selected by group Lasso and obtain a significant improvement (+9% in terms of accuracy) over the baselines.

In the future, we will further explore VC investment in the following directions. First, we will design an SBFG model with an embedded feature selection mechanism, which can better explain the formation of the VC network and further improve the prediction performance. Second, although the proposed model exceeds consistently the baselines in most measures, the precision varies for different datasets, and we plan to study the effect of different datasets on the proposed model. We will also study other structural patterns that may affect the formation of VC network, such as circle with more than three nodes.

Further following the data mining in this article, we would like to investigate the theory underlying these findings. For example, the shortest distance is the number 1 of 10 factors influencing the possibility of coinvestment. As found earlier, when two VCs have the shortest distance equal to or less than 2, they are highly likely to coinvest. But when they have a distance larger than 2, the likelihood of coinvestment decreases rapidly. The possible interpretation behind this finding is that a Chinese investor is unlikely to syndicate with a stranger, unless his or her friends introduce this stranger as a new friend to him or her. In a highly uncertain environment like the VC industry, people need detailed information concerning a new potential partner and personal endorsement provided by trustworthy friends before they can start a new relationship. The evidence from our field studies supports this interpretation. In one case, two investors couldn't make a decision to partner in a venture until a common friend mediated with them to have dinner together.

This interpretation also collaborates with this article's important finding: "when the structural balance factor is removed from the model, the accuracy drops by 12.5% (from 93.85% to 83.85%), which demonstrates the prediction power of structural balance theory." In Figure 6.15b, node A is unlikely to connect with node B and C, since he or she has a high possibility of no common friends with the latter two. In Figure 6.15c, node C is the mediator between A and B, which increases the possibility of A connecting with B, that is, the case in Figure 6.15d.

The theory underlying the findings stated earlier points to an interesting question: "who is a friend for a VC investor?" This is exactly the main topic in Chapter 7, which can be taken as a next-run study for this chapter.

Acknowledgments

This work is supported by the National Natural Science Foundation of China under Grant No. 61303068 and the Research Fund of State Key Laboratory of High Performance Computing under Grant No. 201502-02. We appreciate the help from Jing Zhang, Huaiyu Wan, Zhanpeng Fang, and Ling Zhou at Tsinghua University.

References

1. A. Alesina, A. Devleeschauwer, W. Easterly, S. Kurlat, and R. Wacziarg. Fractionalization. *Journal of Economic Growth*, 8(2):155–194, June 2003.
2. L. Backstrom and J. Leskovec. Supervised random walks: Predicting and recommending links in social networks. In *Proceedings of ACM International Conference on Web Search and Data Mining (WSDM'11)*, pp. 635–644, 2011.

3. P. Breheny, Regularization paths for regression models with grouped covariates, July 2016, http://cran.r-project.org/web/packages/grpreg/index.html, accessed January 4, 2017.

4. P. Breheny and J. Huang. Group descent algorithms for nonconvex penalized linear and logistic regression models with grouped predictors. *Statistics and Computing*, 25:173–187, November 2013.

5. R. Burt. *Structural Holes: The Social Structure of Competition*. Harvard University Press, Cambridge, MA, 1992.

6. N.V. Chawla, N. Japkowicz, and A. Kotcz. Editorial: Special issue on learning from imbalanced data. *ACM SIGKDD Explorations Newsletter*, 6(1):1–6, 2011.

7. Crunchbase Inc., CrunchBase, http://www.crunchbase.com/, accessed March 20, 2014.

8. D. Easley and J. Kleinberg. *Networks, Crowds, and Markets: Reasoning about a Highly Connected World*. Cambridge University Press, Cambridge, U.K., 2010.

9. R.-E. Fan, K.-W. Chang, C.-J. Hsieh, X.-R. Wang, and C.-J. Lin. Liblinear: A library for large linear classification. *Journal of Machine Learning Research*, 9:1871–1874, August 2008.

10. B. Frey and D. MacKay. A revolution: Belief propagation in graphs with cycles. In *Proceedings of Neural Information Processing Systems Conference (NIPS'97)*, pp. 479–485, 1997.

11. J. Hammersley and P. Clifford. Markov field on finite graphs and lattices. Unpublished manuscript, 1971.

12. M. Al Hasan, V. Chaoji, S. Salem, and M. Zaki. Link prediction using supervised learning. In *Proceedings of SDM Workshop of Link Analysis, Counterterrorism and Security*, 2006.

13. H. He and E.A. Garcia. Learning from imbalanced data. *IEEE Transactions on Knowledge and Data Engineering*, 21(9):1263–1284, September 2009.

14. J. Hopcroft, T. Lou, and J. Tang. Who will follow you back? Reciprocal relationship prediction. In *Proceedings of ACM International Conference on Information and Knowledge Management (CIKM'11)*, pp. 1137–1146, 2011.

15. ISO, Country Codes, http://www.iso.org/iso/home/standards/country_codes.htm, accessed December 10, 2016.

16. B. Kogut, P. Urso, and G. Walker. Emergent properties of a new financial market: American venture capital syndication, 1960–2005. *Management Science*, 53(7):1181–1198, July 2007.

17. J. Lerner. The syndication of venture capital investments. *Financial Management*, 16–27, Autumn 1994.

18. J. Leskovec, D. Huttenlocher, and J. Kleinberg. Predicting positive and negative links in online social networks. In *Proceedings of International Conference on World Wide Web (WWW'10)*, pp. 641–650, 2010.

19. D. Liben-Nowell and J. Kleinberg. The link-prediction problem for social networks. *Journal of the American Society for Information Science and Technology*, 58(7):1019–1031, May 2007.

20. R. Lichtenwalter, J. Lussier, and N. Chawla. New perspectives and methods in link prediction. In *Proceedings of ACM SIGKDD International Conference on Knowledge Discovery and Data Mining (KDD'10)*, pp. 243–252, 2010.

21. L. Meier, S. van de Geer, and P. Bühlmann. The group lasso for logistic regression. *Journal of the Royal Statistical Society, Series B*, 70:53–71, 2008.

22. J.M. Mooij and H.J. Kappen. Sufficient conditions for convergence of the sum-product algorithm. *IEEE Transactions on Information Theory*, 53(12):4422–4437, December 2007.

23. J. Pearl. *Probabilistic Reasoning in Intelligent Systems: Networks of Plausible Inference*. Morgan Kaufmann, San Francisco, CA, 1988.

24. M. Piskorski. Networks of power and status: Reciprocity in venture capital syndicates. Unpublished manuscript, 2004.

25. W. Powell, D. White, K. Koput, and J. Owen-Smith. Network dynamics and field evolution: The growth of interorganizational collaboration in the life sciences. *American Journal of Sociology*, 110(4):1132–1205, January 2005.

26. O. Sorenson and T. Stuart. Syndication networks and the spatial distribution of venture capital investment. *The American Journal of Sociology*, 106(6):1546–1588, May 2001.

27. C. Sutton and A. McCallum. An introduction to conditional random fields. *Foundations and Trends in Machine Learning*, 4(4):267–373, 2011.

28. J. Tang, T. Lou, and J. Kleinberg. Inferring social ties across heterogenous networks. In *Proceedings of ACM International Conference on Web Search and Data Mining (WSDM'12)*, pp. 743–752, 2012.

29. R. Tibshirani. Regression shrinkage and selection via the Lasso. *Journal of the Royal Statistical Society, Series B*, 58:267–288, 1996.

30. D. Trapido. Mechanisms of venture capital co-investment networks: Evolution and performance implications. Unpublished manuscript, 2009.

31. Y. Weiss. Correctness of local probability propagation in graphical models with loops. *Neural Computation*, 12(1):1–41, January 2000.

32. R. Wilson. The theory of syndicates. *Econometrica*, 36(1):119–132, January 1968.

33. S. Wu, J. Sun, and J. Tang. Patent partner recommendation in enterprise social networks. In *Proceedings of ACM International Conference on Web Search and Data Mining (WSDM'13)*, pp. 43–52, 2013.

34. Y. Yang, J. Tang, J. Keomany, Y. Zhao, J. Li, Y. Ding, T. Li, and L. Wang. Ming competitive relationships by learning across heterogeneous networks. In *Proceedings of ACM International Conference on Information and Knowledge Management (CIKM'12)*, pp. 1432–1441, 2012.

35. M. Yuan and Y. Lin. Model selection and estimation in regression with grouped variables. *Journal of the Royal Statistical Society, Series B*, 68:49–67, 2006.

Chapter 7

Repeated Cooperation Matters: An Analysis of Syndication in the Chinese VC Industry by ERGM

Jar-Der Luo, Ruiqi Li, Fangda Fan, and Jie Tang

Contents

This chapter reveals a process of integrating qualitative studies and data mining in developing a theory. As suggested in the introduction of this book, the development of theory is always composed of several runs of qualitative and quantitative studies. Based on the guidance of existing theories, this chapter first illustrates some samples of field work to sketch the outline of theory waiting for further development. Then, an exponential random graph model (ERGM) is used to help mine data to find that the indicators categorize various roles in an ego-centered network in the Chinese venture capital (VC) industry. An interpretation then follows this quantitative analysis, and more qualitative studies are conducted to theorize the data mining result and its interpretation.

7.1 Guanxi Circle Phenomenon in the Chinese VC Field

7.1.1 Guanxi in the Chinese VC Industry

Chinese VC is a newly emergent industry, in which government policies keep changing, governance structure is immature, and information asymmetry always bothers investors. All these make the Chinese investment environment highly uncertain, and the short-term rational calculation of investors is often made in vain. Thus, Chinese VCs seek to build up a robust network in which long-term social exchanges help hedging against the impacts of environmental uncertainty. This research thus aims to analyze VCs' consideration behind building relations rather than the motivations for investing behaviors. We adopt both qualitative and quantitative methods to collect data (King et al., 1994; Small, 2011). First, several interviews with three informants help us understand why Chinese VCs build connections with other investors in joint investment (Table 7.1). We then collect the data of 2060 VCs and 12,414 investment events over a period of 17 years from SiMuTon database and analyze the network dynamics of this field in 1995–2011 by using the ERGM method.

There are many excellent researches studying the syndication in the VC industry. Some of them focus on the compensation of each other's insufficiency (Lockett and Wright, 2001), so that rich and diversified resources may increase the probability of

Table 7.1 List of Interviewees

Interviewee	Occupation	Time	Location	Recording Interview
Mr. Z	An junior partner of private VC investor	2012/7	Tianjing	With notes
Mr. Y	A senior partner of a private VC investor	2012/7 and 2013/4	Beijing	With tape-recording
Mr. Liu	A CEO of a state-owned VC firm	2013/10	Tianjing	With notes

success of an investment (Brander et al., 2002). Some studies put emphasis on the motivation of risk-sharing behind joint investments, which generally involve huge uncertainty (Wilson, 1968). In such an environment, the governance mechanism for hedging opportunism behaviors (Williamson, 1996) has also been proposed on the research agenda (Holmstrom, 1982; Admati and Pfleiderer, 1994; Tykvová, 2007). However, a solely performance-focused approach constricts the contribution of syndication research. Comparing scrutinized previous research of syndication, there are few in corporate finance literature due to the difficulties of analyzing syndication patterns empirically and verifying the complexity of motives behind syndication (Lerner, 1994). Attachment patterns and logics behind relation building might be the key to explain this field (see Hochberg et al., 2010). Especially in the context of emerging countries such as China and India, the difficulties of data collection often block the promotion of research.

Although Chinese VCs share some common ground with their Western counterparts, the institution and culture place an emphasis on guanxi (Chinese term, social relations) and networking rather than individual self-interest motivations, which might bring about different activities and relation-building logics (Bruton and Ahlstrom, 2003; Bruton et al., 2005). Relatively less literature has shed light on the VC industry and syndication network in the Chinese context.

In an environment with well-developed markets, personal properties are well defined and resources flow following certain rules. But it is not true for the Chinese VC industry, since unclear property rights and high information asymmetry make access to a good project extremely difficult. Without good *guanxi*, it is almost impossible to get enough information to analyze a project. Especially, whether a project is good or not highly depends on the policies of central or local governments, so it requires good guanxi to get prior information concerning the attitudes of governments. Relation building is thus needed to access good projects.

In addition to searching for good investment opportunities, guanxi building of Chinese VCs is also very helpful for hedging against free-riding (Olson, 1966) and opportunistic behaviors (Williamson, 1985) as well as protecting their own interests collectively from the interference of continuously changing governmental policies (Luo, 2015). Guanxi-building behaviors in the VC community bring about a type of network structure that is centered on one or several leaders with multiple layers of group members. This is what is called a "guanxi circle" (in Chinese, Quan Zi or Xiao Quan Zi) shown in Figure 7.1, as the senior investor, Mr. Y, says that there is a three-layer network structure; as he puts it:

> There are few investors in the first layer [in terms of power and number of projects],…they have unique resources.…In the second layer, some famous PE [private equity] are in this layer.…Those in the third layer are generally not famous nationwide, but even some globally famous investors sometime need their cooperation, [since they may have special resources] such as local government relations, local market knowledge, etc.

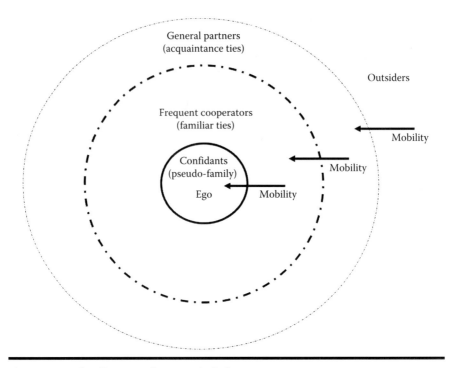

Figure 7.1   The diagram of a guanxi circle.

The following sections will use the method of complex network to investigate the structure of guanxi circles in syndication. But first need to ask what a guanxi circle is.

7.1.2 What Is a Guanxi Circle*

A guanxi circle is a group of people bound together for a common identity and shared interests. It can refer to a large community, such as engineers' circle, lawyers' circle, or professors' circle. But more often, it refers to a small clique in which group members know and interact with each other. This chapter defines the term "guanxi circle" according to its narrow meaning including only small cliques rather than large communities.

A guanxi circle often has a central person as its leader, so it may be named after someone, such as manager Chang's circle and CEO Lin's circle. This means that a leading person accompanied by his or her strong ties forms a guanxi circle in which

---

* Part of the section "What Is a Guanxi Circle" is also used in the following book chapter: Luo, Jar-Der, forthcoming. "Guanxi circle phenomenon in the Chinese Venture Capital Industry" In Wang, Jenn hwan (Ed.), *Social Capital and Entrepreneurship in Greater China*. New York: Routledge.

members share common interests and struggle for these interests together (Luo and Yeh, 2012). Two important Chinese characteristics form the cultural and normative bases for the guanxi circle phenomenon. First, as indigenous sociologist Fei (1992) called "the differential mode of association" (in Chinese, *cha xu ge ju*), a Chinese ego-centered network is comprised of multiple layers of rings in which different behavioral and moral standards are applied for each of these different rings of guanxi.

Second, family ethics is the base for a Chinese person to build and maintain his or her guanxi (Liang, 1983; Bond and Hwang, 1986). Guanxi circles are actually imitated as pseudo-families in his or her working life. Through the process of "familyization" (i.e., turning an outsider to be a family member; Chua et al., 2009), a centered ego may recruit outsiders into his or her pseudo-family in the workplace.

A Chinese person divides his or her social ties into several rings, and different rings imply different moral standards. It is common for indigenous Chinese research to categorize three types of guanxi. For example, guanxi may be classified as expressive, mixed, or instrumental ties, based on the continuum between expressive and instrumental elements (Hwang, 1987, 1988). Or guanxi may be divided into obligatory, reciprocal, and utilitarian ties, according to the degree of obligation (Zhang and Zhang, 2006).

Based on Fei's framework of differential modes of association (1992) and Yang's three categories of Chinese social relations (1993), we propose a framework of differential relationships (Luo, 2005, 2011). Acquaintance ties fit in the outermost ring of an ego-centered network under the "rules of equity" (Hwang, 1987) and may come to be trusted based on general ethical principles of fairness and the conservative process of repeated exchanges. Guanxi of this sort is defined by its short-term duration and rational-based behaviors.

There are two types of strong ties included in a person's guanxi circle. The innermost ring generally consists of family members and fictive kin (Chen, 1994). Chinese psychologist Yang (1993) calls the innermost ring of an ego-centered social network "chia ren," which translates as family ties, including real family and pseudo-family ties, since they may include special intimate relations other than family members (Chen, 1994; Luo, 2005).

Familiar ties, including good friends and persons to whom one feels particularly close, fit in the next ring under the "rules of favor exchange," by which relational trust can be built from frequent exchange of favors (Hwang, 1987; Tsui and Farh, 1997). Familiar ties generally involve instrumental exchanges, but pure rational-choice account cannot explain the behaviors in this ring well.

An actor's motivation is mixed (Granovetter, 2002), since historical, cultural, and normative factors are intertwined with self-interest calculation (Granovetter, 1999). While family ties place emphasis on expressive and normative concerns and acquaintance ties take care of instrumental interests, familiar ties need to balance the two different motivations—expressive and instrumental concerns. A familiar tie by definition is a strong tie (Granovetter, 1973; Marsden and Campbell, 1984). Yet familiar ties are different from family ties, since they are concerned more with instrumental interests and can be broken if there is a lack of trustworthy behavior.

For a centered ego, the ring of acquaintance ties provides abundant opportunities and resources that may be accessed by weak ties (Granovetter, 1973; Burt, 1992). However, the resources in this ring are not guaranteed for successful mobilization. So the acquaintance ties of this sort are outsiders for the guanxi circle's centered ego.

The ring of family ties constructs the core of a guanxi circle. This core may be called the "basic team" (Chen, 1998) or "confidant" (Chi, 1996), since it includes the basic forces and the most intimate relations for the centered ego.

The ring of familiar ties is the interface between a circle core and the outside world, as shown in Figure 7.1. They are more flexible and open than the core but much stronger in mobilizing resources than acquaintance ties. Thus, an important benefit of maintaining familiar ties as the periphery members of a guanxi circle is to keep circle operations flexible and the circle boundary open to the outside world.

Summarizing the arguments stated earlier, there are some static features of a guanxi circle. First, the guanxi circle is centered on an ego. Second, it has a structure with differential modes of association, including an innermost core, which is indicated by loyal, unbreakable, and intimate relationships, and periphery members, mainly composed of long-term relations with limited liability in frequent favor exchanges. Third, the boundary of a guanxi circle is usually open, and thus there may be overlapping areas among several guanxi circles. In the dynamic process, a guanxi circle may absorb outsiders into the inner group and also move trustworthy periphery members into the core. In other words, the boundaries within and outside a guanxi circle are blurred.

Chinese VC investors apply this ripple-like networking to build up their own guanxi circles in the industrial community, as shown in Figure 7.1. The innermost ring is a hard core composed by confidants, who are imitations of family members in the investors' working places. The middle ring is full of frequent cooperators, who conduct both instrumental and expressive exchanges with the circle's center. And the outermost ring is the peripheral members of the circle, in which occasional joint investments occur based on self-interest calculation. As a CEO of a state-owned VC firm, Mr. Liu said:

> …A big brother has reputation and good investment portfolio to support this reputation.… A little brother likes the big brother, because he can use money to exchange reputation. He directly gets reputation from cooperating with a big name.…In addition, a little brother may manipulate guanxi [in the big brother's guanxi circle], and gradually move into the inner rings. It is possible for the little brother someday somehow to become a big brother [the center of his own guanxi circle].

In other words, a "big brother" is the center of a guanxi circle, and "little brothers" join in the circle. The new entrances gradually move to the inner ring and then the hard core, so as to build up their own guanxi and resources in this process. In the following, we will use ERGM to analyze the network structure of joint investments and use the guanxi circle phenomenon to interpret the simulation results.

7.2 Analytical Method: ERGM

7.2.1 Method of ERGM

In general, we describe a network by its statistical features rather than the whole picture of the network in detail. There are many networks sharing a set of common network features. For example, a bunch of networks, or what we call an "ensemble," may meet the requirement of a network structure with 1000 nodes that have the average degree of 10 (we certainly can assume more statistics, such as how many k-stars, cycles, links between certain nodes). An ensemble in the context of this chapter means a set of possible networks good fit for a set of given network features. The ERGM tries to answer the following question: which one best fits the actual network in the ensemble, given a part of statistics of the actual network?

The basic idea of ERGM is to generate all the possible networks, given a set of network statistics, and then measure their difference to the target network (or a certain feature of the target network). We thus get a simulated network that is most likely to be the real one. However, this process is very complex. For example, when the number of nodes is 1000, then the ensemble $\mathcal{Y}$ will contain as many as $2^{C_2^{n(x)}}$ networks. The question is thus how to find the best choice among these networks in an ensemble. We generally compare each simulated network and the real one to get a weight of a network feature, which forms a probability distribution under the condition of a relatively small number of constraints. Then, averaging the simulated networks with their weights will give us the network best fitted for the real one. The way is similar to many physicists' and statisticians' work following Willard Gibbs' provoking innovation, which have been developed for over a hundred years since the late nineteenth century. In practical work, instead of the complex computation enumerating all the network features in an ensemble, we generally employ Monte Carlo random simulation to simplify the computing process (Mark, 2000).

ERGM can also be used to perform sensitivity (significance) analysis for the underlying mechanisms in the network evolution. After adding a new factor into a model, we may prove this factor significantly influences the process of network evolution, if the ERGM gives us a better prediction. On the contrary, if this factor does not improve the predictive ability, then it may not be a significant factor.

In any simulation experiment, there are some network features taken into account, and cycles are certainly one of the most important among these factors. In our experiments, closed quadrangles among four nodes (in brief, it is denoted as "cycle4") are our main concern. An experimental model is defined as a model with all given network features, while in control model "cycle4" is taken out from the experimental model. If the error rate of the control model is significantly worse than that of the experimental model, then we can conclude "cycle4" as an important factor in the network evolution.

The error rate is defined as follows:

$$\text{ErrorRate} = \frac{\text{abs}(\text{simulated} - \text{target})}{\max(\text{target}, \text{simulated})}$$

where

"simulated" means a set of simulated networks

"target" indicates the target network

An exponential model is a statistical model with the probability function satisfying the following:

$$f_X(x|\theta) = h(x)g(\theta)\exp(u(\theta)T(x))$$

ERGM uses exponential models in network analysis. In ERGM, if a target network is denoted as x, then x can be constructed by different networks with various structures, each accompanied with a certain probability. A set of various network structures is g(x) with a set of probability, which is coded as the coefficient θ. Then, we may take x as one of the network families that is randomly generated from the mathematical formula as follows:

$$P(X = x \mid \theta) = \frac{\exp\left(\theta^{\mathrm{T}} g(x)\right)}{\kappa(\theta)}$$

It can also be in a logistic form as follows:

$$\log(P(X = x \mid \theta)) = \theta^{\mathrm{T}} g(x) - \log(\kappa(\theta))$$

where $g(x) = (N_{\text{edge}}(x), N_{\text{VC-concurrent}}(x), N_{\text{kstar2}}(x),...)$ is a statistics vector from a number of various network structures.

$$\theta = \left(\theta_{\text{edge}}, \theta_{\text{VC-concurrent}}, \theta_{\text{kstar2}},...\right)$$

is a coefficient vector.

$$\kappa(\theta) = \sum_{y \in \mathcal{Y}} \exp\left(\theta^{\mathrm{T}} g(y)\right)$$

where g(y) is a statistics vector, which normalizes the probabilities to 1.

$\mathcal{Y}$ is a set of networks that are generated under the constraint of some model parameters (in the following, we will use edges; VC-concurrent; Firm-concurrent; kstar2, kstar3, cycle3, cycle4 as parameters, which are described in the following section), which appear in the network x, too.

We aim to choose the best coefficient $\tilde{\theta}$ to get a family of random-generated networks, which has the largest probability to let x appear. So we regard x as a representative example of the family of random-generated networks, given certain structures (g(x) and $\tilde{\theta}$). Although the theory behind the solution is rather complex, the computing method is actually remarkably simple, that is, the best choice of $\tilde{\theta}$ is to maximize the Gibbs entropy (Newman, 2010) as follows:

$$S = -\sum_{y \in \mathcal{Y}} P(y) \ln P(y)$$

7.2.2 *From an Open Quadrangle to a Closed Quadrangle*

To explore the effect of guanxi circles to a certain joint investment, we will focus our study on how the strength of a syndication tie between two VCs influences the new joint investment between them. In a two-mode network of VCs and invested companies, the basic analytical element for two VCs is an open quadrangle, as shown in the upper-left-hand diagram of Figure 7.2. Whether there is an open quadrangle between two VCs, separately named after VC_1 and VC_2, depends on at least three conditions as follows:

1. $Firm_1$ is invested by VC_1.
2. VC_1 invested another company (or some other companies), such as $Firm_2$.
3. There is another VC, called VC_2, which invested $Firm_1$.

In such an open quadrangle, VC_1 and $Firm_1$ are indirectly connected with VC_2 and $Firm_2$ separately. If VC_2 invests $Firm_2$, then this open quadrangle becomes closed, as illustrated in the upper-right-hand side of Figure 7.2.

For measuring the effect of tie strength between two VCs on the new joint investment between them, we can use open and closed quadrangles as main statistics in ERGM. The more closed quadrangles are formed between two VCs, the stronger the syndication tie is between them. In a small circle of network, joint investment brings about consecutive effects, which introduce more joint investments for syndicated partners and create more closed quadrangles. As shown in the lower-left-hand-side figure, VC_2 accompanied with VC_3 invests in $Firm_3$ and thus introduce $Firm_1$ and $Firm_2$ to VC_3. In the lower-right-hand-side figure, we can see that three more closed quadrangles are therefore created.

Guanxi circle theory assumes that open quadrangles may induce the formation of closed quadrangles, and a syndication tie with more joint investments formed between any pair of VCs will have higher probability to turn their open quadrangles closed. By using ERGM, we can investigate the effects of syndication tie strength on the formation of closed quadrangles, that is, the more joint investments between two VCs, when given open quadrangles and other network features as controls.

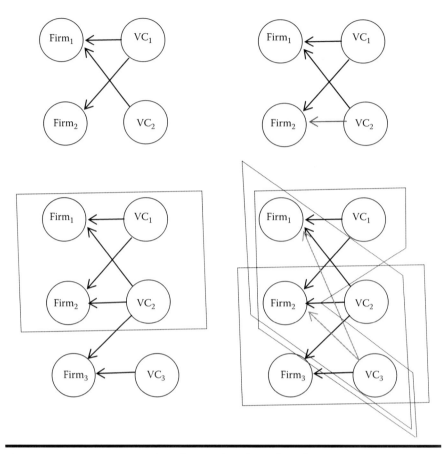

Figure 7.2 From open quadrangles to closed quadrangles.

7.2.3 *Experimental Design*

For controlling other significant factors in network evolution, our previous data mining provides three types of important features affecting the structure of network as shown in the following. To prove the effect of closed quadrangles on the formation of joint investments, we also add them into our ERGM as control variables.

1. *Edge*: In the completely random network of ERGM, each node has a probability of 0.5 to connect another node. But in target network, the density of edge is decided by the ratio of the actual number of joint investment to the maximum number of syndication ties. So the probability of each edge that appears in this network is much lower than 0.5. This is measured by statistics "edge" (the actual number of edges in the target network).

2. *Degree*: In ERGM without any controls given, there can be many totally unconnected nodes, since edges are generated randomly. But in our target network, edges are created by investments, so there are only those connected nodes included. We should add some controls to measure the features of degree in the target network. The network statistics "VC-concurrent" is the number of VCs that have at least two investment ties, while "Firm-concurrent" indicates the number of invested firms that have two or more edges. "kstar2" means the number of 2-stars centered on any type of nodes, while "kstar3" is the number of 3-stars.
3. *Cycles*: The number of open quadrangles is named after "cycle3," since it is a cycle among three nodes in the joint-investment network. A higher number of cycle3 means more chances to bring about closed quadrangles, which is the indicator of joint investment between two VCs.

The focus of this study is syndication tie strength, which is measured by the number of closed quadrangles between two VCs, and this explanatory variable is named after "cycle4." To conduct a significant analysis of guanxi circle theory, the experimental model includes all controls and "cycle4," while the control model excludes "cycle4."

7.3 Data and Analytical Results

In China, existing major VC databases such as ChinaVenture, Zero2IPO, Simuton database, and Venture Capital Research Institute's annual reports release data about all public investments and relevant indexes in the VC field for the years of 1995–2011. For establishing a VC database, we collect both Internet data and secondhand data mainly from the publically available Simuton database. Simuton collects a variety of data from the Internet and modifies it into a structured form.

We first collect 4164 VCs and their investment data to form a 2-mode network. From 1995 to 2009, there were 9305 investment events involved with 2060 VCs and 6569 invested firms. From 1995 to 2011, the investment events increased to 12,414. The joint investments in the mature stage of new star-ups may not imply the cooperation between the two investors, since a "super-star" may attract many investors, who are chosen, rather than choose, to invest in this super-star. So the data of investment events in the mature stage are ruled out of our analysis.

In the following analyses, we compare the statistical information of target network with the experimental and control models. The dependent variable is the number of closed quadrangles between any pair of VCs, that is, the number of their joint investments. First of all, it is necessary to estimate the ERGM coefficients of the two models. By doing that, we simulate the models' 10 runs in each experiment.

Our analyses then average the results of 10-run simulations and finally compare these results with the actual statistics of target network.

We introduce our experimental and control models as follows:

1. *Target network*: The information of original network data
2. *Experimental model*: The ERGM estimation of the target network, with controls of edges; VC-concurrent; Firm-concurrent; kstar2, kstar3, cycle3; and the explanatory variable in our study, that is, cycle4
3. *Control model*: Another ERGM estimation of the target network like the experimental model, except that it does not include the number of closed quadrangles "cycle4"

As shown in Figure 7.3, we take investment network of 1991–2009 data as the target network and compute the statistics of this network listed earlier as the control and explanatory variables. The simulation results show that the error rates between the experimental and control models are not big at the very beginning. Both models can predict the number of joint investment well between any pair of VCs. However, after a threshold value 3, that is, three joint investments between any two VCs, the difference becomes huge. The experiment model is at least 30% better than the control model after the threshold point. In other words, the information of previous joint investments between two VCs indeed influences the model's prediction power. However, this influence is not significant before three joint investments.

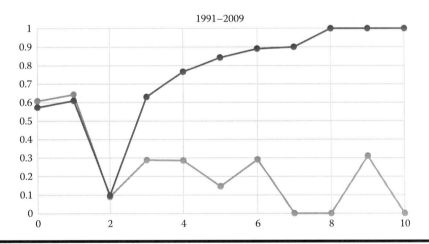

Figure 7.3 The simulation results by using 1991–2009 data. *Note:* Y-axis is the error rate. In other words, 0 is 100% prediction for target network, while 1 means 100% error rate. X-axis is the number of joint investments between any pair of VCs. The black line is the error rate of the control model, while the gray line is that of the experimental model. The difference between the two models is the significant influence of the network statistics cycle4.

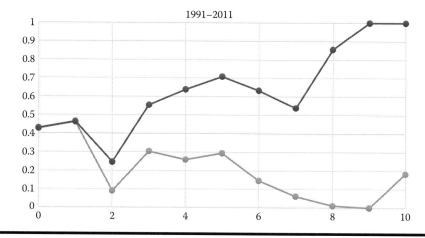

Figure 7.4 **The simulation results by using 1995–2011 data.** *Note:* **Y-axis is the error rate. In other words, 0 is 100% prediction for target network, while 1 means 100% error rate. X-axis is the number of joint investments between any pair of VCs. The red line is the error rate of the control model, while the blue line is that of the experimental model. The difference between the two models is the significant influence of the network statistics cycle4.**

Another interesting finding is that point 4 in the X-axis is another joint investment threshold point, after which the difference of error rates between the two models enlarges to a certain level, until point 7 where the rate of the experiment model drops sharply to 0.

For retesting our simulation results, we use the investment network of 1991–2011 data as the target network and run the ERGMs again. The results show a very similar pattern. At point 2, the difference between the two models becomes significant and increases to a certain level after threshold point 4. Between points 4 and 7, the error rate of the experiment model is around 30%–40%, but then drops sharply again after threshold point 8. In the same stage, the control model's error rate becomes higher and higher, until it reaches 100%.

How can we explain the results of ERGM? Why does the difference between the two models increase sharply at threshold point 4? At point 8, why does the error rate of the experimental model drop sharply? In Figure 7.4, we would like to use the qualitative data to interpret these results.

7.4 Interpretations for Analytical Results

7.4.1 Interpretations

First, in comparison with random-generated network given only "edge" as a control, the control model's error rate is not high in predicting the number of first or second syndication in the Chinese VC network. Second, after threshold point 4, the explanation power of cycle4, that is, the information of joint investments, becomes more and more significant, and at threshold point 7 or 8, the error rate of the experimental model drops sharply to zero, while the control model has about 100% error rate.

For interpreting the first finding, we suggest that the first experience of joint investment between two VCs may not be the starting point of their long-term cooperation. Finding syndication partners is a trial-and-error process, and the first cooperation may not be correlated to more joint investments. That is why the information of joint investments is not very useful for predicting the number of newly formed syndications. However, the information about the number of joint investments turns to be more and more important for predicting the number of high-level syndications after passing threshold point 3. We thus speculate that only two or more runs of joint ventures can make two VCs firmly bonded together in the future. In our interviews, Mr. Y once commented on this phenomenon in the following way:

> Newly emergent VCs are naive, immature, and not so sophisticated. ... it is easy to control them if they are absorbed in my circle [in Chinese terms, small circle or guanxi circle, i.e., a small and comparatively closed group centered on the interviewee]. The relationships among mature VC investors are not stable, and they seldom form a circle... we cooperate with each other for limited reciprocity, such as bringing money in to hedge risk. New VCs are willing to be cannon fodder [the sacrificed side],...they should pay tuition.

In other words, a guanxi circle's leader often finds new entrances, other than mature sophisticated VCs or old friends, as the limited partners in some risky investments, since they may be sacrificed in certain situations. In a highly uncertain environment, a new run of cooperation may be a zero-sum game. Particularly if an investment sometimes involves a huge amount of profit or loss and unfair distribution may hurt friendship between old partners. For the sake of keeping friendship, the focal person sometimes avoids inviting a familiar person to join in such a new investment. Newly formed syndication ties are thus not very stable.

However, a guanxi circle's leader also needs to build up long-term cooperation with certain partners, and the expectation for the next runs of game ensures cooperative relations continue (Axelrod, 1984; Hardin, 2001). This phenomenon may help explain the second finding, which illustrates that a model can't explain high-level cooperation without knowing the information of joint investments. We thus speculate that repeated joint investments foster necessary trust that brings about long-term and stable cooperative ties.

As stated in the guanxi circle theory, the Chinese tend to cooperate with familiar persons in the way of long-term favor exchanges (Hwang, 1987). This may lead us to suggest that a Chinese VC tends to initiate a joint investment with those who had cooperative experience with the focal person (the leader in a guanxi circle) in the past, as a junior partner of a VC firm, Mr. Y, put it:

> First of all, firms [Chinese VCs] generally get bored with these [too detailed contract and too calculative financial arrangements]....Foreign investors pay too much attention on short-term profit...We are not like this. In China, we tend to foster something [in a long period], especially friendship.

7.4.2 Conclusions

Summarizing the analytical results and interpretations stated previously, guanxi is important in the sense of access to valuable projects and introducing new partners for a focal VC. However, in such a highly uncertain environment, the familiar partner may sometimes not be the best choice in a new investment. But strangers or those with high relational distance are not a good choice either, since information asymmetry makes them untrustworthy. So those with a short path of relational distance, such as friends' friends, are chosen in some risky investment. That is why the first or second joint investment may not be a good predictor for more cooperation.

However, previous experience of syndication may transform occasional partners into familiar ties, which breed expressive feelings and trust needed for long-term cooperation in Chinese society. That is why the information of joint investment is necessary to predict frequent cooperation in the network.

At very-high-level cooperation, the guanxi between two VCs changes again. A type of pseudo-family ties is established, which requires each side sharing opportunities with and not betraying its confidant partner.

A robust network, rather than a good contract with careful self-interest calculation, is the best way of hedging the risks in a highly uncertain environment. Guanxi-oriented thinking ensures that a Chinese VC often pays more attention to its network position than the profit or loss in one single transaction. The center position will attract more partners, who are thus invited into a larger network so as to find more chances to get to know new friends. In return, they bring more good projects and key information in this network.

Acknowledgments

We are grateful for the financial support of the Center for Social Network Research, Tsinghua University, and Tsinghua's research project "Trust and Guanxi Studies on Internet," Project Number: 20121088015, as well as the support of the Chinese Natural Science Foundation Project "Social Network in Big Data Analysis: A Case in Investment Network," Project number: 71372053, and National 863 project, Project number: 20141860074.

References

Admati, A., Pfleiderer, P. 1994. Robust financial contracting and the role of venture capitalists. *Journal of Finance*, 49(2):371–403.

Axelrod, R.M. 1984. *The Evolution of Cooperation*. New York: Basic Books.

Bond, M.H., Hwang, K.K. 1986. The social psychology of chinese people. In Bond, M.H. (ed.), *The Psychology of the Chinese People*. Hong Kong: Oxford University Press, pp. 213–266.

Brander, J.A., Amit, R., Antweiler, W. 2002. Venture-capital syndication: improved venture selection vs. the value added hypothesis. *Journal of Economics & Management Strategy*, 11(3):422–452.

Bruton, G.D., Ahlstrom, D. 2003. An institutional view of China's venture capital industry: Explaining differences between China and the West. *Journal of Business Venturing*, 18:233–259.

Bruton, G.D., Fried, V.H., Manigart, S. 2005. An institutional view of the development of venture capital in the U.S., Europe and Asia. *Entrepreneurship Theory and Practice*. http://citeseerx.ist.psu.edu/viewdoc/download?doi=10.1.1.195.8313&rep=rep1&type=pdf.

Burt, R. 1992. *Structural Holes: The Social Structure of Competition*. Cambridge, MA: Harvard University Press.

Burt, R., Knes, M. 1996. The gossip of the third party. In Kramer, R.M. and Tyler, T.R. (eds.), *Trust in Organizations*. London, U.K.: Sage Publications, Inc.

Chen, C.-H. 1994. *Subcontracting Networks and Social Life*. Taipei, China: Lien-Jin Press (in Chinese).

Chen, C.-H. 1998. *Sociological Perspectives on Taiwan's Industries—Transformation of Small and Medium-sized Firms*. Taipei, China: Lien-Jin Press (in Chinese).

Chi, S.C. 1996. The empirical study in roles of leader's confidant. *Management Review* 15(1):37–59.

Chua, R., Morris, M., Ingram, P. 2009. Guanxi vs. networking: Distinctive configurations of affect- and cognition-based trust in the networks of Chinese vs. American managers. *Journal of International Business Studies*, 40:490–508.

Fei, H.T. 1992. *From the Soil: The Foundations of Chinese Society*. Berkeley, CA: University of California Press.

Granovetter, M. 1973. The strength of weak tie. *American Journal of Sociology*, 78:1360–1380.

Granovetter, M. 1999. Coase encounters and formal models: Taking gibbons seriously. *Administrative Science Quarterly*, 44:158–162.

Granovetter, M. 2002. A theoretical agenda for economic sociology. In Guillen, M., Collins, R., England, P., and Meyer, M. (eds.), *The New Economic Sociology: Developments in An Emerging Field*. New York: Russell Sage Foundation, pp. 35–59.

Hardin, R. 2001. Conceptions and explanations of trust. In Cook, K.S. (ed.), *Trust in Society*. New York: Russell Sage Foundation, pp. 3–39.

Hochberg, Y.V., Ljungqvist, A., Lu, Y. 2010. Networking as a barrier to entry and the competitive supply of venture capital. *Journal of Finance*, 65 (3):829–859.

Holmstrom, B. 1982. Moral hazard in teams. *The Bell Journal of Economics*, 13(2):324–340.

Hwang, K.K. 1987. Face and favor: The Chinese power game. *American Journal of Sociology*, 92:944–974.

Hwang, K.K. 1988. *The Chinese Power Game*. Taipei, China: Lien-Jin Press (In Chinese).

King, G., Keohane, R.O., Verba, S. 1994. *Designing Social Inquiry: Scientific Inference in Qualitative Research*. Princeton, NJ: Princeton University Press.

Lerner, J. 1994. The syndication of venture capital investments. *Financial Management*, 23(3):16–27.

Liang, S.-M. 1983. *The Comparison between Chinese and Western Cultures*. Taipei, China: Li-Ren Publishing House (in Chinese).

Lockett, A., Wright, M. 2001. The syndication of venture capital investments. *Omega*, 29:375–390.

Luo, J.-D. 2005. Particularistic trust and general trust—A network analysis in Chinese organizations. *Management and Organizational Review*, 3:437–458.

Luo, J.-D. 2011. Guanxi revisited—An exploratory study of familiar ties in a Chinese workplace. *Management and Organizational Review*, 7(2):329–351.

Luo, J.-D. and Cheng, M.-Y. 2015. Guanxi circles' effect on organizational trust—Bringing power and vertical social exchanges into intra-organizational network analysis. *American Behavioral Scientist*, 59(8):1024–1037.

Luo, J.-D., Yeh, K. 2012. Neither collectivism nor individualism—Trust in Chinese guanxi circles. *Journal of Trust Research*, 2(1):53–70.

Mark, H.S. 2000. Package 'ergm'. http://statnet.org.

Marsden, P., Campbell, K. 1984. Measuring tie strength. *Social Forces*, 63(2):483–501.

Newman, M.E.J. 2010. *Networks: An Introduction*. Oxford, U.K.: Oxford University Press.

Olson, M. 1966. *The Logic of Collective Action*. Cambridge, MA: Harvard University Press.

Small, M.L. 2011. How to conduct a mixed methods study: Recent trends in a rapidly growing literature. *Annual Review of Sociology*, 37:57–86.

Tsui, A.S., J.-L. Farh. 1997. Where guanxi matters—Relational demography and guanxi and technology. *Work and Occupations*, 24(1): 57–79.

Tykvová, T. 2007. Who chooses whom? Syndication, skills and reputation. *Review of Financial Economics*, 16(1):5–28.

Williamson, O. 1985. *The Economic Institutions of Capitalism*. New York: The Free Press.

Williamson, O. 1996. *The Mechanisms of Governance*. New York: Oxford University Press.

Wilson, R. 1968. The theory of syndicates. *Econometrica*, 36(1):119–132.

Yang, G.S. 1993. Chinese social orientation. In Yang, G.S., Yu, A.B. (eds.), *Chinese Psychology and Behavior*. Taipei, China: Laureate Press, pp. 87–142.

Zhang, Y., Zhang, Z. 2006. Guanxi and organizational dynamics in China: A link between individual and organizational levels. *Journal of Business Ethics*, 67(4): 375–392.

SOCIAL NETWORK BEHAVIORS

Chapter 8

Patterns of Group Movement on a Virtual Playfield: Empirical and Simulation Approaches

Margarete Boos, Wenzhong Li, and Johannes Pritz

Contents

8.1 Group Movements in Animals and Humans

Many animals, including humans, live in groups. The last three decades of examining group living (e.g., Alexander, 1974; Krause and Ruxton, 2002; Sumpter, 2010) has revealed advantages and disadvantages to group cohabitation. The disadvantages include squabbles over food and procreation mates as well as increased exposure to parasites and diseases (Alexander, 1974; Altizer et al., 2003; Bertram, 1978; Pitcher et al., 1982; Reebs, 2000; van Schaik, 1989). However, since the advantages outweigh the disadvantages, group living prevails in these species. Advantages include strength-in-number approaches to (1) confounding predators (Hamilton, 1971; Quinn and Cresswell, 2006), (2) foraging (Pitcher et al., 1982), (3) identifying whereabouts of resources and predators (Reebs, 2000), (4) defense of group's foraging and dwelling habitats (Williams et al., 2004), (5) keeping warm (Scantlebury et al., 2006), (6) hunting (Benoit-Bird and Au, 2009), (7) breeding (Meade et al., 2010), (8) identifying danger (Ward et al., 2011), and (9) offspring socialization (Pearson, 2011).

The survival of human and other primate groups depends on the group's ability to remain together by coordinating the varying preferences of its members (Conradt and Roper, 2005; Rands et al., 2003). Studies have shown that decisions in groups are achieved in a variety of manners, being made by consensus involving a majority of group members and sometimes being dictated by a single group member or a small subset of the group (Conradt and Roper, 2005, 2009).

Consensus decisions—widespread decisions reached by the group as a whole—once taken, require that group members become informed about how to cohesively behave. Members of small groups become informed of the consensus decision on how to behave (usually the direction to move in) by globally observing the other group members' behavior (Conradt and Roper, 2005). However, in large groups of animals (e.g., shoals, flocks, and herds), group members are informed about consensus decisions (e.g., what direction to move in) based on local rather than global information transfer. Rather than observing the movements of their group as a whole, members of these larger groups mimic and respond to how their adjacent neighbors behave (overview on vertebrates: Conradt et al., 2009; Couzin and Krause, 2003; Parrish et al., 2002).

8.2 Coordination Processes and Mechanisms for Group Movement

The previously mentioned collective movement of groups toward a physical destiny (Krause et al., 2000; Sumpter, 2010) minimizes the demand for global and even interindividual communication across the group (Conradt and Roper, 2005, 2009). Empirical research (Camazine et al., 2003; Fischer and Zinner, 2011; King et al., 2011) and behavioral modeling (Couzin and Krause, 2003; Guy et al., 2012; Katz et al., 2011) have shown that in diverse species, including humans (Boos et al., 2013; Dyer et al., 2009; Helbing et al., 2001), local individual rules are adequate to generate complex collective behavior at the group level (Conradt and List, 2009; Couzin, 2009; Sumpter et al., 2008). There is increasing evidence (King et al., 2011; Moussaïd et al., 2009) that not only large swarms but also small heterogeneous groups may be coordinated by local interaction rules (Boos et al., 2013).

To explain this phenomenon of "swarming" in animals and humans, Couzin and colleagues created a model in which group movement is formed by group members regulating their movement according to how adjacent members move (Couzin et al., 2005). Their swarm model was composed of three fundamental parameters described by Aoki (1982) and Reynolds (1987): (1) *cohesion* (swarm members become attracted to neighbors' positions within a local range), (2) *alignment* (swarm members align with neighbors' direction and speed), and (3) *collision avoidance* (swarm members avoid neighbors within a predefined radius). Couzin et al. (2005) deduced that a relatively small number of directionally informed individuals can channel the naïve (uninformed) members of the swarm to the target of the directionally informed ones. Neither the informed nor the naïve members need to recognize each other, be aware of the informational gap, or practice active signaling. Assumptions about inherent personal distinctions (e.g., personality traits or social cues) need not be present in order to explain effective movement leadership. To account for this influence of group members being informed about a preferred goal, in a contemporary study on the coordination of group movement of nonhuman primates, a weighted direction vector was added to Couzin et al.'s three fundamental parameters to investigate how these so-called informed individuals manage the pursuit of their preferred goal and do so with the group in tow (Fichtel et al., 2011).

The previously mentioned series of studies summarized in this chapter defines the contextual backdrop of our test of whether these nonglobally informed group member movements and leadership behaviors—known as swarming—empirically hold true for small groups of humans restricted to "reading/transmitting" only movement behavior. To perform such a test, we developed a computer-based HoneyComb© multiagent game (Boos et al., 2013) to serve as our investigative platform. The elements of this virtual platform and the parameters of the myriad of games able to be played on the said platform were designed to eliminate all sensory/communication channels except the perception of participant-assigned avatar movements on the playfield (Figure 8.1). We used this paradigm as an

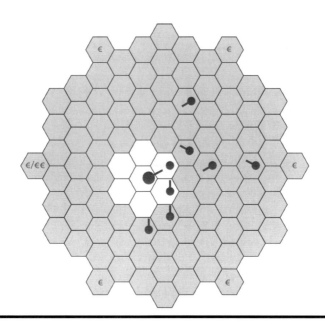

Figure 8.1 **The HoneyComb© virtual playground with monetary goal fields (two different perspectives—from an informed and an uninformed participant—overlain in this picture), avatars representing participants, and lines indicating directions the avatars head from.**

experimental setting where the human participants' avatars move as identical black dots on a virtual playground, deprived of all information sources about their coparticipants except for their movements.

8.3 HoneyComb©: An Experimental Paradigm for Measuring Coordination and Leadership in Group Movement

In the following, we summarize the rationale and the results of a series of experiments that we performed in order to investigate whether two of the three parameters of swarming behavior in large groups of animals—cohesion and alignment—described earlier in the 2005 Couzin and colleagues' study also hold true for small groups of humans. The experiments were conducted in a lecture building of the University of Göttingen between June and July 2010 and again in May 2011. The results of the corresponding Studies 1, 2, and 3 were published in biological journals (Belz et al., 2013; Boos et al., 2014, 2015). A fourth study implemented in order to validate the results of Study 3 will be presented here.

Participants: A total of 400 primarily undergraduate students participated in the study and were randomly assigned into 40 groups of 10 individuals each. These 400 undergraduate students were from 40 different fields of study and were between the ages of 18 and 44 (M = 24.24, SD = 3.16). Of the total sample, 43.6% were female. All participants were naïve regarding the purpose of the experiment, including no immediate post-experiment debriefing to control for possible sharing of information with other potential participants. All participants received payment for their participation (paid *after* the entire experiment was complete), depending on their individual and the whole groups' performance in games 3–6.

The HoneyComb experiments consisted of three phases: pretest, testing, and posttest.

In the *pretest phase*, three assistants randomly recruited participants, providing standardized information about the experiment: (1) duration would be about 25 min; (2) maximum payment would be 13€ (2010 Study) or 8€ (2011 Study), depending on their performance; and (3) it was a multiplayer game to be played on institution-owned laptops. As soon as 10 participants were gathered, they were led into a specified area with individual workstations, each equipped with a laptop. Audiovisual communication between the participants was eliminated by mandatory earplug use and partition-encased workstations. Participants signed a form designating informed consent and were seated in front of the provided laptops.

In the *testing phase*, participants used laptops connected via a local area network (uniform laptops; screen size, 13.3 in.; resolution, 1366 × 768 pixels; all launched in full screen). Participants mouse-controlled a black avatar dot—twice as big as the visible dots (10–15 pixels depending on the number of participants on one hexagon) of the other nine participants—on a virtual 97-hexagon playfield (each hexagon having a radius of 40 pixels), starting in the center of the field and then moving on the virtual playfield. By left-clicking into the respective small hexagon, their black avatar dot could be moved. Only adjacent fields could be chosen for the next move. In one experimental condition (Game 5), a local perception radius (displayed as light fields in Figure 8.1) was implemented in order to amplify the criticality of the game's single communication factor: knowledge of only their neighboring participants' movements.

A movement delay of 1500 ms was implemented in both conditions to prevent experienced computer users from moving systematically faster through the playfield than others. The movement delay was implemented in all conditions and therefore not meant to prevent or encourage moving faster through more rapid decision-making or to impede differences between conditions. After each move, a small tail was blended in for 4000 ms for each participant, indicating the last direction from which he or she hailed. All visual components were displayed in gray, black, and white to avoid the influences of colors.

In the *posttest phase*, participants filled out an online questionnaire assessing demographic data, Big Five personality factors, perceived stress and calmness, and pay satisfaction (to be paid upon completion of the entire experiment).

Data Structure: Each participant's moves were recorded by the server as hexagonal coordinates, with timestamps at an accuracy of 1 ms and individual and group IDs. Thus, a metric could be defined on the playfield and distances between participants over time could be measured. Movement data could be combined with data from the questionnaires.

8.4 Empirical and Simulation Approaches to Collective Movement

8.4.1 Empirical Approach

8.4.1.1 First Swarming Parameter: Cohesion (Study 1)

Flocking behavior, known as a form of self-organized collective behavior, is described as the formation of groups lacking global control and explicit recruitment signals. Flocking behavior is observed in many group-living animals, that is, bird flocks, aquatic shoals, and herds of ungulates. Flocking behavior has been simulated in a number of seminal models but it has not been detected experimentally in human groups thus far. In *Study 1* (Belz et al., 2013), our research question was whether participants moving their avatar on a field with visible coparticipant avatar movements eventually create cohesiveness in the group, even though they were not given any external incentive or instruction to do so.

The participants played two games: (1) *Single Game*, where group members' avatar locations were invisible, and (2) *Joint Game*, where coparticipants' avatar locations were visible in order to find out whether the presence of conspecifics on the playfield would induce flocking behavior in the participants' movements.

The participants in both games were told there was no time limit to complete the task—a feature of our procedural design to avoid any externally imposed competitive factor. Both games were conducted without monetary rewards to reveal whether and to what extent participants would flock when moving freely in a setting with visible versus nonvisible conspecifics on the playfield (cf. Belz et al., 2013).

8.4.1.1.1 Main Results

We found that individuals in virtual human groups approach their neighbors automatically if they can identify where their neighbors' avatars are located, reducing spatial dispersion of the whole group. We also found that this element of flocking behavior was consistent over the entire time the groups moved around the virtual playing field. Furthermore, we were able to show that the visual presence of coparticipants' avatars did not lead to faster, individually competitive movements (Belz et al., 2013).

8.4.1.2 Stability of Cohesion (Study 2)

The next two games were designed to test the stability of this seemingly innate human tendency to flock and whether there were side effects regarding individual perceptions of stress and/or reward dissatisfaction. In *Study 2* (Boos et al., 2015), we introduced a competitive outcome interdependence factor: the chance to compete for virtual coins—in one condition, an inexhaustible amount, and in the other, a limited amount.

8.4.1.2.1 Game 3 "Neutral Game"

In the neutral game (NG), participants could earn coins from an inexhaustible source while moving over the virtual playfield. In the NG, six initially invisible and randomly distributed 50¢ coins could be found by mouse-touching the corresponding hexagon. Participants were not informed about the total number of coins to avoid systematic effects, for example, resignation after all coins had been found. If a participant found a coin, a black framework was displayed permanently at the corresponding hexagon, visible only to the said participant. Participants were informed that each coin spot could be independently exploited, once by each group member. Each participant had a limit of 15 moves, individually displayed by counters in the four corners of the playfield. The NG was over when each participant had made his or her 15 moves.

8.4.1.2.2 Game 4 "Competitive Game"

In the competitive game (CG), coins could only be gained at the expense of other participants in the same game. Again six 50¢ coins were randomly placed by the server but participants were informed that each coin spot could only be exploited by one group member. Collected coins were removed from the playfield, and a black framework—indicating an exploited spot—was visible to all participants.

8.4.1.2.3 Main Results

The results of our *Study 2* (Boos et al., 2015) to test the stability of the tendency to flock showed that introducing competition-inducing factors such as individual-based rewards does lead to individual reward-maximizing behavior, at the expense of group cohesion as well as causing added stress and less calmness for *all* group members. Participants who normally flocked together in our HoneyComb paradigm (see *Study 1*: Belz et al., 2013) adapted their movements to self-benefiting behavior in the competitive setting. CG participants specifically avoided their neighbors so they could find more of the limited amount of virtual coins before the other participants in the same group. Besides the systematic avoidance of neighbors, which was opposite of participant behavior displayed in *Study 1*'s *Game 2 "Joint game,"* we also found the CG participants moved significantly faster. Accelerated movements alone cannot be classified as reward-maximizing behavior, but in combination with spatial avoidance of other group members, the participants who moved faster—and covertly on a different path than their group members—heightened their chance to find virtual coins *before* others did and therefore actively gained an advantage for themselves.

8.4.1.3 Second Swarming Parameter: Alignment (Study 3)

How is movement of individuals toward a spatial goal coordinated as a group? This is the question we addressed in *Study 3* (Boos et al., 2014) using Game 5 described in the succeeding text where we again set monetary incentives. In contrast to *Study 2* (Games 3 and 4), we set fixed and visible goal fields, granting a monetary reward to those participants who reached them. An additional reward for alignment was set by granting participants reaching a goal field a reward calculated by the number of coparticipants ending up on the same field. In order to discover whether leadership as a means of coordinated movement could occur in this restricted virtual environment, we implemented differences in information and reward structures for a minority/majority subgroup of the participants.

In this study, we asked (1) whether an (informed) group *minority* with preference for a specific goal field with a higher reward can lead an (uninformed) group *majority* with no preference to the minority's goal, and if so, (2) how this minority exerts its influence. Additionally, we asked whether coordination and leadership are possible when information is limited to an individual group member's only local observation of adjacent group member movements.

8.4.1.3.1 Game 5 "Minority/Majority Game"

At the beginning of the game, all participants' avatar dots were positioned in the center of the HoneyComb. In each of the 15 available moves, the participants could navigate their avatar dot via mouse-click to one of the six adjacent fields from their respective point of departure. An incentive structure operationalizing the model parameters was implemented via six spatial goal fields, granting monetary payoffs (€ or €€) (*alignment*). If a participant arrived at a payoff field, his or her payoff would be multiplied by the number of coparticipants' avatars standing on this payoff field at the end of the game (*cohesion*), making coordinated choices advantageous. The criterion for ending the game was either that all participants' avatars stood on payoff fields and/or that all participants had used all available moves.

To explore study question (1) regarding whether the informed minority would be able to lead the uninformed majority to their goal field, a minority/majority information differentiation within each of the 10-person groups was established: a minority of two randomly selected participants were informed of the location of their one highly rewarded €€ goal field in addition to five lower-rewarded € fields (Figure 8.1). A majority of eight participants were notified of six equally lower-rewarded goal fields (Figure 8.1). Neither the highly rewarded "informed" nor the lower-rewarded "uninformed" knew whether they were in the majority or in the minority or that there was a reward difference among the participants.

To address whether locomotive coordination and leadership would be possible only within *global* or also within *local* perception radius of the other participants' locations and movements, a second experimental factor was implemented: half of the groups were additionally restricted to being able to perceive only local coparticipants' movement relative to his or her avatar dot's proximity. The 40 ten-person groups were randomly allotted to either the *local condition* (*n* = 20 groups) limiting the participants' sight to coparticipant locations and movements only on adjacent fields to their avatar dot's position or the *global condition* (*n* = 20 groups) disclosing an overview of all coparticipants' avatar dot locations and movements on the playfield.

To find out which characteristics of the informed minority's movement behavior made them more successful in terms of monetary rewards, we analyzed a set of variables describing their movement behavior: first-mover behavior, similarity of movement paths and directions of the two informed minority participants, path length, mean latency between moves, starting order, personality variables (extraversion, openness to experience, etc.), and computer literacy.

8.4.1.3.2 Main Results

We showed that in a virtual human group—on the basis of movement alone—a minority can successfully lead a majority, even in the restricted condition of local visual perspective to only adjacent fields. Minorities lead successfully when (1) their members chose similar initial steps toward their goal field and (2) they were among the first in the entire group to make a move (Boos et al., 2013). Personality traits and computer literacy of informed participants were not crucial to their success in pulling the uninformed majority's avatars to their preferred goal field.

8.4.1.4 Leadership in Group Movement: Optimal Strategies via Programmed Leaders (Study 4)

Our objective in *Study 4* was to validate the results of *Study 3*'s *Game 5* by introducing two programmed avatars into *Game 6* with what we considered to be superior movement behaviors and then observe the results. These programmed avatars were inserted into *Game 6* by randomly exchanging two human participants who then played a separate game (*Game 7*) with eight programmed avatars (*Game 7* is not included in the focus of this contribution). The programmed avatars inserted into *Game 6* were programmed to exhibit ideal movement patterns apt for leading the majority of the eight human participants to their goal field. We furnished the two programmed avatars with the first mover, and other successful movement behavior styles that we had observed in *Study 3* were used by the human informed minority participants to lead the human naïve majority participants to the higher-rewarded goal field.

We also added two features derived from the literature and from the empirical results of our *Study 3* (Boos et al., 2014) that reflected additional effective leadership movement behavior styles for this virtual platform: (1) the shortest possible path to the goal field and (2) short latencies between two moves. For example, honeybees disposing of exact knowledge of a proliferous food resource not only manage to get their swarm there by enacting their waggle dance but also show a discriminable—that is, faster and more determined—movement behavior compared to their conspecifics (Beckman et al., 2006). Although the variables "shortest possible path" and "short latencies" had not been statistically significant predictors of the leadership success of the informed players in *Study 3* (Boos et al., 2014), they indicated a tendency in this direction. Therefore, we decided to use these movement characteristics as additional features of the programmed avatars' behavior inserted into Study 4's *Game 6*.

8.4.1.4.1 Game 6: "Programmed Minority Avatars"

Study 4's *Game 6* offered the same parameters as *Study 3*'s *Game 5*: six visible goal fields would render monetary rewards, these rewards to be multiplied by the number of coparticipants who ended up on the respective goal field. The difference to Study 3's *Game 5* was that the two minority players were programmed based on a program simulating the optimal leadership movement behavior described in the previous paragraph. This program was implemented in two versions, creating two experimental conditions for 10 ten-agent groups each: (A) the shortest possible latency of 1.5 s and (B) mean empirical latencies per move based on the results of *Study 3* (min = 3.05, max = 5.85 s). For *Study 4*'s *Game 6*, we implemented only the local vision radius for the participants.

8.4.1.4.2 Main Results

As only the reward-rendering depots had a subjective value for the participants, we did not expect any participant (0%) to arrive elsewhere in the virtual playing field (Table 8.1). For the uninformed majority with their six equally rewarded €ates goal fields, the one "€€" money depot (known only to the informed minority in *Game 5* and preset goal of the programmed players in *Game 6*) was expected to be

Table 8.1 Arrival Rates (%) of Uninformed Players Ending Up on Goal Depots in *Games 5* and 6

Goal Fields	Stochastically to Be Expected	Observed Game 5	Observed Game 6 (Both Latency Conditions)
€€ field (higher reward)	16.67	34.40	57.50
€ field (lower reward)	83.33	63.40	42.50
Elsewhere (no reward)	00.00	2.20	00.00

as attractive as each of the five "€" money depots, leading to a predicted probability of a sixth (16.67%) of the uninformed majority to inadvertently arrive at the "€€" money depot by the end of the game. However, not only did the human minority participants who ended up with a higher reward lead a higher than stochastically to-be-expected proportion of majority players to their goal field (*Study 3*; Boos et al., 2014, p. 4), but the two programmed avatars equipped with optimal movement behavior were even more successful (Table 8.1). The differences, based on chi-square and *t*-tests, between the expected and the observed arrival rates were statistically significant on a level of at least $p < 0.01$. The observed values between the leadership of the human versus the programmed avatars did not differ significantly ($t(38) = 1.559$; $p = .127$ two-tailed). Also, there were no differences in the (high) success rates of the programmed minority players in Condition A with minimal latency and those of Condition B with empirically based per-move latencies taken from *Study 3* ($t(18 = -0.77, p = .226$).

In summary, our results show that participants with a distinct preference for a direction—here the higher-rewarded goal field—exert substantial influence on the movement of the whole group. They can exert this influence by their movement behavior, by moving first, by moving the shortest possible way toward their goal, by doing so in a determined manner, and—if they are in a minority of several players—using the same path toward their goal.

It is interesting that the programmed avatars were not more successful than the human participants in leading a majority to their goal field. This brings us to the conclusion that factors other than their movement behavior likely influenced the majority. One of these factors could be the tendency shown in our *Study 1* of human participants to flock on the playfield, that is, their swarming (minimizing distance between participants) behavior to maintain group cohesion.

In a computer simulation approach, we tried in a subsequent step to differentiate between these two strategies—determined goal-directed movement toward the goal versus a tendency to stay cohesive within the group—as well as a possible mixture of the two strategies. Based on the HoneyComb paradigm, these two strategies were modeled in a computer simulation in order to identify—in terms of leadership success respective of monetary rewards—the most effective movement strategy.

8.4.2 Computer Simulation Approach

8.4.2.1 Introduction

The previous sections describe our empirical testing and subsequent observations of swarm-like movement behavior of humans. This section describes our modeling of group movement in order to quantify the proposed system parameters (e.g., cohesion and alignment) and to further study the mechanisms of swarming behavior by computer simulation.

In the HoneyComb computer simulation model, the movement of agents is described by discrete time series. In each time slot, an agent can decide whether to *stay* or to *move* based on a probabilistic model. If an agent stays, the assumption is it stays in order to observe the movement of its neighbors so that it can follow its neighbors in a subsequent move. If an agent moves, its movement is determined by two parameters: *cohesion* (the agent follows the majority of neighbors moving toward the same goal field) and *alignment* (the agent aligns its movement direction with the majority of its neighbors). By analyzing the probabilities of stay, move, cohesion, and alignment from the empirical data in Game 5, we applied a model to generate the movement trajectories of the simulation agents. We will illustrate in this section that the occurrence of human swarm-like movement and the forming of leadership are well simulated by the HoneyComb computer simulation model. The simulated collective behavior is coincident with the empirical results from the experiments with human-directed avatars in Study 4.

8.4.2.2 General Concepts

We use the following concepts for simulation:

Agent: Each agent in these computer simulations corresponds to a human participant in the HoneyComb games of our empirical experiments, simulating the movement behavior of said participant-directed avatars.

Hexagonal coordinate system: In the computer simulation, we applied the same hexagonal coordinate system used in the HoneyComb games of our experiments (see Figure 8.2). As shown in Figure 8.2, the point of origin (an agent's starting point) is labeled (0,0). From each field labeled by (x,y) in the hexagonal coordinate system, an agent can move to one of the six neighboring fields $(x,y - 1)$, $(x + 1, y)$, $(x + 1, y + 1)$, $(x, y + 1)$, $(x - 1, y)$, and $(x - 1, y - 1)$.

Playground: The movement area for all agents is called the playground. The boundary of the playground in our experiments and our simulations is

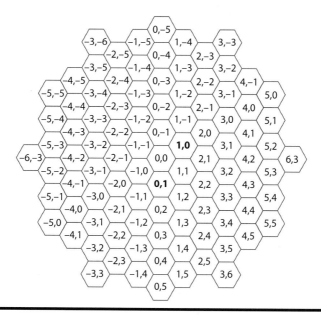

Figure 8.2   The hexagonal coordinate system.

illustrated in Figure 8.1 (radius highlighted), where the movements of agents are restricted to the labeled area of hexagons.

Goal fields: In our experiments as well as our simulations, we set six goal fields in the corners of the playground with the coordinates (3, –3), (6, 3), (3, 6), (–3, 3), (–6, –3), and (–3, –6). We assumed that when an agent enters a goal field, the agent will remain on this field for the rest of the game because of the reward structure of the game.

Rewards: For each goal field, there was a bonus of either 1 € or 2 €. If an agent arrived at a goal field, the agent would receive rewards depending on the bonus and the number of other agents arriving on that field as well.

Incentive mechanism: To enable the agents to move in a group without coordination, the game devised a group incentive mechanism, which rewards the agent in a goal field by *bonus in that field × the number of arrivals*. Thus, to receive a higher reward, the assumption was that the agents would tend to move to the goal with higher reward and that there would also be a greater amount of arrivals of other participants at this higher-reward goal.

Local view: The agents did not have global information about the movement of all other agents; they were privy only to local information about events on neighboring fields. In our games, each agent could observe the movement of the neighboring agents within a 1-step distance and decided its movement based on this local view information.

Informed agents: There was a minority of two informed agents out of a total of 10 agents, named "informed" because they have been informed about the difference in rewards rendered by the six goal fields, with one goal field providing a reward of €2 and five goal fields with a reward of €1 each.

Uninformed agents: The remaining eight agents were known as uninformed agents because even though they also knew the coordinates of the six goal fields, they were uninformed about the one goal i field rendering the higher €2 reward.

8.4.2.3 Group-Cohesion Mobility Model

In the hexagonal coordinate system, the movement trajectory of an agent could be represented by a sequence of moves $\{\langle goal_1, \theta_1 \rangle, \langle goal_2, \theta_2 \rangle, ..., \langle goal_n, \theta_n \rangle\}$, where $\langle goal_i, \theta_i \rangle$ meant that in the ith step, the agent moved toward goal i; therefore, this agent's movement angle was θ_i in the hexagon coordinate system.

We introduced a probabilistic mobility model to generate the movement trajectories of the group of agents. The model used *cohesion*, *alignment*, and *stay* to describe the behaviors of participants during movement in the game, each behavior type occurring with different probabilities. We quantified the behaviors and their probabilities as follows:

Cohesion: This parameter describes the agents moving toward the same goal as a group. Since each agent knew the coordinates of the six goal fields, in each step it would choose one of the goal fields and move toward it. Since each participant only had local view, we assumed *max_goal* to be the goal chosen by the maximum number of neighboring agents. We used $p_{cohesion}$ to denote the probability that an agent moved to the same goal as other agents, thus forming a moving group. That is, in each step, the agent would choose *max_goal* as its goal with probability $p_{cohesion}$ and move closer to the goal field.

Alignment: This parameter describes how an agent aligned its direction with the others during movement. We assumed *max_angle* be the observed movement angle with the maximum number of neighboring agents. We defined *palignment* (θ) as the probability that the move direction of an agent had drift θ to *max_angle*, where θ is the included angle between the movement direction and *max_angle*. That is, in each step, an agent would choose its movement angle as *max_angle* ± θ with probability *palignment* (θ). Note that because there are six movement directions in the hexagon coordinate system, the absolute value of the included angle θ can take one of the four values $\{0°, 60°, 120°, 180°\}$, where $\theta = 0°$ indicates that the agent aligned its movement direction with the majority of agents and $\theta = 180°$ implies that the agent moved in the opposite direction of the other agents.

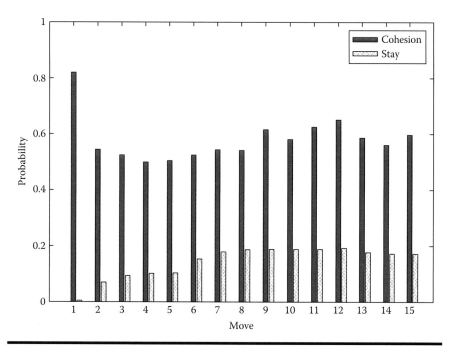

Figure 8.3 **The probability of** *cohesion* **and** *stay* **for each move in Game 5 (empirical data, averaged over 20 rounds).**

Stay: An agent could choose to stay in a field without movement and observe the status of its neighbors. In each step, we assumed that an agent would choose to stay with probability p_{stay}.

We calculated the probabilities mentioned earlier by analyzing the dataset of *Game 5*. The results are discussed in the following text.

Figure 8.3 shows the average $p_{cohesion}$ and p_{stay} of 20 round tests in *Game 5*. According to the figure, the cohesion probability was very high for each step, varying from 0.5 to 0.8, which meant the participants tended to move to the same goal as a group. In the first step, since all participants were concentrated in the origin and could observe the goal of each other, the cohesion probability was high (larger than 0.8) and the stay probability was very low. During subsequent moves, there were less neighbors to be observed, thus the cohesion probability lessened, but most of the time its probability remained above 0.5. The stay probability was estimated to be between 0.1 and 0.2 for most moves, which meant in each step, there would be a small number of participants staying still and observing the movement of others so that they could follow their movement.

Figure 8.4 shows the probability of *alignment* $p_{alignment}(\theta)$ for Game 5. According to the figure, more than half the agents had drift angle 0, which meant that the

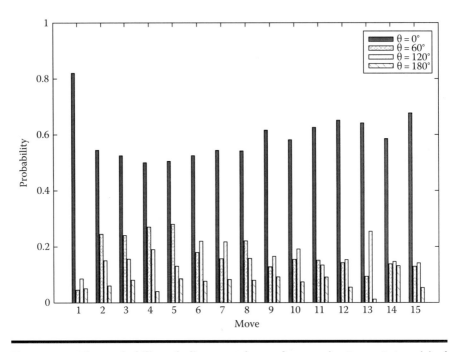

Figure 8.4 The probability of alignment for each move in Game 5 (empirical data, averaged over 20 rounds).

probability of aligning to the same angle was very high. About 20% of the agents had drift angle $\theta = 60°$. Such agents may not have followed the majority of agents, but they approached the same or the neighboring goal field as most of their neighbors. This meant the probability of a higher drift angle was very low, and the probability of $\theta = 180°$ (choosing the opposite direction of the majority of its neighbors) remained below 0.08.

The average values (from the empirical data) of the parameters are summarized in Table 8.2, which will be used in the rest of our simulation illustration.

For informed agents, their movement was straightforward: they moved directly to the €2 field without considering the movement of other neighbors. The uninformed agents determined their moves according to the group-cohesion mobility model, whose pseudocode is illustrated in Algorithm 8.1.

Table 8.2 Simulation Parameters and Their Values

Simulation Parameter	$p_{cohesion}$	p_{stay}	$p_{alignment}(\theta)$			
			$\theta = 0°$	$\theta = 60°$	$\theta = 120°$	$\theta = 180°$
Value	0.582	0.145	0.592	0.171	0.166	0.071

Algorithm 8.1: Pseudocode of the Movement of Uninformed Agents

Begin

    While (true)

    {

        (1) If a goal field is reached, return;

        (2) With probability p_{stay} stay still; break;

        (3) With probability $p_{cohesion}$ let my_goal=majority_goal, and move one step closer to my_goal; break;

        (4) With probability $p_{alignment}(\theta)$ let my_angle=*max_angle* $\pm$ θ, and move toward my_angle; break;

    }

End

8.4.2.4 Simulation Results

With the proposed group-cohesion mobility model, we conducted computer simulations to study human group movement. At the beginning, all agents were located in coordinate (0,0). For the informed agents, their goal field was the €2 field and they moved toward this goal directly. For the uninformed players, they were randomly assigned a goal and a direction initially. In each time slot, they determined their actual goal and direction according to the proposed probability mobility model. The simulation tested the following results of our empirical study:

1. *The group incentive mechanism can produce swarm-like human movement without coordination.*
2. *A minority number of informed participants with a preference can lead the majority of uninformed participants without preference to their preferred goal field.*

To test the first result, we set the number of informed agents to be 0; that is, all agents were aware of the coordinates of six goal fields but assumed an equal bonus (€1) for each goal field.

Figure 8.5 shows the distribution of final rewards of the simulation for three rounds. In the first round, there were nine agents concentrating on a €1 field (reward = €9) and one agent reached the €2 field (reward = €2). In the second round, seven agents arrived at the €2 field (reward = €14), two agents arrived at a €1 field, and one agent arrived at another €1 field. In the third round, eight agents and two agents arrived at two different €1 fields accordingly. In all the cases mentioned earlier, there was a goal field receiving the majority number of agents, which verifies that the agents moved as a group without coordination under the applied group incentive mechanism.

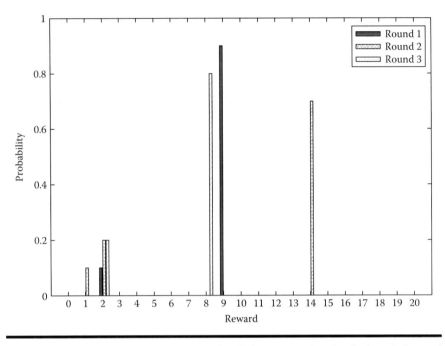

Figure 8.5 The distribution of rewards of three rounds (simulation, informed agents = 0).

We repeated the simulation for 1000 rounds; the average distribution of rewards is shown in Figure 8.6. As shown, most agents received reward 10 (with probability 0.55) and the second most received reward 9 (with probability 0.2). Figure 8.7 compares the probability of arrivals in the six goal fields. The distribution of arrivals is almost even, with probability ranging between 0.15 and 0.2. The goal field with lower ID has higher probability, since the agents chose the goal with lower ID to break the tie (i.e., if they observed two goals with the equal number of neighbors, they chose the one with lower ID).

Figure 8.8 shows the distribution of arrivals in the preferred field (€2 field). It is shown that the probability of no agent arriving there was higher than 0.8. The reason is that all agents were unaware of the €2 field, so they chose their goals at random.

The simulated collective behaviour is coincident with the empirical results from the experiments with human-directed avatars described in paragraph 4.1.3 of this chapter. Since the informed agents knew the exact bonus of each goal field, they would choose the €2 field at the beginning and move directly toward that goal without considering the movement of their neighbors. We repeated the simulation for 1000 rounds; the results are shown in Figures 8.8 through 8.10. In Figure 8.9, the probability of gaining a reward of 20 (probability = 0.28) and

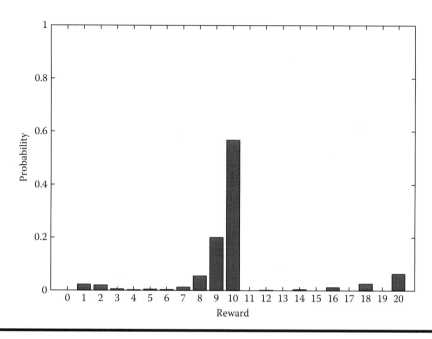

Figure 8.6 The distribution of rewards (simulation, informed agents = 0, averaged over 1000 rounds).

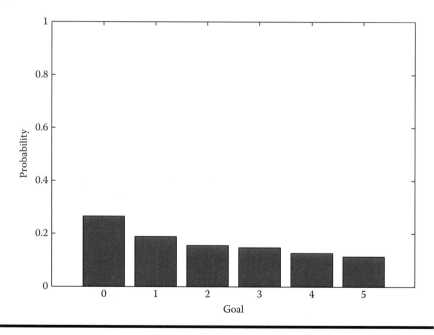

Figure 8.7 The distribution of arrivals in the six goal fields (simulation, informed agents = 0, averaged over 1000 rounds).

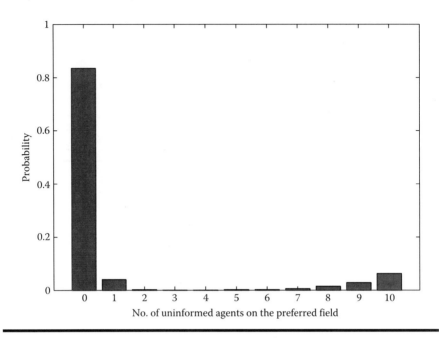

Figure 8.8 **The distribution of uninformed agents on the preferred goal fields (simulation, informed agents = 0, averaged over 1000 rounds).**

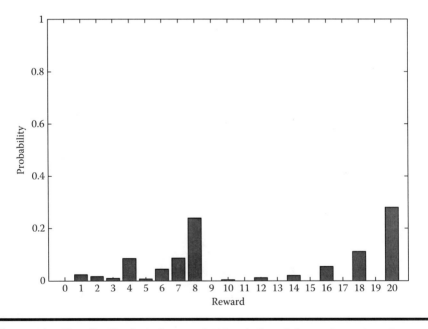

Figure 8.9 **The distribution of rewards (simulation, informed agents = 2, averaged over 1000 rounds).**

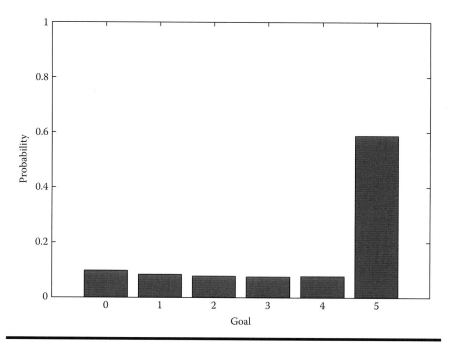

Figure 8.10   The distribution of arrivals in the six goal fields (simulation, informed agents = 2, averaged over 1000 rounds).

18 (probability = 0.11) was significantly higher than that in Figure 8.6, which meant that the overall group would receive much higher rewards when there were two informed agents involved.

Figure 8.10 shows the probability of arrivals in the different goal fields. It illustrates that the probability of arriving at goal 5 (the €2 field) was higher than 0.6, which is seven times higher than that of the other five goal fields. The distribution of arrivals in the preferred €2 goal field is illustrated in Figure 8.11. Compared to the result shown in Figure 8.8, the probability of uninformed agents arriving the €2 field was significantly increased (with probability 0.28 that eight uninformed players would arrive at the preferred €2 field). The experiments confirmed that the existence of two informed agents has significant influence on the group movement and that a minority can lead the majority to arrive at the preferred goal fields with high probability.

8.4.3 Comparison of Empirical and Simulation Results

We compared the simulation results with the empirical data, which are shown in Table 8.3. According to the table, the percentage of agents achieving a higher reward (arriving at the 2€ field) was 38.8% in simulation and 34.4% in

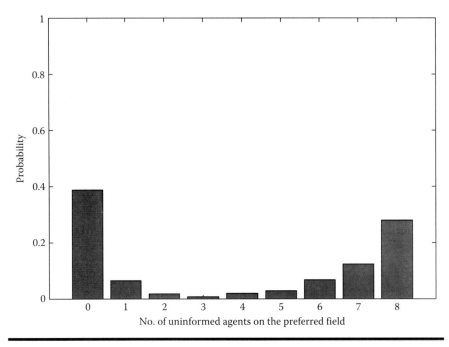

Figure 8.11 **The distribution of uninformed players on the preferred goal fields (simulation, informed agents = 2, averaged over 1000 rounds).**

Table 8.3 **Comparison of the Simulation and Empirical Results for the Arrival Rates (%) of Uninformed Players Ending Up on the Preferred €2 Goal Field in *Games 5***

Goal Fields	Empirical Results of Game 5	Simulation of Game 5
€2 field (higher reward)	34.40	38.80
€1 field (lower reward)	63.40	61.20
Elsewhere (no reward)	2.20	0.00

empirical data. The percentage of achieving a lower reward was 61.20% for simulation and 63.40% in empirical data. The simulation results fit the empirical statistics very well, confirming the effectiveness of the proposed group-cohesion mobility model.

Also, the distribution of arrival rates of uninformed majority agents on the preferred goal field of the informed minority agents (Figure 8.11) fits the empirical distribution of the human participants in our experiment (Figure 8.12).

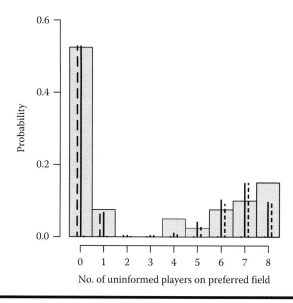

Figure 8.12 Histogram of arrivals (*n* = 40), fitted mixture of two binomials (solid lines), and contribution to probability mass function of the two binomials (dashed and dotted lines, respectively). (From Boos, M. et al., *PLoS Comput. Biol.*, 10(4), e1003541, 2014.)

8.5 Discussion

In our empirical studies reported here, we could demonstrate that self-organized patterns of collective movement emerge in groups of participants moving their avatars on a virtual playground without any other sort of communication than the pure movement behavior itself. We were also able to describe which movement behavior of a minority of participants with a preferred goal field turned out to be the most effective in influencing the majority's avatar movements toward the said preferred goal field of the minority.

Furthermore, using our computer simulation model, we were able to reproduce these empirical findings of how movement—specifically movement expressing leadership behavior—can be effective in terms of affecting arrival rates on goal fields with preferred monetary rewards. The simulation model was brought in line by probability distributions concerning cohesion and alignment behavior derived from the empirical data. Our results showed that if a minority of agents with a preferred goal field moves toward said field and majority agents without preference "vote" for one of the six possible fields and then move cohesively toward it, high arrival rates of majority agents at the goal field of the minority can be produced. In the game experiment conducted with human participants, this was achieved by "simply" using the immediacy of the initial move of an informed minority participant and the influence of an analogous movement path of the two members of the minority. We concluded from the similar distributions of participants/agents on the higher-rewarded goal field (Figures 8.11 and 8.12) that the overall behavior of human and simulated agents produces the same results.

These results of our combination of experimental research with human participant avatars and the simulation of movement behavior using the same HoneyComb paradigm demonstrate a significant advantage of this approach: The back-and-forth of empirical and simulation approaches can be very productive in identifying behavioral patterns that are not only empirically valid but also effective in terms of preset criteria. Additionally, computer simulation offers the opportunity to mix human participant avatars in our experiments with computer-simulated agents, as there are three types of move-producers who can be brought into interaction with simulated agents:

1. Random move sequence (testing for patterned behavior)
2. Move sequence out of a file of empirical or constructed data
3. Strategic move sequence computed intelligently (their move sequence conditionally computed according to past or actual movement on the playground)

To what extent is our work compatible with social network approaches? The proposed probabilistic model for computer simulation can be interpreted from a social network analysis approach. If we consider neighboring agents (whose distance is within an agent's visual radius) as socially connected, we predict that applying the proposed probabilistic computer simulation model will reveal the emergence of paths of agents who do not see each other and that from those emergences we will be able to determine the grade of connectivity of the whole or parts of the network. The local view perspective of an agent corresponds to its "egocentric" social network. An example of the egocentric network of a hypothetical agent A is illustrated in Figure 8.13, where only the agent itself and its neighbors are included. In this figure, Agent A has six neighbors, forming a network structure from its local view information. The links between nodes indicate neighboring relationships (e.g., impulses to align) during movement, and two agents can observe the behavior of each other or influence each other if and only if there is a link between them (note the exponential nature of the spread of their influence).

According to the theory of social influence (Kempe et al., 2003), the decision of a person to adopt an innovation is influenced by his or her friends. In the case of our Game 5, the participants' choice of which goal field to move toward is similarly influenced by his or her neighbors. The *independent cascade model* (Kempe et al., 2003) can be used to describe this social influence. In Figure 8.13, if a neighbor N_i chooses goal field G, its influence on Agent A to choose goal field G can

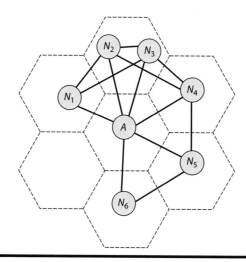

Figure 8.13   The egocentric network of an agent.

be quantified as a condition probability $P_{A,N_i} = Pr\{A \text{ chooses } G \mid N_i \text{ chooses } G\}$. However, the pairwise social influence is difficult to calculate from the empirical data of Game 5; thus, we quantify the influence of Agent A's neighbors. In our simulation model, Agent A's choice of goal field is influenced by the choice of the majority of its neighbors, which is called "cohesion," and is quantified by the probability $p_{cohesion} = Pr\{A \text{ chooses } G \mid$ the majority neighbours choose $G\}$. By using the cohesion approach to quantify agents' choices of goal fields to move toward, our probabilistic model mimics the directional alignment strategies used by humans in the social network analysis approach.

In future research, we plan to extend the social network analysis approach described earlier to reveal additional theoretical characteristics and patterns of group movement. First, we will study the *exponential increase of social influence* in group movements, since it is feasible that an individual can be influenced by not only his or her direct neighbors but also by "neighbors of neighbors." Exploring the spread of social influence of multiple hops can potentially explain how leaders can influence the choice of nonadjacent neighbors and lead them to the preferred goal field. Second, we will introduce the *cluster coefficient* to describe the regulation of distance maintained between individuals moving as a group. A higher cluster coefficient theoretically means that individuals remain relatively closer during movement; a lower cluster coefficient means that they maintain a greater distance to the other individuals in the group. Third, the evolution of *community structure* of the social network can theoretically further explain how/why the players of Game 5 divided into subgroups and arrived at different goal fields in the end.

References

Alexander, R.D. 1974. The evolution of social behavior. *Annual Review of Ecology and Systematics* 5:325–383.

Altizer, S., Nunn, C.L., Thrall, P.H. et al. 2003. Social organization and parasite risk in mammals: Integrating theory and empirical studies. *Annual Review of Ecology, Evolution and Systematics* 34:517–547.

Aoki, I. 1982. A simulation study on the schooling mechanism in fish. *Nippon Suisan Gakkai Shi* 48(8):1081–1088.

Beckman, H., Suchman, A.L., Curtin, K., and Greene, R.A. 2006. Physician reactions to quantitative individual performance reports. *American Journal of Medical Quality* 21(3):192–199.

Belz, M., Pyritz, L.W., and Boos, M. 2013. Spontaneous flocking in human groups. *Behavioural Processes* 92:6–14.

Benoit-Bird, K.J. and Au, W.W. 2009. Cooperative prey herding by the pelagic dolphin, *Stenella longirostris*. *The Journal of the Acoustical Society of America* 125(1):125–137.

Bertram, B.C.R. 1978. Living in groups: Predators and prey. In: Krebs, J.R. and Davies, N.B. (eds.), *Behavioural Ecology: An Evolutionary Approach*. Blackwell Scientific Publications, Oxford, U.K., pp. 64–96.

Boos, M., Franiel, X., and Belz, M. 2015. Competition in human groups—Impact on group cohesion, perceived stress and outcome satisfaction. *Behavioural Processes* 120:64–68.

Boos, M., Pritz, J., Lange, S., and Belz, M. 2014. Leadership in moving human groups. *PLoS Computational Biology* 10(4):e1003541.

Boos, M., Schauenburg, B., Strack, M., and Belz, M. 2013. Social validation of shared and nonvalidation of unshared information in group discussions. *Small Group Research* 45:1–15.

Camazine, S., Deneubourg, J.L., Franks, N.R., Sneyd, J., Theraulaz, G., and Bonabeau, E. 2003. *Self-Organization in Biological Systems*, 2nd edn. Princeton University Press, Princeton, NJ.

Conradt, L., Krause, J., Couzin, I.D., and Roper, T.J. 2009. Leading according to need in self-organizing groups. *The American Naturalist* 173:304–312.

Conradt, L. and List, C. 2009. Group decisions in humans and animals: A survey. *Philosophical Transactions of the Royal Society of London B: Biological Sciences* 364:719–742.

Conradt, L. and Roper, T.J. 2005. Consensus decision making in animals. *Trends in Ecology & Evolution* 20(8):449–456.

Conradt, L. and Roper, T.J. 2009. Conflicts of interest and the evolution of decision sharing. *Philosophical Transactions of the Royal Society B: Biological Sciences* 364(1518):807–819.

Couzin, I.D. 2009. Collective cognition in animal groups. *Trends in Cognitive Sciences* 13:36–43.

Couzin, I.D. and Krause, J. 2003. Self-organization and collective behavior in vertebrates. *Advances in the Study of Behavior* 32:1–75.

Couzin, I.D., Krause, J., Franks, N.R., and Levin, S.A. 2005. Effective leadership and decision-making in animal groups on the move. *Nature* 433:513–516.

Dyer, J.R.G., Johansson, A., Helbing, D., Couzin, I.D., and Krause, J. 2009. Leadership, consensus decision making and collective behaviour in humans. *Philosophical Transactions of the Royal Society B: Biological Sciences* 364(1518):781–789.

Fichtel, C., Pyritz, L., and Kappeler, P.M. 2011. Coordination of group movements in non-human primates. In: Boos, M., Kolbe, M., Kappeler, P.M., and Ellwart, T. (eds.), *Coordination in Human and Primate Groups*. Springer, Berlin, Germany, pp. 37–56.

Fischer, J. and Zinner, D. 2011. Communication and cognition in primate group movement. *International Journal of Primatology* 32(6):1279–1295.

Guy, S.J., Curtis, S., Lin, M.C., NS Manocha, D. 2012. Least-effort trajectories lead to emergent crowd behaviors. *Physical Review E* 85:016110.

Hamilton, W.D. 1971. Geometry for the selfish herd. *Journal of Theoretical Biology* 31:295–311.

Helbing, D., Molnár, P., Farkas, I.J., and Bolay, K. 2001. Self-organizing pedestrian movement. *Environment and Planning B* 28:361–383.

Katz, Y., Tunstrøm, K., Ioannou, C.C., Huepe, C., and Couzin, I.D. 2011. Inferring the structure and dynamics of interactions in schooling fish. *Proceedings of the National Academy of Sciences of the United States of America* 108:18720–18725.

King, A.J., Sueur, C., Huchard, E., and Cowlishaw, G. 2011. A rule-of-thumb based on social affiliation explains collective movements in desert baboons. *Animal Behaviour* 82:1337–1345.

Krause, J., Hoare, D.J., Croft, D. et al. 2000. Fish shoal composition: Mechanisms and constraints. *Proceedings of the Royal Society of London B: Biological Sciences* 267:2011–2017.

Krause, J. and Ruxton, G.D. 2002. *Living in Groups*. Oxford University Press, Oxford, U.K.

Kempe, D., Kleinberg, J., and Tardos, É. 2003. Maximizing the spread of influence through a social network. In *Proceedings of the Ninth ACM SIGKDD International Conference on Knowledge Discovery and Data Mining*, ACM, pp. 137–146.

Meade, J., Nam, K.B., Beckerman, A.P., and Hatchwell, B.J. 2010. Consequences of 'load-lightening' for future indirect fitness gains by helpers in a cooperatively breeding bird. *Journal of Animal Ecology* 79:529–537.

Moussaïd, M., Helbing, D., Garnier, S., Johansson, A., Combe, M., and Theraulaz, G. 2009. Experimental study of the behavioural mechanisms underlying self-organization in human crowds. *Proceedings of the Royal Society of London B: Biological Sciences* 276(1668): 2755–2762.

Parrish, J.K., Viscido, S.V., and Grünbaum, D. 2002. Self-organized fish schools: An examination of emergent properties. *The Biological Bulletin* 202:296–305.

Pearson, H.C. 2011. Sociability of female bottlenose dolphins (*Tursiops* spp.) and chimpanzees (*Pan troglodytes*): Understanding evolutionary pathways toward social convergence. *Evolutionary Anthropology: Issues, News, and Reviews* 20:85–95.

Pitcher, T.J., Magurran, A.E., and Winfield, I.J. 1982. Fish in larger shoals find food faster. *Behavioral Ecology and Sociobiology* 10:149–151.

Quinn, J.L. and Cresswell, W. 2006. Testing domains of danger in the selfish herd: Sparrowhawks target widely spaced redshanks in flocks. *Proceedings of the Royal Society of London B: Biological Sciences* 273:2521–2526.

Rands, S.A., Cowlishaw, G., Pettifor, R.A., Rowcliffe, J.M., and Johnstone, R.A. 2003. Spontaneous emergence of leaders and followers in foraging pairs. *Nature* 423:432–434.

Reebs, S.G. 2000. Can a minority of informed leaders determine the foraging movements of a fish shoal? *Animal Behaviour* 59:403–409.

Reynolds, C.W. 1987. Flocks herds, and schools: A distributed behavioral model. *ACM Siggraph Computer Graphics* 21:25–34.

Scantlebury, M., Bennett, N.C., Speakman, J.R., Pillay, N., and Schradin, C. 2006. Huddling in groups leads to daily energy savings in free-living African four-striped grass mice, Rhabdomys pumilio. *Functional Ecology* 20:166–173.

Sumpter, D.J.T. 2010. *Collective Animal Behavior*. Princeton University Press, Princeton, NJ.

Sumpter, D.J.T., Buhl, J., Biro, D., and Couzin, I.D. 2008. Information transfer in moving animal groups. *Theory in Biosciences* 127:177–186.

van Schaik, C.P. 1989. The ecology of social relationships amongst female primates. In: Standen, V. and Foley, R.A. (eds.), *Comparative Socioecology: The Behavioral Ecology of Humans and Other Mammals*. Blackwell, Oxford, U.K., pp. 195–218.

Ward, A.J., Herbert-Read, J.E., Sumpter, D.J., and Krause, J. 2011. Fast and accurate decisions through collective vigilance in fish shoals. *Proceedings of the National Academy of Sciences of the United States of America* 108:2312–2315.

Williams, J.M., Oehlert, G.W., Carlis, J.V., and Pusey, A.E. 2004. Why do male chimpanzees defend a group range? *Animal Behaviour* 68:523–532.

Chapter 9

Social Spammer and Spam Message Detection in an Online Social Network: A Codetection Approach*

Fangzhao Wu and Yongfeng Huang

Contents

---

* This chapter is an extended version of our previous work published in *CIKM'15* (Wu et al. 2015a).

9.1 Social Spammer and Spam Message Detection

9.1.1 Background and Motivation

Microblogging websites, such as Twitter and Sina Weibo, have become popular platforms for information dissemination (Hu et al. 2013). Hundreds of millions of users frequently post short messages on these websites to release latest news and share their opinions on various topics, such as political events, companies, and daily life. However, microblogging websites are also recognized as ideal places to conduct spamming due to their popularity (Stringhini et al. 2010; Zhang et al. 2012; Hu et al. 2013). Massive fake microblogging accounts, which are known as social spammers (Webb et al. 2008), post masses of spam messages for various purposes, such as conducting social advertising, collecting users' personal information, and promoting affiliate websites (Bilge et al. 2009; Lee et al. 2010). These spam messages may contain dangerous content and URLs that are related to scams, malware, and phishing (Grier et al. 2010; Lee et al. 2010; Hu et al. 2013). Spam messages are also used to conduct political astroturfing (Bilge et al. 2009; Ratkiewicz et al. 2011). These massive social spammers and spam messages seriously hurt the user experience and hinder the healthy development of microblogging systems (Lee et al. 2010). Thus, effectively detecting social spammers and spam messages is beneficial to both microblogging websites and users.

In addition, social spammer detection and spam message detection can facilitate the research on microblogging platforms significantly. For example, microblog sentiment analysis is a hot research topic and has wide applications in both academic and industrial fields (Wu et al. 2016). However, since masses of social spammers frequently post massive spam messages to conduct social advertising, the sentiments in these spam messages are usually fake and misleading. Thus, detecting social spammers and spam messages is also useful for scientific research on microblogging platforms, such as network analysis and opinion mining (Wu et al. 2016).

9.1.2 Social Spammer Detection

Social spammer detection is an important research topic and has been studied in various social networking websites, such as Twitter (Benevenuto et al. 2010), Facebook (Brown et al. 2008), YouTube (O'Callaghan et al. 2012), and Sina Weibo (Lin et al. 2013). Existing studies on social spammer detection can be roughly divided into two categories. The first category uses social network analysis to detect social spammers (Oscar and Roychowdbury 2005; Danezis and Mittal 2009; Ghosh et al. 2012). The assumption behind these methods is that social spammers cannot build a large number of social relations with legitimate users (Hu et al. 2013). However, due to the special characteristics of microblogging websites, this assumption may not hold true (Weng et al. 2010) and these methods cannot be applied to microblog spammer detection directly (Hu et al. 2013). The second category of methods is to extract effective features from users' attributes, online behaviors, and the textual contents of the messages they post and build a classifier using machine learning techniques (Benevenuto et al. 2010; Stringhini et al. 2010; Wang 2010; Lin et al. 2013; Hu et al. 2014a,b). For example, McCord and Chuah proposed to extract two kinds of features, that is, user-based features and content-based features, and use traditional classifiers, such as support vector machine (SVM) and Naive Bayes, for detecting social spammers in Twitter (McCord and Chuah 2011). The user-based features they used include the numbers of friends and followers and reputation score. The content-based features contain the numbers of URLs, key words, and hashtags in users' messages. Hu et al. (2014a) proposed to detect social spammers according to users' textual content and explored to utilize the resources from e-mail, SMS, and web spam detection fields to help train the classifier. However, social spammers may continuously change their behaviors and attributes to pretend to be normal users. In addition, they may post some normal messages besides the spam messages. These strategies may make methods mentioned earlier less accurate.

Social contexts have also been explored for social spammer detection. In Hu et al. (2013), the authors proposed to incorporate the following relations between users into the classifier learning stage by constraining that the users with social relations are assigned similar scores by the learned classifier. When a new user comes, only the textual content of his or her messages is used to classify this user. In their method, the social contexts are incorporated into the model learning stage. Even with the help of social contexts, it is still difficult to train an accurate enough social spammer classifier, since spammers' attributes, behaviors, and textual contents are continuously evolving (Hu et al. 2014b). However, the social contexts of the unseen users and messages can provide some useful information for classifying them into spam or nonspam. Thus, we believe that it is more appropriate to utilize social contexts in the prediction stage than in the model training stage.

9.1.3 Spam Message Detection

Spam detection has been extensively studied on various kinds of texts, such as e-mail (Blanzieri and Bryl 2008), web page (Gyongyi et al. 2004; Becchetti et al. 2006; Ntoulas et al. 2006), SMS (Gomez Hidalgo et al. 2006), and review (Jindal and Liu 2007). There are two main kinds of methods for spam detection, that is, link-based methods and content-based methods. Link-based methods are widely used for detecting spams in linked texts, such as web pages (Gyongyi et al. 2004; Becchetti et al. 2006). These methods are based on the assumption that spam web pages have different link patterns compared with normal web pages and they are seldom linked to high-quality web pages. For example, Becchetti et al. (2006) found that degree correlations, number of neighbors, and TrustRank score are effective metrics for web spam detection. However, since not all microblog messages contain URLs, and URLs in microblogs usually point to web pages rather than other microblog messages, these link-based methods cannot be directly used to detect spam microblog messages.

Content-based methods are extensively studied and popularly used for spam detection (Blanzieri and Bryl 2008; Ntoulas et al. 2006; Gomez Hidalgo et al. 2006; Jindal and Liu 2007; Gao et al. 2012). In these methods, effective features are first extracted from the content. Then spam classifiers are trained on labeled data using machine learning techniques. These classifiers are used to classify unseen texts into spam or nonspam according to their content. For example, Ntoulas et al. (2006) designed various features for web spam detection, such as the number of words in the page, amount of anchor text, and fraction of visible content. Then they used the C4.5 algorithm to train the classifier.

Many microblog spam message detection methods also belong to content-based methods (Song et al. 2011; Liu and Jia 2012; Martinez-Romo and Araujo 2013). For example, in order to detect malicious tweets in trending topics, Martinez-Romo and Araujo proposed to extract language model–based features, for example, the K-L divergence between a tweet and the thread of tweets in this topic. They also incorporated other content-based features, such as the numbers of URL, hashtags, and numeric characters (Martinez-Romo and Araujo 2013). However, since microblog messages are very short and noisy (Hu et al. 2013), it is quite difficult to detect all the spam messages purely according to their textual content. Different from the methods mentioned earlier, our method combines spam message detection with social spammer detection and exploits various social contexts to refine the spam message detection results.

The benefit of combining spam detection and spammer detection on web data has been observed by Chen et al. (2009). Given a set of labeled bookmarks and a set of labeled users, they trained a SVM classifier for spam detection and a SVM classifier for spammer detection simultaneously by utilizing the user–user relations and user–bookmark relations. The users with fans relation are constrained to have similar scores during training. Similarly, a user and a bookmark are constrained to be assigned similar scores by the classifiers if the bookmark is created by this user. Different from this method, our method utilizes the social context information in the prediction stage rather than the model learning stage.

9.1.4 Social Spammer and Spam Message Codetection

In general, in existing studies, social spammer detection and spam message detection are mainly regarded as two separate tasks. However, in microblogging websites, a common phenomenon is that social spammers tend to post more spam messages and spam messages have high probabilities to be posted by social spammers. Thus, there are strong connections between social spammers and spam messages. Detecting social spammers and spam messages simultaneously may achieve better performance than conducting each task in isolation. In addition, the social connections between users and those between messages may also be helpful for social spammer detection and spam message detection. For example, social spammers are often followed by other spammers because they frequently collaborate in this way to build more social relations and pretend to be normal users. Many spam messages contain the same URLs because they belong to the same promoting campaigns (Zhang et al. 2012). Some spam messages contain the same hashtags for the purpose of advertising for a brand.

Motivated by these observations, we propose here a unified framework for social spammer and spam message codetection in microblogging with various social contexts. In our framework, social spammer detection and spam message detection are bridged by the posting relations between users and messages. The results of social spammer detection can help refine the results of spam message detection and vice versa. Both the performance of social spammer detection and that of spam message detection can be boosted. In addition, our framework can incorporate the social contexts of user–user relations and message–message relations by modeling them as regularizations over the prediction results.

9.2 Social Context Extraction

9.2.1 User–Message Relation

The first kind of social contexts used in our framework is the posting relations between users and messages, that is, the user–message relations, as shown in Figure 9.1. It has been widely recognized in social spammer detection and spam filtering fields that social spammers tend to post more spam messages than legitimate users, and spam messages have higher probabilities to be posted by social spammers rather than legitimate users (Zhang et al. 2012; Hu et al. 2013). Thus, social spammer detection and spam message detection are not independent tasks. In fact, they are closely connected by the social connections between users and messages. Detecting

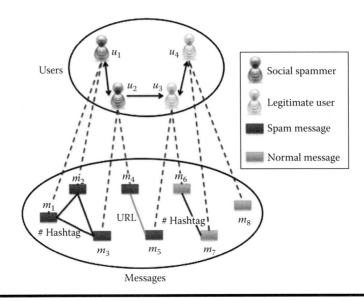

Figure 9.1 An illustrative example of the social contexts used in our framework.

spam messages can help identify more potential social spammers. In turn, if we find that some users are social spammers, we can obtain more candidate spam messages.

Denote $\mathcal{U}$ as the set of users and $\mathcal{M}$ as the set of messages. $U = |\mathcal{U}|$ and $M = |\mathcal{M}|$ are the numbers of all users and messages. We model the user–message relations using matrix $\mathbf{P} \in \mathbb{R}^{U \times M}$. If message j is posted by user i, then $P_{i,j} = 1$. Otherwise, $P_{i,j} = 0$. For example, in Figure 9.1, messages m_1 and m_3 are posted by u_1 and u_2, respectively, and then $P_{u_1, m_1} = 1$ and $P_{u_2, m_3} = 1$.

9.2.2 User–User Relation

Microblogging platform is one kind of online social networks (OSNs) and microblog users are networked. If a user wants to receive messages from some other users, he or she can just follow them. However, different from other OSNs such as Facebook, a user in microblogging platforms can follow anyone without the followee's prior permission. Thus, the social relations among microblogging users are directed.

A common observation in social spammer detection is that social spammers usually follow each other in order to gain more followers and pretend to be normal users (Hu et al. 2013). Legitimate users also follow each other frequently, partially because they know each other offline. Thus, if two users follow each other, they have a high probability to be both social spammers or both legitimate users. However, it is also frequently observed in microblogging platforms that some social spammers follow a large number of legitimate users in order to gain enough social relations with legitimate users and obtain high social influence (Weng et al. 2010). Although social spammers can follow legitimate users, it is not very likely that legitimate users will follow them.

Motivated by observations mentioned earlier, we extract two kinds of user–user relations. The first kind is friend relation, which means that two users follow each other. We use matrix $\mathbf{F} \in \mathbb{R}^{U \times U}$ to denote friend relation. If users i and j follow each other, then $F_{i,j} = 1$ and $F_{j,i} = 1$. Otherwise, $F_{i,j} = 0$ and $F_{j,i} = 0$. The second kind of user–user relation is following relation. Different from friend relation, following relation is directed. We use $\mathbf{D} \in \mathbb{R}^{U \times U}$ to denote this relation. If user i follows user j, but user j does not follow user i, then $D_{i,j} = 1$ and $D_{j,i} = 0$. Otherwise, $D_{i,j} = 0$.

9.2.3 Message–Message Relation

Normal messages may be related to various topics. However, masses of spam messages share the same targets. This is because spam messages are usually not used independently. In fact, many of them are used collectively to promote the same products, services, or websites. For example, researchers have found that many spam accounts are manipulated by a small group of spammers. They use these accounts to post massive spam messages for some promoting campaigns by adding the same URLs into these messages (Zhang et al. 2012). In addition, some researchers have found that spam messages share highly similar content and the same hashtags (Beck 2011; Lin et al. 2013).

Motivated by these observations, we propose to extract social connections for microblog messages. We define that the message–message relations are undirected, and if two messages are related to the same target, then they are connected. Denote $\mathbf{T} \in \mathbb{R}^{M \times M}$ as the social connections between messages. If message i and message j share the same target, then $T_{i,j} = 1$ and $T_{j,i} = 1$. Otherwise, $T_{i,j} = 0$ and $T_{j,i} = 0$. In this chapter, if two messages contain the same URL or hashtag, then we consider them to be related to the same target and connected with each other. For example, in Figure 9.1, since messages m_4 and m_5 have the same URL, and messages m_6 and m_7 contain the same hashtag, then T_{m_4,m_5}, T_{m_5,m_4}, T_{m_6,m_7}, T_{m_7,m_6} all equal to 1.

9.3 Social Spammer and Spam Message Codetection

9.3.1 Notations

First, we introduce several notations that will be used in the following discussions. Denote the set of microblog users to be classified as $\mathcal{U}$ and the size of $\mathcal{U}$ as U. Similarly, denote $\mathcal{M}$ as the set of microblog messages to be classified and the size of $\mathcal{M}$ as M. Following the notations used in the previous section, we denote here $\mathbf{P} \in \mathbb{R}^{U \times M}$ as the user–message relation matrix, $\mathbf{F} \in \mathbb{R}^{U \times U}$ as the friend relation between users, $\mathbf{D} \in \mathbb{R}^{U \times U}$ as the following relation between users, and $\mathbf{T} \in \mathbb{R}^{M \times M}$ as the message–message relation. Assuming that we already have a social spammer classifier $f_U(\cdot)$ and a spam message classifier $f_M(\cdot)$, which are trained on labeled datasets using machine learning techniques, denote $\mathbf{u} \in \mathbb{R}^{U \times 1}$ as the classification results of $\mathcal{U}$ using the social spammer classifier $f_U(\cdot)$, where positive values indicate social spammers and negative values indicate normal users. Similarly, denote $\mathbf{m} \in \mathbb{R}^{M \times 1}$ as the classification results of $\mathcal{M}$ using the spam message classifier $f_M(\cdot)$, where positive values indicate spam messages and negative values indicate normal messages. Since the features of social spammers and spam messages are continuously evolving, the social spammer classification results $\mathbf{u}$ and the spam message classification results $\mathbf{m}$ may not be accurate enough. So we incorporate the social contexts to refine them. Denote $\mathbf{x} \in \mathbb{R}^{U \times 1}$ and $\mathbf{y} \in \mathbb{R}^{M \times 1}$ as the final classification scores of $\mathcal{U}$ and $\mathcal{M}$ outputted by our framework.

9.3.2 Model

Our solution to the problem of social spammer and spam message codetection in microblogging with various social contexts is a unified framework defined as follows:

$$\arg\min_{\mathbf{x},\mathbf{y}} \mathcal{L}(\mathbf{x},\mathbf{y}) = \sum_{i=1}^{U}(x_i - u_i)^2 + \sum_{i=1}^{M}(y_i - m_i)^2 + \alpha \sum_{i=1}^{U}\sum_{j \neq i} F_{i,j}\left|x_i - x_j\right|$$

$$+ \beta \sum_{i=1}^{U}\sum_{j \neq i} D_{i,j}\left(x_j - x_i\right) - \lambda \sum_{i=1}^{U}\sum_{j=1}^{M} P_{i,j} x_i y_j + \gamma \sum_{i=1}^{M}\sum_{j \neq i} T_{i,j}\left|y_i - y_j\right|$$

$$(9.1)$$

where α, β, λ, and γ are nonnegative regularization parameters. The terms $\sum_{i=1}^{U}(x_i - u_i)^2$ and $\sum_{i=1}^{M}(y_i - m_i)^2$ mean that we hope the final prediction results do not differ too much from the original classification results. In other words, we take the classification results generated by the existing social spammer classifier and spam message classifier as the prior knowledge. The terms $\sum_{i=1}^{U}\sum_{j \neq i} F_{i,j}\left|x_i - x_j\right|$ and $\sum_{i=1}^{M}\sum_{j \neq i} T_{i,j}\left|y_i - y_j\right|$ are motivated by graph-guided fused lasso (Chen et al. 2012), which can exploit the graph structure over the output variables for structured regression and classification. $\sum_{i=1}^{U}\sum_{j \neq i} F_{i,j}\left|x_i - x_j\right|$ means that if two microblog users follow each other, then their spam scores should be similar, that is, they tend to be both social spammers or legitimate users. $\sum_{i=1}^{M}\sum_{j \neq i} T_{i,j}\left|y_i - y_j\right|$ is introduced to constrain that if two microblog messages contain the same hashtag or refer to the same URL, then these messages tend to be both spam or nonspam and should be assigned similar spam scores. $\sum_{i=1}^{U} \sum_{j \neq i} D_{i,j} (x_j - x_i)$ incorporates the directed following relations between users. The insight behind this term is that if user i follows user j while user j does not follow user i, then user i has a higher probability to be a social spammer than user j. Thus if the spam score of user j exceeds that of user i, a penalty will occur. The term $\sum_{i=1}^{U} \sum_{j=1}^{M} P_{i,j} x_i y_j$ is introduced to combine the social spammer classification results with spam message classification results. This term constrains that if a message j is posted by user i, then they should have the same spam label, that is, be both positive (spam) and negative (nonspam). This is motivated by the observation that social spammers tend to post spam messages, while legitimate users tend to post more normal messages. If message j is posted by user i, but they are assigned different spam labels, then a penalty will be triggered (note that there is a minus sign before this term in Equation 9.1). Thus, our model defined in Equation 9.1 can incorporate various social contexts into a unified framework for social spammers and spam messages codetection.

9.3.3 Optimization Method

Next, we discuss how to solve our framework in Equation 9.1 efficiently. The optimization problem in Equation 9.1 is convex with respect to $\mathbf{x}$ and $\mathbf{y}$, respectively. However, it may be nonconvex with respect to $\mathbf{x}$ and $\mathbf{y}$ together, which can be verified using the second-order condition (Boyd and Vandenberghe 2004). Thus, there is no analytical solution for the optimization problem in Equation 9.1. Here we introduce an iterative optimization method to solve our framework.

First, we introduce several new notations. Assuming that there are n_F nonzero elements in $\mathbf{F}$, then we define $\mathbf{A} \in \mathbb{R}^{n_F \times U}$ as an equivalent representation of $\mathbf{F}$. If $F_{i,j}$ is the nth nonzero element in $\mathbf{F}$, then $A_{n,i} = 1$ and $A_{n,j} = -1$. Other elements in the nth row of $\mathbf{A}$ are all zeros. Similarly, we define $\mathbf{B} \in \mathbb{R}^{n_D \times U}$ and $\mathbf{C} \in \mathbb{R}^{n_T \times M}$ as the equivalent representations of $\mathbf{D}$ and $\mathbf{T}$, respectively, where n_D and n_T are the numbers of nonzero elements in $\mathbf{D}$ and $\mathbf{T}$. Then the optimization problem in Equation 9.1 can be equivalently reformulated as follows:

$$\arg\min_{\mathbf{x},\mathbf{y}} \mathcal{L}(\mathbf{x}, \mathbf{y}) = \|\mathbf{x} - \mathbf{u}\|_2^2 + \|\mathbf{y} - \mathbf{m}\|_2^2 + \alpha \|\mathbf{Ax}\|_1 - \beta \mathbf{1}^T \mathbf{Bx} - \lambda \mathbf{x}^T \mathbf{Py} + \gamma \|\mathbf{Cy}\|_1 \quad (9.2)$$

Inspired by Ding et al. (2010), we propose to optimize $\mathbf{x}$ and $\mathbf{y}$ alternatively. When updating $\mathbf{x}$, $\mathbf{y}$ will be fixed. Similarly, $\mathbf{x}$ will be fixed when updating $\mathbf{y}$. The optimization problem in each step of the alternative algorithm is convex, and a unique optimal solution exists. The alternative algorithm continues until converges.

Next, we introduce how to update $\mathbf{x}$ and $\mathbf{y}$, respectively.

9.3.3.1 Updating x

When updating **x** in the tth iteration, we fix **y** as $\mathbf{y}^t$, and optimizing the objective function in Equation 9.2 is equivalent to the following optimization problem:

$$\arg\min_{x} \mathcal{L}(x) = \|x - u\|_2^2 + \alpha\|Ax\|_1 - \beta\mathbf{1}^T Bx - \lambda x^T Py^t \tag{9.3}$$

We can prove that the optimization problem in Equation 9.3 is convex (Boyd and Vandenberghe 2004; Ding et al. 2010). However, the objective function in Equation 9.3 is not smooth with respect to **x**, due to the term $\|Ax\|_1$. Thus, it cannot be solved using the standard gradient descent method. Although we can solve Equation 9.3 using subgradient descent method, the convergence rate of subgradient descent method is O(1/k) (Beck and Teboulle 2009), where k is the number of iterations, which is unsatisfactory. In order to solve the optimization problem in Equation 9.3 more efficiently, here we propose to solve it using alternating direction method of multipliers (ADMM) (Boyd et al. 2011), which has a convergence rate of O(1/k). The detailed algorithm can be found in Wu et al. (2015a).

9.3.3.2 Updating y

Next, we discuss how to update **y** in Equation 9.2. Since **x** is fixed to be $\mathbf{x}^{t+1}$ when updating **y** in the tth iteration, minimizing the objective function in Equation 9.2 is equivalent to the following optimization problem:

$$\arg\min_{y} \mathcal{L}(y) = \|y - m\|_2^2 - \lambda \mathbf{x}^{{t+1}^T} Py + \gamma\|Cy\|_1 \tag{9.4}$$

We can verify that this is a convex optimization problem. It is also nonsmooth due to the term $\|Cy\|_1$. Thus, again, we can apply ADMM to solve this optimization problem efficiently. The detailed algorithm can also be found in Wu et al. (2015a).

9.4 Experimental Evaluation

9.4.1 Dataset

In this section, we introduce the dataset used in our experiments. We first crawled a large microblog dataset using API from Sina Weibo, which is the most popular microblogging website in China. The time period of this data crawling process is from January 1, 2015, to February 1, 2015. Then we randomly selected 200 users who frequently used some third-party APIs to automatically post microblog messages in our dataset. We found that these users tend to be social spammers. In addition, we randomly selected 200 verified users from our dataset, since verified users have a high probability to be legitimate users. We merged these 400 users together and used them as seed users. Then we crawled followers and followees of these users. Finally, we obtained 5090 users in total including the seed users. Among these users, there are 433 friend relations and 4748 following relations. We also crawled the profiles and recent microblog messages of these users from their microblogging homepages. We obtained 53,484 messages in total. We used the URLs and hashtags contained in these messages to build connections between them and obtained 234,375 message–message relations. We manually labeled each user and each message into spam or normal. We used +1 as the spam label and –1 as the normal label.

Several preprocessing steps were conducted before experiments. First, feature vectors were extracted for each user and each message. User features were extracted according to the suggestions in Benevenuto et al. (2010), which contain both content attributes and behavior attributes. Message features were constructed using term frequency–inverse document frequency (TF–IDF). Stop words were removed. Fivefold cross-validation was used in all our experiments. The dataset was randomly divided into five parts with equal size, where three for training, one for validation, and one for test. The parameters of our approach and all the baseline methods were tuned on validation sets. All the experiments were repeated ten times independently, and the average results on test sets were reported.

9.4.2 Model Comparison

The model of our approach (Equation 9.1) is motivated by graph-guided fused lasso. In our model, the three kinds of social contexts, that is, the user–message relations, the user–user relations, and the message–message relations, are regarded as the graph structure over the spam scores of users and messages and incorporated into our model as regularization terms. In order to verify the advantage of our graph-guided fused lasso–based model, here we introduce an interesting alternative model for our approach by replacing all the L_1-norm regularization terms with L_2-norm regularization terms. This L_2-norm regularization model is motivated by label propagation, where each user and each message are regarded as the nodes of a bipartite graph, and the social contexts are regarded as the edges between these nodes. The initial spam scores of these nodes are propagated over the graph along these edges until converge. We can verify that the optimization problem in this model is convex, and we apply the gradient descent method to solve it. The performance of the L_2-norm regularization model (denoted as L_2 model) and our graph-guided fused lasso–based model in Equation 9.1 (denoted as L_1 model) is shown in Table 9.1.

Table 9.1 shows that the L_1-norm regularization model (Equation 9.1) performs consistently better than the L_2-norm regularization model. It indicates that graph-guided fused lasso is more suitable for our social spammer and spam message codetection approach than label propagation. Thus, in all the following experiments, we used the graph-guided fused lasso–based model for our approach.

Table 9.1 Comparison between Two Different Types of Models for Our Approach

	Half Training Data		All Training Data	
Method	*Spammer*	*Spam*	*Spammer*	*Spam*
L_2 model	0.8546	0.9122	0.8582	0.9186
L_1 model	0.8637	0.9228	0.8673	0.9297

9.4.3 Performance Evaluation

In this section, we evaluate the performance of our framework on both social spammer classification and spam message classification by comparing it with several baseline methods. The methods to be compared are listed as follows:

- *SVM*: A standard supervised classification method, widely used in social spammer detection and spam message classification (Blanzieri and Bryl 2008; Chen et al. 2009; McCord and Chuah 2011).
- *Logistic regression* (*LR*): Another widely used supervised classification method (Blanzieri and Bryl 2008; Liu and Jia 2012).
- *LS_Lasso*: Least squares method with lasso regularization (Tibshirani 1996). Some researchers found that since microblog data are noisy and sparse, it is beneficial to use sparse learning techniques such as lasso for social spammer detection and spam message classification (Hu et al. 2013).
- *SSDM*: Social Spam Detection in Microblogging, which is proposed in Hu et al. (2013). This method is based on LS_Lasso and incorporates the social relations between users into the model learning stage.
- *Coclassify*: The method proposed in Chen et al. (2009), which trains a social spammer SVM classifier and a spam message SVM classifier simultaneously by incorporating the user–message relations. Note that in this method the social contexts are also used in the model learning stage.
- *S3MCD*: This is our proposed framework for *s*ocial *s*pammer and *s*pam *mes*sage *co*detection in microblogging. The initial classification results used in our approach were generated using LR.

The experimental results are shown in Figures 9.2 and 9.3. By comparing the accuracies of different methods in Figures 9.2 and 9.3, we have the following observations:

First, our S3MCD method achieves the best performance among all the methods compared here on both social spammer detection and spam message classification with different sizes of training data. We used two-sample one-tail *t*-tests to compare the results of our S3MCD method with those of the baseline methods. The hypothesis testing results show that our S3MCD method performs

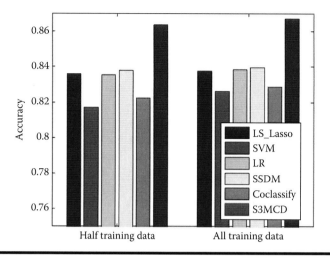

Figure 9.2   **The performance of different methods on social spammer detection.**

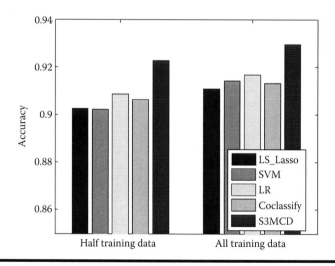

Figure 9.3   **The performance of different methods on spam message detection.**

significantly better than all the baseline methods with the significance level 0.01. Our S3MCD method can outperform traditional classification methods (such as SVM and LR) and the method based on sparse learning (LS_Lasso) because the attributes and content of social spammers and spam messages are various and evolving, and it is quite difficult to build an accurate enough classifier for social spammer detection and spam message detection using traditional classification methods. Our S3MCD method tries to alleviate this difficulty by exploiting the social contexts of users and messages to refine the classification results, which can provide additional information besides the attributes, behaviors, and textual content information. The experimental results show that incorporating social contexts into our framework can improve the classification accuracy significantly. These results validate the usefulness of social contexts in social spammer detection and spam message detection. SSDM and coclassify methods also incorporate social contexts for social spammer detection and/or spam message detection. The main difference between these methods and our method is the way of utilizing social contexts. In SSDM and coclassify, the social contexts are used in the model learning stage to constrain the user–user pair or user–message pair with social relations to have similar scores. However, in the prediction stage, only the textual content and attributes are considered. Due to the same reasons mentioned previously, it is still difficult to train an accurate enough classifier even with the help of social contexts. Different from these methods, in our S3MCD framework, the social contexts are used in the prediction stage. We exploit the graph structure over the output variables extracted from the various kinds of social connections between users and messages to make more accurate predictions. The superior performance of our S3MCD method compared with those of SSDM and coclassify validates the advantage of our S3MCD framework in utilizing social contexts for social spammer detection and spam message detection.

9.4.4 Influence of Classifier Type

In our social spammer and spam message codetection approach, supervised social spammer classifier and spam message classifier are used to assign the initial spam scores to users and messages. Thus, the type of the social spammer classifier and

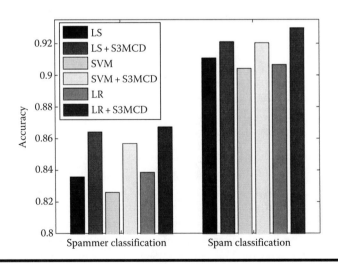

Figure 9.4 The performance of our approach with different kinds of classifiers.

spam message classifier is an important factor that may influence these spam scores and further influence the performance of our approach. Thus, in this section, we conducted experiments to explore the influence of classifier type on our S3MCD approach. We want to verify whether our approach can work under different types of classifiers. Three kinds of popular classifiers in social spammer detection and spam message detection are introduced and compared here, that is, SVM, least squares method with L_1-norm regularization (LS), and LR. The performance of our approach with different kinds of classifiers is summarized in Figure 9.4.

Figure 9.4 illustrates that our approach can consistently improve the performance of both social spammer detection and spam message detection tasks, no matter what kind of classifier is used to assign the initial spam scores. Thus, the experimental results validate that our approach is robust to the type of the social spammer classifier and spam message classifier.

9.5 Conclusion

Due to the popularity of microblogging websites, there are a large number of social spammers on them. These social spammers post massive spam messages to conduct social spamming, which contain noisy, even dangerous content. Detecting these social spammers and spam messages can help improve user experience and is beneficial to the healthy development of microblogging websites.

Here we present a unified framework for social spammer and spam message codetection in microblogging. Our framework can incorporate various social contexts of the microblog users and messages and refine the results of social spammer classification and spam message classification by exploiting their social connections. Three kinds of social contexts are extracted, that is, the friend and following relations between users, the posting relations between users and messages, and the connections between messages. In our framework, the social spammer detection and spam message detection are combined using the posting relations between users and messages. The friend and following relations between users and the connections between messages are modeled as regularization terms over the prediction results in our framework. Extensive experiments on a real-world microblog dataset show that our framework can improve the performance of social spammer detection and spam message detection effectively.

References

Becchetti, L.; Castillo, C.; Donato, D.; Leonardi, S.; and Baeza-Yates, R. A. 2006. Link-based characterization and detection of web spam. In *AIRWeb*, Seattle, WA, pp. 1–8.

Beck, A. and Teboulle, M. 2009. A fast iterative shrinkage thresholding algorithm for linear inverse problems. *SIAM Journal on Imaging Sciences* 2(1):183–202.

Beck, K. 2011. Analyzing tweets to identify malicious messages. In *IEEE International Conference on Electro/Information Technology (EIT)*, Mankato, MN, pp. 1–5. IEEE.

Benevenuto, F.; Magno, G.; Rodrigues, T.; and Almeida, V. 2010. Detecting spammers on twitter. In *Collaboration, Electronic Messaging, Anti-abuse and Spam Conference (CEAS)*, Redmond, WA, Vol. 6, p. 12.

Bilge, L.; Strufe, T.; Balzarotti, D.; and Kirda, E. 2009. All your contacts are belong to us: Automated identity theft attacks on social networks. In *WWW*, Madrid, Spain, pp. 551–560. ACM.

Blanzieri, E. and Bryl, A. 2008. A survey of learning-based techniques of email spam filtering. *Artificial Intelligence Review* 29(1):63–92.

Boyd, S.; Parikh, N.; Chu, E.; Peleato, B.; and Eckstein, J. 2011. Distributed optimization and statistical learning via the alternating direction method of multipliers. *Foundations and Trends R in Machine Learning* 3(1):1–122.

Boyd, S. and Vandenberghe, L. 2004. *Convex Optimization*. Cambridge University Press, Cambridge, England.

Brown, G.; Howe, T.; Ihbe, M.; Prakash, A.; and Borders, K. 2008. Social networks and context-aware spam. In *Proceedings of the 2008 ACM Conference on Computer Supported Cooperative Work*, San Diego, CA, pp. 403–412. ACM.

Chen, F.; Tan, P.-N.; and Jain, A. K. 2009. A coclassification framework for detecting web spam and spammers in social media web sites. In *CIKM*, Hong Kong, China, pp. 1807–1810. ACM.

Chen, X.; Kim, S.; Lin, Q.; Carbonell, J. G.; and Xing, E. P. 2012. Smoothing proximal gradient method for general structured sparse regression. *The Annals of Applied Statistics* 6(2):719–752.

Danezis, G. and Mittal, P. 2009. Sybilinfer: Detecting sybil nodes using social networks. In *NDSS*, San Diego, CA.

Ding, C.; Li, T.; and Jordan, M. I. 2010. Convex and seminonnegative matrix factorizations. *TPAMI* 32(1):45–55.

Gao, H.; Chen, Y.; Lee, K.; Palsetia, D.; and Choudhary, A. N. 2012. Towards online spam filtering in social networks. In *NDSS*, San Diego, CA.

Ghosh, S.; Viswanath, B.; Kooti, F.; Sharma, N. K.; Korlam, G.; Benevenuto, F.; Ganguly, N.; and Gummadi, K. P. 2012. Understanding and combating link farming in the twitter social network. In *WWW*, Lyon, France, pp. 61–70. ACM.

Gomez Hidalgo, J. M.; Bringas, G. C.; Sánz, E. P.; and Garcıa, F. C. 2006. Content based sms spam filtering. In *Proceedings of the 2006 ACM Symposium on Document Engineering*, Amsterdam, the Netherlands, pp. 107–114. ACM.

Grier, C.; Thomas, K.; Paxson, V.; and Zhang, M. 2010. @ spam: The underground on 140 characters or less. In *Proceedings of the 17th ACM Conference on Computer and Communications Security*, Chicago, IL, pp. 27–37. ACM.

Gyongyi, Z.; Garcia-Molina, H.; and Pedersen, J. 2004. Combating web spam with trustrank. In *VLDB*, Toronto, Ontario, Canada, pp. 576–587. VLDB Endowment.

Hu, X.; Tang, J.; and Liu, H. 2014a. Leveraging knowledge across media for spammer detection in microblogging. In *SIGIR*, Gold Coast, Queensland, Australia, pp. 547–556. ACM.

Hu, X.; Tang, J.; and Liu, H. 2014b. Online social spammer detection. In *AAAI*, Québec City, Québec, Canada.

Hu, X.; Tang, J.; Zhang, Y.; and Liu, H. 2013. Social spammer detection in microblogging. In *IJCAI*, Beijing, China, pp. 2633–2639. AAAI Press.

Jindal, N. and Liu, B. 2007. Review spam detection. In *WWW*, Banff, Alberta, Canada, pp. 1189–1190. ACM.

Lee, K.; Caverlee, J.; and Webb, S. 2010. Uncovering social spammers: Social honeypots+ machine learning. In *SIGIR*, UniMail, Geneva, Switzerland, pp. 435–442. ACM.

Lin, C.; He, J.; Zhou, Y.; Yang, X.; Chen, K.; and Song, L. 2013. Analysis and identification of spamming behaviors in sina weibo microblog. In *Proceedings of the Seventh Workshop on Social Network Mining and Analysis*, Chicago, IL, p. 5. ACM.

Liu, L. and Jia, K. 2012. Detecting spam in chinese microblogs-a study on sina weibo. In *Eighth International Conference on Computational Intelligence and Security (CIS)*, Guangzhou, China, pp. 578–581. IEEE.

Martinez-Romo, J. and Araujo, L. 2013. Detecting malicious tweets in trending topics using a statistical analysis of language. *Expert Systems with Applications* 40(8):2992–3000.

McCord, M. and Chuah, M. 2011. Spam detection on twitter using traditional classifiers. In *Autonomic and Trusted Computing,* Lecture Notes in Computer Science, pp. 175–186. Springer, Berlin, Germany.

Ntoulas, A.; Najork, M.; Manasse, M.; and Fetterly, D. 2006. Detecting spam web pages through content analysis. In *WWW*, Edinburgh, Scotland, U.K., pp. 83–92. ACM.

O'Callaghan, D.; Harrigan, M.; Carthy, J.; and Cunningham, P. 2012. Network analysis of recurring youtube spam campaigns. In *ICWSM*, Dublin, Ireland.

Oscar, P. and Roychowdbury, V. 2005. Leveraging social networks to fight spam. *IEEE Computer* 38(4):61–68.

Ratkiewicz, J.; Conover, M.; Meiss, M.; Gonçalves, B.; Patil, S.; Flammini, A.; and Menczer, F. 2011. Truthy: Mapping the spread of astroturf in microblog streams. In *WWW*, Hyderabad, India, pp. 249–252. ACM.

Song, J.; Lee, S.; and Kim, J. 2011. Spam filtering in twitter using sender-receiver relationship. In *Recent Advances in Intrusion Detection*, Lecture Notes in Computer Science, pp. 301–317. Springer, Berlin, Germany.

Stringhini, G.; Kruegel, C.; and Vigna, G. 2010. Detecting spammers on social networks. In *Proceedings of the 26th Annual Computer Security Applications Conference*, Orlando, FL, pp. 1–9. ACM.

Tibshirani, R. 1996. Regression shrinkage and selection via the lasso. *Journal of the Royal Statistical Society. Series B (Methodological)* 58: 267–288.

Wang, A. H. 2010. Don't follow me: Spam detection in twitter. In *Proceedings of the 2010 International Conference on Security and Cryptography*, Athens, Greece, pp. 1–10. IEEE.

Webb, S.; Caverlee, J.; and Pu, C. 2008. Social honeypots: Making friends with a spammer near you. In *CEAS*, San Francisco, CA.

Weng, J.; Lim, E.-P.; Jiang, J.; and He, Q. 2010. Twitterrank: Finding topic-sensitive influential twitterers. In *WSDM*, New York, pp. 261–270. ACM.

Wu, F.; Huang, Y.; and Song, Y. 2016. Microblog sentiment classification with contextual knowledge regularization. *Neurocomputing* 175: 599–609.

Wu, F.; Shu, J.; Huang Y.; and Yuan, Z. 2015a. Social spammer and spam message co-detection in microblogging with social context regularization. In *CIKM*, Melbourne, Victoria, Australia, pp. 1601–1610. ACM.

Wu, F.; Song, Y.; and Huang, Y. 2015b. Microblog sentiment classification with contextual knowledge regularization. In *AAAI*, Austin, TX, pp. 2332–2338. AAAI.

Zhang, X.; Zhu, S.; and Liang, W. 2012. Detecting spam and promoting campaigns in the twitter social network. In *ICDM*, Brussels, Belgium, pp. 1194–1199.

SOCIAL NETWORKS IV

AS COMPLEX

SYSTEMS AND THEIR

APPLICATIONS

Chapter 10

Cultural Anthropology through the Lens of *Wikipedia*

Peter A. Gloor, Joao Marcos, Patrick M. de Boer, Hauke Fuehres, Wei Lo, and Keiichi Nemoto

Contents

10.1 Introduction

Over the last 10 years, the web has become a mirror of the real world (Gloor et al. 2009, 2015). More recently, the web has also begun to influence the real world: societal events such as the Arab Spring and the Chilean student unrest have drawn a large part of their impetus from the Internet and online social networks. In the meantime, *Wikipedia* has become one of the top 10 websites,* occasionally beating daily newspapers in the actuality of most recent news. Be it the resignation of German national soccer team captain Philipp Lahm or the downing of Malaysian Airlines Flight 17 in Ukraine by a guided missile, the corresponding *Wikipedia* page is updated as soon as the actual event happens (Becker 2012, Futterer et al. 2013).

In an ongoing project at the MIT Center for Collective Intelligence started in 2008 (Iba et al. 2010, Gloor et al. 2005), we are using *Wikipedia* as a "socioscope" to study different aspects of intercultural human evolution. We draw on different-language Wikipedias to provide a mirror of today's historical understanding of world history through different cultures to measure differences in gender equality, track emotionality and positive sentiment in different-language news, and assess whether war and conquest or science and art are considered more important in different cultures.

We are using Wikipedia in different languages as a window into the "soul" of different cultures, replacing anthropological fieldwork with statistical analysis of the treatment given by native speakers of a culture to different subjects in *Wikipedia*. One of the most popular categories in *Wikipedia* is the people pages, talking about the most important people of all ages. Wikipedians have put together "notability criteria" that clearly define if a person deserves inclusion into *Wikipedia* or not. In earlier work, we have used the people pages in *Wikipedia* to identify the most influential thought leaders, idea givers, and academics through social network analysis techniques (Frick et al. 2013) and have calculated maps of the most influential people in the different-language Wikipedias (Kleeb et al. 2012).

In this chapter, we introduce Wikihistory, a dynamic temporal map of the most influential people of all times in four different Wikipedias (English, German, Chinese, and Japanese) and then look at gender distribution in the English, Portuguese, Spanish, and German Wikipedias among people considered noteworthy, resulting in a comparison among cultures on the subject of gender equality. In addition, we also compare sentiment and emotionality of news articles in the English, Spanish, Portuguese, and German Wikinews, a hand-curated news page that is part of *Wikipedia*.

---

* http://www.alexa.com/topsites.

10.1.1 Bias of Wikipedia

For different parts of our analysis, we rely on the English, German, Chinese, Japanese, Portuguese, and Spanish Wikipedias. While the German, Japanese, and Portuguese Wikipedias are more or less representative of their language spaces, things are more complex for the English, Chinese, and Spanish Wikipedias. Owing to the global dominance of the English language, the English *Wikipedia* is by far the largest, with 1.4 million monthly page edits in the United States (with U.S. population of 308 million) and 486,000 page edits in the United Kingdom (with a UK population of 62 million). To a smaller extent, English Wikipedians also exhibit some political bias, as they have a reputation of having a leftist liberal bent. In a study, Greenstein and Zhu (2012) found that compared to the early days of *Wikipedia*, the liberal bias, while still there, has been reduced. They found that phrases like "civil rights" and "trade deficit" favored by Democrats are still more prominent than phrases like "economic growth" and "illegal immigration" favored by Republicans. We speculate that the other Wikipedias we analyzed might exhibit a similar bias, as most editors are intellectuals, journalists, and academics, which have been shown to have left-leaning sympathies in general (Brint 1984, Blodget 2009).

While the English *Wikipedia* could claim to reflect the dominant view of the world, it comes with a heavy bias toward the worldview of the United States and United Kingdom. This is in contrast to the Chinese *Wikipedia*, with 51,000 monthly edits in Hong Kong (with a population of 7 million), 46,000 monthly edits in Taiwan (with a population of 23 million), and 35,000 monthly edits in mainland China (with a population of 1.3 billion people). As *Wikipedia* is officially blocked in China, editing is done to a large part in Hong Kong and Taiwan; however, as we will see in the following, based on the importance of communist heroes in the Chinese *Wikipedia*, we suspect that Chinese censors are actively editing the Chinese *Wikipedia*.

The Spanish *Wikipedia* on the other hand draws on not only a widely distributed editor base in Spain, but also many contributors in more populous Latin American countries such as Colombia and Mexico and some very active editor communities in Chile and Argentina.

10.2 Methodology for Network Creation

Our goal was to identify a social network of all notable people in the history of mankind. Given our subjective view of the past and the fact that our collective memory forgets facts over time, we had to approximate this social network using a proxy: we only consider people that made it into *Wikipedia*, for whom we assume that they fulfill Wikipedia's notability criteria. In this social graph,

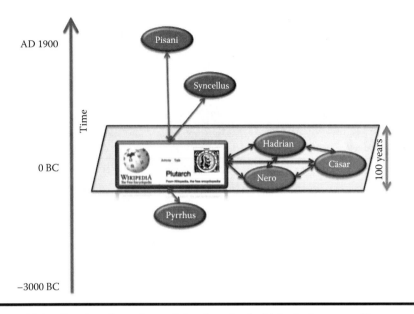

Figure 10.1 Construction of a social network of a historical personality.

people are considered vertices. For every underlying people page on *Wikipedia*, all references to other people are used to infer edges to other vertices. To put it in simple words, a link between two people is constructed if one is mentioned on the *Wikipedia* page of the other. The amount of mentions is used to calculate the weight of each directed edge. As a second requirement, a link between two people can only exist if both of them were living at the same time. This is done to keep the "social element," as a relationship embodies some sort of interaction between two people, which is hard to imagine if one interaction partner is dead. Of course, this connectivity is filtered through the eyes of the twenty-first-century *Wikipedia* editors. For the English *Wikipedia*, we therefore start with the 900,000 pages tagged as "people pages." All 900,000 people pages are dated by extracting the dates of birth and death of each individual. Using this information, 4900 networks through history, from 3000 BC to 1950 CE, are calculated, as shown in Figure 10.1.

For instance, in the graph shown in Figure 10.1, from all the links to the page about Plutarch, only the links from and to Hadrian, Caesar, and Nero are kept, while the links to Pyrrhus, who died well before Plutarch was born, and the pages to medieval historian Syncellus and modern historian Pisani are ignored. Repeating this process leads to the 4900 unique networks mentioned earlier (less for the Chinese and Japanese *Wikipedia*, as their history does not go as far back). For each of these networks, the most central people in the graph are determined using the PageRank algorithm (Page et al. 1999). To get a second selection criterion among all the influencers, their indegree, that is, other people pages pointing back to them, is taken. As has been shown in 30 years of social network analysis research, the structural properties of individual actors correspond to their real-world influence (Wassermann and Faust 1994).

10.3 The Top 50 of All Times

Who are the most important people of all times? The answer to this question is quite different in the United States, the United Kingdom, and German-speaking countries than it is in China and Japan. Looking at the top 10 and top 50 people lists also confirms that most English language *Wikipedia* editors come from the United States and the United Kingdom, while Chinese language editors come from Taiwan, Hong Kong, and mainland China.

10.3.1 *English* Wikipedia *Analysis*

The 50 most important people in the English *Wikipedia* from 3000 BC to AD 1900 are primarily politicians (26 kings and generals), followed by religious leaders (13), and poets and historians (11) (Table 10.1).

The disproportionally large role of historians clearly stands out as they shape our view on the past. It seems that it pays to be a historian, to write one's own place in history. This is clearly shown by Sidney Lee, a Victorian professor of English and history, who wrote 800 biographies and thereby secured his place in the annals.

Not only is a nineteenth-century biographer under the top 10 influencers of all times (which is also an artifact of our collection method), but also classical historians like Polybius, Tacitus, and Plutarch get very high ranks. Treating biographers and historians well so they write positively about world leaders is of course no new insight: Roman emperor Vespasian was paying historians Tacitus, Suetonius, Josephus, and Pliny the Elder, and in return they speak suspiciously well about him, shaping his positive image in history. Caesar and Winston Churchill took this concept one step further, writing their history themselves. As today's history is written in *Wikipedia*, the conclusion seems obvious: treat Wikipedians well! This means for example to give them more recognition or provide research funding for *Wikipedia*-related work.

The next three networking pictures illustrate the English *Wikipedia* Leadership networks through the ages, with snapshots taken at 600 BC (Figure 10.2), at AD 0 (Figure 10.3), and at AD 600 (Figure 10.4). In correspondence with the availability of written records, in 600 BC the Greek philosophers, documented in classical texts by Roman librarians, and Babylonian kings, documented in writings on the walls of historical buildings, are in the center, but there is also a noticeable cluster of Chinese leaders, as well as historical figures around Buddha.

Table 10.1 Top 50 Most Important People of All Times in Four Wikipedias (Most Important at the Top)

	English	Chinese	Japanese	German
1.	George W. Bush	Mao Zedong	Ikuhiko Hata	Adolf Hitler
2.	William Shakespeare	Yuan Shikai	Tokugawa Ieyasu	Johann Wolfgang von Goethe
3.	Sidney Lee	Jay Chou	Toyotomi Hideyoshi	Aristotle
4.	**Jesus**	Oda Nobunaga	Adolf Hitler	Benedikt XVI.
5.	Charles II of England	Tokugawa Ieyasu	Oda Nobunaga	Platon
6.	Aristotle	Emperor Gaozong of Tang	Hirohito	Martin Luther
7.	Napoleon	Cao Cao	Tokugawa Hidetada	Otto von Bismarck
8.	Muhammad	Kangxi Emperor	Tokugawa Iemitsu	Johannes Paul II.
9.	Charlemagne	Emperor Huizong of Song	Chiang Kai-shek	Johann Heinrich Zedler
10.	Plutarch	Yongle Emperor	Tokugawa Ienari	Johann Sebastian Bach
11.	Julius Caesar	Kangxi Emperor	Emperor Meiji	Wilhelm II. (Deutsches Reich)
12.	William III of England	Hongwu Emperor	Tokugawa Tsunayoshi	Karl V. (HRR)
13.	Homer	Jiajing Emperor	Tokugawa Yoshimune	Wolfgang Amadeus Mozart
14.	**Bede**	Koxinga	Emperor Go-Daigo	Napoleon Bonaparte
15.	**Athanasius of Alexandria**	Wang Shichong	Minamoto no Yoritomo	Richard Wagner

(Continued)

Table 10.1 (*Continued*)   Top 50 Most Important People of All Times in Four Wikipedias (Most Important at the Top)

	English	Chinese	Japanese	German
16.	Dante Alighieri	*Emperor Daizong of Tang*	*Emperor Go-Shirakawa*	Georg Wilhelm Friedrich Hegel
17.	**Gautama Buddha**	*Emperor Xuanzong of Tang*	*Ashikaga Takauji*	*Marcus Tullius Cicero*
18.	*Tiberius*	*Zhengtong Emperor*	*Ashikaga Yoshimitsu*	Pius XII.
19.	**Cyril of Alexandria**	*Emperor Xizong of Tang*	*Emperor Go-Toba*	Ludwig van Beethoven
20.	**Bernard of Clairvaux**	*Qianlong Emperor*	*Emperor Saga*	Karl Marx
21.	**Moses**	*Dong Zhuo*	*Ashikaga Yoshimasa*	Friedrich Schiller
22.	*Tacitus*	*Yuwen Tai*	*Ashikaga Yoshinori*	*Joseph Goebbels*
23.	*Edward III of England*	*Qianlong Emperor*	*Emperor Toba*	*Abraham Lincoln*
24.	*Justinian I*	*Huan Xuan*	*Emperor Kanmu*	*Heinrich Himmler*
25.	*David*	*Emperor Huizong of Song*	*Emperor Ninmyō*	Denis Diderot
26.	*Ashoka*	*Emperor Xuanzong of Tang*	*Emperor Daigo*	*Benito Mussolini*
27.	Origen	*Emperor Renzong of Song*	*Emperor Junna*	*Thomas Jefferson*
28.	*Septimius Severus*	*Temür Khan, Emperor Chengzong of Yuan*	*Emperor Seiwa*	Immanuel Kant
29.	Polybius	*Emperor Taizong of Song*	*Emperor Wu of Liu Song*	*Friedrich II. (HRR)*
30.	Confucius	*Fu Jian*	*Emperor Montoku*	Heinrich Heine

(Continued)

Table 10.1 (*Continued*)   Top 50 Most Important People of All Times in Four Wikipedias (Most Important at the Top)

	English	Chinese	Japanese	German
31.	Alexander Severus	Sima Ying	Emperor Uda	Bertolt Brecht
32.	**Patriarch Eutychius of Alexandria**	Emperor Taizong of Song	Fujiwara no Michinaga	Andrew Jackson
33.	Tutankhamun	Wang Mang	Emperor Wen of Liu Song	Gerhart Hauptmann
34.	Akhenaten	Emperor Shunzong of Tang	Cao Cao	Franziskus (Papst)
35.	Ramesses II	Shi Jingtang	Emperor Xiaowu of Liu Song	Ludwig XIV.
36.	**Pope Benjamin I of Alexandria**	Wang Yangming	Emperor Xiaowen of Northern Wei	Franz Liszt
37.	Teti	Hong Xiuquan	Emperor Ming of Liu Song	Konrad Adenauer
38.	Amenemhat II	Napoleon III	Emperor Wu of Southern Qi	Plutarch
39.	Pepi II Neferkare	Emperor Xiaowu of Liu Song	Emperor Wu of Liang	George Washington
40.	Merneith	Sima Shi	Sun Quan	Pablo Picasso
41.	Terence	Möngke Khan	Augustus	Friedrich Nietzsche
42.	Cato the Elder	Chang Yuchun	Pompey	Albert Einstein
43.	Charles Martel	Emperor Ming of Han	Tiberius	Barack Obama
44.	Gilgamesh	Tuoba Huang	Mark Antony	Augustus
45.	**Deborah**	Yuwen Huaji	Alexander the Great	Alexander von Humboldt

(*Continued*)

Table 10.1 (*Continued*)   Top 50 Most Important People of All Times in Four Wikipedias (Most Important at the Top)

	English	Chinese	Japanese	German
46.	*Lugalbanda*	*Mu Ying*	Plato	*Josef Stalin*
47.	*Kubaba*	*Emperor Wen of Liu Song*	Cicero	*Heinrich IV. (HRR)*
48.	*Fu Xi*	Zhu Xi	*Emperor Wu of Han*	*Benjamin Franklin*
49.	*Henry I of England*	**Confucius**	*Ptolemy I Soter*	*Angela Merkel*
50.	Petrarch	*Emperor Ming of Southern Qi*	*Octavia the Younger*	Friedrich Engels

Italics denote politicians, bold religious leaders, and normal font scientists and artists.

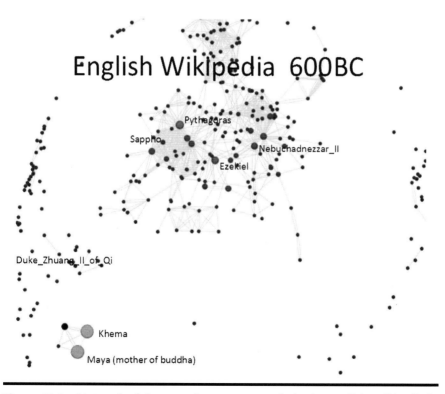

Figure 10.2   Network of the most important people in the English *Wikipedia* in 600 BC.

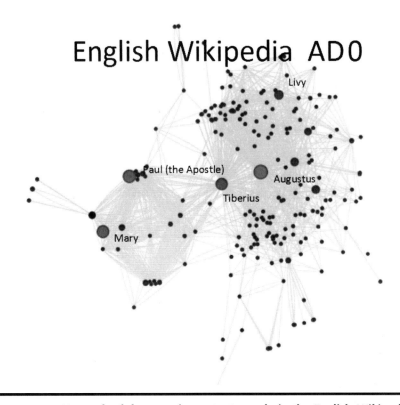

Figure 10.3   Network of the most important people in the English *Wikipedia* in AD 0.

Around AD 0, Roman emperors, consuls, and writers are in the center, as well as biblical figures. Jesus has not been born yet, but his mother Mary has a prominent position in the biblical cluster.

Around AD 600, the Catholic Church with popes, monks, and saints stands out. Greek Orthodox church fathers around Babai the Great form a separate cluster. The Chinese emperors and generals form another cluster of almost similar size, representative for the subsequent blossoming of the Tang dynasty starting in 618, commonly seen as the high point in Chinese civilization.

10.3.2 Chinese **Wikipedia** *Analysis*

Eminent leaders in the Chinese *Wikipedia* show a markedly different picture. Other than in the English *Wikipedia*, the top 50 leaders of all times are mostly emperors and generals. While in the English *Wikipedia* only 26 out of 50 people fell into that category; in the Chinese *Wikipedia*, there are only 4 people who are not political and military leaders, among them are 3 Confucian scholars including

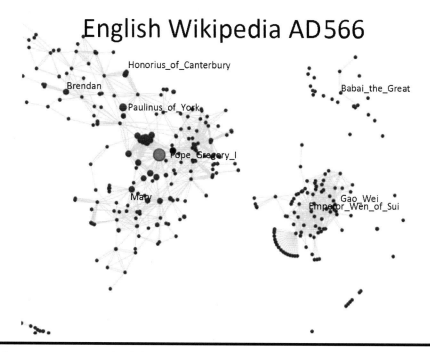

Figure 10.4   Network of the most important people in the English *Wikipedia* in AD 566.

Confucius himself, plus one of the most popular Chinese pop musicians (who is mostly unknown outside Chinese-speaking countries).

As Tables 10.1 and 10.2 illustrate that in China and Japan only famous warriors and politicians had a chance to make it into the top 10 and top 50—the East seems far less religious than the West in their view on the past—while the Western Wikipedias are more balanced with half of the top 10 and the top 50 of all times being religious leaders, artists, or scientists. Historians play a special role. Both Sidney

Table 10.2   Distribution of Different People Categories in Four Wikipedias among the Top 50 People of All Times

	English	*Chinese*	*Japanese*	*German*
Politicians	26	46	47	23
Religious leaders	11	1	0	5
Artists/scientists	13	3	3	22
Cultural in-group	10	48	31	31

Lee and Ikuhiko Hata, a nineteenth-century Japanese military biographer, owe their prominent position to their prolific biography writing, as they get many backlinks from the references on the pages of contemporary politicians they wrote about.

Note that due to the smaller size of the Chinese *Wikipedia*, the indegrees of the top 50 Chinese leaders are much lower than for the English *Wikipedia* leaders. This means that in the lower ranks of the top 50 a few more incoming links can have a large effect on the ranking of a person. Furthermore, Chinese leaders do not go back as far in history as the Egyptian pharaohs and the ancient kings of the Middle East, where a combination of year-ring dating and listing of dynasties allows to date ancient leaders back to 3000 BC. The oldest entries in both Wikipedias that are Chinese are from about the time 800 BC. Mythical earlier emperors like the Yellow Emperor who might have reigned around 3000 BC are not included in the dead people category, as historians are not certain if he ever really existed as a single real person.

The Chinese *Wikipedia* leaders have far fewer links to people outside China than leaders in the non-Asian Wikipedias we have looked at. One could therefore see them as more inward-looking, that is, China-focused. Napoleon III (not Napoleon I) and Tokugawa Ieyasu are the only non-Chinese/Japanese among the top 50 leaders. The English *Wikipedia* is far more diverse, including Confucius, Buddha, and Fu Xi besides military leaders from ancient Egypt and Sumeria together with the leaders of the Western world.

A big restriction of the Chinese *Wikipedia* is the censorship executed by the Chinese government, which might influence the scant inclusion of Western politicians, scientists, and religious leaders.

10.3.3 Japanese Wikipedia Analysis

Other than the Chinese *Wikipedia*, the Japanese *Wikipedia* is not subject to any censorship and can thus rightfully claim to represent the opinion and collective intelligence of the Japanese population. The top person article by indegree, just like the article about the historian Sidney Lee in the English *Wikipedia*, is about a military historian who wrote about all the politicians, mostly generals, referenced in the Japanese *Wikipedia*. Amazingly, the fourth most central article in the Japanese *Wikipedia* is about Adolf Hitler.

10.3.4 Cultural Chauvinism

There are striking differences in the number of out-group leaders, that is, leaders not part of the language sphere of a particular *Wikipedia*, included among the top 50. While the English *Wikipedia* includes 80% non-English leaders among the top 50, only two non-Chinese made it into the top 50 of the Chinese *Wikipedia*: Napoleon III and Tokugawa Ieyasu. The Japanese *Wikipedia* is slightly more balanced, with almost 40% non-Japanese leaders, half of them being Chinese Emperors and people like Adolf Hitler, Plato, Cicero, and Augustus.

A part of that effect might also come from the different sizes and ethnic profiles of the editors of the different Wikipedias, as the English *Wikipedia* probably includes articles written about Chinese leaders written by Chinese and Japanese living abroad, while the articles in the Chinese and Japanese *Wikipedia* are most likely written by the ethnic Chinese and Japanese.

10.4 Differences in Gender Equality

In a subsequent analysis, we studied the percentage of important female people in different cultures. Although, in theory, *Wikipedia* people pages are tagged by gender, many of them do not include this mapping. We therefore created a heuristic algorithm that collects key words in different languages and analyzes the frequency of those words on each page. It counts, for example, "she," "he," and "herself," for the English *Wikipedia*. In the Portuguese *Wikipedia*, we used words such as "ela" and "ele." The same approach was used for the German and Spanish Wikipedias. To verify the accuracy of this method, we compared the results with a subset of people pages that include the gender tag. We found that this approach got the gender right in more than 90% of the people pages in those four languages.

10.4.1 Top 50 Gender Analysis

While many societies have made great progress toward gender equality over the last 100 years, we wanted to measure the pace of this progress. We tracked the evolution of the share of women among the people represented in the different Wikipedias. We found that the 50 most important women in the Wikipedias from 2000 BC to AD 2000 are almost exclusively in two categories, namely, politicians (mostly queens) and artists (e.g., writers, actresses, and singers) (Table 10.3).

Table 10.4 lists all the names in the four Wikipedias. The first group consists of politicians and queens. In this group, the most prominent member is Queen Elizabeth II, showing that people's fascination with the British Royals is unbroken.

Table 10.3 Split between Politicians and Artists among the Top 50 Most Influential Women of All Times in Different Wikipedias

	German	English	Spanish	Portuguese
Politicians	10	14	12	11
Artists	38	36	35	34
Others	2	0	3	5
% Politicians	20.83	28.00	25.53	24.44

Table 10.4 Top Most Important Female Leaders of All Times in Four Wikipedias

	German	English	Spanish	Portuguese
1.	**Elizabeth II.**	**Elizabeth II**	**Michelle Bachelet**	**Maria II de Portugal**
2.	**Angela Merkel**	**Queen Victoria**	Marilyn Monroe	Madonna
3.	**Maria Theresia**	Joan Baez	**Isabel I de Inglaterra**	**Isabel II do Reino Unido**
4.	Katie Fforde	Simone Signoret	**María Teresa I de Austria**	**Dilma Rousseff**
5.	Marlene Dietrich	**Benazir Bhutto**	Mary Pickford	**Maria I de Portugal**
6.	Rosamunde Pilcher	Eudora Welty	Katharine Hepburn	**Vitória do Reino Unido**
7.	**Margaret Thatcher**	Gertrude B. Elion	Elizabeth Taylor	Judy Garland
8.	Hannah Arendt	Betty White	**Hillary Clinton**	Cher
9.	Greta Garbo	Annette Bening	**Margaret Thatcher**	Fernanda Montenegro
10.	Elfriede Jelinek	Eunice Kennedy Shriver	Greta Garbo	Barbra Streisand
11.	Sigrid Roth	**Ruth Bader Ginsburg**	**María Estela Martínez de Perón**	Meryl Streep
12.	Maria (Mutter Jesu)	Susan Hayward	**Vivian Malone Jones**	Marilyn Monroe
13.	Thea Leitner	Mary J. Blige	**Eva Perón**	Gal Costa
14.	Ella Fitzgerald	**Margaret Beckett**	Madonna	Sophia Loren
15.	**Maria Stuart**	**Barbara Jordan**	Gabriela Mistral	Britney Spears
16.	Marilyn Monroe	Zora Neale Hurston	Barbra Streisand	**Marta Suplicy**

(Continued)

Table 10.4 (*Continued*)   Top Most Important Female Leaders of All Times in Four Wikipedias

	German	English	Spanish	Portuguese
17.	Jane Fonda	Rosalynn Carter	Britney Spears	Christina Aguilera
18.	Bette Davis	Sarah Vaughan	Jane Fonda	Roberta Flack
19.	Elizabeth Taylor	Heidi Klum	Marlene Dietrich	Maggie Smith
20.	Billie Holiday	**Helen Clark**	**Juana de Arco**	Rihanna
21.	Nelly Sachs	Donna de Varona	Whitney Houston	Helen Mirren
22.	Liza Minnelli	Julie Walters	Virginia Woolf	Elis Regina
23.	Diana Ross	Patti Smith	Christina Aguilera	Kate Winslet
24.	Katharine Hepburn	**Harriet Tubman**	Mariah Carey	**Maria Teresa da Áustria**
25.	**Beatrix (Niederlande)**	Michelle Pfeiffer	George Sand	Angelina Jolie
26.	Joan Crawford	Allison Janney	Meryl Streep	Lauren Bacall
27.	Katarina Witt	Carole King	Aretha Franklin	Whitney Houston
28.	Shirley MacLaine	Alice Munro	Ella Fitzgerald	Judi Dench
29.	**Elizabeth I.**	Faye Dunaway	Shakira	Marília Pêra
30.	Romy Schneider	Willa Cather	**Josefina de Beauharnais**	Janet Jackson
31.	Claudette Colbert	**Margaret Sanger**	Ingrid Bergman	**Isabel I de Castela**
32.	Toni Morrison	Kirstie Alley	Judy Garland	Nigar Jamal
33.	Ingrid Bergman	**Joanna of Castile**	Liza Minnelli	Jennifer Lawrence
34.	Barbra Streisand	Sheryl Crow	Simone de Beauvoir	Cate Blanchett

(*Continued*)

Table 10.4 (*Continued*) Top Most Important Female Leaders of All Times in Four Wikipedias

	German	*English*	*Spanish*	*Portuguese*
35.	Whoopi Goldberg	Sally Ride	**María Josefa de Austria**	Mary Pickford
36.	Sigrid Undset	Jennifer Hudson	Ava Gardner	**Maria Antonieta**
37.	George Sand	Serena Williams	Billie Holiday	Penélope Cruz
38.	Nadine Gordimer	**Donna Shalala**	Samuel Johnson	Sissy Spacek
39.	Gabriela Mistral	**Shirley Chisholm**	Lady Gaga	Whoopi Goldberg
40.	Doris Lessing	Olivia Newton-John	**Angela Merkel**	**Hillary Clinton**
41.	Pearl S. Buck	Kristin Scott Thomas	Nicole Kidman	Jennifer Lopez
42.	**Marie Antoinette**	**Margaret, Maid of Norway**	Maria Callas	Ingrid Bergman
43.	Helen Hayes	Candice Bergen	Vanessa Redgrave	Barbara Stanwyck
44.	Meryl Streep	Wilma Rudolph	Joan Crawford	**Isabel I de Inglaterra**
45.	**Hillary Clinton**	**Martha Griffiths**	Mercedes Sosa	Jodie Foster
46.	Judy Garland	Antonina Houbraken	Janet Jackson	Shirley MacLaine
47.	Alice Munro	Claire Danes	Rita Hayworth	**Francisca de Bragança**
48.	Britney Spears	Marion Cotillard	Julia Roberts	Sandra Bullock
49.	Goldie Hawn	Sappho	Tina Turner	**Januária Maria de Bragança**
50.	**Isabella I. (Kastilien)**	Alice Hamilton	Rihanna	Lady Gaga

Politicians in bold.

In our metrics, she consistently leads the female leadership ranking. Moreover, in the German and Portuguese Wikipedias, we find German chancellor Angela Merkel and Brazilian president Dilma Rousseff among the top five positions in their corresponding countries, illustrating that in the last decades women have been accumulating more influence in global politics. Another interesting result is the position of American politician Hillary Clinton. She is present among the top 50 most influential women in all Wikipedias but the English. We can speculate that maybe she has more influence overseas than inside her own country due to her position as a foreign minister. We also have to note that this analysis was completed 2 years before Hillary announced her aspirations for the U.S. 2016 presidential race.

In the art categories, we find a more diversified distribution between writers, singers, and actresses. It also seems that the United States exerts a dominating influence in this area in the rest of the world. Many actresses who worked or work in the U.S. show business, such as Marilyn Monroe, Judy Garland, or Barbra Streisand, have a high PageRank in the different Wikipedias.

10.4.2 Longitudinal Gender Analysis

By analyzing the percentage of women over the last century, we can see how the fraction of women among the world's leaders is increasing over time (Figure 10.2). Our data show the Portuguese *Wikipedia* having the highest percentage of women among the Wikipedias we analyzed, followed by the Spanish and English.

One fact that may have influenced this result is the number of total people pages in the Portuguese *Wikipedia* (93,000), which is significantly lower than that in the English *Wikipedia*, which has 10 times more people pages, translating to a lower sample size. The graph shows a linear increase in the percentage of women until 1995 (Figure 10.5), when the percentage really explodes to parity between women and men in the English, Spanish, and Portuguese Wikipedias. This explosion, however, might also be an artifact of the smaller number of people pages for the last 20 years, as there are very few people, other than Justin Bieber or Malala Yousafzai (the youngest ever Nobel Peace Prize winner), that fulfill the notability criteria of *Wikipedia* at such a young age. Nevertheless, it seems that in this smaller sample of young high achievers we attain gender equality.

10.5 Comparing Different Cultures through Wikinews

We complement our historical analysis of *Wikipedia* with an analysis of the treatment of late breaking news by Wikipedians in Wikinews, a hand-curated news page of whatever Wikipedians consider most newsworthy on any given day. In particular, we use Wikinews to analyze sentiment and emotion in different cultures. Wikinews is part of *Wikipedia*. It is a free and open news website where users create the content based on digesting news from sources such as Reuters, Bloomberg, and CNN.

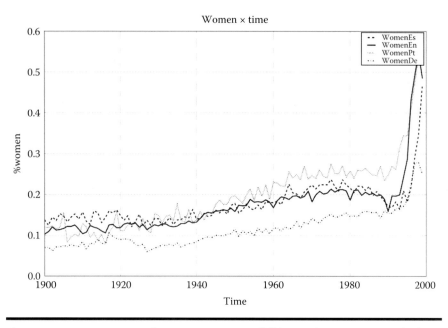

Figure 10.5 Percentage of women among Wikihistory important people from 1900 to 2000. Each line shows the ratio of women to men for the particular language.

The main focus in this project is to analyze what kinds of news are more relevant in each culture and the sentiment related to those news. For example, we want to investigate if some cultures focus more on bad or good news or whether some topics are considered more newsworthy in some cultures than in others.

10.5.1 Data Collection

We collected the news using the Wikinews pages in English, German, Spanish, and Portuguese. In those pages, we can find the most relevant events of each year through the eyes of the Wikipedians. In particular, whenever they consider a particular topic newsworthy, they will add a short sentence on the Wikinews page as an anchor and create a new *Wikipedia* page for the entire event. For each language, we collected all the links to the pages in *Wikipedia* and connected those links with each other. This approach creates four distinct networks, one for each language (see Figures 10.6 through 10.9). As we can see, some Wikipedias have a more complex and connected news network. This is not surprising because, for example, the English *Wikipedia* has more content and is more updated than the Portuguese. The total number of articles is also quite different between the different Wikipedias.

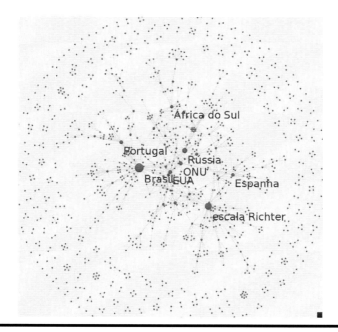

Figure 10.6   Portuguese Wikinews network.

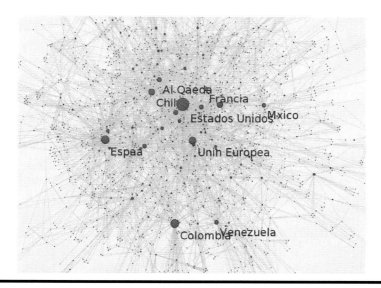

Figure 10.7   Spanish Wikinews network.

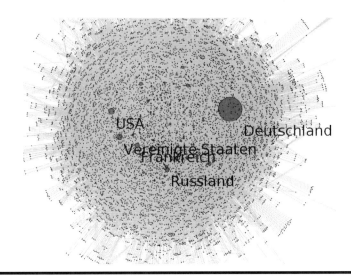

Figure 10.8   German Wikinews network.

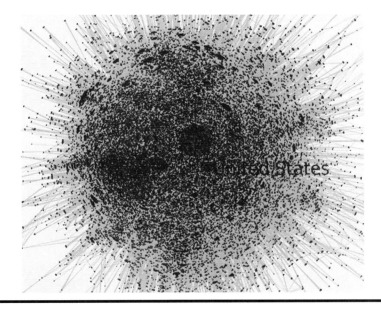

Figure 10.9   English Wikinews network.

As we can see in the network pictures in Figures 10.6 through 10.9, the most central nodes are usually countries. News are linked to location pages related to where an event happened as opposed to one main subject like war, company names, or people. Unsurprisingly, we observe a heavy location bias, in which intracultural news get a much more detailed treatment. This means that *Wikipedia* editors of one language upload news that happened in the country with the same language more frequently than outside news (Figure 10.10). For the Spanish *Wikipedia*, due to the many countries sharing the same language, we observe a more equal distribution of topics by betweenness centrality. As many different countries are appearing on the Spanish Wikinews with similar centrality, this illustrates that people from many of those countries seem to be contributing. The "popularity" of one country in other cultures and languages can show how one country has the attention of others. For

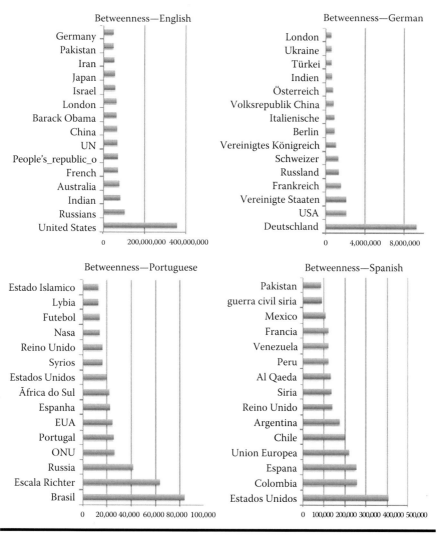

Figure 10.10 **The most important topics by betweenness in the different-language Wikinews.**

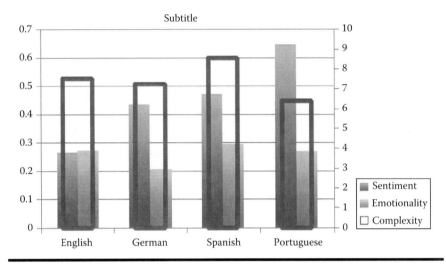

Figure 10.11 **Sentiment, emotionality, and complexity of the pages linked to Wikinews in the different languages.**

example, we can see how the United States is a big player on all Wikinews, illustrating U.S. dominance in global politics across all languages and cultures.

We not only looked at the key topics in the different-language versions but also compared the sentiment in the news, using automatic sentiment analysis (Brönnimann 2014). Using a machine learning approach, the computer measured the density of positive words like "great," "wonderful," and negative words like "horrible" or "bad." Emotionality is defined as the variation in positive and negative sentiment. Complexity measures the use of rare words compared to a simple standardized vocabulary. We used the sentiment, emotionality, and complexity functions of the tool Condor (Brönnimann 2014) to calculate these metrics for all four Wikinews data sets. The overall negativity of sentiment stands out, below the neutrality threshold of 0.5. While the text has been written by Wikipedians, they base their selection on general sources such as Bloomberg, Reuters, and CNN. This confirms the popular belief that people are much more interested in negative than in positive news. However, we also notice that some Wikinews data sets are more positive than others (Figure 10.11). For instance, the English language *Wikipedia* is the most negative while Portuguese and Spanish are the most positive. It also seems that Spanish Wikinews uses more complex language than the others, which might be due to the many countries that share the same language. Spanish speakers in Spain might be saying similar things in other words than the speakers in Mexico, Chile, or Argentina. The same could be claimed for the English Wikinews, due to the United States, the United Kingdom, Australia, Canada, and New Zealand editing. However, in this case, the population of the United States is considerably larger than that of the others combined. German and Portuguese Wikinews basically just cover one country, where words might be used more consistently, leading to lower complexity measures as calculated by our software. On the other hand, the Germans seem to be less emotional than the Spanish, Portuguese, or English, confirming a national stereotype of dry and matter-of-fact behavior.

10.6 Related Work

Charles Murray's list of "Human Accomplishments" (2003) shows the most innovative people in history. The list is led by Isaac Newton and Galileo Galilei. It is based on a compilation of history textbooks, where "accomplished" people have to be listed multiple times in different languages and sources. Murray's list has been combined in the Pantheon with *Wikipedia* (http://pantheon.media.mit.edu/methods). Pantheon is based on a list created from 11,340 *Wikipedia* people pages, where a person has to be listed in at least 25 different-language Wikipedias. The list has been hand-curated to remove obviously nonsignificant characters. Our analysis approach is purely based on data and not hand-curated, making a claim to higher objectivity. Second, to be included into the Pantheon, a person also needs to be listed in the Charles Murray's book whose inclusion criteria are to be listed in multiple school textbooks. Consistent with traditional western education, Pantheon seems to be biased toward Greek philosophers, as the top five entries are Aristotle, Plato, Jesus Christ, Socrates, and Alexander the Great.

10.7 Conclusions

The Internet enables researchers to more easily compile rankings of the most important people of all times (Murray 2003, Hidalgo 2014). Our work is unique in that we extract language-specific rankings that allow us to compare the worldview for dozens of different cultures. Probing the historical perspective of many different-language-specific Wikipedias enables an x-ray view into cultural and national characteristics, giving some confirmation to national stereotypes of Germans as "people of the book" or the Japanese placing heavy emphasis on their warlike past.

We think that our preliminary research has just scratched the surface of digital humanities, illustrating the potential of employing the different-language versions of *Wikipedia* as a socioscope into the different facets of human nature and culture.

References

Becker, M. (2012) Die Aktualität von Online-Enzyklopädien—Eine empirische Analyse am Beispiel Wikipedia. Diploma thesis, University of Cologne, Köln, Germany.

Blodget, H. (2009) Who the hell writes Wikipedia, anyway? *Business Insider*, January 3, 2009. http://www.businessinsider.com/2009/1/who-the-hell-writes-wikipedia-anyway?

Brint, S. (1984) "New-Class" and cumulative trend explanations of the liberal political attitudes of professionals. *American Journal of Sociology*, 90, 30–71.

Brönnimann, L. (2014) Analyse der Verbreitung von Innovationen in sozialen Netzwerken. MSc thesis, University of Applied Sciences Northwestern Switzerland, Basel, Switzerland. http://swarmcreativity.blogspot.com/2014/03/how-to-measure-influence-in-social.html.

Frick, K., Guertler, D., Gloor, P. (2013) Coolhunting for the world's thought leaders. *Proceedings Fourth International Conference on Collaborative Innovation Networks (COINs 2013)*, Santiago de Chile, August 11–13, 2013.

Futterer, T., Gloor, P., Malhotra, T., Mfula, H., Packmohr, K., Schultheiss, S. (2013) WikiPulse—A news-portal based on Wikipedia. *Proceedings Fourth International Conference on Collaborative Innovation Networks (COINs 2013)*, Santiago de Chile, August 11–13, 2013.

Gloor, P., De Boer, P., Lo, W., Wagner, S., Nemoto, K., Fuehres, H. (2015) Cultural anthropology through the lens of Wikipedia—A comparison of historical leadership networks in the English, Chinese, and Japanese Wikipedia. *Proceedings of the Fifth International Conference on Collaborative Innovation Networks (COINs15)*, Tokyo, Japan, March 12–14, 2015.

Gloor, P., Krauss, J., Nann, S., Fischbach, K., Schoder, D. (2009) Web Science 2.0: Identifying trends through semantic social network analysis. *IEEE Conference on Social Computing (SocialCom-09)*, Vancouver, British Columbia, Canada, August 29–31, 2009.

Greenstein, S., Zhu, F. (2012) Collective intelligence and neutral point of view: The case of Wikipedia. NBER Working Paper No. 18167.

Hidalgo, C. (2014) Pantheon: Mapping historical cultural production. http://pantheon.media.mit.edu. Accessed July 1, 2015.

Iba, T., Nemoto, K., Peters, B., Gloor, P. A. (2010) Analyzing the creative editing behavior of Wikipedia editors: Through dynamic social network analysis. *Procedia-Social and Behavioral Sciences*, 2(4), 6441–6456.

Kleeb, R., Gloor, P., Nemoto, K., Henninger, M. (2012) Wikimaps: Dynamic maps of knowledge. *International Journal of Organisational Design and Engineering*, 2(2), 204–224.

Murray, C. (2003). *Human Accomplishment: The Pursuit of Excellence in the Arts and Sciences, 800 BC to 1950*. HarperCollins, New York.

Page, L., Brin, S., Motwani, R., Winograd, T. (1999) The PageRank citation ranking: Bringing order to the Web. Stanford InfoLab, Palo Alto, CA.

Wasserman, S., Faust, K. (1994) *Social Network Analysis: Methods and Applications*, Vol. 8. Cambridge University Press, Cambridge.

Chapter 11

From Social Networks to Time Series: Methods and Applications

Tongfeng Weng, Yaofeng Zhang, and Pan Hui

Contents

11.1 Background

Social networks is an important branch in network science and has attracted continuous attention since the discovery of six degrees of separation (Milgram, 1967). Substantial progress has been made in the area of network science, among which two representatives are the small-world phenomenon and the scale-free property (Barabási and Albert, 1999; Watts and Strogatz, 1998). These findings have deeply altered our understandings of relations encoded in large data from social relationships in terms of community structure, hierarchical structure, clustering coefficient, and assortativity (Barabási and Albert, 1999; Newman, 2002; Watts and

Strogatz, 1998). In this sense, network science provides us with a new perspective to describe and characterize relationships and behaviors among individuals in society.

However, almost all measures devised for characterizing the structural properties of social networks are of a purely topological character—many of these measures are derived from mathematical graph theory. Obviously, only these topological measurements are not enough for fully characterizing the underlying mechanism governing complex systems. Recently, characterizing network structure from the dynamical perspective certainly provides us with a new channel. On this issue, Liu et al. (2010) proposed to study networks constructed from various types of music through mapping music into time series by a stochastic method. Later, Shimada et al. (2012) introduced a deterministic method (as opposed to a previous stochastic method) by using the multidimensional theory and the perturbation theory of linear operators. In such a situation, the dynamical properties of the transformed time series properly reflect the structure organization of small-world networks. However, the deterministic method has a very limited utility when applied to real-world, scale-free networks directly. An important issue is how to assign a proper temporal order for a given network in the transformation process. Indeed, the network representation of real networks has no temporal information. To address this issue, Weng et al. (2014) provided a transformation method from networks to time series based on a finite-memory random walk. It is found that the self-similar features of the obtained time series reveal the mixing patterns of real-world networks. Moreover, there is a unified dynamical mechanism hidden in various networks with the same function that uncovers the essential differences among social, biological, and technological networks.

In this chapter, we first introduce two methods of transforming networks (graphs) into time series. Then, we analyze the long-range correlation and the multiscale feature of time series transformed from social networks to show their dynamical properties beyond purely topological viewpoints. Finally, we give a conclusion and discussion regarding the benefits of analyzing social networks from the time series perspective.

11.2 Methods for Mapping Networks into Time Series

11.2.1 Deterministic Method

The deterministic method for transforming graphs to time series is introduced by using a multidimensional scaling method (Shimada et al. 2012). Let $A = \{a_{ij}\}$ be an adjacency matrix of a network, whose entry $a_{ij} = 1$ (0) if nodes i and j are (not) connected. Then, define a distance d_{ij} between nodes i and j according to

$$d_{ij} = \begin{cases} a_{ij} & a_{ij} = 1 \\ \omega & a_{ij} = 0 \end{cases}$$

where the parameter ω is an adjustable factor taking from the interval (1,2). In this situation, it guarantees the distance relationship among nodes satisfying the triangle inequality on the network. The adjacency matrix A is then mapped into a distance matrix $D = \{d_{ij}^2\}$. Next, the distance matrix is transformed to a centralizing gram matrix S as follows:

$$S = -\frac{1}{2}HDH$$

where $H = E - \frac{1}{N}I$, E is an N-dimensional identity matrix, and I is an N-dimensional matrix of ones. Note that it is possible to select an appropriate value of ω such that the centralizing gram matrix S is positive semidefinite. Consequently, the matrix S can be rewritten in the form of its eigenvalues and eigenvectors:

$$S = P\Lambda^{(1/2)}(P\Lambda^{(1/2)})^T$$

where
$P = (p_1, p_2, \dots, p_N)$
$\Lambda = \mathrm{diag}(\lambda_1, \lambda_2, \dots, \lambda_N)$
p_i is the corresponding eigenvector of the eigenvalue λ_i of the matrix S

The first vector of matrix $P\Lambda^{(1/2)}$ is defined as the transformed time series represented as $\{x_i\}_{i=1}^n$. In this paradigm, the small-world property of a network is reinterpreted as the periodicity of the transformed time series, see in Figure 11.1. It is shown that a regular network is mapped into a periodic time series, whereas small-world networks are transformed into noisy time series. These relationships are held with the help of the circulant-matrix theory and the perturbation theory of linear operators. More detailed analysis can be seen in the reference (Shimada et al. 2012).

However, such elegant transformation method has very limited utility. One apparent drawback is how to assign the temporal information for a given network. If we change the temporal sequence, the obtained time series as well as their dynamics may vary dramatically. It is comparable to the surrogate method (Theiler et al., 1992). So wide adoption of this method is hindered by such defect.

11.2.2 Finite-Memory Random Walk Method

The deterministic method has very limited utility when applied to social networks. Here, we present an alternative approach for transforming graphs into time series using the finite-memory random walk (Weng et al., 2014).

Let $A = \{a_{ij}\}$ denote an adjacency matrix of a network defined as before. The degree of node i is given by $k_i = \sum_{l=1}^{N} a_{li}$. Typically, the degree distribution of a real network follows the power law property, which means a large majority of nodes

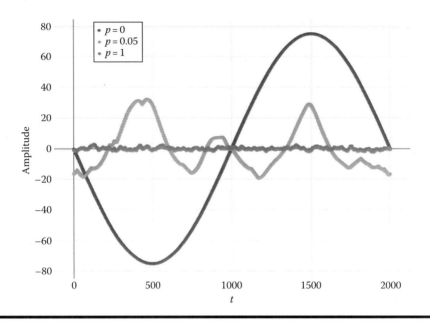

Figure 11.1 **The diagram of the transformed time series from small-world models based on the deterministic method.** *Note:* **Examples of transformed time series form the small-world model with different rewiring probabilities *p* ranging from ring lattice (*p* = 0) to small world (*p* = 0.05) to random network (*p* = 1).**

have low degrees while a small amount of nodes (known as "hub" nodes) have vast degrees. Indeed, the power law feature is a common characteristic of most social networks (Barabási and Albert, 1999; Newman, 2001).

We then perform the finite-memory random walk traversing the network and define its trajectory as a time series (i.e., the value of the time series being a function of the degree of the currently visited node). Certainly, the behavior of such random walk is fully determined by its transition probability. At time t, the transition probability of a walker moving from the current node i to node j depends on the previously visited nodes information such that

$$\pi_{ij}(t) = \frac{a_{ij}\left|k_j - \tilde{k}(t)\right|}{\sum_{j=1}^{N} a_{ij}\left|k_j - \tilde{k}(t)\right|}$$

where $\tilde{k}(t) = \max_{l=1,2,\ldots,\tau} k(t-l)$. Here, $k(t-1), k(t-2),\ldots, k(t-\tau)$ are degrees of nodes being visited by the walker at past τ interval times. So the parameter τ controls how much information may be used at each step and further influences the trajectory of the walker. Clearly, when the walker visits a high-degree node, it usually departs from this high-degree node for the next τ interval times and then prefers to revisit high-degree nodes again. Thus, the transformed time series shows a pseudoperiodic behavior reminiscent of the appearance of various real time series such as human electrocardiograph, annual sunspot numbers, and laser output (Kantz and Schreiber, 2004).

In Figure 11.2, we show a schematic illustration from the synthetic network to time series based on a finite-memory random walk approach. The transformed time series presents a pseudoperiodic behavior in which each high-amplitude point is usually followed by a small amount of lower-amplitude points. In the next section, we will show that the transformed time series can provide us with abundant structural and functional properties of synthetic and social networks.

However, we cannot reconstruct the original network structure from the transformed time series as this approach uses a random way to assign the temporal order of time series. A desirable solution is a transformation method that assigns the temporal order deterministically, which is still a challenging problem.

11.3 Long-Range Correlation Analysis of Social Networks

For the transformed time series, we can use various nonlinear statistics to uncover dynamical properties hidden in network structure. Among them, the long-range correlation is a fundamental feature of most time series. Thus, we first investigate long-range correlations of the transformed time series by using the detrended fluctuation analysis (DFA) method (Peng et al., 1994).

For a time series $\{x_i\}_{i=1}^{n}$, we first integrated them according to

$$y(k) = \sum_{i=1}^{k}(x_i - \bar{x})$$

where $\bar{x}$ is the average value of time series $\{x_i\}_{i=1}^{n}$. The integrated time series is then divided into several overlapping boxes of the same size l. In each box, a polynomial function $y_l(k)$ is fitted to the previously integrated data $y(k)$. Finally, we calculate the mean fluctuation function between $y(k)$ and $y_l(k)$ as follows:

$$F(l) = \sqrt{\frac{1}{n}\sum_{k=1}^{n}\left(y(k) - y_l(k)\right)^2}$$

Repeat this process over a number of box sizes varying from 2 to n. Generally, the mean fluctuation $F(l)$ shows a power law function of size, that is, $F(l) \propto l^{\alpha}$. Typically, $\alpha \approx 0.5$ indicates there is no correlation, $0.5 < \alpha < 1$ indicates long-range correlation, and $0 < \alpha < 0.5$ indicates anticorrelation.

We then apply the DFA method to the transformed time series constructed from the Barabási–Albert (BA) model to show the relationship between the mixing

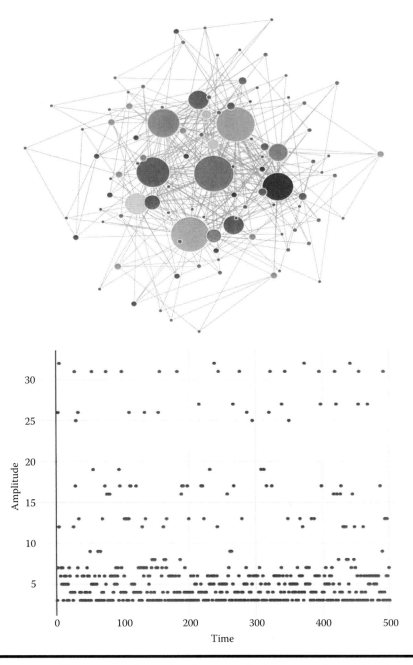

Figure 11.2 **The scheme of mapping from a scale-free network to a transformed time series based on the finite-memory random walk.** *Note*: The synthetic network composed of 100 nodes and 315 edges. The associated time series based on finite-memory random walk method shows a seemingly pseudoperiodic behavior.

patterns of networks and the long-range correlation of the transformed time series. For generating an ensemble of networks with different mixing patterns, we use the link rewiring method to adjust network structure (Maslov and Sneppen, 2002). This method randomly chooses a pair of links and swaps the four end nodes. Repeating the process for a sufficient number of times, we can obtain a network with a desirable mixing pattern. To quantify the mixing pattern of a network, we adopt assortativity coefficient r defined as follows:

$$r = \frac{M^{(-1)} \sum_l k_l j_l - \left[M^{(-1)} \sum_l \frac{1}{2}(k_l + j_l) \right]^2}{M^{(-1)} \sum_l \frac{1}{2}(k_l^2 + j_l^2) - \left[M^{(-1)} \sum_l \frac{1}{2}(k_l + j_l) \right]^2}$$

where
k_l and j_l are degrees of two end points of the lth link
M is total number of links in the network (Newman, 2002)

Especially, when $r > 0$, the network is claimed to exhibit assortative mixing (i.e., high-degree nodes tend to connect to other high-degree nodes). In contrast, if $r < 0$, the network is called disassortative (i.e., high-degree nodes prefer to attach to low-degree nodes).

Figure 11.3 shows the results of all the DFA of the constructed time series from a disassortative mixing network, a neutral mixing network, and an assortative mixing network, respectively. Clearly, we see that the scaling exponent α of assortative mixing networks is larger than 0.5, whereas that of the disassortative networks is less than 0.5, as demonstrated in Figure 11.3. It shows that the long-range correlations of the transformed time series can reflect the mixing pattern of networks properly.

We now consider the application of the DFA technique to various real-world networks, including social (jazz [Pablo and Danon, 2003], cond [Newman, 2001], hep [Newman, 2001], e-mail [Guimerà et al., 2003], coauthorships [Newman, 2006], dolphin [Lusseau et al., 2003]), biological (*Caenorhabditis elegans* [Jeong et al., 2000]), and technological (language [Milo et al., 2004]) to explore the underlying long-range correlation feature. We repeat the previous calculation applied to these real networks. An apparent scaling between the mean fluctuation $F(l)$ and the box size l emerges for time series transformed from three social networks, as seen in Figure 11.4. Also, we notice that these profiles exhibit slightly different scaling exponents, meaning that their corresponding network structures have some differences.

To check whether or not the previous relationship between the mixing pattern and the scaling exponent still established real networks, we further plot the scaling exponent as a function of the mixing pattern. As expected, the scaling

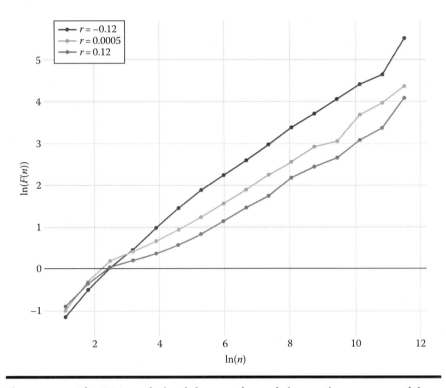

Figure 11.3 The DFA analysis of the transformed time series constructed from the BA model. *Note:* DFA of time series of 20.000 points, derived from the BA model with distinct mixing patterns.

exponent shows a strong positive correlation with the assortativity coefficient *r* (as shown in Figure 11.4). Their correlation coefficient and *P*-value are 0.878 and 0.004, suggesting the confidence level of our conclusion. Besides the scale-free (SF) property, the coauthorships' network has some other specific substructures such as community structure and the group leaders are the community centralities in this network (Newman, 2006). Thus, the scaling behavior of the coauthorships' network deviates remarkably from our expectation. These results uncover the long-range correlations of social networks that certainly characterize the underlying possible mechanism from a new perspective. Sometimes, the scaling relationship between $F(l)$ and l may not satisfy for the transformed time series generated from some social networks, for example, the occurrence of the crossover phenomenon. In such a case, we may refer to check the coupling of different dynamics for the transformed time series (Chen et al., 2005). Alternatively, we can use the diffusion entropy method to examine the long-range property of the transformed time series, which can eliminate the effect of the "Lévy" scaling (Scafetta and Grigolini, 2002).

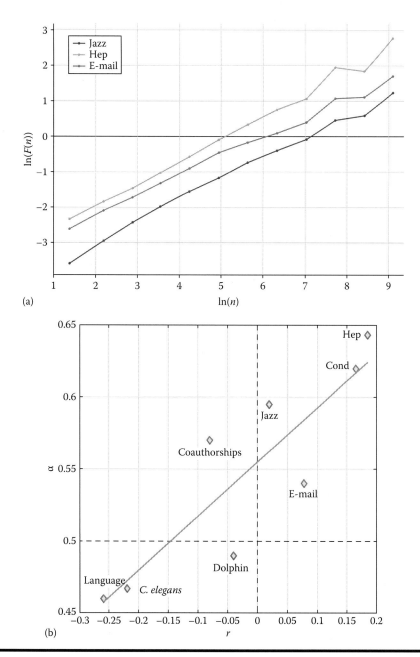

(a)

(b)

Figure 11.4 **The DFA analysis of the transformed time series derived from real networks.** *Note:* DFA of three social networks (a). Scaling exponent of the transformed time series versus the assortativity coefficient *r* of real networks (b).

11.4 Multiscale Properties of Social Networks

The DFA analysis has already provided some self-similarity properties of time series constructed from social networks. However, it is not enough to explore the underlying mechanism of these time series. Next, we employ multiscale entropy (MSE) to extract multiscale features of these social networks' structure that are absent from the purely topological aspect. The MSE defines a complexity measurement based on quantifying the sample entropy (SampEn) over multiple scales (Costa et al., 2002). Given a transformed time series $\{x_i\}_{i=1}^{N}$, we first construct consecutive coarse-grained time series $y_i^{(\varepsilon)}$ as follows:

$$y_i^{(\varepsilon)} = \frac{1}{\varepsilon} \sum_{i=(j-1)\varepsilon+1}^{j\varepsilon} x^i$$

where ε is a scale factor. For each coarse-grained time series $\{y_i^{(\varepsilon)}\}$, we construct m-dimensional vector $Y_i = \left[y_i^{(\varepsilon)}, y_{i+1}^{(\varepsilon)}, \ldots, y_{i+m-1}^{(\varepsilon)} \right]$. Then, we calculate the distance between Y_i and Y_j as follows:

$$d[Y_i, Y_j] = \max_{k=0,1,\ldots,m-1} \left| y_{i+k}^{(\varepsilon)} - y_{j+k}^{(\varepsilon)} \right|$$

For a given threshold value r, we use $N_i^m(r)$ to represent the number of vectors Y_j that satisfies $d[Y_i, Y_j] < r$. Thus, we can calculate the ratio $C_i^m(r) = N_i^m(r)/(n/\varepsilon - m + 1)$. The complexity function $\Phi^m(r)$ is

$$\Phi^m(r) = \frac{1}{n/\varepsilon - m + 1} \sum_{i=1}^{n/\varepsilon - m + 1} C_i^m(r)$$

Repeat the procedure earlier to the $m + 1$ dimensional vector $\tilde{Y}_i = \left[y_i^{(\varepsilon)}, y_{i+1}^{(\varepsilon)}, \ldots, y_{i+m}^{(\varepsilon)} \right]$ and the sample entropy is

$$ApEn(m,r) = \lim_{n/\varepsilon \to \infty} \Phi^m(r) - \Phi^{m+1}(r)$$

Generally, the sample entropy reflects the complexity of the underlying time series. A smaller value of $ApEn(m,r)$ means it is easier to capture the underlying mechanism of time series, while a large value of $ApEn(m,r)$ shows that time series is more likely to be unpredictable. Finally, we plot the sample entropy as the function of the scale factor ε and observe the profile of the MSE curve.

To better describe the results obtained from the BA network model and various social networks, we show profiles of three typical dynamical systems to serve as a benchmark. The selected time series are white noise, discrete chaotic map, and continuous chaotic time series. The discrete chaotic map is Ikeda map given as follows:

$$x_{n+1} = 1 + 0.9 x_n e^{\left(0.4i - \frac{6i}{1+|x_n|} \right)}$$

Meanwhile, the continuous chaotic time series is generated from the Lorenz system defined by

$$\begin{cases} \dot{x} = 10(y - x) \\ \dot{y} = x(28 - z) - y \\ \dot{z} = xy - 8/3z \end{cases}$$

Clearly, it is shown that different dynamical systems exhibit distinct profiles, as shown in Figure 11.5. Especially, the sample entropy of white noise monotonically decreases with the increasing scale factor ε. However, for discrete chaotic maps, the sample entropy markedly increases at small scales and then gradually increases at large scales. In contrast, the continuous chaotic map shows it monotonically increases in the whole scale range. The results show that profiles of MSE analysis can well characterize and classify different dynamical systems.

Now, we apply the MSE technique to analyze time series constructed from the BA model with different mixing patterns. Here, we also adopt the link rewiring method to adjust network structure for a desired mixing pattern (Maslov and Sneppen, 2002). Interestingly, we observe that the sample entropy of time series derived from disassortative mixing pattern networks shows a similar profile to that of white noise, while the behavior for assortative mixing pattern networks presents the same behavior as the discrete-time chaotic system for small value r and resembles the feature of the continuous-time chaotic system when r is extremely large, as shown in Figure 11.5. These findings uncover potential dynamical properties of network mixing patterns that are absent merely based on the often-studied global network measurements. This also suggests that there is a dynamical mechanism governing the structural evolution of different mixing pattern networks. The time series–based analysis provides a new perspective of network structure transition that enriches our understanding of network structure organization.

Next, we apply the MSE technique to five social networks (i.e., jazz [Pablo and Danon, 2003], cond [Newman, 2001], hep [Newman, 2001], e-mail [Guimerà et al., 2003], coauthorships [Newman, 2006]). We find that networks derived from the social networks show similar profiles, as shown in Figure 11.6. The similarity in profiles uncovers a fundamental mechanism underlying the organization of various social systems. In fact, the social networks reflect the behavior among persons driven by basic interpersonal relationships. Moreover, the profiles of MSE analysis uncover the underlying mechanism that governs different functions of networks (Weng et al., 2014). Here, to take advantage of MSE analysis, we also exhibit the degree distribution of these selected social networks as a comparison. It is shown that different social networks present clearly distinct degree distributions, as shown in Figure 11.6. Thus, the MSE technique indeed allows us to characterize social networks according to their original functions efficiently beyond the solely topological aspect.

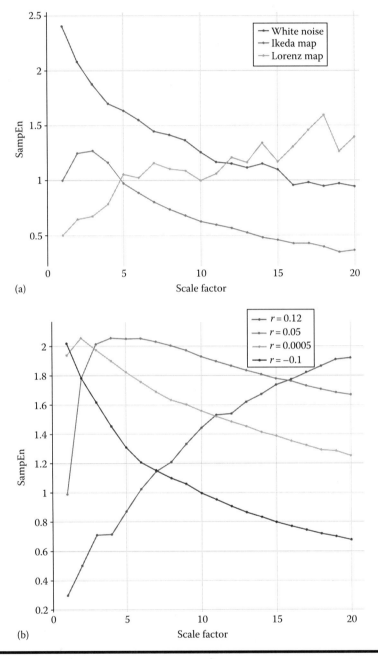

Figure 11.5 **The MSE analysis of typical dynamical systems and transformed time series constructed from the SF model.** *Note*: MSE analysis of time series derived from three typical dynamical systems (a) and the SF network model (b). Symbols represent mean values of the sample entropy for each network over 100 tests.

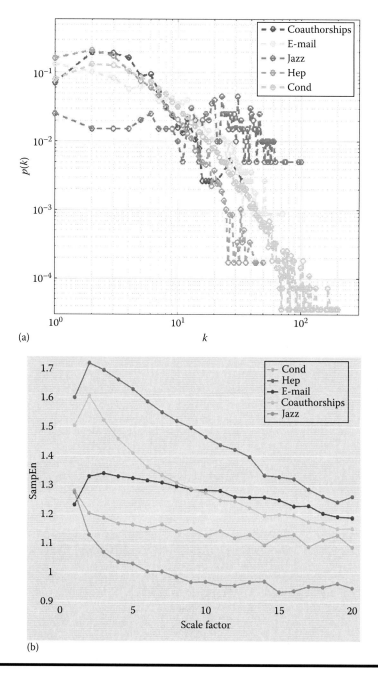

Figure 11.6 **The MSE analysis of the transformed time series constructed from real networks and their degree distributions.** *Note*: Degree distribution (a) and MSE analysis of time series derived from social networks (b). Symbols represent mean values of the sample entropy for each network over 100 tests.

11.5 Conclusion and Discussion

In this chapter, we have summarized two possible methods of transforming networks into time series. The deterministic method is only suitable to small-world models as it does not provide a unique way of assigning the temporal information. Nevertheless, it indeed develops the relationship between periodicity of time series and randomness of network structure analytically. Another method based on a finite-memory random walk is more practical. In such paradigm, the long-range correlations of transformed time series can reflect the mixing pattern of networks. Specifically, the long-range correlation shows an assortative mixing pattern, while anticorrelation corresponds to a disassortative one. These relationships are consistent across various social networks. Moreover, the MSE analysis allows us to uncover possible dynamical properties of social networks. Meanwhile, the random sampling inherent to the random walk also implies that this approach is useful for characterizing extremely large networks for which an exhaustive computation may be prohibitive. However, one possible drawback is that it is not a one-to-one map between social networks and time series, which may result in inequivalent underlying information.

Furthermore, there are some interesting issues needed to be addressed. The first one is how to detect the community structure of social networks based on the time series–based analysis. The second one is to construct an analytical formula for describing social networks based on their dynamical properties. The last one is to extend this method to the study of generic networks beyond social ones.

References

Barabási, A., Albert, R., Emergence of scaling in random networks, *Science*, 1999, 286:509–512.

Chen, Z., Hu, K., Carpena, P., Galvan, P., Stanley, H., Ivanov, P., Effect of nonlinear filters on detrended fluctuation analysis, *Physical Review E*, 2005, 71:011104.

Costa, M., Goldberger, A. L., Peng, C. K., Multiscale entropy analysis of complex physiologic time series, *Physical Review Letters*, 2002, 89:068102.

Guimerà, R., Danon, L., Díaz-Guilera, A., Giralt, F., Arenas, A., Self-similar community structure in a network of human interactions, *Physical Review E*, 2003, 68:065103.

Jeong, H., Tombor, B., Albert, R., Oltvai, Z. N., Barabási, A. L., The large-scale organization of metabolic networks, *Nature*, 2000, 407:651–654.

Kantz, H., Schreiber, T., *Nonlinear Time Series Analysis*. Cambridge, U.K.: Basic Books, 2004.

Liu, X. F., Tse, C. K., Small, M., Complex network structure of musical compositions: Algorithmic generation of appealing music, *Physica A: Statistical Mechanics and Its Applications*, 2010, 389:126–132.

Lusseau, D., Schneider, K., Boisseau, O. J., Haase, P., Slooten, E., Dawson, S. M., The bottlenose dolphin community of doubtful sound features a large proportion of long-lasting associations, *Behavioral Ecology and Sociobiology*, 2003, 54:396–405.

Maslov, S., Sneppen, K., Specificity and stability in topology of protein networks, *Science*, 2002, 296:910–913.

Milgram, S., The small world problem, *Psychology Today*, 1967, 2:60–67.

Milo, R., Itzkovitz, S., Kashtan, N., Levitt, R., Shen-Orr, S., Ayzenshtat, I., Sheffer, M., Alon, U., Superfamilies of evolved and designed networks, *Science*, 2004, 303:1538–1542.

Newman, M. E. J., The structure of scientific collaboration networks, *Proceedings of the National Academy of Sciences*, 2001, 98:404.

Newman, M. E. J., Assortative mixing in networks, *Physical Review Letters*, 2002, 89:208701.

Newman, M. E. J., Finding community structure in networks using the eigenvectors of matrices, *Physical Review E*, 2006, 74:036104.

Pablo, M. G., Danon, L., Community structure in jazz, *Advances in Complex Systems*, 2003, 6:565.

Peng, C. K., Buldyrev, S. V., Havlin, S., Simons, M., Stanley, H. E., Goldberger, A. L., Mosaic organization of DFA nucleotides, *Physical Review E*, 1994, 49:1685–1689.

Scafetta, N., Grigolini, P., Scaling detection in time series: Diffusion entropy analysis, *Physical Review E*, 2002, 66:036130.

Shimada, Y., Ikeguchi, T., Shigehara, T., From networks to time series, *Physical Review Letters*, 2012, 109:158701.

Theiler, J., Eubank, S., Longtin, A., Galdrikian, B., Farmer, J. D., Testing for nonlinearity in time series: The method of surrogate data, *Physica D*, 1992, 58:77–94.

Watts, D., Strogatz, S., Collective dynamics of small-world networks. *Nature (London)*, 1998, 393:440–442.

Weng, T. F., Zhao, Y., Small, M., Huang, D. F., Time series analysis of networks: Exploring the structure with random walks, *Physical Review E*, 2014, 90:022804.

Chapter 12

Population Growth in Online Social Networks

Konglin Zhu,* Xiaoming Fu, Wenzhong Li, Sanglu Lu, and Jan Nagler

Contents

---

* Part of this work was conducted while KZ was affiliated at the University of Göttingen.

285

12.1 Introduction

Online social networks (OSNs) are now among the most popular services on the web, which are regarded as a great source of news and entertainment. With the increasing attention drawn by social networks, more and more social network platforms and applications appear and grow rapidly. The user population of OSNs is growing expeditiously. It is reported that Facebook has reached 2.2 billion users in July 2014. Meanwhile, Twitter has also surpassed 500 million users in 2015. This urges researchers to seek a better understanding of the laws and patterns of social network population growth. The benefits of investigation on social network population growth are threefold: (1) It reveals the dynamics and evolution of social networks [13]. Adding a new user to a social community or creating a new social link will impact the online and offline social structures and behaviors, which are interesting study subjects for physicists, sociologists, computer scientists, etc. (2) It is important for city planning and resource allocation [31]. For instance, the knowledge of geographical population growth of OSNs will provide valuable information to predict network traffic and to optimize the placement of routers and servers. (3) It may provide guidance for the design of future social systems. One example that considers the population dynamics is presented in Reference [22]. However, most existing social-inspired systems such as reliable e-mail (RE) [7] and SybilGuard [32] are designed based on static social populations, which ignore population growth. The growth of population will increase the workload and hence lead to essential impacts to the system performance. Therefore, it is necessary to design social systems taking account of dynamic population growth.

Previous researches show that population growth in human society follows Gibrat's law [8]: the average and standard deviation of growth rate are constant and independent of initial population size. Following the methodology of Gibrat's law, Hernan et al. study the population growth in cities [25], which demonstrates that the standard deviation of growth rate is a power-law decay as a function of the initial size that deviates Gibrat's law. Similar conclusions are found in the study of human interactions [26] and scientific output [19]. Over the past years, researches on population growth in OSNs mainly focus on the general tendency of population dynamics. [10,15,23,29].

In this chapter, we study the characteristics of population growth in OSNs, and several classical growth models, as well as how the population growth in OSNs fits the classical growth model.

12.2 Related Works

Population growth describes the increase of population size. Studies related to population growth in the real world go as far back as the 1930s [8]. Gibrat's law states that the growth rate of an entity (firm, mutual fund, city, population, etc.) has a distribution function with mean and variance that are constant with the initial size of the entity, which indicates the growth rate of an entity is independent of its initial size. It has significant influence on later studies and has been well exploited in population growth models such as in References 6, 11, and 16.

Based on the methodology of Gibrat's law, several recent studies [19,25,26] demonstrate that the standard deviation of growth rate is a power-law distribution as a function of the initial size of entities. In particular, Hernan et al. [25] claim that the standard deviation of population growth rate by city clustering algorithm is a power-law distribution in terms of the initial population size in cities. It infers that population growth by city clustering is a spatial correlation. Meanwhile, Rybski et al. [26] discover the standard deviation of interaction growth rate is a power-law scaling as a function of the initial number of interactions of individuals.

A number of population studies in OSNs mainly focused on the general tendency of population growth [10,15,23,29]. Jure et al. [15] study population growth as a function of time. Through capturing the best fits of population growth in different OSNs, they draw the conclusion that population growth in different OSNs performs wide variations on the growth tendency as time. Mojtaba et al. [29] and Reza et al. [23] show that aggregate population growth in MySpace experienced a slow growth in the beginning, following a period of exponential growth, and finally a significant and sudden slowdown in the growth of the population, known as an S-shaped curve. They further argue that the observed slowdown is directly related to the emergence of other OSNs, such as Facebook. Furthermore, Hu et al. [10] present the aggregated population growth in Wealink is an S-shaped curve as a function of time, which has a similar growth trend as MySpace. Overall, all these works concentrate on the general tendency of aggregate population growth.

12.3 The Data

To conduct the growth analysis in OSNs, we use the data collected from three OSN sites: Renren, Twitter, and Gowalla. We introduce the three data sets and the data collection methodology.

12.3.1 Three Online Social Networks

The data sets are collected from three OSNs: Renren, a social-based application service; Twitter, a social-based media service; and Gowalla, a location-based online social service. Renren, established in December 2005 and now with 160 million users, is a Chinese OSN that organizes users into membership-based networks representing schools, companies, and geographic locations. It allows users to post short messages known as status, blogs, and pictures. It also allows people to share contents such as videos, articles, and pictures. Twitter, with over 300 million users, launched in July 2006, is known as its microblogging services by which users can write any topic within the 140-character limit. Such kind of short message is known as tweet. It allows users to create personal profiles and their own pages inside the site. A follower can follow any other users and receive any kind of tweets from his or her followings. Varied from earlier mentioned two OSNs, Gowalla is a location-oriented online social service. People are allowed to check in their visiting places via mobile devices. It was launched in 2007 and closed in 2012 with approximately 600,000 users.

12.3.2 Data Collection Method

We collect the Renren and Twitter data sets by crawling from their sites accordingly. We start our crawling with randomly selected users from the largest weakly connected component (WCC) in Renren and Twitter, respectively. We follow friends' links in the forward direction in a breadth-first search (BFS) fashion. In this way, we collect a sample of each social network. To eliminate the degree bias caused by BFS, we launch the BFS-bias correction procedure described in Reference [14]. Furthermore, according to the estimation method of the size of social networks by Katzir et al. [12], we believe the quality and quantity of our data sets are enough to reveal the laws of population growth in OSNs. In order to capture the growth of population in different geographic locations, we need to know the account creation time and geographic information of each user. We trace the user account creation time in Twitter from the user profile. However, we cannot explicitly retrieve the user account creation time from the Renren user profile. To estimate a new user's registration date precisely in the Renren data set, we use the time of the user's first activity such as updating status, posting a blog, or interacting with friends as the account creation time. Meanwhile, we seek users' geographic location from user profiles and choose users with valid geographic information to compose our data sets.

The Gowalla data set, obtained from a public source [3], contains about 200,000 users, as well as their social relations and check-in histories. Unfortunately, there are no explicit data showing user home locations. Similar as Reference [3], we infer user home locations by compartmentalizing the globe into 25 km by 25 km cells and defining the home location as the cell with the most check-ins.

The statistics of the three data sets are shown in Table 12.1. The Renren data set (Renren) contains around 1 million of users and covers 10,039 locations. It records

Table 12.1　Statistics of Data Sets

	Renren	Twitter	Gowalla
Nodes	997,849	257,929	196,591
Locations	10,039	8,929	5,088
Period	01/06−12/10	08/06−10/10	02/09−10/10

user activities over the period of January 2006 to December 2010 (60 months). The Twitter data set (Twitter) consists of more than 250 thousand of users covering 8929 locations. We collect user activities over the period of August 2006 to October 2010 (51 months). The Gowalla data set (Gowalla) has around 200 thousand of nodes, with 5088 populated locations. The period of check-ins ranges from February 2009 to October 2010 (21 months).

12.4 Population Growth and Its Laws

To understand the population growth, we discuss the regional population, growth rate, laws of population growth, and models for the growth.

12.4.1 Regional Population

The regional population suggests the population size in each geographical area or region. Specifically, we divide the social networks into numerous cells geographically. As we mentioned earlier, Renren has 10,039 populated geographical locations, Twitter contains 8,929 populated locations, and Gowalla covers 5,088 populated locations. We use regional population to describe the geographic population. Table 12.2 shows the population of the top five populated regions in the data sets and their evolution over time. According to the table, the distribution of the population in various locations is uneven. The population size varies from locations to locations in different time periods. The population growth in different locations generally follows the rule that "rich gets richer". That is, a location with larger population size attracts more people to join in the OSN. However, the growth rate fluctuates at the early time of the OSNs, and it tends to be stable as the time increases. For example, the population size of the second largest city surpasses the first largest city in the 20th month of Twitter, whereas the overall population rank does not change after the 30th month.

12.4.2 Power-Law Distribution

The population distribution reveals the proportions of different population sizes in an OSN. We investigate the population distribution by drawing the log-log plots of the probability density function of populations in different geographic locations of the three data sets as shown in Figure 12.1 with respect to different time points. The observation to the figures shows that the population distributions are close to each other in different time periods. In particular, the population distributions of Renren are close to each other from the 10th month to the 50th month, as shown in Figure 12.1a. A similar phenomenon can also be observed from Twitter from the 8th month to the 48th month in Figure 12.1b and Gowalla from the 5th month to the 20th month in Figure 12.1c. It allows us to use one distribution curve

Table 12.2 The Five Largest Locations in the Three Data Sets

Rank	Renren				Twitter				Gowalla			
	10th	*20th*	*30th*	*40th*	*10th*	*20th*	*30th*	*40th*	*5th*	*10th*	*15th*	*20th*
1	892	5243	12,380	17,892	81	138	389	3,767	41	137	2,282	2,408
2	735	3952	11,069	15,456	57	262	3020	12,128	17	102	680	1,252
3	474	3168	9,868	12,060	53	231	1473	18,368	13	62	359	696
4	405	2842	6,219	8,040	45	153	792	11,367	12	370	1,476	2,016
5	404	2576	5,591	7,488	42	92	442	9,185	7	44	200	350

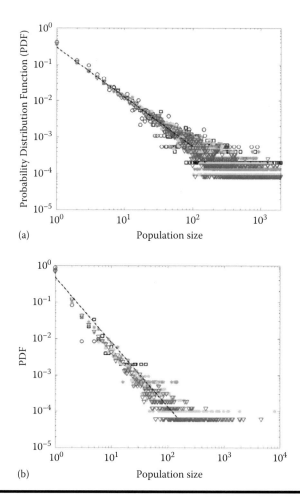

Figure 12.1 Population distribution of various periods in the three data sets. (a) Renren, the distribution of population size in the 10th month (circle), 20th month (square), 30th month (star), 40th month (solid circle), and 50th month (triangle). Five curves are close to each other and seemingly follow the same distribution. The dashed line is the power-law distribution: $y \sim x^{-1.4}$. (b) Twitter, the distribution of population size in the 8th month (circle), 18th month (square), 28th month (star), 38th month (solid circle), and 48th month (triangle). Five curves are close to each other and seemingly follow the same distribution. The dashed line is $y \sim x^{-1.78}$. **(*Continued*)**

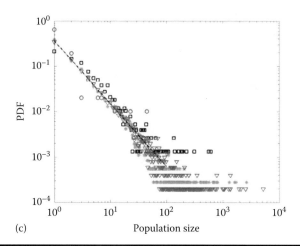

(c)   Population size

Figure 12.1 (*Continued*)   Population distribution of various periods in the three data sets. (c) Gowalla, the distribution of population size in the 5th month (circle), 10th month (square), 15th month (star), and 20th month (triangle). Four curves are close to each other and seemingly follow the same distribution. The dashed line is $y \sim x^{-1.4}$.

approximately to fit all population distributions in one data set, which means the population distributions of various periods roughly can be fitted with one identical distribution function. Then we find that the population distribution of each data set is seemingly a straight line in the log-log scale, which indicates that the distribution can be fitted with a power-law function. To confirm this observation, we conduct the hypothesis testing, which uses a *goodness-of-fit test* to determine plausibility of the power-law fit. It generates a p-value to quantify the plausibility. If p-value is close to 1, the fit is considered as plausible to the empirical data. Otherwise, it is considered as implausible. The results of the hypothesis tests show that $p = 1.0$ for Renren, $p = 0.90$ for Twitter, and $p = 0.95$ for Gowalla. All three values are close to 1. This suggests that the power-law function is plausible to fit the three data sets.

In addition, we conduct the alternative hypothesis testing regarding the population distribution by the *likelihood ratio test*, which suggests that the distribution is a power law given the likelihood ratio between the alternative and power-law distribution is positive. We calculated the likelihood ratio of exponential distribution compared with power-law distribution, which is 2.23, and the likelihood ratio of log-normal distribution compared with power-law distribution, which is 0.12. The result also suggests that power law is the best distribution to represent population distribution.

We fit each distribution in figures with maximal likelihood estimation (MLE). The fitting results are shown in dashed lines. It shows that the Renren data set has a power-law exponent of 1.4, Twitter has a power-law exponent of 1.78, and Gowalla has a power-law exponent of 1.4. We devise the mathematical model of the population distribution in different time periods as

$$P(s) = \varphi * s^{-\lambda},$$
(12.1)

where
φ is the scaling factor
λ is the power-law exponent

The equation suggests that the distribution of population size is a power law function in different time periods. It draws conclusion that the distribution of population size is independent of time.

12.4.3 Population Growth Rate

We denote the population size, that is, the number of users with home location index $1 \le l \le l_{max}$ at time $0 < t \le T$, by $S^l(t)$. Following References [6,11,16], we define the logarithmic growth rate r between time t_0 and $t_1(t_0 < t_1 \le T)$ as

$$r(S_0) = \ln \frac{S_1}{S_0},$$
(12.2)

where $S_0 = S^l(t_0)$ and $S_1 = S^l(t_1)$ are the population sizes at a location l but at different time points t_0 and t_1 [26], where t_0 and t_1 are the time points constraining the analysis time window of data sets. t_1 is chosen as the end point of the data set, $t_1: = T$. For the choice of t_0, we consider two factors: the number of populated locations in the time window and the size of the time window. A too small t_0 would lead to only a few populated locations, whereas any large t_0 would reduce the width of the window. Following the methodology of studies in human population growth in the real world [25] and the human interaction activities in OSNs [26], we determined t_0 as a result from time when the number of locations with growing populations reaches the peak. That is, $t_0: = 35$ for Renren, $t_0: = 36$ for Twitter, and $t_0: = 14$ for Gowalla, respectively (see Figure 12.2).

12.4.4 Laws of Population Growth

We investigate the mean growth rate and its fluctuation in OSN populations and ask the question how these observables depend on the initial population size.

To characterize fluctuations, we study the average growth rate $\langle r(S_0) \rangle$ and the standard deviation

$$\sigma(r|S_0) = \sqrt{\langle (r(S_0) - \langle r(S_0) \rangle)^2 \rangle}$$
(12.3)

as a function of the initial population size S_0 (see Figure 12.1). In other words, the average growth rate $\langle r(S_0) \rangle$ corresponds to only those online populations with the

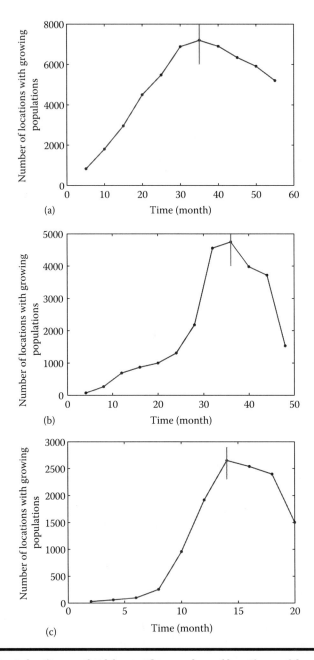

Figure 12.2 Selection method for t_0. The number of locations with growing populations ($S(t_1) > S(t_0)$) as a function of time. We account for the trade-off between a large number of populated locations and a large time series length $t_1 - t_0$ by choosing t_0 close to the maximum. This results (a) for Renren to t_0: = 35, (b) for Twitter to t_0: = 36, and (c) for Gowalla to t_0: = 14.

size of at least S_0 until time t_0. The conditional standard deviation of the growth rate $\sigma(r|S_0)$ for those populations expresses the statistical spread or fluctuation of growth among populations with S_0. Both quantities show a power-law dependence on the initial population size

$$\langle r(S_0) \rangle \sim S_0^{-\alpha} \quad \text{and} \quad \sigma(r|S_0) \sim S_0^{-\beta} \tag{12.4}$$

with positive exponents $\alpha, \beta > 0$ ($P < 0.05$), which suggests a deviation from the independence of Gibrat's law that would imply $\alpha_{\text{Gibrat}} = \beta_{\text{Gibrat}} = 0$. Scale-invariant growth instead of Gibrat's proportionate growth has been reported for economic systems such as firms [28] and countries ($\beta = 0.15 - 0.18$) [2], research and development expenditures at universities ($\beta \approx 0.25$) [21], scientific output ($\beta = 0.28 - 0.40$) [19], and more recently city population growth ($\beta = 0.19 - 0.27$) [25] and online communities ($\beta = 0.15 - 0.22$) [26].

The range of β for Renren and Twitter is in agreement with those previously reported exponents for β. However, in contrast to the previous work mentioned earlier, our analysis (employing MLE and bootstrapping) does not suggest significant deviations from $\beta = 0.5$, which would indicate uncorrelated growth. In contrast, for Gowalla, we find β significantly smaller than $\beta = 0.5$ ($P < 0.05$).

Second, we find the range of exponents for the average growth rate for all studied OSNs significantly above $\alpha = 0$ ($P < 0.05$) indicating a violation of Gibrat's proportionate growth, which is in agreement with social and economic systems [2,19,21,25,26,28].

The average growth rate $\langle r(S_0) \rangle$ and the conditional standard deviation of the growth rate $\sigma(r|S_0)$ allow for direct comparison with the literature for other social systems and Gibrat's law but are only averages. As suggested by studies of certain assets in economic systems, the distribution of the variance can often expose important information that cannot be seen in averages [18].

Since for a given S_0 there is only a single value of $\sigma(r|S_0)$ (see Figure 12.3), we ask what is the relative variation of $\sigma(r|S_0)$ across all values of $\sigma(r|S_0')$ that occur in a given data set. We thus focus on the relative fluctuation function (rff)

$$\text{rff}(S_0) = \frac{\sigma(r|S_0)}{\sum_{S_0'} \sigma(r|S_0')} \tag{12.5}$$

as a function of S_0. Specifically, we study the complementary cumulative relative fluctuation function (ccrff), which is given by the complement of the integrated rff:

$$\text{ccrff}(S_0) = 1 - \sum_{S_0' \leq S_0} \text{rff}(S_0') \tag{12.6}$$

We chose the ccrff representation because it shows (if exists) a clearer scaling than the rff and thus better exposes different (scaling) regimes. The ccrff is obtained by

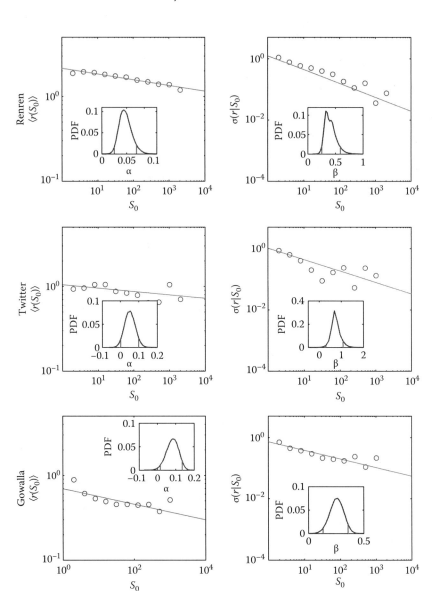

Figure 12.3 Scaling in average growth rate and standard deviation. Both $\langle r(S_0)\rangle$ and $\sigma\langle r|S_0\rangle$ as a function of the initial population size S_0 exhibit a power law, $\langle r(S_0)\rangle \sim S_0^{-\alpha}$, $\sigma(r|S_0) \sim S_0^{-\beta}$. Renren: $\langle r(S_0)\rangle \sim S_0^{-0.07}$ ($R^2 = 0.326$), $\sigma(r|S_0) \sim S_0^{-0.45}$ ($R^2 = 0.526$), that is, $\alpha_{rr} = 0.07$, $\beta_{rr} = 0.45$; Twitter: $\alpha_{tw} = 0.04$ ($R^2 = 0.142$), $\beta_{tw} = 0.37$ ($R^2 = 0.531$); Gowalla: $\alpha_{gw} = 0.09$ ($R^2 = 0.343$), $\beta_{gw} = 0.35$ ($R^2 = 0.625$). All values are obtained from MLE. Bootstrapping suggests 95% confidence for $\alpha > 0$ (violation of Gibrat's law) and for $\beta_{gw} < 0.5$ (suggesting long-range correlations). No statistical significance is found for $\beta < 0.5$ for Renren and Twitter. Vertical lines indicate 5% marks (insets).

collecting all locations with a given value of S_0 using exponential binning, by which the bins are evenly distributed on a logarithmic scale. Specifically, the beginning of each bin is $b^j = [cR^j]$, exponentially increasing in j, with constants c and $R > 1$, so that bins have size $b_{j+1} - b_j \approx b_j(R-1)$.

As shown in Figure 12.4, in contrast to Renren and Twitter where we find no significant bimodality, for Gowalla the ccrff as a function of S_0 exhibits a remarkable bimodal behavior.

For Gowalla, Figure 12.4c suggests a bimodal distribution of standard deviations, characterized by an exponential decay that is followed by a power law:

$$\text{ccrff}(S_0) = \begin{cases} e^{-\mu S_0} & (S_0 < S^*) \\ S_0^{-\nu} & (S_0 \geq S^*) \end{cases} \tag{12.7}$$

To determine the best value for S^*, we fit the distribution of standard deviation with respect to S_0 ranging from 0 to 300 by using MLE. For each S_0, we calculate R^2 for exponential and power-law fitting, denoted as $R^2_{\exp}$ and R^2_{pow}, respectively. To characterize the overall fitting quality (FQ), we use

$$FQ = R^2_{\exp} R^2_{\text{pow}}, \tag{12.8}$$

where we use log-log scaling for determining the coefficient of determination for the power law, and log-linear scaling for the exponential.

We choose $S^* = \text{argmax}\ (FQ(S_0))$ where FQ takes its maximum at the value of $S^* = 93$, as shown in Figure 12.5. MLE suggests that the power-law decay is characterized by the exponent $\nu_{\text{gw}} = 0.13$ ($R^2 = 0.966$).

12.4.5 Gowalla: Correlations in the Growth Rate

The findings mentioned earlier suggest to consider two groups of locations: one group with initial population size $S_0 < S^*$, and the other one with initial population size $S_0 \geq S^*$. We call this a dichotomy. We conduct a study to seek the origin of the observed dichotomy phenomenon. Specifically, we investigate the dichotomy phenomenon by examining the correlation of regional population growth. To understand the relation between the dichotomy phenomenon and correlations, we first introduce several definitions of correlation. [1,4,27].

The autocorrelation function (ACF) is used to measure the self-correlation as a function of a time lag τ. For a process $x(t)$, the definition of ACF is denoted as

$$C(\tau) = \frac{\langle (x(t) - \langle x(t) \rangle)(x(t+\tau) - \langle x(t) \rangle) \rangle}{\sigma_x^2} \tag{12.9}$$

where τ is the time lag and σ_x is the standard deviation of $x(t)$. $C(\tau)$ ranging from −1 to 1 measures the interdependencies between the values of $x(t)$.

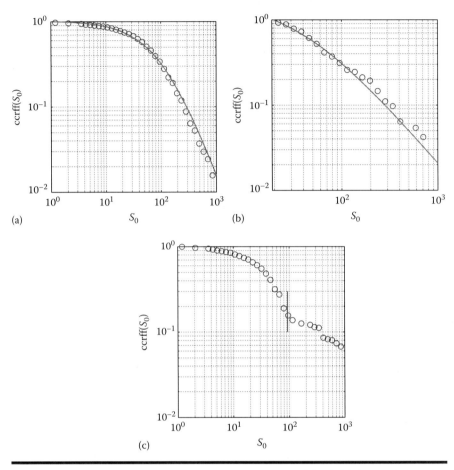

Figure 12.4 The ccrff, Equation 12.6, as a function of the initial population size S_0. For Renren and Twitter, the ccrff is well fitted by shifted power law $\sim (S_0 - C)^{-\nu}$, with C a constant: (a) Result for Renren: $\nu_{rr} = 1.828$ ($R^2 = 0.997$). (b) Result for Twitter: $\nu_{tw} = 1.324$ ($R^2 = 0.995$). (c) For Gowalla, the ccrff is bimodal with a cutoff point at $S^* \approx 93$ (obtained from MLE, see Methods): the left part is well fitted by an exponential and the right part is in good agreement with a power-law decay, $\mathrm{ccrff}(S_0) \sim e^{-\mu S_0}$ for $S_0 < S^*$ and $\mathrm{ccrff}(S_0) \sim S_0^{-\nu}$ for $S_0 \geq S^*$. Fit exponents $\mu_{gw} = 0.009$ ($R^2 = 0.997$) and $\nu_{gw} = 0.13$ ($R^2 = 0.966$).

Stochastic processes can exhibit short- and/or long-term correlations [1,27]. In short-term correlation processes, the coupling between values at different times decreases rapidly as the time lag increases. The ACF has an exponential decay. In long-term correlation processes, the corresponding ACF is a power-law decay. We give the mathematical expression of the short-term correlation and the long-term correlation in the following:

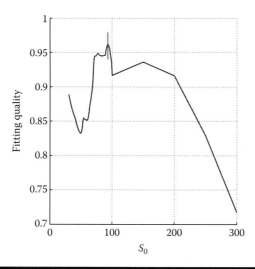

Figure 12.5 **The selection of S^* for Gowalla. The FQ as a function of S_0. S^* is defined as the position (argmax) of the maximum, which is $S^* = 93$ for Gowalla.**

Short-term correlation: If a process is short-term correlated, the ACF eventually decays exponentially, namely,

$$C(\tau) \sim e^{-\omega\tau}. \tag{12.10}$$

Long-term correlation: The ACF follows a power law if the process is long-term correlated, which is presented as

$$C(\tau) \sim \tau^{-\gamma}, \tag{12.11}$$

with the correlation exponent $0 < \gamma < 1$.

We study the monthly population growth rates for each location and calculate their ACF [1,4,27]. For $S_0 < S^*$, the ensemble averaged ACF exhibits an exponential decay, $C(\tau) \sim e^{-\gamma\tau}$, indicating that the population growth is short-term correlated (see Figure 12.6a). We obtain the exponent $\gamma = 0.13$ ($R^2 = 0.992$ from MLE), which is equivalent to a correlation time constant of about 2 weeks.

In contrast, for $S_0 \geq S^*$, the ACF is well described by a power law, $C(\tau) \sim \tau^{-\delta}$ with a power-law exponent $\delta = 0.73$ ($R^2 = 0.955$ from MLE) (see Figure 12.6b).

This is consistent with long-term correlations characterized by $\sum_{\tau=-\infty}^{\infty} C(\tau) = \infty$; see Reference 9 and references therein.

12.4.6 Superposition Model

Seemingly, long-range correlations can often be explained by a finite set of independent processes whose superposition accounts for the algebraic decay in the ACF

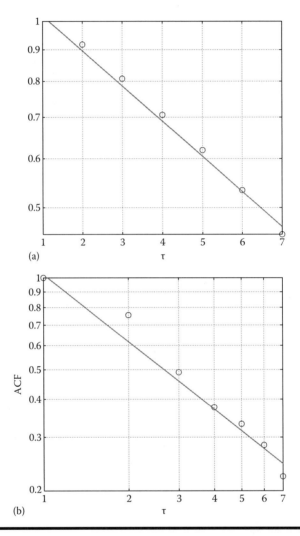

Figure 12.6 *Gowalla*: **Temporal short- and long-term correlations in the population growth rate. (a) Short-term correlations for $S_0 < S^*$ (log-lin plots), $C(\tau) \sim e^{-\gamma\tau}$; (b) long-term correlations for $S_0 \geq S^*$ (log-log plots), $C(\tau) \sim \tau^{-\delta}$. Fits using MLE suggest $\gamma = 0.13$ ($R^2 = 0.992$), $\delta = 0.73$ ($R^2 = 0.955$); log-log scaling for determining the coefficient of determination for the power law, and log-linear scaling for the exponential.**

and the divergence of its infinite sum. In 1979, Van der Ziel established that any ensemble of uncoupled, short-range correlated stochastic oscillators is sufficient for explaining long-range correlations in their superposition, if and only if the time constants of the mixed processes are sufficiently broadly distributed [30]. More recently, it has been shown that a superposition of Poisson processes, together with circadian activity, very likely accounts for many scaling laws of human activity patterns [17]. Here, as the growth rates are broadly distributed, we follow this spirit by considering a superposition of populations and surrogate time series from these.

To establish superpositions, we select all populations at locations with $S_0 < S^*$. The randomized surrogate data set is created by shuffling these entries and creating a time series from these shuffled entries as follows. (1) From the set of populations with $S_0 < S^*$, we select randomly a population and add up its initial population size S_0, irrespective of its location. (2) We repeat (1) until the sum exceeds S^*. This results in a set of locations whose total initial population size equals or slightly exceeds S^*. We call this set of locations one realization of a superposition. (3) For each realization, we study the temporal development with respect to the total population's size of the thereafter fixed selected locations. For each superposition, we construct a time series, that is, the population growth rates in monthly resolution, from t_0 to t_1. For this set of time series, we obtain the ensemble averaged ACF.

Gowalla's population growth of the superposition ensemble obtained from a random selection of population with $S_0 < S^*$ results in the occurrence of seemingly long-term correlations for locations with $S_0 \geq S^*$. The exponents δ^{sur} for the surrogate superpositions (sur) are obtained from fitting the superposition ensemble averaged ACF by MLE with $R^2 = 0.986$, $\delta^{sur} = 0.59$ ($R^2 = 0.986$, $\delta = 0.73$); see Figure 12.7.

This suggests that the seemingly long-term correlated population growth found for locations with $S_0 \geq S^*$ results from superpositions of short-term correlated growing populations.

12.4.7 Spatial Dependence

To study geographical factors, we investigate correlations of the population growth rates r_i and r_j between different places [20,24]. For each location with integer ID l, we extract a time series from t_0 to t_1 of the monthly population growth rate according to Equation 12.2 as $r_t = \ln \dfrac{S_{t+1}}{S_t}$, $t_0 \leq t < t_1$ being the tth month. We therefore study Pearson's correlation coefficient:

$$c = \frac{\langle (r_i - \langle r_i \rangle)(r_j - \langle r_j \rangle) \rangle}{\sigma_i \sigma_j}, \tag{12.12}$$

where $\sigma_{i,j} = \sqrt{\langle (r_{i,j} - \langle r_{i,j} \rangle)^2 \rangle}$ is the standard deviation of r_i and r_j, respectively.

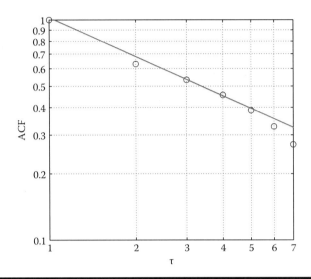

Figure 12.7 *Gowalla*: **Decomposition of the growth into independent short-term correlated population growth processes. The ACF for the three data sets according to the superposition scheme explained in the text. The power-law exponents from fitting** $C(\tau) \sim \tau^{-\delta^{sur}}$ **obtained from the decomposition via surrogate data (sur). Best fits from MLE:** $\delta^{sur} = 0.59$ **(** $R^2 = 0.986$ **).**

We investigate the monthly population growth rates and Pearson's correlation coefficient between a pair of locations as a function of the geographic distance of the users. Figure 12.8 shows Pearson's correlation coefficients for the three data sets. The average correlation $\langle c \rangle$ is found at a level of about 0.7–0.8, effectively independent of the geographic distance. The high value of the cross-correlation agrees well with the plausible assumption that individuals join OSNs collectively but independent of the geographic distance to each other.

12.5 Conclusion and Discussion

In this chapter, we address the population distribution and the population growth in OSNs. First, we study the population distribution in OSNs. We find the population size in OSNs is a power-law distribution, with a power-law exponent from 1.4 to 1.8, which is smaller than that of population in the real world. This may suggest that network effect is not so strong in three networks. They does not act as the maintainer of social networks, while they are the network relying on information diffusion. Therefore, it is also necessary to study the social networks such as Facebook, WeChat and etc. We find scaling in the population growth rate and variance in OSNs. Our results suggest that the population growth in OSNs is significantly determined neither by population size [5] nor by spatial factors. The results

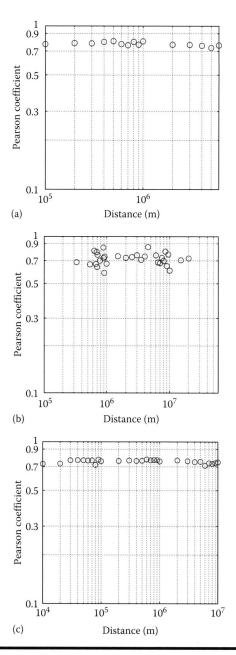

Figure 12.8 Spatial independence of the population growth rates. The mean correlation coefficient $\langle c \rangle$ of the population growth rate as a function of geographic distance (log-log plot). (a) For Renren, plateau at about $\langle c_{rr} \rangle \approx 0.80$; (b) for Twitter, $\langle c_{tw} \rangle \approx 0.73$; and (c) for Gowalla, $\langle c_{gw} \rangle \approx 0.76$.

deviate from Gibrat's law as previously found in many social and economic systems. The seemingly long-term correlated growth behavior for Gowalla suggested scaling in the standard deviation is explained by a simple decomposition into short-term correlated population growth with broadly distributed growth rates. Our method may help in interpreting (seemingly) long-range correlations in the growth of large heterogenous (online) social and economic systems. Seemingly collective behavior in online social systems may result from the high variability of loners' actions and not from correlated collective behavior.

The diversity between short-range correlation and long-range correction suggests that the initial size of population is important, which confirms that s-curve may appear when the initial size surpass S_0. The superposition of small size of locations showing the same seemingly long-range correlations suggests the population growth is independent in spatial perspective, which collaborative with the conclusion we have drawn when discussing the spatial dependency. The analysis results show that Gowalla has different patterns compared with Renren and Twitter data sets. However, the reason why some data sets exhibit different patterns is not fully revealed yet. One possible explanation is that some data sets (e.g., Twitter and Renren) are crawled from the websites, which only contain less than 10% of whole social network users, while some other data sets (e.g., Gowalla) contain the full size of the network. Our conjecture is that the seemingly long-term correlated growth behavior may only occur in the whole data but not obvious in the crawled data. However, due to the significant large size of both Twitter and Renren networks, it is impossible to collect all users from these two websites. Further analysis, experiments on other data sets, and possibly dialogues with social science knowledge and models are needed.

References

1. J. Beran, R. Sherman, M.S. Taqqu, and W. Willinger. Long-range dependence in variable-bit-rate video traffic. *IEEE Transactions on Communications*, 43(234):1566–1579, 1995.
2. D. Canning, L.A.N. Amaral, Y. Lee, M. Meyer, and H.E. Stanley. Scaling the volatility of gdp growth rates. *Economics Letters*, 60(3):335–341, 1998.
3. E. Cho, S.A. Myers, and J. Leskovec. Friendship and mobility: User movement in location-based social networks. In *Proceedings of the 17th ACM SIGKDD International Conference on Knowledge Discovery and Data Mining (KDD'11)*, pp. 1082–1090, ACM, New York, 2011.
4. P.F. Dunn. *Measurement and Data Analysis for Engineering and Science*. CRC Press/ Taylor & Francis, Boca Raton, FL, 2010.
5. D. Easley and J. Kleinberg. *Networks, Crowds, and Markets: Reasoning about a Highly Connected World*. Cambridge University Press, New York, 2010.
6. X. Gabaix and Y. Ioannides. The evolution of city size distributions. In J.V. Henderson and J.F. Thisse, eds., *Handbook of Regional and Urban Economics*, 1st edn., vol. 4, Chapter 53, pp. 2341–2378. Elsevier, Amsterdam, the Netherlands, 2004.

7. S. Garriss, M. Kaminsky, M.J. Freedman, B. Karp, D. Maziéres, and H. Yu. Re: Reliable e-mail. In *Proceedings of NSDI*, San Jose, CA, pp. 297–310, 2006.

8. R. Gibrat. Les ingalits conomiques. Libraire du Recueil Sierey, Paris, France, 1931.

9. H. Hennig, R. Fleischmann, A. Fredebohm, Y. Hagmayer, J. Nagler, A. Witt, F.J. Theis, and T. Geisel. The nature and perception of fluctuations in human musical rhythms. *PLoS One*, 6(10):e26457, 2011.

10. H. Hu and X. Wang. Evolution of a large online social network. *Physics Letters A*, 373(12–13):14, 2009.

11. Y.M. Ioannides and H.G. Overman. Zipf's law for cities: An empirical examination. *Regional Science and Urban Economics*, 33:127–137(11), 2003.

12. L. Katzir, E. Liberty, and O. Somekh. Estimating sizes of social networks via biased sampling. In *Proceedings of the 20th International Conference on World Wide Web (WWW'11)*, pp. 597–606, ACM, New York, 2011.

13. R. Kumar, J. Novak, and A. Tomkins. Structure and evolution of online social networks. In P.S. Yu, J. Han, and C. Faloutsos, editors, *Link Mining: Models, Algorithms, and Applications*, pp. 337–357. New York: Springer New York, 2010.

14. M. Kurant, A. Markopoulou, and P. Thiran. Towards unbiased BFS sampling. *IEEE Journal on Selected Areas in Communications*, 29(9):1799–1809, 2011.

15. J. Leskovec, L. Backstrom, R. Kumar, and A. Tomkins. Microscopic evolution of social networks. In *Proceedings of the 14th ACM SIGKDD International Conference on Knowledge Discovery and Data Mining (KDD'08)*, Las Vegas, NV, pp. 462–470, 2008.

16. M. Levy. Gibrat's law for (all) cities: Comment. *American Economic Review*, 99(4):1672–1675, 2009.

17. R.D. Malmgren, D.B. Stouffer, A.E. Motter, and L.A.N. Amaral. A poissonian explanation for heavy tails in e-mail communication. *Proceedings of the National Academy of Sciences of the United States of America*, 105:18153–18158, November 2008.

18. R.N. Mantegna and H.E. Stanley. *Introduction to Econophysics: Correlations and Complexity in Finance*. Cambridge University Press, New York, 2000.

19. K. Matia, L.A.N. Amaral, M. Luwel, H.F. Moed, and H.E. Stanley. Scaling phenomena in the growth dynamics of scientific output. *Journal of the American Society for Information Science and Technology*, 56(9):893–902, 2005.

20. D. Nikolic, R.C. Muresan, W. Feng, and W. Singer. Scaled correlation analysis: A better way to compute a cross-correlogram. *European Journal of Neuroscience*, 35(5):742–762, 2012.

21. V. Plerou, L.A.N. Amaral, P. Gopikrishnan, M. Meyer, and H.E. Stanley. Similarities between the growth dynamics of university research and of competitive economic activities. *Nature*, 400(6743):433–437, 1999.

22. J.M. Pujol, V. Erramilli, G. Siganos, X. Yang, N. Laoutaris, P. Chhabra, and P. Rodriguez. The little engine(s) that could: Scaling online social networks. In *Proceedings of the ACM SIGCOMM 2010 Conference (SIGCOMM'10)*, pp. 375–386, New Delhi, India, 2010.

23. R. Rejaie, M. Torkjazi, M. Valafar, and W. Willinger. Sizing up online social networks. *Network, IEEE*, 24(5):32–37, IEEE Press Piscataway, NJ, 2010.

24. J.L. Rodgers and W.A. Nicewander. Thirteen ways to look at the correlation coefficient. *The American Statistician*, 42(1):59–66, 1988.

25. H.D. Rozenfeld, D. Rybski, J.S. Andrade Jr., M. Batty, H.E. Stanley, and H.A. Makse. Laws of population growth. *Proceedings of the National Academy of Sciences of the United States of America*, 105:18702–18707, 2008.

26. D. Rybski, S.V. Buldyrev, S. Havlin, F. Liljeros, and H.A. Makse. Scaling laws of human interaction activity. *Proceedings of the National Academy of Sciences of the United States of America*, 106(31):12640–12645, 2009.

27. G. Samorodnitsky. Long range dependence. *Foundations and Trends in Stochastic Systems*, 1:163–257, January 2007.

28. M.H.R. Stanley, L.A.N. Amaral, S.V. Buldyrev, S. Havlin, H. Leschhorn, P. Maass, M.A. Salinger, and H.E. Stanley. Scaling behaviour in the growth of companies. *Nature*, 379(6568):804–806, 1996.

29. M. Torkjazi. Hot today, gone tomorrow: On the migration of myspace users. In *Proceedings of the Second ACM Workshop on Online Social Networks (WOSN'09)*, Barcelona, Spain, 2009.

30. A. van der Ziel. Unified presentation of 1/f noise in electron devices: Fundamental 1/f noise sources. *Proceedings of the IEEE*, 76(3):233–258, IEEE Press Piscataway, NJ, 1988.

31. M.P. Wittie, V. Pejovic, L. Deek, K.C. Almeroth, and B.Y. Zhao. Exploiting locality of interest in online social networks. In *Proceedings of the Sixth International Conference on Emerging Networking EXperiments and Technologies (CoNEXT'10)*, Philadelphia, PA. ACM Press, New York, 2010.

32. H. Yu, M. Kaminsky, P.B. Gibbons, and A. Flaxman. Sybilguard: Defending against sybil attacks via social networks. In *ACM SIGCOMM 2006*, Pisa, Italy, pp. 267–278. ACM Press, New York, 2006.

COLLABORATION AND INFORMATION DISSEMINATION IN SOCIAL NETWORKS

V

Chapter 13

Information Dissemination in Social-Featured Opportunistic Networks

Wenzhong Li, Sanglu Lu, Konglin Zhu,
Xiao Chen, Jan Nagler and Xiaoming Fu

Contents

13.1 Introduction

In recent years, opportunistic networks have emerged as a mechanism for infrastructure-free communications in wireless networks. An opportunistic network is a sparse dynamic wireless network where mobile nodes work in ad hoc mode and can communicate with each other only when they move into their communication range [7]. The communication in opportunistic networks is disruption tolerant, and there is no need of establishing end-to-end message routing paths. Since opportunistic networks allow people to communicate without network infrastructure, they are widely used in wildlife tracking sensor networks, vehicular ad hoc networks, pocket switched networks, and mobile social networks.

Information dissemination addresses the issue of sending a piece of information from a source node to one or more destination(s), which is a key function of communication in opportunistic networks. Since mobile devices can exchange information only when humans come into contact, such networks are tightly coupled with human social networks [23]. Therefore, an opportunistic communication network can be described as a complex network with social features, and the methodologies for interdisciplinary social networks research can be applied to analyze the structure and dynamics of such network and further to provide guidelines and principles to improve information dissemination in opportunistic communication. Specifically, the application of social network analysis approach in our communication network is twofold. First, social profiles can be addressed to study the encounter opportunities of human beings. According to the principle of homophily, people tends to be associated with similar others regarding age, gender, class, and organizational role. This inspires us to study the *social profile similarity*, which is the quantification of the homophily between users in the opportunistic network and can be used as a good indicator to infer the future communication opportunities between individuals. Second, social network structure has great impact on the efficiency of information dissemination process. One of the most important aspects of social network is the community structure. A social network naturally forms different communities due to the clustering of individuals for different reasons. In the context of mobile opportunistic communication, community structure occurs due to the regional characteristics of human movement and the local and remote contact patterns of individuals. We apply distributed community detection algorithm to reveal the community structure in opportunistic network, based on which we can devise several principles to improve the efficiency of information dissemination for intracommunity and intercommunity communications.

In this chapter, we introduce two types of information dissemination in social-featured opportunistic networks: *unicast* and *multicast.*

Unicast enables one-to-one communication in opportunistic networks, where one mobile node sends information to another node. Based on characterizing users' social interactions and mobility patterns, we propose a *s*ocial- and *m*obile-*a*ware message *r*ou*t*ing strategy called "SMART." It exploits a distributed community partitioning algorithm to divide an opportunistic network into smaller communities based on user movements and interaction routines. Then, according to the positions of the destination nodes, it performs either the intracommunity communication or the intercommunity communication process to disseminate information. For intracommunity communications, a decayed routing utility combining social similarity and social centrality is calculated, which is used to decide relay nodes efficiently inside the community. To enable efficient intercommunity communications, it chooses the fringe nodes that travel remotely as relays, and the community-degree utilities are calculated for routing decision across communities. The efficiency of SMART is evaluated by extensive trace-driven experiments, which illustrate that it outperforms other unicast strategies in various opportunistic network traces.

Multicast enables one-to-many communication where one mobile node sends information to a set of destinations. We introduce the concept of dynamic social features and its enhancement to capture nodes' dynamic contact behavior and social relationships. Based on the derived dynamic social features and the community structure, we adopt the compare–split scheme to select the best relay node for each destination in each hop to construct a multicast tree. Specifically, we propose two *c*ommunity and *s*ocial feature–based multicast algorithms named "Multi-CSDO," which involves *d*estination nodes *o*nly in community detection, and "Multi-CSDR," which involves both the *d*estination nodes and *r*elay candidates in community detection in case the relay candidates are also socially similar. The performance of the algorithms is evaluated by simulations with a real trace of a mobile social network, which shows that the proposed multicast algorithms outperform the existing ones in terms of delivery rate, latency, and number of forwardings.

The rest of the chapter is organized as follows. Section 13.2 presents the modeling of opportunistic network as a social graph. Section 13.3 introduces the definitions of social features and social properties. Section 13.4 proposes the information dissemination strategies for unicast. Section 13.5 proposes the information dissemination strategies for multicast in opportunistic networks. The chapter is concluded in Section 13.6.

13.2 Model

We model an opportunistic network as a social graph $G = \langle V, E \rangle$, which is illustrated in Figure 13.1. In the graph, V is a set of nodes representing mobile users. Each user has a set of personal information forming his social profile. The *encounter event* is defined as the event that two nodes enter the communication range of each other. If a node encountered another node in the past, there is a link between them indicating their social relationship. E is the set of links/edges in the graph.

The following glossary is used to describe the social properties of social-featured opportunistic networks:

Social ties: Represent the social interaction between two nodes, which is quantified by the frequency of their encounters.
Neighbors: Represent the set of nodes that have direct contact to a user in the network.
Communities: Represent the clustering structure of the social network. Nodes within the same community are closely connected to each other by either direct linkage or intermediates.

Social features of opportunistic network are defined in the next section.

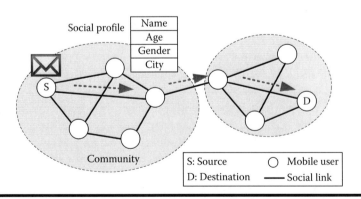

Figure 13.1   The social graph of an opportunistic network.

13.3 Social Features

Since information diffusion in opportunistic networks is based on the contacts of mobile devices carried by human individuals, the speed and range of diffusion are dependent upon the frequency and the patterns of intercontacts of individuals, which are affected by the social features of individuals. In this section, we introduce the representation of social features in opportunistic networks. Specifically, we explore two types of social features: social profiles and social network structures.

13.3.1 Social Profiles

Social profiles are the properties associated with individuals in the social life. For example, node i (an individual) may be a *female* working as a *faculty* member in a *university in the United States*, while node j may be a *male* working as a *manager* in a *company in China*. The two nodes have different gender, profession, affliction, and locations that form their social profiles. According to the study of [25,26], people come in contact more frequently if they have more social profile features in common.

We use a vector $E_i = \langle E_{i1}, E_{i2}, \ldots, E_{im} \rangle$ to indicate the social profiles of node i, where $E_{i1}, E_{i2}, \ldots$ can refer to the information of *nationality, city, language, gender, profession, affliction*, etc. Each social feature E_{ik} can take multiple values. For example, a social feature E_{ik} can be language and its values can be English, Spanish, and so on. The social profile of a person is time variant. For example, the *age* and *location* of a person will change over time. Thus, we use $E_{ik}(\tau)$ to indicate the value of the *kth* social feature of node i at time τ. We introduce the *social profile similarity* to represent the similarity of two individuals regarding their social profiles.

Definition 13.1 Social profile similarity Assume $E_i(\tau) = \langle E_{i1}(\tau), E_{i2}(\tau), \ldots, E_{im}(\tau) \rangle$ and $E_j(\tau) = \langle E_{j1}(\tau), E_{j2}(\tau), \ldots, E_{jk}(\tau) \rangle$ are the social profiles of nodes i and j at time τ, the social profile similarity of the two nodes is defined as

$$S_{i,j}(\tau) = dist(E_i(\tau), E_j(\tau)), \tag{13.1}$$

where $dist(X, Y)$ are the distance measurements of the two vectors.

Based on the definition, the social profile similarity can be measured by the distance of two vectors. There are a variety of distance measurements such as Euclidean distance and Mahalanobis distance, which can be used to quantify the social profile similarity.

Another metric to evaluate the closeness of two nodes is *social neighbor similarity*, which is defined as the number of neighbors they shared.

Definition 13.2 Social structure similarity Assume $\mathcal{F}_i(\tau)$ and $\mathcal{F}_j(\tau)$ are the sets of neighbors of nodes n_i and n_j at time τ accordingly, the social neighbor similarity of the two nodes is defined as

$$S_{i,j}(\tau) = \left| \mathcal{F}_i(\tau) \cap \mathcal{F}_j(\tau) \right|. \tag{13.2}$$

Social neighbor similarity infers the reachability of two nodes for information dissemination in opportunistic networks. The higher the social neighbor similarity of two nodes is, the more likely they can communicate with each other via the common neighbors.

13.3.2 Social Network Structures

Social network structure represents the position of a node in the social network and how the nodes connect with each other in the network. We use *centrality* and *community* to specify such social features.

Social centrality refers to the position and the relative importance of a node in the social network structure. There are various definitions of centrality, which include degree centrality [10] and betweenness centrality [9].

Definition 13.3 Degree centrality Degree centrality is simply defined as the proportion of the number of links incident upon a node. Assume $G = \langle V, E \rangle$ is a social graph; d_{ik} is an indicator to represent the existence of a link between two nodes, where $d_{ik}(\tau) = 1$ if there exists a link between node i and node k at time τ, and $d_{ik}(\tau) = 1$ otherwise. The degree centrality of node i at time τ is calculated by

$$C_i(\tau) = \frac{\sum_{\forall k \in V} d_{ik}(\tau)}{\sum_{\forall j \in V} \sum_{\forall k \in V} d_{jk}(\tau)}, \tag{13.3}$$

where $\sum_{\forall j \in V} \sum_{\forall k \in V} d_{jk}(\tau)$ is the total number of links in the social network.

Definition 13.4 Betweenness centrality Betweenness centrality measures the importance of a node that acts as a bridge along the shortest path between two other nodes in the social graph. For a social graph $G = \langle V, E \rangle$, assume at time τ the set of nodes on the shortest path from node s to node t is indicated by $V_{s \to t}$. The betweenness centrality of node i at time τ is calculated by

$$C_i(\tau) = \frac{\sum_{\forall s \in V \& s \neq i} \sum_{\forall t \in V \& t \neq i} \left| \{i\} \cap V_{s \to t} \right|}{(n-1)(n-2)/2}, \tag{13.4}$$

where the upper part calculates the total times that node i lies on the shortest path from s to t, and the lower part is the total number of source–destination pairs in the social graph.

In the context of information diffusion in social networks, the degree centrality and betweenness centrality can be interpreted in terms of the ability of a node for holding information flowing through the network.

The community structure refers to the property that nodes of the network forming subgroups with which vertex–vertex connections are dense, but between which connections are less dense [11]. According to [20], the community structure of a social network can be defined as follows.

Definition 13.5 Community A community is a local densely connected subgraph in a network. For a subgraph $G' = \langle V', E' \rangle$ of a social graph $G = \langle V, E \rangle$, assume d_i^{in} is the number of connections from node i to the other nodes in V' and d_i^{out} is the number of connections from i to the nodes in $V-V'$. G' is a community of G if it satisfies

$$\sum_{i \in V'} d_i^{in} > \sum_{i \in V'} d_i^{out}, \qquad (13.5)$$

that is, the total number of internal connections in G' should be larger than the total number of external connections to the rest of the network.

Community detection algorithms have been well studied in the past. Typical approaches include the min-cut technique [5] that partitions a connected graph into subgraphs recursively, the Girvan–Newman algorithm [11] that removes the edges with the highest edge betweenness gradually, and the label propagation algorithm [19] that provides a near-linear time solution for community detection in large-scale networks.

13.4 Unicast

Unicast refers to one-to-one communication in a network. When a piece of information is sent by a source node, a unique destination address is specified. Unicast in opportunistic networks employs the "store-carry-forward" manner: when information is sent by a source node, it traverses several intermediate nodes that store and carry data while moving and forward the data to the next relay node upon encountering, until eventually the destination is reached.

To achieve unicast information delivery in opportunistic networks based on user contacts, we propose a *social-* and *mobile-a*ware message *rou*ting strategy called "SMART". The basic idea of SMART is to exploit community structure in opportunistic networks and choose relay nodes to route data adaptively according to social features and mobility characteristics. The SMART scheme first applies a *distributed community partitioning* algorithm to divide mobile nodes into communities, and then based on the positions of the destination nodes, it performs either an *intracommunity communication* or an *intercommunity communication* process to disseminate information. The details are presented as follows.

13.4.1 Distributed Community Partitioning

In opportunistic networks, communities are formed based on the locations and movement trajectories of users. Intuitively, people staying in closer geographic areas or sharing similar location interests tend to meet each other more often [8,15,16]. According to the observation in [27], about 80% of trajectory coordinates of a user appear within 5 km from its *centroid* (or known as *geographic mass point*), and the encountering probability of two nodes is high only when their mass points are close enough. Inspired by the previous observation, we propose a dynamic and distributed community partitioning algorithm called "m-partition" to detect the clusters of frequently encountering nodes.

Given the number of community m, the community partitioning process contains two stages: the bootstrap stage and the evolution stage. In the *bootstrap stage*, m nodes are randomly selected and each node is assigned with a unique community ID. A node without community affiliation will be assigned the ID of the node with known community it first encountered. After this stage, each node has an initial

---

Algorithm: m-partition

Require: Node N_i and AP vector;

Ensure: The community ID of node N_j;

  1: Assume there are m communities to be detected;

  2: **for** Each encounter event (with N_j) **do**

  3:    **if** $N_i.communityID = null$ **then**

  4:      $N_i.communityID = N_j.communityID$

  5:    **else**

  6:      $y \leftarrow N_j.communityID$

  7:      $x \leftarrow N_i.communityID$

  8:      **if** $y = x$ **then**

  9:        $ap_{xi} = ap_{xi} + 1$

 10:      **else**

 11:        $ap_{yi} = ap_{yi} + 1$;

 12:      **end if**

 13:      **if** $ap_{yi} > ap_{xi}$ **then**

 14:        $N_i.communityID = y$

 15:      **end if**

 16:    **end if**

 17: **end for**

Figure 13.2   The m-partition algorithm.

community ID. In the *evolution stage*, each node keeps counting the affiliation parameters (APs), which indicate the number of encounters with nodes in different communities. Then, it adjusts its community affiliation according to the updated AP values. Specifically, we use a vector to depict the APs of node n_i:

$$E_i = \{ap_{1_i}, ap_{2_i}, \ldots, ap_{m_i}\},$$

where ap_{j_i} is the AP of n_i connecting to community C_j, which denotes the number of encounters between n_i and nodes in C_j. The AP vector is updated each time an encounter occurs, and the node adaptively changes its community affiliation to the community with the maximal AP value in the vector. The detailed process of the algorithm is illustrated in Figure 13.2.

The algorithm is run in a distributed way, and each node keeps recording the community affiliations of other nodes it encounters. Since community is formed by a group of frequently encountering nodes, the community members will be known to each other after running the algorithm long enough.

After dividing mobile users into communities, we consider two cases of unicast: the *intracommunity communication* where the source and destination are in the same community and the *intercommunity communication* where the source and destination are in different communities. The principles of information dissemination for the two cases are discussed in the following sections.

13.4.2 Intracommunity Communication

In the social graph of an opportunistic network, the links between nodes indicate the encountering events of the nodes in the past. If a source node n_s and a destination node n_d are in the same community, they will encounter each other or other nodes in the same community more often; thus, the structure of the social graph can be exploited to form a routing path between n_s and n_d. Intuitively, we can choose relay nodes based on social features such as centrality and similarity. On one hand, if a node has more links to the other nodes, it is more likely to encounter the destination, so social centrality is a good indicator of the ability to serve as a hub for information exchange. On the other hand, if a node has more common friends with the destination node, it will have higher probability to reach the destination directly or indirectly (via a common friend); thus, social neighbor similarity can also be used as a metric to choose relay nodes. In this section, we will combine the two metrics to form a utility function for routing decision.

According to Section 13.3.2, social centrality can be represented by the degree centrality of a node. However, to multigate the accumulative effect that a node may encounter many other nodes in the history but become less active in the recent, we introduce a decayed degree centrality of node i to overcome the accumulative effect of historical encounter events, which is calculated by

$$C_i'(\tau) = \frac{C_i(t)}{\tau - t}, \tag{13.6}$$

where

τ is the current time

t is the most recent time that node i encounters another node

According to the equation, $C_i'(\tau)$ is a decay function of $C_i(t)$

Social neighbor similarity is given by Equation 13.2. We calculate the decayed social neighbor similarity as

$$S_{i,j}'(\tau) = \frac{S_{i,j}(t)}{\tau - t}, \tag{13.7}$$

where

τ is the current time

t is the most recent time that node i encounters j or j's friends

Since social centrality and social structure similarity describe different aspects of social features of a mobile node, there need to be a way to combine the two different metrics to form a utility function. Inspired by the concept of convolution in signal processing, which provides a mathematical operation on two functions to produce the weighted average over time, the utility function at time T is formulated as

$$Y_{i,d}(T) = S_{i,d}'(T) \otimes C_i'(T) = \int_{\tau=0}^{T} S_{i,d}'(\tau) * C_i'(T - \tau). \tag{13.8}$$

In the real implementation, time is divided into slots and the utility can be calculated in a discrete way and can be updated whenever an encountering event occurs:

$$U_{i,d}(T) = \sum_{\tau=0}^{T} X_{i,d}(\tau) * S_{i,d}'(\tau) * C_i'(T - \tau), \tag{13.9}$$

where $X_{i,d}(\tau) = 1$ when an encounter occurs at time τ; otherwise, $X(\tau)_{id} = 0$.

The utility function describes that when each encounter occurs, it yields an addictive effect represented by social structure similarity and social centrality decaying over time. According to the utility function, a node with higher degree and more common friends with the destination decays slower than a node with poor connection to the network, and a node with more recent encounters decays slower than a less active one.

With the derived utility function, we propose the routing principle for intra-community communication.

Intracommunity forwarding principle: In opportunistic networks, if a source node sends a message to a destination within the same community, whenever an intermittent node n_i is encountered, utility function in Equation 13.9 is applied and the message is forwarded to the node with higher utility until the destination is reached.

13.4.3 Intercommunity Communication

If the destination node n_d does not belong to the same community as the source node n_s, we need to choose some relay nodes to forward the message across communities. The idea is to use "fringe nodes" to bridge the communication of intercommunities.

A fringe node is a node that is capable of remote contact with other communities. It is measured by the number of links that it connects to other communities. We select nodes with a higher number of links to outside communities as fringe nodes. Each fringe node is represented by its ID and its remote contact table is shown in Table 13.1, where $\mathcal{X}_k (k = 1, ..., M)$ is the community ID and $\eta_{ik}(k = 1, ..., M)$ is the frequency that n_i encounters nodes in $\mathcal{X}_k$.

Each community maintains a set of fringe nodes $\mathcal{F}$. The set $\mathcal{F}$ is calculated and updated periodically. During a period, each node compares the contact frequencies in its remote contact table with those of the fringe nodes in $\mathcal{F}$. If a node n_i finds that it has better connection with outside communities than a fringe node n_j, it will announce itself as a new fringe node by broadcasting its ID and remote contact table to the community. The process is described in the succeeding text.

Assume $\eta_{i1}, \eta_{i2}, ..., \eta_{iM}$ are the remote contact frequencies of n_i and $\eta_{j1}, \eta_{j2}, ..., \eta_{jM}$ are the remote contact frequencies of n_j. Define a function $\phi(x, y) = 1$ if $x \geq y$, and otherwise, $\phi(x, y) = -1$. The relative ability for remote contact of the two nodes is evaluated by

$$\mathfrak{F}_{i,j} = \sum_{k=1}^{M} \phi(\eta_{ik}, \eta_{jk}).$$

If $\mathfrak{F}_{i,j}$ is larger than 1, it means n_i has better remote connection than n_j; thus, n_i will announce itself a fringe node for the community.

According to the report in [24], a small fraction of the remote links are enough to form a small-world network with a small network diameter. In our network, we set the number of fringe nodes as 10% of the community size. If the community size is smaller than 10, the number of fringe nodes is set as 1.

Intercommunity forwarding principle: For intercommunity communication, a source node n_s in community C sends a message to the destination n_d in community C',

Table 13.1 Remote Contact Table of Node n_i

$\mathcal{X}_1$	$\mathcal{X}_2$	...	$\mathcal{X}_k$	...	$\mathcal{X}_M$
η_{i1}	η_{i2}	...	0	...	η_{iM}

where $C \neq C'$. With the set of fringe nodes derived, it applies the following principles to forward the message from C to C':

1. If C and C' are directly connected, that is, there exists a nonempty set $\mathbb{C} = \{n_j | \forall\ n_j \in \mathcal{F}\ and\ n_j\ connects\ to\ C'\}$, the principle is to choose the fringe node with the maximum connection to C' as relay. That is, the message will be forwarded to the fringe node with higher degree centrality to C'.

2. If C and C' are not directly connected, the message will be forwarded across multiple communities. Similar to the definition of the degree centrality, we define the *community-degree centrality* as follows:

$$\mathcal{D}_i = \frac{\sum_{k=1}^{M} \eta_{ik}}{\sum_{\forall j \in F} \sum_{k=1}^{M} \eta_{jk}}. \tag{13.10}$$

A higher $\mathcal{D}_i$ value indicates more connections from n_i to the outside communities. Thus, the principle for cross-community communication is to forward the message to the fringe node with a higher community-degree centrality. The message will be forwarded in multiple hops, until it reaches the destination community. After that, the intracommunity forwarding principle will be applied to keep forwarding the message to the destination eventually.

13.4.4 Performance Evaluation

13.4.4.1 Data Sets

Our study is based on three publicly available opportunistic network traces: MIT Reality [6], DieselNet [2], and Cabspotting [18]. The MIT Reality data set consists of the location traces of 97 users with Nokia 6600 smartphones at MIT during the 2004–2005 academic year. DieselNet logs mobility traces of 34 buses in Amherst. Each bus is equipped with a computer and a GPS. It records the GPS locations of all the buses during the 20 days from October to November in 2007. Cabspotting is a mobility trace of taxicabs in San Francisco. Each taxi is outfitted with a GPS

Table 13.2   Statistics of the Data Sets

Traces	MIT Reality	DieselNet	Cabspotting
Network type	Bluetooth	802.11b	None
No. devices	97	34	536
No. contacts	54,667	2284	111,153
Duration (days)	246	20	30

tracking device. It contains GPS coordinates of 536 taxis collected over 30 days in San Francisco Bay Area. The statistics of the three data sets are summarized in Table 13.2.

13.4.4.2 Experiment Setup

We launch the experiment on the HaggleSim simulator [13]. It takes the discrete sequential encounter events and the corresponding social graph as the inputs and makes data forwarding decisions using various routing algorithms. For each experiment, we emulate 1000 messages with 1-week lifetime sent from a randomly selected source to destination. We run every experiment 20 times for statistical convergence. The following performance metrics are used to evaluate the performance of the routing algorithms:

- *Delivery ratio*: The ratio of the number of destinations having received the data to the total number of destinations.
- *Average delay*: The average time delay for each data item delivered from the source to the destination.
- *Average cost*: The average number of relays used for data delivery from the source to the destination.

We extract a 2-week session from MIT Reality, DieselNet, and Cabspotting, respectively and run the simulator over the selected sessions with uniformly generated traffic. The SMART algorithm is implemented and is compared to other existing routing algorithms.

13.4.4.3 Impact of Community Numbers

We first investigate the impact of the number of communities on the performance of SMART. We apply the proposed m-partition algorithm for community partitioning on the three mobility traces and then use SMART to route messages.

Figure 13.3 shows the performance metrics as a function of community number m (varying from 1 to the size of the data sets) and time on MIT Reality trace. The delivery ratio of MIT Reality trace is shown in Figure 13.3a. According to this figure, when no community partitioning algorithm is applied ($m = 1$), the delivery ratio is quite low and increases slowly with time. As the community number is set to an appropriate value (e.g., $m = 10$), the delivery ratio increases dramatically, which is almost two times as much as that when $m = 1$. For $10 \leq m \leq 90$, the delivery ratio becomes stable and has only small fluctuation. When the community number approaches the size of the data set ($m = 97$), the performance drops dramatically since the impact of the community structure disappears. The average delay is illustrated in Figure 13.3b. It is seen that the average delay is almost the same for all community numbers and it only varies with time. The average cost is shown in 13.3c. Similar to delivery ratio, the average cost is influenced by m and increases to a stable value when

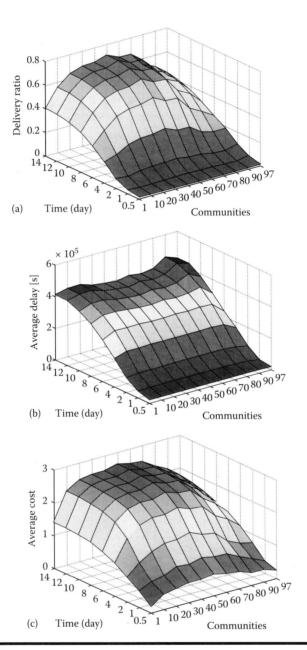

Figure 13.3 The performance metrics as a function of community number and time (MIT Reality). (a) Delivery ratio, (b) average delay, (c) average cost.

$10 \leq m \leq 90$. Similar results are also found in DieselNet and Cabspotting. The results suggest that SMART performs better when the community structure is outlined, while the performance of SMART is low when no community structure is indicated in the network. It also reveals that the proper value of m is within a wide range. In the rest of our experiments, we fix our community number to $m = 10$.

13.4.4.4 Impact of Community Partitioning Algorithms

We show the impact of community partitioning algorithms on the SMART routing scheme in this group of experiments. We evaluate the performance of SMART using different community partitioning algorithms, including m-partition, k-clique percolation algorithm [17] (which considers the adjacent k-cliques as communities), and Girvan–Newman algorithm [11] (which continues removing edges with the highest betweenness until a certain threshold is reached).

Figure 13.4 presents the experimental results of the MIT Reality trace. As shown in Figure 13.4a, the m-partition method outperforms Girvan–Newman by 10% and k-clique percolation by 2% in delivery ratio. In terms of average delay, as shown in Figure 13.4b, m-partition performs slightly better than the other two algorithms. The three algorithms produce similar average costs as shown in Figure 13.4c. Similar results are also observed in DieselNet and Cabspotting data traces. Despite the different algorithms used for community partitioning, the routing performance is quite similar for all three data sets. It indicates that the proposed SMART routing mechanism is not sensitive to community partition. Since Girvan–Newman and k-clique percolation need global network topology information, which is difficult to obtain in opportunistic networks, the proposed m-partition algorithm is more suitable for distributed implementation in the real world.

13.4.4.5 Performance Comparison

We compare SMART with five existing routing strategies for opportunistic networks: PROPHET [14], SimBet [3], Bubble Rap [12], friendship-based routing (FBR) [1], and Epidemic routing [22]. PROPHET is a utility-based strategy according to encounter history. It forwards data to the nodes with higher delivery rate based on contact history. SimBet is a utility-based strategy according to social features. It considers social properties including similarity and centrality to make data forwarding decisions. Bubble Rap is a community-based strategy. It depends on community structure and routes data based on rankings calculated from social centrality. FBR algorithm is another community-based algorithm. It constructs temporal community and uses the nodes with direct connection to the destination community for data delivery. Epidemic routing is a flooding strategy. It has high delivery cost, but its delivery ratio and delay approach the theoretical bounds. To show the amount of traffic in the routing algorithms, we add control overhead as an additional metric to evaluate different routing strategies.

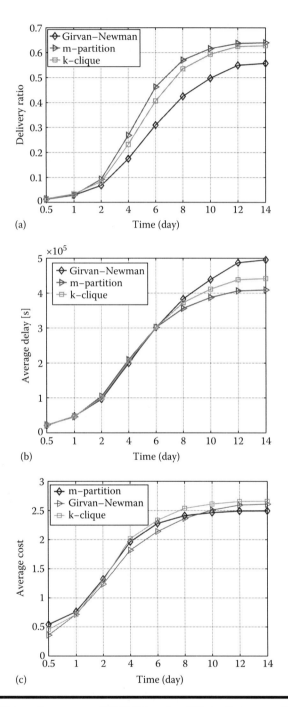

Figure 13.4 The performance of SMART under different community partitioning algorithms (MIT Reality). (a) Delivery ratio, (b) average delay, (c) average cost.

Figure 13.5 shows the performance of various algorithms as a function of time on MIT Reality trace. The delivery ratio is compared in Figure 13.5a. It shows that SMART outperforms PROPHET, SimBet, FBR, and Bubble Rap. The delivery ratio of SMART is about 10% higher compared to those of Bubble Rap and FBR, 15% higher than that of SimBet, and nearly 20% higher than that of PROPHET. The reason that PROPHET performs the worst is due to the reason that it fails to adapt to the community structure of the mobility trace. SimBet exploits social properties to enhance the delivery ratio but it cannot adapt to the decaying effect of social features. Bubble Rap and FBR take advantages of the community structure, so they perform better than PROPHET, but not as well as SMART. Since Epidemic routing represents the theoretical upper bound of the delivery ratio, the performance of SMART is below that

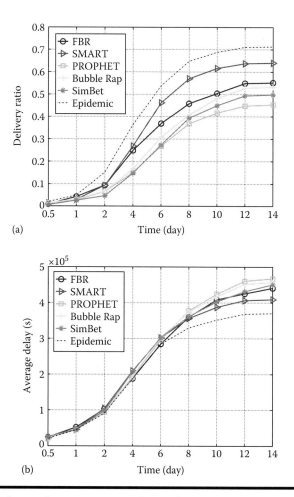

Figure 13.5   The performance comparison of various strategies on MIT Reality Mining trace. (a) Delivery ratio, (b) average delay.   (*Continued*)

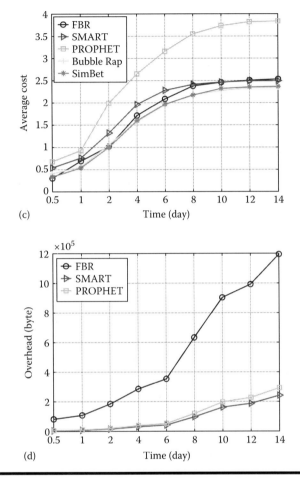

Figure 13.5 (*Continued***)** **The performance comparison of various strategies on MIT Reality Mining trace. (c) average cost, (d) control overhead.**

of the Epidemic routing. Average delay is compared in Figure 13.5b. Again, the delay of SMART is lower than the other four strategies (most of the time their performance is very close) but higher than the lower bound (Epidemic routing). The average cost is compared in Figure 13.5c. The cost of PROPHET is the highest. The cost of SMART is slightly higher than those of the others due to the decaying effect, which makes SMART take more relays for data delivery. The comparison of the control overhead on MIT Reality data trace is shown in Figure 13.5d. The overhead of SMART is around 20 kB at the end of the experimental period, which is mainly caused by the exchange of the friend list. PROPHET has over 10% higher overhead than SMART since it needs to exchange transitivity information. FBR takes 4 times more control overhead than SMART because it requires the encounter information from the neighbors.

Figure 13.6 presents the performance results of various algorithms as a function of time on the DieselNet data set. The delivery ratio is depicted in Figure 13.6a. SMART outperforms Bubble Rap by 3%, FBR by 5%, and PROPHET by 8%. It has nearly 20% higher delivery ratio than SimBet. Regarding the average delay and the average cost of each strategy shown in Figure 13.6b and c, SMART has very close average delay to Epidemic, which is less than those in the other strategies. The average cost of SMART is about 50% of that of PROPHET and higher than those of FBR and SimBet. DieselNet has very similar network structure with MIT Reality and thus has a similar trend on delivery ratio with MIT Reality. However, due to the regular and repetition routine of buses in DieselNet, it makes the SimBet meet dead ends quite often and takes more time to wait until reaching

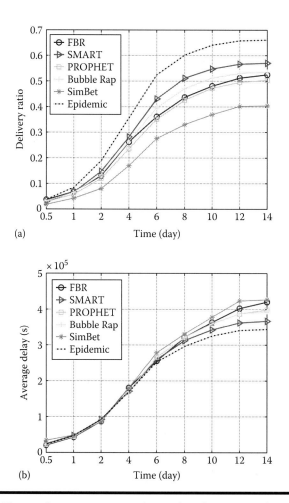

(a)

(b)

Figure 13.6 The performance comparison of various strategies on DieselNet trace. (a) Delivery ratio, (b) average delay. **(*Continued*)**

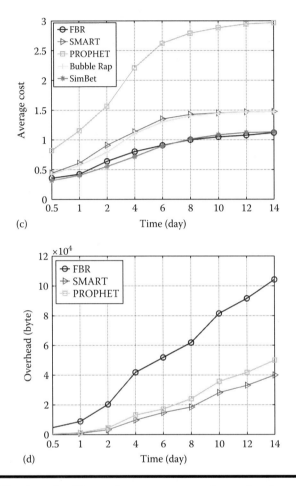

Figure 13.6 (*Continued*)   The performance comparison of various strategies on DieselNet trace. (c) average cost, (d) control overhead.

the destinations. Therefore, it has lower delivery ratio and higher average cost. Since DieselNet has tighter clustering structure, it makes Bubble Rap and FBR perform close to SMART. SMART has similar cost with social-related strategies but much lower cost than PROPHET. The overhead is presented in Figure 13.6d. The overhead of SMART is the lowest, which is 4 kB at the end of the experimental period. PROPHET has 25% higher overhead than SMART and the overhead of FBR is 2.5 times of that of SMART.

The comparison of the different algorithms' performance on Cabspotting trace is shown in Figure 13.7. Figure 13.7a depicts the delivery ratio of the various algorithms as a function of time. The SMART algorithm has very similar performance as PROPHET. It outperforms FBR by 5%. The Bubble Rap algorithm is affected by weak community structure, which lowers down its delivery ratio around 10% compared to SMART. SimBet has the lowest delivery ratio, among all other strategies. In terms of the average delay shown in Figure 13.7b, the delay of SMART is as low as that of Epidemic and is much lower than those of others. The average costs of various algorithms are similar as shown in Figure 13.7c. The overhead is shown in Figure 13.7d. The overhead of SMART is around 20 kB at the end of the experimental period, while the overhead of FBR and PROPHET is much higher than that of SMART.

In summary, the proposed SMART strategy outperforms the utility-based and community-based strategies on various opportunistic network data sets in most of the performance metrics.

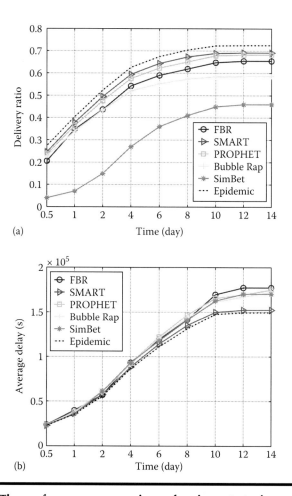

(a)

(b)

Figure 13.7 The performance comparison of various strategies on Cabspotting trace. (a) Delivery ratio, (b) average delay.   (*Continued*)

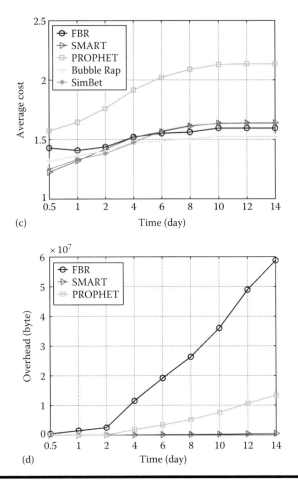

Figure 13.7 (*Continued*) **The performance comparison of various strategies on Cabspotting trace. (c) average cost, (d) control overhead.**

13.5 Multicast

Multicast refers to one-to-many communication in a network. The sender may specify a group of destination addresses for a single piece of information. For multicast in opportunistic networks, it also applies the "store-carry-forward" approach to relay information among mobile nodes. Different from unicast, when a node encounters another node, it decides whether to create a new copy of the data or simply hands over the data to the other nodes. In multicast, more and more copies of the original information are created and propagated in the network, until all the destinations receive a copy of the original information.

In multicast, a message holder is expected to forward a message to multiple destinations. To reduce the overhead and forwarding cost, the destinations will share the routing path until the point that they have to be separated, which usually results in a tree structure. The basic idea of our scheme is to improve multicast efficiency by exploring node social features and community structure. We first introduce the definition of *dynamic social features*, which represents the dynamic social characteristics of mobile users regarding their social profiles and encountering behaviors. And then, we present *enhanced dynamic social features*, an improved version of dynamic social features. Based on the enhanced dynamic social features, we apply the compare–split scheme using community detection to form a multicast tree. Specifically, we propose two *community and social feature–based multicast algorithms named "Multi-CSDO,"* which involves *destination nodes only* in community detection, and "Multi-CSDR," which involves both the *destination nodes* and the *relay candidates* in community detection in case the relay candidates are also socially similar. The details are presented as follows.

13.5.1 Dynamic Social Features

Suppose the social profile of a mobile user is represented by m social features $\langle E_1, E_2, ..., E_m \rangle$. The social profile similarity can be calculated using Equation 13.1. However, such social features are static and cannot represent the encountering behavior of mobile users. In this section, we introduce the dynamic social features and enhanced dynamic social features to incorporate the behavior dynamics.

Definition 13.6 Dynamic social features Assume a mobile node x has social profiles $E_x(\tau) = \langle E_{x1}(\tau), E_{x2}(\tau), ..., E_{xm}(\tau) \rangle$, its dynamic social features can be represented by a vector $\tilde{E}_x(\tau) = \langle \tilde{E}_{x1}(\tau), \tilde{E}_{x2}(\tau), ..., \tilde{E}_{xm}(\tau) \rangle$, where $\tilde{E}_{xk}$ ($0 \le \tilde{E}_{xk} \le 1$) is the ratio of node x encountering other nodes having the same social profile E_{xk}, which is computed by

$$\tilde{E}_{xk}(\tau) = \frac{M_k(\tau)}{M_{total}(\tau)},$$

(13.11)

where
   $M_k(\tau)$ is the number of meetings of node x with other nodes having social feature value E_{xk}
   $M_{total}(\tau)$ is the total number of nodes x has met in the duration τ

Dynamic social features not only record if a node has certain social feature values but also record the frequency this node has met other nodes with the same social feature values. Unlike the static ones, they are time-related and adjusted to the user contact behavior change over time.

   The definition of dynamic social features is based on frequency, which cannot distinguish the cases, for example, if A has met 1 *student* out of 2 people it has met in total and B has met 5 *students* out of 10 people it has met in total in the history we observe. Both of them have the same frequency of 1/2 to meet a *student*, but B is more active in meeting people. To break the tie and favor the more active node, there are many formulas we can design. Here, we come up with the following enhanced dynamic social features to serve our purposes.

Definition 13.7 Enhanced dynamic social features Following the notations in Definition 13.6, the enhanced dynamic social features of mobile node x are defined as $\hat{E}_x(\tau) = \langle \hat{E}_{x1}(\tau), \hat{E}_{x2}(\tau), ..., \hat{E}_{xm}(\tau) \rangle$, where

$$\hat{E}_{xk}(\tau) = \left(\frac{M_k(\tau)+1}{M_{total}(\tau)+1} \right)^{p_k} * \left(\frac{M_k(\tau)}{M_{total}(\tau)+1} \right)^{1-p_k}, \tag{13.12}$$

where $p_k = (M_k(\tau)/M_{total}(\tau))$.

This definition predicts $\hat{E}_{xk}$ by looking at the next meeting probability of node x with another node having the same social feature value. In the next time, the total meeting times will be $M_{total}(\tau) + 1$. The first part $((M_k(\tau)+1)/(M_{total}(\tau)+1))^{p_k}$ means that there will be p_k probability that x will have a "good" meeting with another node having the same social feature value next time. In this case, M_k will also be incremented by 1. The second part $(M_k(\tau)/(M_{total}(\tau)+1))^{1-p_k}$ means that there will be $1-p_k$ probability for x not to meet a node with the same social feature value next time. In that case, M_k will remain the same. The definition for $\hat{E}_{xk}$ then takes the geometric mean of the two parts.

With the definitions mentioned earlier, the social similarity of two nodes x and y regarding their enhanced dynamic social features is defined as follows.

Definition 13.8 Enhanced social similarity Following the notations in Definition 13.7, the enhanced social similarity of nodes x and y is computed by their Euclidean distance subtracting from 1:

$$S_{x,y}(\tau) = 1 - \frac{\sqrt{\sum_{k=1}^{m} (\hat{E}_{yk}(\tau) - \hat{E}_{xk}(\tau))^2}}{\sqrt{m}}. \tag{13.13}$$

Based on the enhanced dynamic social features and similarity measurement, we proposed two multicast algorithms in the following subsections.

13.5.2 Multi-CSDO *Algorithm*

The first proposed multicast algorithm is called Multi-CSDO as shown in Figure 13.8. Its basic idea is as follows: First, a source node s has a destination set to multicast a message to and s is the initial message holder or relay node x. When x meets a node y,

---

Algorithm Multi-CSDO: community and social feature–based multicast involving destinations only in community detection

---

Require: The source node s and its destination set $D_s = \{d_1, d_2, ..., d_n\}$; s is the initial message holder x

1: **while** not all of the destinations receive the message **do**
2:     On contact between a message holder x and node y:
3:     **if** $y \in D_x$ **then**
4:         /* Found destination y */
5:         y gets the message and x removes y from D_x
6:     **end if**
7:     /* Compare node social similarity and split the destinations */
8:     Construct a weighted graph and a distance matrix of the destination nodes only as explained in Section 1.5.2
9:     Feed the distance matrix to the hierarchical clustering algorithm to generate two communities C_1 and C_2 as explained in Section 1.5.2
10:     Compare the social similarity of C_1 and C_2 with x and y using enhanced dynamic social features, respectively
11:     Whichever (x or y) is more socially similar to each of the communities will be the message carrier for that community
12: **end while**

Figure 13.8   The Multi-CSDO multicast algorithm.

if y is one of the destinations, y gets the message and is removed from the destination set. Next, we use a compare–split scheme to make a decision of whether it is better to pass some destinations to y. Both x and y are called relay candidates in the decision. To separate the destinations into x's community or y's community, we use a community detection algorithm involving only the destination nodes based on their social similarities. The community detection algorithm we use takes a distance matrix coming from a similarity weighted graph as an input. The following are the details.

13.5.2.1 Similarity Weighted Graph and Distance Matrix

In Multi-CSDO, as shown in an example in Figure 13.9, when a message holder x encounters a node y, we construct a similarity weighted graph involving only the destination nodes. The weight of the edges is the social similarity of the two connected destination nodes calculated using static social features (denoted by dashed edges in Figure 13.9) as their dynamic social features are not known to the relay candidates in a distributed algorithm. With the similarity weighted graph, we can create a distance matrix as shown in Table 13.3 to indicate the social difference or distance between each pair of destinations. The social distance between two destinations d_i and d_j is defined as $1 - S(d_i, d_j)$ here. The distance matrix will be used in the following community detection algorithm to separate the destinations into two communities.

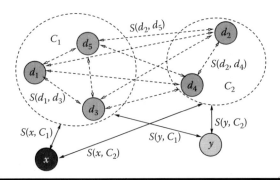

Figure 13.9 **The similarity weighted graph and community detection involving destination nodes only. Node *x* is a message holder and *y* is a newly met node. The green nodes are the destinations. The weight of a dashed edge is the social similarity calculated using static social features, while the weight of a solid edge is the social similarity calculated using the enhanced dynamic social features. The destinations are split into two communities C_1 and C_2 based on their social similarities.**

Table 13.3 The Distance Matrix

	d_1	d_2	d_3	d_4	...
d_1	0	$1-S(d_1, d_2)$	$1-S(d_1, d_3)$	$1-S(d_1, d_4)$	
d_2	$1-S(d_1, d_2)$	0	$1-S(d_2, d_3)$	$1-S(d_2, d_4)$	
d_3	$1-S(d_1, d_3)$	$1-S(d_2, d_3)$	0	$1-S(d_3, d_4)$	
d_4	$1-S(d_1, d_4)$	$1-S(d_2, d_4)$	$1-S(d_3, d_4)$	0	
⋮					

The distance between destination nodes d_i and d_j is $1-S(d_i, d_j)$ if $i \neq j$; otherwise, 0.

13.5.2.2 Community Detection Algorithm

We use a hierarchical clustering algorithm called complete-linkage clustering [4] to split the destinations into two communities. We choose this one because it best matches our needs and there is an existing Python package [28] available for this algorithm so that we do not have to reinvent the wheel.

The idea of the complete-linkage hierarchical community detection algorithm we adopt is as follows: At the beginning of the process, each node is in a community of its own. The communities are then sequentially combined into larger communities, until all nodes end up being in one community. At each step, the two communities separated by the shortest distance are combined. The distance between communities is defined as the distance between those two nodes (one in each community) that are farthest away from each other. Using the distance matrix as input, we run the Python package with cluster number being 2, and as a result we can obtain two communities of the destinations.

13.5.2.3 Destinations Split

After applying the community detection algorithm, the destinations are separated into two communities C_1 and C_2. Next, we decide which relay candidate, x or y, should carry the destinations in which community. We compare the social similarity of each relay candidate with each community using enhanced dynamic social features (denoted by the solid edges in Figure 13.9). The social similarity between a node and a community should include all of the social feature values of the nodes involved. After calculation, whichever is more socially similar to a community will be the relay node for the destinations in that community.

In Multi-CSDO, x and y are supposed to be in different communities, which may not be true if they are socially similar. Thus, in the next section, we introduce the Multi-CSDR algorithm by incorporating both x and y in the community detection and make our decision more accurate by considering more node relationships.

13.5.3 Multi-CSDR *Algorithm*

The second multicast algorithm is called Multi-CSDR. It has a similar structure with the first algorithm but has several differences. As shown in the example in Figure 13.10, first, the community detection algorithm involves both the destination nodes and the relay candidates x and y. Thus, the similarity weighted graph adds the social similarity

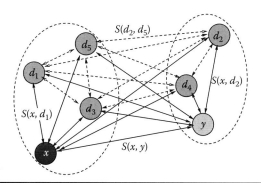

Figure 13.10 **The similarity weighted graph and community detection involving both destination nodes and relay candidates x and y. Node x is a message holder and y is a newly met node. The green nodes are the destinations. The weight of a dashed edge is the social similarity calculated using static social features, while the weight of a solid edge is the social similarity calculated using the enhanced dynamic social features. The nodes are split into two communities based on their social similarities.**

between each relay candidate and each destination node. The social similarity between two destination nodes is still calculated using static social features and is denoted by a dashed edge in Figure 13.10. However, the social similarity between a relay candidate and a destination is calculated using enhanced dynamic social features as they can be obtained and is denoted by a solid edge in Figure 13.10. We still use the same community detection algorithm. But the distance matrix now also includes the distance between each relay candidate and each destination. After applying the community detection algorithm, the destinations in x's community will be carried by x and those in y's will be carried by y. For other cases, for example, if x and y are in the same community, then x will still be the carrier for the original destination set.

In this algorithm, by adding the social similarity of each relay node with each destination using enhanced dynamic social features, we hope to improve the accuracy of the compare–split scheme.

13.5.4 Performance Evaluation

We evaluate the performance of the proposed multicast algorithms by comparing them with the existing ones using a simulator written in Python. The simulations were conducted using a real conference trace [21] reflecting an opportunistic network created at IEEE Infocom 2006 in Miami. The trace recorded conference attenders' encounter history using Bluetooth small devices (iMotes) for four days at the conference. The trace data set consists of two parts: *contacts* between iMote devices that were carried by participants and self-reported *social features* of the participants collected using a questionnaire form. The six social features extracted from the data set were *affiliation*, *city*, *nationality*, *language*, *country*, and *position*. In this trace, 62 nodes with complete social feature information were considered in the simulation.

We compare our algorithm with the following existing multicast algorithms:

- *The epidemic algorithm (epidemic)* [22]: The message is spread epidemically throughout the network until it reaches all of the destinations.
- *The social-similarity-based multicast algorithm (Multi-Sosim)* [26]: The multicast algorithm based on dynamic social features in our previous work.

Three important metrics are used to evaluate the performance of the multicast algorithms:

- *Delivery rate:* The ratio of the number of successful multicasts (where the message is delivered to all the destinations) to the number of total multicasts generated.
- *Delivery latency:* The time from the start of multicast to when all of the multicast destinations have received the message.
- *Number of forwardings:* The number of hops needed to deliver a message to all of the multicast destinations.

13.5.5 Simulation Setup

In our simulations, we divided the whole trace time into 10 intervals. Thus, 1 time interval is 1/10 of the total time length. For each algorithm, we tried 5 and 10 destinations. In each experiment, we randomly generated a source and its destination set. Since the whole trace only contains 4 days of node contact history, the time interval we observed to calculate the dynamic and enhanced dynamic social features was counted from the beginning of the trace up until the time we needed to make a routing decision. For a community detection algorithm, we adopted the Python package available at [28] for complete-linkage hierarchical clustering algorithm. We ran each algorithm 300 times and averaged the results.

13.5.6 Simulation Results

The simulation results comparing our algorithms with others using 5 and 10 destinations are shown in Figures 13.11 and 13.12, respectively. For the Epidemic algorithm, as expected, it has the highest delivery rate (100%) and lowest delivery latency (almost close to 0) but the highest number of forwardings.

With both 5 and 10 destinations, Multi-CSDO and Multi-CSDR consistently outperform Multi-Sosim in terms of delivery rate, latency, and number of forwardings. In the 5-destination case, Multi-CSDR and Multi-CSDO improve the delivery rate of Multi-Sosim by as much as nine times and seven times, respectively, reduce the latency of Multi-Sosim by as much as 47% and 43%, respectively, and decrease the number of forwardings of Multi-Sosim by as much as 29% and 18%, respectively. Similarly, in the 10-destination case, Multi-CSDR and Multi-CSDO improve the delivery rate of Multi-Sosim by as much as 11 times and 6 times, respectively, reduce the latency of Multi-Sosim by as much as 51% and 38%, respectively, and decrease the number of forwardings of Multi-Sosim by as much as 40% and 28%, respectively. These tell us that adding the social relationships among destinations in the compare–split scheme can facilitate multicast.

Furthermore, Multi-CSDR has better delivery rate, lower latency, and lower number of forwardings than Multi-CSDO with both 5 and 10 destinations. In the 5-destination case, Multi-CSDR improves the delivery rate of Multi-CSDO by as much as 5%, reduces the latency of Multi-CSDO by as much as 11%, and decreases the number of forwardings of Multi-CSDO by as much as 13%. Similarly, in the 10-destination case, Multi-CSDR improves the delivery rate of Multi-CSDO by as much as 69%, reduces the latency of Multi-CSDO by as much as 22%, and decreases the number of forwardings of Multi-CSDO by as much as 17%. These verify that considering the social relationship between each relay candidate and each destination and calculating their social similarity using enhanced dynamic social features can improve multicast performance.

In summary, these results confirm that obtaining more accurate dynamic information and using better compare–split schemes can make multicast more efficient.

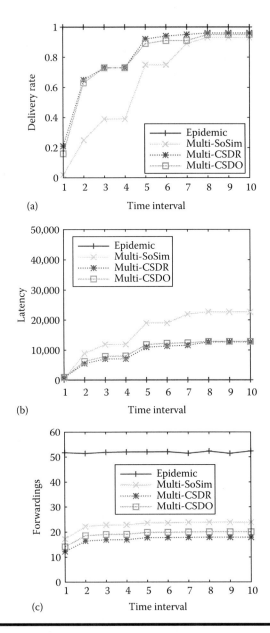

Figure 13.11 Comparison of different algorithms with 5 destinations using all devices in the trace. (a) Delivery rate, (b) delivery latency, (c) number of forwardings.

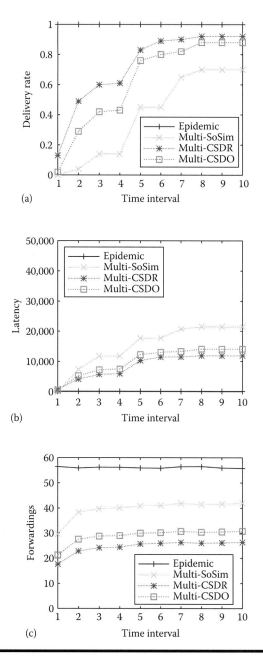

Figure 13.12 Comparison of different algorithms with 10 destinations using all devices in the trace. (a) Delivery rate, (b) delivery latency, (c) number of forwardings.

13.6 Conclusion

In this chapter, we studied information dissemination mechanisms in opportunistic networks. Based on the coupling of opportunistic networks and human social networks, we modeled the opportunistic network as a social graph and exploited social features such as users' social profiles, social relationships, and network structures to build more efficient information dissemination schemes.

Specifically, we explored the unicast and multicast information dissemination in opportunistic networks. For one-to-one communication (unicast), we proposed a social- and mobile-aware message routing strategy called SMART. In this strategy, an opportunistic network is divided into a number of communities using adaptive community partitioning algorithms. Two data routing processes were introduced: intracommunity communications and intercommunity communications. It was shown that SMART adopts both community structure and social similarities to enhance data forwarding efficiency. Extensive trace-driven experiments showed that SMART outperforms other unicast strategies in various opportunistic network traces. For one-to-many communication, we proposed two social feature–based multicast algorithms named Multi-CSDO and Multi-CSDR. The proposed algorithms used enhanced dynamic social features to capture nodes' contact behavior and applied a compare–split scheme based on community detection to select the best relay node for multiple destinations in each hop to improve multicast efficiency. Simulations using a real trace of a mobile social network showed that the proposed algorithms outperform the existing ones in various performance metrics.

Our work revealed the possibility of exploiting social features to facilitate communication networks. By incorporating the social properties such as centrality, similarity, and community structure into algorithm and protocol design, the efficiency of information dissemination in mobile and wireless networks achieved great improvement.

Acknowledgments

This work was partially supported by the National Natural Science Foundation of China (Grant Nos. 61373128, 91218302, 61321491), the EU FP7 IRSES MobileCloud Project (Grant No. 612212), and the Collaborative Innovation Center of Novel Software Technology and Industrialization, and the Sino-German Institutes of Social Computing.

Glossary

Mobile social network: A mobile communication system focusing not only on the interactions but also on the social aspects of the users.

Multicast: One-to-many communication where one mobile node sends information to a set of destinations.

Opportunistic network: A sparse dynamic wireless network where mobile nodes work on ad hoc mode and can communicate with each other when they move into their communication range.

Unicast: One-to-one communication in opportunistic networks, where one mobile node sends information to another node.

References

1. SciPy.org Hierarchical clustering. http://docs.scipy.org/doc/scipy/reference/cluster.html, March 2014.
2. Bulut E. and B. Szymanski. Exploiting friendship relations for efficient routing in mobile social networks. *IEEE Transactions on Parallel and Distributed Systems*, PP(99):1, 2012.
3. Burgess J., B.N. Levine, R. Mahajan, J. Zahorjan, A. Balasubramanian, A. Venkataramani, Y. Zhou, B. Croft, N. Banerjee, M. Corner, and D. Towsley. CRAWDAD data set umass/diesel (v. 2008-09-14). http://crawdad.cs.dartmouth.edu/umass/diesel, 2008.
4. Daly E.M. and M. Haahr. Social network analysis for routing in disconnected delay-tolerant manets. In *Proceedings of the Eighth ACM International Symposium on Mobile Ad Hoc Networking and Computing (MobiHoc'07)*, pp. 32–40, ACM, New York, 2007.
5. Defays D. An efficient algorithm for a complete link method. *The Computer Journal*, 20(4):364–366, 1977.
6. Ding C.H.Q., X. He, H. Zha, M. Gu, and H.D. Simon. A min-max cut algorithm for graph partitioning and data clustering. In *IEEE ICDM'01*, San Jose, CA, pp. 107–114, 2001.
7. Eagle N. and A.S. Pentland. CRAWDAD data set mit/reality (v. 2005-07-01). http://crawdad.cs.dartmouth.edu/mit/reality, 2005.
8. Fall K. A delay-tolerant network architecture for challenged internets. In *Proceedings of the 2003 Conference on Applications, Technologies, Architectures, and Protocols for Computer Communications (SIGCOMM'03)*, pp. 27–34, ACM, New York, 2003.
9. Fortunato S. Community detection in graphs. *Physics Reports*, 486(3C5):75–174, 2010.
10. Freeman L. A set of measures of centrality based on betweenness. *Sociometry*, 40(1):35–41, 1977.
11. Freeman L. Centrality in social networks: Conceptual clarification. *Social Networks*, 1(3):215–239, 1979.
12. Girvan M. and M. E. J. Newman. A set of measures of centrality based on betweenness. *Proceedings of National Academy of Science of the Unites States of America*, 99(12):7821–7826, 2002.
13. Hui P., J. Crowcroft, and E. Yoneki. Bubble rap: Social-based forwarding in delay tolerant networks. In *Proceedings of the Ninth ACM International Symposium on Mobile Ad Hoc Networking and Computing (MobiHoc'08)*, pp. 241–250, ACM, New York, 2008.
14. Hui P. and J. Crowcroft. How small labels create big improvements. In *PerCom Workshops'07*, White Plains, NY, pp. 65–70, 2007.
15. Lindgren A., A. Doria, and O. Schelén. Probabilistic Routing in Intermittently Connected Networks. In *Lecture Notes in Computer Science*, Vol. 3126, pp. 239–254, Springer-Verlag GmbH, Berlin, Germany, 2004.

16. Newman M.E.J. Fast algorithm for detecting community structure in networks. *Physical Review E*, 69(6):066133, 2004.
17. Nguyen N.P., T.N. Dinh, Y. Xuan, and M.T. Thai. Adaptive algorithms for detecting community structure in dynamic social networks. In *IEEE INFOCOM'11*, Shanghai, China, pp. 2282–2290, 2011.
18. Palla G., I. Derenyi, I. Farkas, and T. Vicsek. Uncovering the overlapping community structure of complex networks in nature and society. *Nature*, 435:814, 2005.
19. Piorkowski M., N. Sarafijanovic-Djukic, and M. Grossglauser. CRAWDAD data set epfl/mobility (v. 2009-02-24). http://crawdad.cs.dartmouth.edu/epfl/mobility, 2009.
20. Raghavan U.N., R. Albert, and S. Kumara. Near linear time algorithm to detect community structures in large-scale networks. *Physical Review E*, 79(3):7821–7826, 2007.
21. Reichardt J. *Structure in Complex Networks*. Lecture Notes in Physics, Springer-Verlag, Berlin, Germany, 2009.
22. Scott J., R. Gass, J. Crowcroft, P. Hui, C. Diot, and A. Chaintreau. Crawdad trace cambridge/haggle/imote/infocom2006 (v. 2009-05-29). http://crawdad.cs.dartmouth.edu/cambridge/haggle/imote/infocom2006, May 2009.
23. Vahdat A., D. Becker et al. Epidemic routing for partially connected ad hoc networks. Technical report, CS-200006, Duke University, Durham, NC, 2000.
24. Vastardis N. and K. Yang. Mobile social networks: Architectures, social properties, and key research challenges. *IEEE Communications Surveys Tutorials*, 15(3):1355–1371, 2013.
25. Watts D.J. and S.H. Strogatz. Collective dynamics of 'small-world' networks. *Nature*, 393(6684):440–442, 1998.
26. Wu J. and Y. Wang. Social feature-based multi-path routing in delay tolerant networks. In *Proceedings of IEEE INFOCOM'12*, Orlando, FL, pp. 1368–1376, March 2012.
27. Xu Y. and X. Chen. Social-similarity-based multicast algorithm in impromptu mobile social networks. In *IEEE Globecom*, Austin, TX, 2014.
28. Zhu K., W. Li, and X. Fu. SMART: A social- and mobile-aware routing strategy for disruption-tolerant networks. *IEEE Transactions on Vehicular Technology*, 63(7):3423–3434, September 2014.

Chapter 14

Information Flows in Patient-Oriented Online Media and Scientific Research

Philip Makedonski, Tim Friede, Jens Grabowski, Janka Koschack, and Wolfgang Himmel

Contents

14.1 Introduction

In the last decades, we have witnessed a powerful movement toward an active, self-managing, and responsible patient, that is, the so-called expert patient (Donaldson, 2003). A key element in this process is an unlimited access to and intelligent use of health-related information, particularly such that it is widely available on websites, in online forums on the Internet, and in the new social media. As a result of this movement, today, patients and their advocates can influence both public and scientific debates (Chafe et al., 2011). However, there is considerable concern that patients can be easily misguided by pseudoscientific information or that they cannot interpret complex scientific statements and studies correctly (e.g., Brunson, 2013). These assumptions will remain speculative as long as we do not develop a comprehensive understanding of the dissemination of health information in the scientific and lay communities. This task requires quantitative methods to extract information on the posting behavior in online forums on a large scale as well as the intimate study of the social exchange processes and argumentative strategies in online health forums. Therefore, we decided to start the research with a case study and to combine qualitative and quantitative research in a mixed-methods approach.

We selected the so-called liberation treatment (also sometimes referred to as the "liberation procedure") in multiple sclerosis (MS) as a suitable case for an exemplary analysis of the information flow in patient-oriented online media and scientific research. The liberation treatment is based on the chronic cerebrospinal venous insufficiency (CCSVI) hypothesis in MS, claiming that obstruction to venous drainage in the neck is linked to MS (Zamboni et al., 2009a). The CCSVI hypothesis was fiercely debated in the scientific community (Valdueza et al., 2013) but also—and for our purposes, far more importantly—in patient online communities, such as the online forums of the Deutsche Multiple Sklerose Gesellschaft (DMSG, German Multiple Sclerosis Society) or the UK MS Society. CCSVI may be a good example to better understand how the scientific and the lay community deal with ambiguous and controversial information and how this controversial information is disseminated and communicated. This exploratory study focused especially on the following research questions:

■ Which CCSVI-related information flows exist in the scientific and lay communities and how do they work?
■ What are the CCSVI-related topics being discussed and how important are these topics for scientists, doctors, patients, and the public?
■ What are the timelines of the scientific and the lay discussions on CCSVI-related topics?
■ What are the line of argumentation and strategies in the discussions in patient-oriented online media for MS, especially when new CCSVI-related topics are introduced and contributors try to persuade others to follow their own position?
■ What are the dependencies between the discussion timelines identified in the scientific and the lay community?

Insights into the information flows in the scientific and the lay communities may, in the end, help us to answer the main question, that is, how the two communities exchange information and influence each other, and to weigh the risks and benefits of the "expert patient" in the Internet era.

14.2 Studying Information Flows in Online Social Media and Research

In order to gain insights into the information flows in the scientific and lay communities, we designed a mixed-methods framework based on a combination of quantitative and qualitative analysis methods from medicine, biostatistics, patient education and health services research, and computer science. The overall framework is outlined in Figure 14.1. It comprises the following tasks:

■ Task 1: *Setting the scene* defines the domain of interest (the discussion of CCSVI within the MS community), identifies the stakeholders, and analyzes the relations among the stakeholders.
■ Task 2: *User pattern analysis* studies the behavior of the various stakeholders with respect to the domain of interest within an online discussion forum.

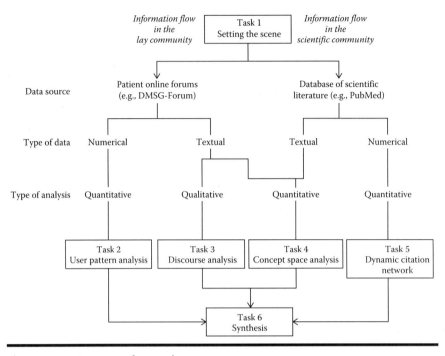

Figure 14.1   Framework overview.

- Task 3: *Discourse analysis* investigates how new scientific topics in the domain of interest diffuse the real-life world as reflected in discussions in an online forum.
- Task 4: *Concept space analysis* identifies the most important topics in the domain of interest, both in the scientific and the public discussions.
- Task 5: *Dynamic citation network* highlights citation dependencies among scientific literature, based on which of the most influential papers in the domain of interest are identified and characterized.
- Task 6: *Synthesis* combines the results of Tasks 1–5 in an integrated view of the information flows in domain of interest to provide a comprehensive understanding of how the two communities exchange information and influence each other and develop the CCSVI hypothesis into a topical concept in MS.

In this chapter, we briefly outline the domain of interest as the result of Task 1 and summarize our methods and findings from Tasks 2 and 3, which have been published in Sudau et al. (2014) and Koschack et al. (2015), respectively. We also provide a first glimpse into our approach to Task 5 and its preliminary outcomes. Finally, we indicate how the results from the different tasks could be merged to a synthesis, including some critical comments on shortcomings and future research directions, such as incorporating the outcomes of Task 4 into the synthesis.

14.3 Setting the Scene

The first step involves the identification of the CCSVI stakeholders, the relations among the stakeholders, the media used by the stakeholders to communicate, and the motivations of the stakeholders. We have initially restricted our scope of analysis to (1) an analysis of an online forum and (2) a systematic review of scientific literature in scientific databases. In the future, it may be worthwhile to expand the scope to include further online social media platforms such as Facebook.

14.3.1 Scientific Community

The CCSVI hypothesis was first proposed by Paolo Zamboni (Zamboni et al., 2009a), who suggested that obstruction to venous drainage in the neck and spinal cord, termed chronic cerebrospinal venous insufficiency, was linked to MS (Thapar et al., 2011, 2012). Although the association between MS and sonographic features of CCSVI is variable (Thapar et al., 2012), some institutions have even begun to offer angioplasty and endovenous stenting of CCSVI, often referred to commercially as "the liberation procedure" (Tumer, 2012). The CCSVI waves seem to have calmed down since and some consider the hypothesis—in a retrospective view of the CCSVI hype—as a waste of valuable time, money, and intellectual energy (Ghezzi, 2013).

14.3.2 Online Community

In Germany, a significant online discussion of CCSVI among different stakeholders took place on the online forum of the DMSG (DMSG, 2015). The DMSG is a nonprofit stakeholder of MS patients and their families, founded by clinical and scientific experts in MS in 1952. It is a registered charity with 16 regional branches and over 900 community contact groups (www.dmsg.de).

Among other features, the DMSG provides on its website two different kinds of freely accessible forums: one is expert forum with time-limited chats between experts and users about different issues (e.g., cognitive deficits in MS or pregnancy in MS). The other forum is unstructured, not moderated, and open for anonymous registration. It is targeted at laypeople, mostly people with MS. The forum consists of threads, which in turn contain sequences of posts. These posts may contain hyperlinks and may cite any number of previous posts.

14.4 Characterizing Sources of Information and User Behaviors

To get a first insight into the information flow in the lay community, we performed a quantitative analysis of the evolving behavior of the various participants within the selected patient online forum.

14.4.1 Methods

The analysis involved different methods for collecting material, searching for scientific publications, studying other web resources referenced in discussions, and ultimately characterizing user behavior, both in terms of sources of information being referenced and in terms of overall behavior.

14.4.1.1 Collecting Materials

All 139,912 posts from 11,997 threads published within the time period between January 1, 2008, and August 17, 2012, were extracted for analysis. Since the forum is about MS in general, only a fraction of the extracted posts were expected to be about the topic of primary interest, that is, CCSVI. A custom information retrieval algorithm (Sudau et al., 2014) was developed to classify individual posts as either relevant ("discussing CCSVI at least partially") or irrelevant. The algorithm identified 8628 posts as relevant, which were used during the subsequent analysis steps.

14.4.1.2 Searching for Scientific Publications

Users occasionally included hyperlinks in their posts and these links referred to content the users based their opinions on. We analyzed which of these links could be identified as references to scientific publications in order to assess the degree to which users relied on scientific sources.

First, we generated a presumably exhaustive list of publications dealing with CCSVI. A citation network starting from Zamboni's original publication and using the CiteXplore web service was constructed (CiteXplore, 2015). These publications were then merged with a second list that was obtained by a search for "CCSVI" in the PubMed database via the Entrez interface (Sayers, 2008). The data set covered articles published between September 1, 2009 and July 31, 2012.

Second, a program fetched every hyperlink (also those in "irrelevant" posts) from the corpus, extracted the textual content from the referenced webpage or PDF document, and searched it for titles or publication IDs from the publication list.

14.4.1.3 Searching for Other Web Resources Used and Their Classification

Apart from searching for scientific information sources in the posts, we also strived to identify what other kinds of information sources were referenced in the posts.

14.4.1.4 Characterizing User Behavior

Since nothing was known in advance about the behavior patterns of forum users, we employed a method of exploratory data analysis to reveal possible patterns.

A clustering algorithm was applied to group users based on their similarity according to a set of predefined characteristics calculated from the available data.

Two behavioral aspects in particular were analyzed in detail by means of separate clustering: (1) the preference for referenced sources of information and (2) the general contribution behavior or posting habits. In the first clustering, we focused on the distribution of referenced sources of information, which were assigned to eight primary domain classes characterizing the kind of information that the source provided:

1. Organization (including foundations, associations, and unions)
2. Commerce (private business selling products or services that do not include treatment)
3. Health care provider (both generic and specialized institutions)
4. News (commercial news providers)
5. Scientific (sources of scientific work and knowledge)
6. Social (social media websites)
7. Personal (content from a single person)
8. Others (not classifiable into one of the categories mentioned earlier)

The second clustering focused on nine quantitative features describing the way a user was most likely to post:

1. Average message length (Brush et al., 2005)—as an indicator of the amount of effort that is put into a post by a user
2. Average number of posts per day (Jones et al., 2011)—as the most important activity feature of a user indicating their selectiveness and frequency of posting
3. Average number of references per post—as an indicator of a user's interest in bringing new sources of information to the forum and preferences for using external evidence
4. Average number of threads per day (Jones et al., 2011)—as an indicator of a user's focus of interest in discussions
5. Days active (Brush et al., 2005)—as an indicator of the consistency of the contribution behavior of a user
6. Fraction of posts that were cited—as an indicator of the tendency to provoke direct responses from other forum participants
7. Fraction of relevant posts—as an indicator of the user's interest in CCSVI
8. Fraction of initiated threads (Chan et al., 2010)—as an indicator of a user's interest to start discussions, often related to the introduction of new information to the forum
9. Coverage of users in relevant parts per post—as an indicator of the efficiency in opinion exchange about CCSVI

In both cases, we assigned names to the clusters based on manual assessment of the results. The definition of these names is based on which characteristics "stand out" for a given cluster.

14.4.2 Results

14.4.2.1 Searching for Scientific Publications

We detected hyperlinks pointing to CCSVI-related scientific publications in 31 posts. The timeline of the references to scientific sources is visualized in Figure 14.2. Interestingly, Zamboni's original publication (Zamboni et al., 2009a) was brought to the forum no later than two months after publication and referenced repeatedly, often indirectly. Another four publications in favor of the CCSVI hypothesis (Singh and Zamboni, 2009; Zamboni et al., 2009a; Al-Omari and Rousan, 2010; Malagoni et al., 2010) were cited by September 30, 2010. The period from July 1, 2009 to September 30, 2010, can thus be described as a "boom phase" of the CCSVI hypothesis in the forum. However, after September 30, 2010, critical publications appeared and were brought to the forum. In fact, all except one (Zamboni et al., 2011) of the referenced publications after September 30, 2010 (Doepp et al., 2010; Yamout et al., 2010; Baracchini et al., 2011; Bastianello et al., 2011; Centonze et al., 2011; Mayer et al., 2011; Wattjes et al., 2011), strongly oppose CCSVI. At this time, the series of repeated references to Zamboni's original publication stopped.

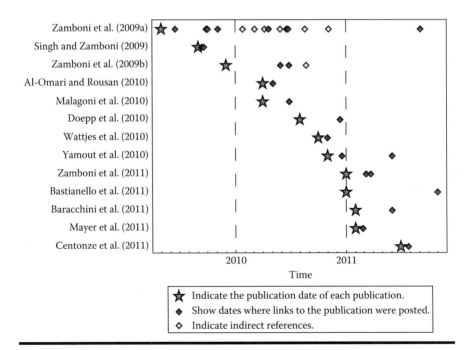

Figure 14.2 Timeline of references to scientific publications in the DMSG patient forum.

14.4.2.2 Searching for Other Web Resources Used and Their Classification

The evolution of the number of references to sources from the different domain classes in relevant posts is summarized in Figure 14.3. At any given point in time, social media websites were the most widely used type of web resource. Similar to the low number of referenced scientific publications, science-based resources were generally not used very often. About half of the posted hyperlinks from the domain class "scientific" refer to Wikipedia articles. Organization-related websites and news sites were the second and third most important ones.

14.4.2.3 Characterizing User Behavior

Only a fraction of all users were included in the clustering because we wanted to focus on those who actively participated in CCSVI discussions. In addition, a sufficient amount of information about each user was required. Therefore, to establish a threshold for active participation, based on observations on the data, we clustered only users who had posted at least five relevant hyperlinks, in the case of hyperlink use (first clustering). Similarly, in the case of posting habits (second clustering), we included only users who had made at least five relevant posts. As a result, from the initial pool of 13,072 users, 1,169 were classified as participants in CCSVI discussions, of which 64 were considered for the clustering in terms of preferred kinds

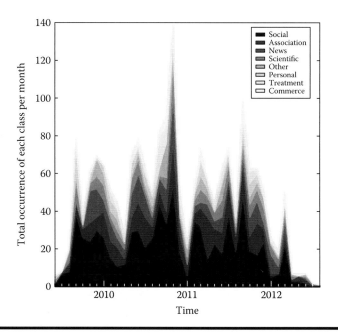

Figure 14.3 Timeline of references to sources from different domain classes.

of referenced sources. With regard to overall behavior, 171 users were considered for the clustering. Among the users considered for each clustering, 57 were in both subsets.

The clustering based on preferred kinds of referenced sources yielded six distinct reference use groups. The distribution of the users among these groups is shown in Figure 14.4 and the preferences of the members of each group are shown in Figure 14.5. Roughly half of the users can be described as *social media fans*. For example, *social media fans* prefer video-sharing websites (such as YouTube.com), Facebook pages, and blogs over more traditional sources. *balanced source users* cite sources from different classes equally often, including scientific ones. *Organization followers* mainly refer to content published by organizations; we also identified a group that uses sources that do not fit well into the classification scheme. *Homepage promoters* post links to websites featuring static content authored by a single person. *Seekers of health care* discuss doctors and clinics. *Users of uncommon sources* focus on religion, esotericism, complementary or alternative medicine, or unrelated resources.

In terms of overall behavior, the clustering yielded six distinct behavior groups. The distribution of the users among these groups is shown in Figure 14.6 and the defining characteristics for each group are highlighted in Figure 14.7. About two-thirds of the users could only be described as "average." This means that they do not stand out, but the characteristics of these

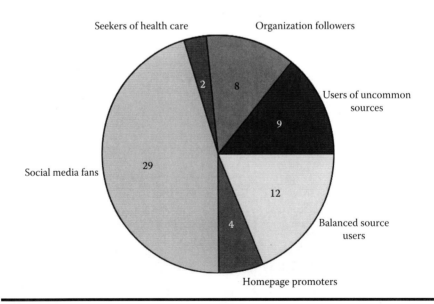

Figure 14.4　Clustering by domain references.

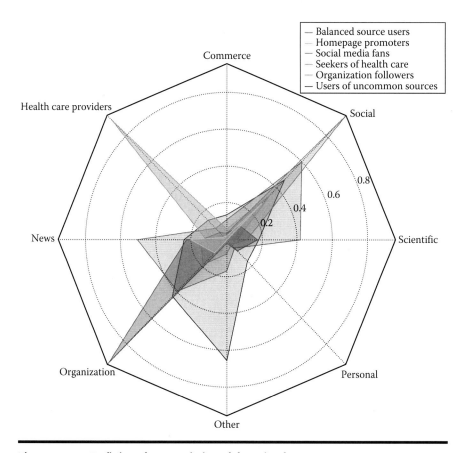

Figure 14.5 Defining characteristics of domain clusters.

users provide a baseline for comparison with the other user roles. Twenty-eight users were CCSVI-focused responders, who were active for less than a year on average. What defines them is the low level of posts per day, the low fraction of initiated threads, and the high fraction of CCSVI-related posts. Ten users were highly active relational posters, who show the highest level of posting activity (about four posts per day). They posted in lots of different threads but rarely initiated them. Another 17 users are CCSVI activators, who stand out due to their high fraction of initiated threads, their high percentage of CCSVI-related posts, and the fact that they included three times as many references as the average user. The four sophisticated contributors are known for making posts that are three times as long as those of average users and include five times more references. The remaining four short-lived CCSVI spammers were active for a few days only and, during their short contribution period, created many posts about CCSVI.

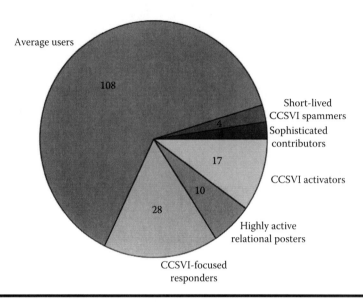

Figure 14.6   Clustering by overall behavior.

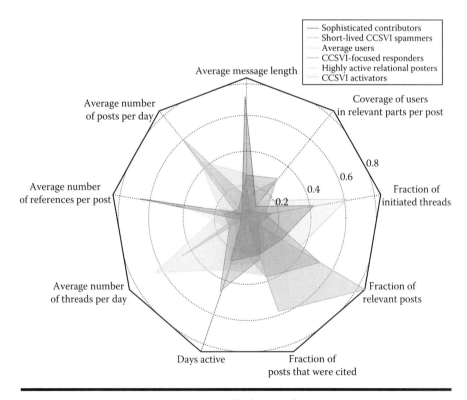

Figure 14.7   Defining characteristics of behavior clusters.

14.5 Characterizing the Discourse about CCSVI in an Online Forum

Next, we performed a discourse analysis of the CCSVI-related posts in the MS patient forum with the aim to explore the content, structure, and substructure of the information flow about CCSVI in a lay community.

14.5.1 Methods

The analysis involved the application of different methods for data reduction, structural analysis of the discourse strand, and detailed analysis of typical discourse fragments (Jäger, 2001).

14.5.1.1 Data Reduction

Initially, all contributions between January 1, 2008 (the starting point of the forum), and August 17, 2012 (the date of the extraction), were extracted. This initial database consisted of 139,912 postings and was reduced first to postings contributing to the CCSVI discussion (see Chapter 14.4.1.1). The first CCSVI-related posting determined the beginning of our data analysis. To define the end of the chronological analysis, we followed the concept of saturation, a guiding principle in qualitative research (Flick, 2014, 170ff.). Six months after the first CCSVI-related posting, we could not identify further discourse fragments that provided new information or put the data already gathered into perspective (Figure 14.8).

14.5.1.2 Structural Analysis of the Discourse Strand

We analyzed the CCSVI-related threads of the patient forum in a chronological order. We identified significant users (i.e., users who posted very often) or whose postings started lively discussions to outline the structure of the discourse strand on CCSVI.

14.5.1.3 Detailed Analysis of Typical Discourse Fragments

We first described the thread, including the number of contributing users, whether it was from a well-known user (i.e., from a user who often posted and elicited many responses from other users), the number of postings, the course of the thread (e.g., whether it meandered or was concise), and whether it mentioned subtopics that were discussed previously. Then, we described the context of the thread, including information about whether the thread was triggered by a real-life event. Next, we analyzed the thread chronologically to reveal its inherent structure. Subtopics were scrutinized for their meaning (i.e., which emotions and connotations were addressed) and how a subtopic was related to other subtopics. After that, we analyzed

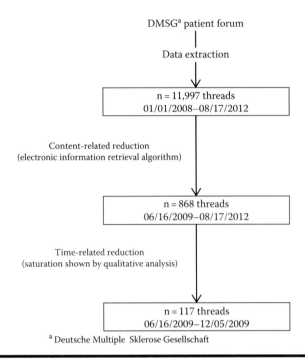

DMSG[a] patient forum

Data extraction

n = 11,997 threads
01/01/2008–08/17/2012

Content-related reduction
(electronic information retrieval algorithm)

n = 868 threads
06/16/2009–08/17/2012

Time-related reduction
(saturation shown by qualitative analysis)

n = 117 threads
06/16/2009–12/05/2009

[a] Deutsche Multiple Sklerose Gesellschaft

Figure 14.8   Discourse analysis data reduction.

the arguments used to justify attitudes or emotions. We flagged the strategy of how the users tried to support their arguments (e.g., by quoting an expert who stated it). Finally, we determined whether cultural stereotypes, such as figures of speech and allegories that seemed to be a common ground for the users in the forum, signified something specific and were therefore used to popularize knowledge.

14.5.2 Results

We identified two main discourse strands. We became aware of some collective symbols that attracted our attention during the detailed analysis. Finally, we report on certain dimensions of reasoning and reconciliation that were useful for interpreting discourse positions within the CCSVI discourse:

1. *The downfall of the professional knowledge providers*: Like scientists usually do, some of the users also began to discuss the CCSVI hypothesis and Zamboni's study (Zamboni et al., 2009a) against the background of evidence-based medicine, using terms such as "placebo," "number of cases," and "blinded." However, this parascientific discourse was not continued; the lack of any further evidence-based information may be the reason. Although users clearly

understood more evidence was needed, some of them argued that the progressive course of their disease did not allow them to wait until the scientific community produced better knowledge. A feeling of distrust toward the scientific community or, more precisely, toward the neurological scientific community tainted the ongoing discussion and the following events were mainly interpreted as confirmation of this feeling.

2. *The rise of the nonprofessional treasure trove of experience*: From the beginning of the CCSVI debate, forum users tried to validate the CCSVI hypothesis against their knowledge about MS in general (e.g., by citing epidemiological facts such as the unequal sex ratio in MS) and their own illness experiences, such as symptom improvement by certain yoga techniques that are claimed to alter blood flow. In parallel to this embedding of CCSVI into the existing knowledge, users began to construct new experience-based knowledge about CCSVI. Two months after the first CCSVI-related posting, they began to publish the first- or secondhand results of diagnostic and therapeutic procedures in the forum.

14.5.2.1 Collective Symbols

Many contributions to the CCSVI debate were accompanied by emotions, as could be observed from the frequent use of collective symbols, such as the German figure of speech "Halbgott in Weiß" ("demigod in white") used for degrading medical experts. Another example was the repeated use of "Bahnhof" ("railroad station"), a metaphor with connotations of "getting lost" or "being left behind." We analyzed one figure of speech to reveal the underlying images from which the users constructed the picture of CCSVI and MS. The German expression "eine neue Sau durchs Dorf treiben" literally translates as "to chase a new sow through the village" and means to make a big fuss about something new, with a clearly negative connotation, and is often associated with the feeling that it distracts the audience's attention from the topic that really matters. In the context of CCSVI, the expression was always used to describe exactly this; the course of the CCSVI debate was sensed as familiar and repetitive, such as many other etiologic or therapeutic breakthroughs that were unable to keep the promise to heal MS. The figure of speech portrays a certain emotional tableau of being disenchanted, hopeless, and being tired from past disappointments.

14.5.2.2 Characterization of Discourse Positions

We detected four different positions from which users participated in the CCSVI discussion and evaluated the associated incidents: "hostile," "frustrated," "wait and see," and "enthusiastic." The positions differed in their orientation toward or against evidence-based and experience-based knowledge as reflected by the discourse strands described previously. During lively debates of the significance of individual experiences or the trustworthiness of scientific information, the discussion became often highly emotional. These feelings accompanied the arguments or were directly verbalized. At some points in the discussion, the emotional coloring developed into a subjectivity, which often manifested itself in insults against others. A conspiracy theory seemed to exist on both sides: The pro-CCSVI side contested "Big Pharma" to the point of felonies like murder. However, the anti-CCSVI side also doubted the motives of CCSVI-promoting doctors and scientists. Economic interests were the main argument of both sides.

14.6 Constructing a Dynamic Citation Network for the CCSVI Discussion in the Scientific Community

To describe and understand the evolving scientific literature on CCSVI, we constructed a dynamic citation network for the domain of interest to identify "communities" (clusters) in the literature and characterize these across different dimensions.

14.6.1 Methods

The dynamic citation network approach was described in (Bommarito et al., 2010). A citation network can be defined as an acyclic directed graph where the nodes represent publications and the arcs describe citations from one publication to another. A dynamic citation network $G := \{G_1, G_2, \ldots, G_n\}$ is a set of increasing citation networks where G_i is a copy of G_{i-1} with the addition of the ith document and its corresponding arcs. The most natural ordering of the citation networks in G is the chronological ordering.

The analyses of the dynamic citation network show the dynamics (e.g., growth over time) of scientific publications on CCSVI and help in discovering the influential CCSVI-related publications and identifying clusters in this literature. Such clusters may show the scientific discussion of new or controversial aspects of CCSVI.

The data were collected from CiteXplore (CiteXplore, 2015), which is a scientific search engine aggregating literature from MEDLINE and PubMed Central (ca. 24 million citations for biomedical literature). The process of data collection involved recursive construction of the citation graph beginning with Zamboni's original publication (Zamboni et al., 2009a) resulting in 120 publications with 229 citations among them until July 9, 2012. Next, the data were processed by means of graph layout algorithms in order to determine the position of each publication in the graph. Important publications were identified by means of the HITS authority score (Kleinberg, 1999) emphasizing the relative importance based on the number of citations and the importance of citing publications, determining their "size" in the graph. Finally, clusters were identified based on the calculation of modularity classes (Blondel et al., 2008), determining the "color" of the publications.

Off-topic satellite clusters from the initial data set were filtered out from further analysis, leaving 59 publications for further analyses, based on graph structure, as well as a version of the SeBriNA approach (Kho and Brouwers, 2012) when considering the publication time, publication type, size of study, and sentiment toward CCSVI.

14.6.2 Results

The 59 publications identified as the core group in the data preparation were very closely connected (graph diameter = 3). As a result, no successful clustering was possible based on structure alone. The evolution of publications over time is shown in Figure 14.9 as color coding of the citation network. Naturally, older publications tend to get more citations, hence their larger size; however, certain publications do stand out when compared to other publications from the same time period.

The results in terms of types of publications over time are shown in Figure 14.10. There was one major publication of each of the following types, original research, review, and opinion in 2010 that gained some attention in terms of the number of subsequent citations. Most of the publications were of type original research, followed by review publications, and an increasing number of letters and editorials in 2011.

We looked at the size of the studies in terms of the reported number of participants in each study. The results are shown in Figure 14.11 where the color intensity corresponds to the number of participants (the darker the color, the higher the number of participants), with black being set as the highest number reported (i.e., 710). While one could expect that a large number of participants are prerequisites for acceptance in major publications, the size of a study did not correlate with the importance of a publication in the case of CCSVI.

Finally, we looked at the sentiments toward CCSVI expressed in the publications based on a manual inspection of the abstracts (Figure 14.12). We observed

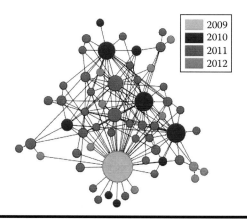

Figure 14.9   Citation network by year.

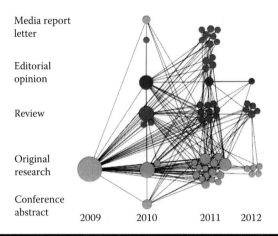

Figure 14.10   Types of publications by year.

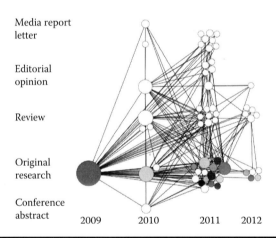

Figure 14.11   Study sizes.

that while, after the initial publication supporting CCSVI in 2009, there were mostly strong sentiments against CCSVI in 2010 (4 to 2), the sentiments were more balanced in 2011 (9 to 7), across all publication types, accompanied by a significant number of publications (20) not expressing any strong sentiments for or against CCSVI. This may have contributed to some of the confusion in the lay communities. The available data for 2012 indicated only sentiments against CCSVI (3 to 0) or no sentiments expressed at all (8).

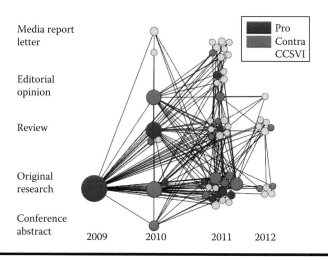

Figure 14.12 **Sentiments toward CCSVI.**

14.7 Summary and Outlook

Our results provide initial insights into the information flow within and between the scientific community and the lay community in the case of a new and fiercely debated treatment option. We were especially interested in the role of the so-called expert patient and the role of scientific information in online health-related discussions. Our results can be summarized as follows.

The user pattern analysis showed that the bulk of the observed contributions in the online forum were not based on scientific publications but on various social media sources. These sources are often regarded as containing mostly opinions and personal experience. A small group of people, the *CCSVI activators,* played a core role in fueling the discussion about CCSVI. Some of the participants in the forum, especially the *sophisticated contributors*, could be considered experts based on the nature of their contribution behavior and their overall behavior, with rather extensive posts often including scientific and other references. They, however, only represent a tiny fraction of the users involved in online discussions.

The discourse analysis made us aware that the users of the MS forum discussed the advantages and disadvantages of scientific research and the quality criteria of clinical studies in a sophisticated manner. They also searched for the latest results of clinical research in scientific databases. At this point, the ideal of the "expert patient" seems to come true. In addition to pursuing scientific knowledge, the users have gained experiential knowledge by (1) making various personal experiences by themselves as patients suffering from MS and (2) listening to the experiences of other patients. We could reveal that the users showed both scientific and experiential knowledge in the CCSVI discussion at different levels of elaboration and deliberation.

The results from Task 2 (*user pattern analysis*) and Task 3 (*discourse analysis*) are in many ways complementary to each other, providing different perspectives at different levels of observation. The closer look at the discourses in the online forum reveals a tension that emerges between the two different forms of knowledge based on, that is, evidence-based and experience-based medicine, respectively. The competition between these two forms of knowledge has a long tradition, with formally acquired knowledge (typified by science) being valued, and naturalistic knowledge (typified by subjective experience) being devalued. Experiential knowledge is associated with unconscious or implicit thinking that does not involve explicit, expressible, and analyzable systems of knowledge. At the same time, the users, or at least some of them, ascribed evidentiary value to experiential knowledge and to scientific knowledge. This could be interpreted as a kind of justification to choose the party of experiential knowledge. This evidence could be called "experiential evidence" (Ziebland and Herxheimer, 2008).

Our third method, the dynamic citation network together with the analysis of the user pattern analysis, also helped to better understand the information flow during the CCSVI debate. The dynamic citation network approach provides some perspective on the relative importance of publications and their position in the network. We could show, at least by time patterns and temporal relationships, how the uncertainty in the scientific discourse gave rise to the controversial discussions in lay communities, with different sentiments expressed in a roughly equal number of publications, and traditional indicators of importance such as study sizes being subdued in favor of other factors. Without this method, it may be difficult to judge the merits of each publication on its own, especially without the necessary training.

Our approach also has some limitations. There is some evidence of a feedback loop, where lay communities or, more generally, the public also influences the scientific community, at least in the case of CCSVI (Chafe et al., 2011). To date, our analysis did not gather any evidence to support this feedback loop. Concept space analysis may be a suitable method to provide some further insights into the importance and perception of different topics and concepts within the different discourses in the domain of interest. As part of our framework for studying information flows in online media and research, we intend to perform concept space analyses for MS and CCSVI as discussed by patients and by the scientific community and investigate how these evolve—and influence each other—over time in future work.

To study the information flow within scientific and lay communities and between these communities is challenging. These communities are different in many ways—in their style of reasoning, in their needs, in their pace, and in their use of the media, among other things. Our framework is designed as a structured approach to identifying and analyzing the interests of the different stakeholders. We tested several methods in a mixed-methods approach that helped us to find global patterns, such as the use of scientific sources in lay communities, by searching through thousands of entries in a large database. At the same time, we also obtained a deeper insight into the content and structure of the discourse of a rather experienced lay community. While in its infancy, we think this framework could be enhanced and expanded to other discourses within and between other online communities in the health care domain and beyond. Extending the application of our framework to further patient online forums will help in validating our findings and may provide the necessary evidence regarding the rising influence of the public on medical debates in scientific communities.

In the future, it will be of increasing importance to anticipate unwelcome or controversial developments in the dissemination of health-related information and to support especially those information channels and dissemination paths that may help patients to become well informed and active partners in health care decisions.

References

Al-Omari, M.H. and L.A. Rousan. Internal jugular vein morphology and hemodynamics in patients with multiple sclerosis. *Int Angiol* 2010;29(2):115–120 [Medline: 20351667].

Baracchini, C., P. Perini, M. Calabrese, F. Causin, F. Rinaldi, and P. Gallo. No evidence of chronic cerebrospinal venous insufficiency at multiple sclerosis onset. *Ann Neurol* 2011;69(1):90–99. doi: 10.1002/ana.22228 [Medline: 21280079].

Bastianello, S., A. Romani, G. Viselner, E.C. Tibaldi, E. Giugni, M. Altieri et al. Chronic cerebrospinal venous insufficiency in multiple sclerosis: Clinical correlates from a multicentre study. *BMC Neurol* 2011;11(132):e7. doi: 10.1186/1471-2377-11-132 [Medline: 22029656].

Blondel, V.D., J.L. Guillaume, R. Lambiotte, and E. Lefebvre. Fast unfolding of communities in large networks. *J Stat Mech: Theor Exp* 2008; (10):P10008.

Bommarito, M.J., D.M. Katz, J.L. Zelner, and J.H. Fowler. Distance measures for dynamic citation networks. *Physica* 2010;A389:4201–4208.

Brunson, E.K. The impact of social networks on parents' vaccination decisions. *Pediatrics* 2013;131(5):e1397–e1404. doi: 10.1542/peds.2012-2452.

Brush, A.J., X. Wang, T.C. Turner, and M.A. Smith. Assessing differential usage of Usenet social accounting meta-data. Presented at *Proceedings of the SIGCHI Conference on Human Factors in Computer Systems*, Portland, OR, 2005, pp. 889–898.

Centonze, D., R. Floris, M. Stefanini, S. Rossi, S. Fabiano, M. Castelli et al. Proposed chronic cerebrospinal venous insufficiency criteria do not predict multiple sclerosis risk or severity. *Ann Neurol* 2011;70(1):51–58. doi: 10.1002/ana.22436 [Medline: 21786298].

Chafe, R., K.B. Born, A.S. Slutsky, and A. Laupacis. The rise of people power. *Nature* 2011;472(7344):410–411. doi: 10.1038/472410a.

Chan, J., C. Hayes, and E.M. Daly. Decomposing discussion forums and boards using user roles. Presented at *AAAI Conference*, George Washington University, Washington, DC, 2010.

CiteXplore. 2015. Web-based PubMed interface. http://www.ebi.ac.uk/citexplore/webservice.jsp (accessed January 31, 2013) [WebCite Cache ID 6M0vmBswA].

Deutsche Multiple Sklerose Gesellschaft/German Multiple Sclerosis Society. DMSG-Forum, 2015. http://www.dmsg.de/multiple-sklerose-forum/index.php?kategorie=msforen (accessed July 6, 2015) [WebCite Cache ID 6IfNcEH1V].

Doepp, F., F. Paul, J.M. Valdueza, K. Schmierer, and S.J. Schreiber. No cerebrocervical venous congestion in patients with multiple sclerosis. *Ann Neurol* 2010;68(2):173–183. doi: 10.1002/ana.22085 [Medline: 20695010].

Donaldson, L. Expert patients usher in a new era of opportunity for the NHS. *BMJ* 2003;326(7402):1279–1280. doi: 10.1136/bmj.326.7402.1279.

Flick, U. *An Introduction to Qualitative Research*, 5th edn. London, U.K.: Sage; 2014.

Ghezzi, A. Funding CCSVI research is/was a waste of valuable time, money and intellectual energy: Yes. *Mult Scler* 2013;19(7):855–857. doi: 10.1177/1352458513479825 [Medline: 23712524].

Jäger, S. Discourse and knowledge: Theoretical and methodological aspects of critical discourse analysis. In: Wodak, R., Meyer, M., editors. *Methods of Discourse Analysis*. London, U.K.: Sage; 2001, pp. 32–62.

Jones, R., S. Sharkey, J. Smithson, T. Ford, T. Emmens, E. Hewis et al. Using metrics to describe the participative stances of members within discussion forums. *J Med Internet Res* 2011;13(1):e3. doi: 10.2196/jmir.1591 [Medline: 21239373].

Kho, M.E. and M.C. Brouwers. The systematic review and bibliometric network analysis (sebrina) is a new method to contextualize evidence. Part 1: Description. *J Clin Epidemiol* 2012;65:1010–1015.

Kleinberg, J.M. Authoritative sources in a hyperlinked environment. *J ACM* 1999; 46(5):604–632.

Koschack, J., L. Weibezahl, T. Friede, W. Himmel, P. Makedonski, and J. Grabowski. Scientific versus experiential evidence: Discourse analysis of the chronic cerebrospinal venous insufficiency debate in a multiple sclerosis forum. *J Med Internet Res* 2015;17(7):e159. doi: 10.2196/jmir.4103.

Malagoni, A.M., R. Galeotti, E. Menegatti, F. Manfredini, N. Basaglia, F. Salvi et al. Is chronic fatigue the symptom of venous insufficiency associated with multiple sclerosis? A longitudinal pilot study. *Int Angiol* 2010;29(2):176–182 [Medline: 20351673].

Mayer, C.A., W. Pfeilschifter, M.W. Lorenz, M. Nedelmann, I. Bechmann, H. Steinmetz et al. The perfect crime? CCSVI not leaving a trace in MS. *J Neurol Neurosurg Psychiatry* 2011;82(4):436–440. doi: 10.1136/jnnp.2010.231613 [Medline: 21296899].

Sayers, E.; NCBI (National Center for Biotechnology Information). Entrez programming utilities help, 2008. http://www.ncbi.nlm.nih.gov/books/NBK25501/ (accessed December 20, 2013) [WebCite Cache ID 6M0w3Mlp4].

Singh, A.V. and P. Zamboni. Anomalous venous blood flow and iron deposition in multiple sclerosis. *J Cereb Blood Flow Metab* 2009;29(12):1867–1878. doi: 10.1038/jcbfm.2009.180 [Medline: 19724286].

Sudau, F., T. Friede, J. Grabowski, J. Koschack, P. Makedonski, and W. Himmel. Sources of information and behavioral patterns in online health forums: Observational study. *J Med Internet Res* 2014;16(1):e10. doi:10.2196/jmir.2875.

Thapar, A., T. Lane, and R. Nicholas. Chronic cerebrospinal venous insufficiency: It is an entity and a subset of multiple sclerosis—Against the motion. In: R.M. Greenhalgh (ed.), *Vascular and Endovascular Controversies Update*. London, U.K.: BIBA Publishing; 2012, pp. 696–705.

Thapar, A., T. Lane, R. Nicholas, T. Friede, M. Ellis, J. Assenheim et al. Systematic review of sonographic chronic cerebrospinal venous insufficiency findings in multiple sclerosis. *Phlebology* 2011;26(8):319–325. doi: 10.1258/phleb.2011.011098 [Medline: 22021635].

Turner, L. Beyond "medical tourism": Canadian companies marketing medical travel. *Global Health* 2012;8(16):11. doi: 0.1186/1744-8603-8-16 [Medline: 22703873].

Valdueza, J.M., F. Doepp, S.J. Schreiber, B.W. van Oosten, K. Schmierer, F. Paul, and M.P. Wattjes. What went wrong? The flawed concept of cerebrospinal venous insufficiency. *J Cereb Blood Flow Metab* 2013;33(5):657–668. doi:10.1038/jcbfm.2013.31 [Medline: 23443168].

Wattjes, M.P., B.W. van Oosten, W.L. de Graaf, A. Seewann, J.C. Bot, R. van den Berg et al. 2011.No association of abnormal cranial venous drainage with multiple sclerosis: A magnetic resonance venography and flow-quantification study. *J Neurol Neurosurg Psychiatry* 2011;82(4):429–435. doi: 10.1136/jnnp.2010.223479 [Medline: 20980483].

Yamout, B., A. Herlopian, Z. Issa, R.H. Habib, A. Fawaz, J. Salame et al. Extracranial venous stenosis is an unlikely cause of multiple sclerosis. *Mult Scler* 2010;16(11):1341–1348. doi: 10.1177/1352458510385268 [Medline: 21041329].

Zamboni, P., R. Galeotti, E. Menegatti, A.M. Malagoni, G. Tacconi, S. Dall'Ara et al. Chronic cerebrospinal venous insufficiency in patients with multiple sclerosis. *J Neurol Neurosurg Psychiatry* 2009a;80(4):392–399. doi: 10.1136/jnnp.2008.157164 [Medline: 19060024].

Zamboni, P., R. Galeotti, E. Menegatti, A.M. Malagoni, S. Gianesini, I. Bartolomei et al. A prospective open-label study of endovascular treatment of chronic cerebrospinal venous insufficiency. *J Vasc Surg* 2009b;50(6):1348–1358. doi:10.1016/j.jvs.2009.07.096 [Medline: 19958985].

Zamboni, P., E. Menegatti, B. Weinstock-Guttman, M.G. Dwyer, C.V. Schirda, A.M. Malagoni et al. Hypoperfusion of brain parenchyma is associated with the severity of chronic cerebrospinal venous insufficiency in patients with multiple sclerosis: A cross-sectional preliminary report. *BMC Med* 2011;9:22. doi: 10.1186/1741-7015-9-22.

Ziebland, S. and A. Herxheimer. How patients' experiences contribute to decision making: Illustrations from DIPEx (personal experiences of health and illness). *J Nurs Manag* 2008;16(4):433–439. doi: 10.1111/j.1365–2834.2008.00863.x.

Chapter 15

Mining Big Data for Analyzing and Simulating Collaboration Factors Influencing Software Development Decisions

Philip Makedonski, Verena Herbold, Steffen Herbold, Daniel Honsel, Jens Grabowski, and Stephan Waack

Contents

15.1 Introduction and Motivation

Software development is inherently a collaborative activity, where different stakeholders communicate and collaborate in order to achieve a common goal in the form of a software product. Intrinsically, as with any human activity, human factors play a major role in software development and both researchers and practitioners need to take these into account when studying software development phenomena, on the one hand, and designing collaborative tools and platforms, on the other. Consequently, de Souza et al. (2005) note two fundamental sources of complexity in software development. On the one hand, they contemplate the complexity of the artifacts, including the design and use of algorithms, architectures, and scale. On the other hand, they also consider the complexity of the activities surrounding the artifacts, including concurrent creation and modification of artifacts by multiple people, coordination, conflict management, and goal and strategy definition, in order to ultimately achieve coherent concerted effect.

With the rise of open source development, there has also been an increasing availability and usage of open source portals and platforms, such as SourceForge, GitHub, and Google Code. Such platforms enable convenient sharing, discovery, and contribution. As a consequence, even the smallest personal projects have the potential to gain exposure and become collaborative endeavors. This has led to the emergence of the "social coding" phenomenon in recent years, which has contributed to a massive proliferation of open source software products and components and staggering growth in their both contributors and users. As a side effect, an unprecedented amount of information related to the very phenomenon has become available in the process. Such information provides researchers with a large amount of material for studying human- and collaboration-related topics in the domain of software development. Information related to the contributions and collaborations of individual developers to the software products as well as their communications across various media is recorded and publicly available due to the very nature of the phenomenon. Such information is typically stored in so-called software repositories of various kinds, serving different primary purposes, such as logging who did what, when, where, and for what reason and discussing issue reports and feature requests and similar information. The same repositories can be mined to extract facts related to the different artifacts, activities, and people involved. The extracted facts can then be used in different assessment tasks in order to aid decisions, such as resource allocation, task and activity prioritization, and team reorganization.

Moreover, we present two applications in this chapter, where we harness the collaboration aspects of software development to improve existing approaches from software engineering. First, we discuss how we can improve the prediction of the location of defects through developer-centric metrics. Second, we present an approach for the simulation of software processes that is partially founded on the mining of collaboration between developers and the impact of single developers on the resulting software product.

In this chapter, we present a multifaceted and interdisciplinary approach for studying collaboration factors by mining big data collected from software repositories for the purposes of analyzing and simulating collaboration activities in order to aid evidence-based decisions in software development. We first summarize related work in the study of social networks in software development. Then we outline our approach for mining diverse software repositories. The facts extracted from software repositories are then used for defect prediction and simulation parameter estimation. We conclude with a summary and an outlook on future work.

15.2 Social Networks in Software Development

Social networks in software development have been the subject of numerous studies over the past few years. Wiese et al. (2014) presented a good systematic overview of the use of social metrics in prediction models in software engineering by conducting a mapping study. They observed that while quantitative data related to social networks in the form of social metrics were often contemplated, they were usually considered as part of process-, history-, or change-related characteristics and rarely used individually. In their mapping study, the authors identified 48 primary studies and 51 social metrics organized across nine categories. The term "social metrics" itself is rather loosely defined, which is part of the reason why social metrics have been considered as part of different dimensions in the literature. Wiese et al. (2014) consider "any metric that measures aspects of the interactions between developers" to be a social metric. This includes the number of comments (e.g., to an issue) or the number of developers that collaborated on an artifact. But the authors also consider experience-related aspects, such as ownership and the number of contributions to an artifact. In contrast, Ibrahim et al. (2010) restrict their notion of "social dimension" only to metrics related to the communication activities between developers and their impact. Emphasizing the lack of systematic studies investigating the impact of social metrics, Hall et al. (2012) noted that few studies that did use developer and social information in fault prediction models reported conflicting results. Radjenovic et al. (2013) also observed that the applicability of developer information in software fault prediction models remains an open research question.

Individual studies considering social metrics include

- Pinzger et al. (2008) investigating the use of developer-module networks for defect prediction
- Rahman and Devanbu (2011) studying the impact of ownership and developer experience on software defects, using human-centered process metrics, some of which can be classified as social metrics
- Shihab et al. (2012) studying the impact of developer experience among other characteristics on the predictability of risky changes

Social network analysis has also been applied in a number of studies, including Meneely et al. (2008) and Bird et al. (2009), where different types of social networks are constructed based on collaborations on artifacts or discussions of issues in order to predict failures.

Miranskyy et al. (2014) propose a temporal collaboration network model based on the history of collaboration among developers, testers, and other stakeholders to estimate the defect exposure for the next month. The authors note that while in reality team structures do change over time, the commonly used static collaboration models that capture interactions between team members over the complete lifespan of a software project fail to take this into account. In their study, the authors observed that the proposed temporal collaboration network provides a more realistic picture than a static one, where the best predictions for the next month are obtained by looking at the collaboration data from the previous month, and can thus be more helpful in aiding evidence-based decisions in software development.

Celik et al. (2010) proposed a novel workforce assignment framework based on a notion of position in a social network and the application of agent-based simulation and multiobjective optimization. The proposed framework is used to aid project managers of globally distributed software development in conducting optimal workforce assignment, while considering both short-term (productivity) and long-term (organizational robustness) benefits.

There also exist approaches simulating developer collaboration for open source software. For example, Gao and Madey (2007) performed a study on agent-based simulation of open source software focusing on developer collaboration networks. In this work, they simulate the SourceForge.net community. With visual inspection and hypothesis testing, they matched the network measures under examination to the reality.

Finally, Timchuk et al. (2014) investigated the extent to which collaboration data mined from software repositories represent the actual collaboration between developers in an open source community. They concluded that data mined from individual software repositories likely do not represent the actual collaboration and advised researchers and practitioners to proceed with caution and consider relying on a combination of multiple sources of information, such as version control systems (VCSs), mailing lists (MLs), and issue tracking systems (ITSs), rather than a single source of information, in order to obtain a more complete and realistic picture of the actual collaborations taking place.

15.3 Concepts and Characteristics

In this work, we are concerned with studying collaboration factors in software development and their influence on decision-making. To better understand the domain of software development, we first identify the relevant concepts of the domain and how they are related to each other.

15.3.1 Domain Concepts

Conceptually, the behavior of a developer is defined as a sequence of activities, performed on different artifacts. Developers and artifacts are described by sets of attributes. Since both artifacts and developers evolve after each activity in that the values for the respective attributes change after each activity, both artifacts and developers have a sequence of states, which is extended with each activity. Artifact states are then described by a set of quantitative and qualitative values of the attributes characterizing the corresponding artifact at a certain point in time. Similarly, developer states are described by a set of values that characterize the corresponding developer at a certain point in time, indicative of their experience and collaborations at that point. Consequently, an activity is performed in a given context defined by the state of the artifact on which it is performed and the state of the developer performing the activity, resulting in a new state for the artifact and potentially also for the developer. Activities are described by a set of deltas, which describe the quantitative changes between the state of the artifact in which the activity was performed and the state resulting after the activity was performed. Activities are also described by a set of activity values of activity attributes that do not translate to states directly but rather relate to the transition between the states. A conceptual overview for the characterization of developer behavior in software development is shown in Figure 15.1.

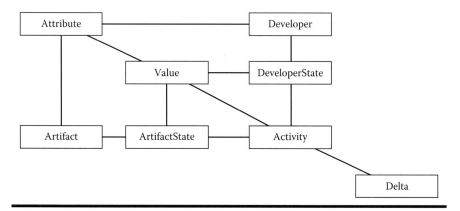

Figure 15.1   Characterizing developer behavior.

15.3.2 *Collaboration Characteristics*

The characterization of collaboration behavior in our work is based on the following premise built on top of the conceptual characterization of developer behavior: a developer *pat* working on an artifact *a* at time point *t* + 2 is considered to *collaborate directly* with a developer *tom* who was the last one to work on the artifact *a* at a time point *t* + 1, and *pat* is considered to *collaborate indirectly* with a developer *joe* who worked on the artifact *a* at some time point *t*, where there was further work on the artifact *a* between time points *t* and *t* + 2. Both artifacts and developers are in corresponding states at the different time points reflecting the values for the different collaboration characteristics at these time points. Thus, a dynamic collaboration graph evolving over time is constructed as a projection based on traces from the interactions of developers with artifacts. The conceptual overview of this premise is illustrated in Figure 15.2, with the developers and their corresponding collaboration relationships visualized at the top, based on their activities on the subsequent states of the artifact visualized at the bottom.

Based on this notion of collaboration and the resulting collaboration graph, we define a set of characteristics that describe the collaboration behavior from both the perspective of an artifact and the perspective of a developer. Consequently, each

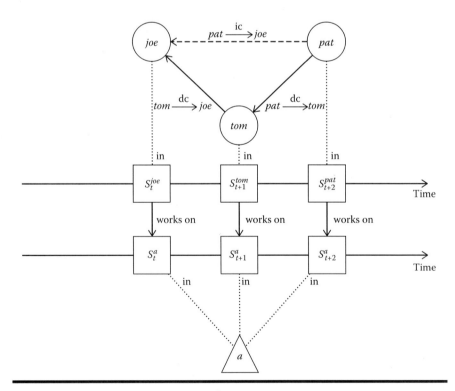

Figure 15.2 Collaboration concepts.

state of an artifact is characterized by a set of values related to the collaborators working on that artifact up to the point in time in which the state was created. These include the following:

- *Artifact collaborator count* (*ACC*): Value indicating the number of developers that have worked on the artifact up to the given state.
- *Relative developer experience on artifact* (*REXP*): Value indicating the ratio of the number of states of the artifact that the developer of a given state worked on to the total number of states up to the given state.
- *Direct collaborations with last author* (*DCLA*): Value indicating the number of times the developer working on a given state of an artifact has directly collaborated with the author of the previous state of the artifact up to the given state.
- *Fractal distribution of relative experience* (*FREXP*): Value indicating the distribution of experience of the developers with a given artifact in a given state. This characteristic is based on the notion of fractal values as defined by D'Ambros et al. (2005), taking into account the fraction of states that each collaborating developer worked on, where a high value would indicate a large number of equally contributing developers and a low value would indicate a major contributor working on a large proportion of the states up to the given state.

Similarly, each state of a developer is characterized by a set of values related to the collaborations of the developer up to the point in time of the state. These include

- *Indirect collaborator count*: Value indicating the number of developers that have indirectly collaborated with the developer on artifacts up to a given point in time
- *Direct collaborator count*: Value indicating the number of developers that have directly collaborated with the developer on artifacts up to a given point in time
- *Artifact ratio* (*AR*): Value indicating the proportion of artifacts that the developer has worked on up to a given point in time, relative to the total number of artifacts up to that point in time

15.4 Mining Approach

In order to obtain the necessary data for the characterization and analysis of the collaboration behavior of developers, we need to mine different sources of information related to software development. There are two fundamental aspects of software mining. The first is related to facts extraction, which involves obtaining measurable data about different entities. The second is related to knowledge derivation, which involves obtaining additional information about software artifacts and development activities through the application of different analysis methods on the extracted facts in order to gain further insights and aid decision-making. Typically, activities directly related to the development of a software product are recorded in VCSs, that store the entire history of software-related artifacts. This includes information about the point in time when an artifact was created, the developer who created it, the points in time it was subsequently modified, the developers that performed these modifications, and the purpose of the modifications. VCSs already provide a wealth of information that can be exploited for characterization and analysis. However, in practice, this is not the primary intended purpose of VCSs. In addition, VCSs come in a variety of flavors; thus, a scalable and widely applicable approach needs to take the heterogeneity of the VCSs into consideration. While there are different approaches, they are typically tailored to a specific VCS and often a specific mining task. In addition, the resulting extracted facts are also heterogeneous in format and content. Another important source of information are ITSs, which record issues related to a software product. Issues may be reported by users, testers, developers, or other stakeholders. There may be comments associated with an issue as well as additional metainformation related to the status and nature of the issue. Issues are assigned to developers to work on and are often associated with a corresponding activity in the VCSs, indicating that a particular issue has been addressed. Similar to VCSs, ITSs also come in a variety of flavors and corresponding approaches also produce heterogeneous output. Thus, one of the challenges for both sources of information is harmonization and homogenization of the resulting facts. Further sources of information such as mailing lists and user forums (UFs) can be used to complement facts obtained from VCSs and ITSs, but they also face the same challenges. In addition, finer granularity processing of the sources of information makes the facts extraction a laborious and complex activity.

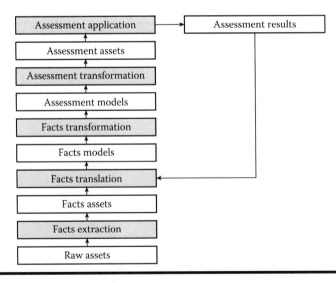

Figure 15.3 Mining approach.

Extracted facts can be used for a wide variety of analysis and assessment tasks. Often the sheer amount of data can be daunting to comprehend and time-consuming to process. In addition, only a fraction of the data may be of relevance to a specific assessment task.

To address these challenges, we propose a multilayered mining approach that systematically addresses different mining challenges and decouples the different mining activities so that addressing a particular assessment task becomes a feasible and approachable task.

At the core of the mining approach, assessment-related concepts and extracted facts are described formally by means of high-level metamodels. Instances of these metamodels are used to abstract away from the concrete low-level representations of extracted facts. By means of model transformations, related facts are consolidated and relevant facts are mapped to the corresponding concepts from the assessment domain resulting in assessment model instances. Similarly, the assessment model instances are then transformed in assessment assets, which are used in the various assessment applications. The mining approach comprises five steps (visualized as gray boxes in Figure 15.3) for obtaining derived knowledge from raw assets:

1. *Facts extraction*: The facts extraction step handles processing of heterogeneous raw assets, such as VCS repositories and logs, ITS databases, source code files, and ML archives, in order to obtain basic facts and metadata stored as facts assets in a structured machine (and human-)-readable format, which are usually independent from one another.

2. *Facts translation*: The facts translation step translates heterogeneous facts assets into homogeneous facts model instances conforming to a set of metamodels describing the structure of the corresponding facts assets.

3. *Facts transformation*: The facts transformation step consolidates and aggregates relevant facts from different facts model instances into assessment model instances according to the assessment task in question, enabling assessment-specific consolidation of relevant data only and stepwise enrichment of the assessment model instances as new facts become available or necessary.

4. *Assessment transformation*: The assessment transformation step uses queries and transformations over the assessment model instances to answer assessment-related questions directly or to produce application-specific assessment assets.

5. *Assessment application*: The assessment application step feeds the assessment assets into corresponding assessment-specific applications, such as clustering, prediction, simulation, and visualization applications, which produce assessment results assets containing derived knowledge. These results assets can then be used as new facts assets, translated into new facts models, and integrated back into the assessment model, for example, using cluster assignments for defect prediction or for visualization.

With the abstraction facilities provided by this mining infrastructure, practitioners can focus on working with relevant concepts at a higher level of abstraction without the need to deal with lower-level concrete representations and technical details.

To exemplify the mining of the collaboration characteristics identified earlier, we rely primarily on facts extracted from a VCS, but the same approach can be pursued to integrate facts extracted from a VCS and an ITS or to use facts from an ITS or a different source for a different assessment task. Once we have extracted and translated the facts extracted from the VCS into a corresponding model instance describing the concepts related to VCSs, we transform the model instance into an instance of the assessment metamodel. This process is sketched in Figure 15.1.

By querying the assessment model instance, we obtain values for attributes described earlier and assign them the corresponding artifact and developer states, thus further enriching the assessment model instance.

Depending on the assessment task and corresponding assessment applications, further information may be required. One of the applications we consider next is defect prediction. In defect prediction, known information about a property of each instance in a given data set (referred to as the training data set) is used to build a prediction model that can then be applied on a new data set for which the information regarding the defect information is not available and instead predicted using the model. The instances in the data sets can be constructed by querying the assessment model instance and combining information about the state of the artifact, the activity, and the state of the developer. The prediction model trained on the available data is used to compute whether performing an activity on a particular state of an artifact can be considered risky with regard to introducing a defect in the future. The prediction depends on the state of the performing developer.

Similarly, by exploiting the information in the assessment model, we can also estimate simulation parameters as discussed in the second application scenario (see Section 15.5.2).

Beyond the collaboration characteristics considered earlier, further collaboration characteristics can be obtained by making use of the facts extracted from ITSs, MLs, UFs, or other sources.

15.5 Applications

Within this section, we will present two concrete applications of social data in software engineering. First, we discuss how defect prediction can be improved through social factors, and then we consider the estimation of simulation parameters for software process simulation.

15.5.1 Software Defect Prediction

One of the key challenges of software quality assurance is the appropriate allocation of the available resources. Usually, there are heavy time and costs constraints.

Therefore, the quality assurance cannot cover all aspects of a system equally and the project and test management must define priorities, which define where to test. Defect prediction is a power vehicle for this. Defect prediction models provide derived knowledge on which parts of a software are defect prone. This knowledge gain can be used for the prioritization of testing efforts and, thereby, exploited to focus the quality assurance efforts.

There are multiple ways to build defect prediction models, for example, based on the number of defects found in a region and the number of changes to a file (Bell et al., 2006), based on software metrics (e.g., Menzies et al., 2007; Catal and Diri, 2009; Herbold, 2013), and based on collaboration aspects (e.g., Bicer et al., 2011, Hu and Wong, 2013). It is the latter that we are primarily interested in within this chapter: How can social networks and collaboration aspects be used to improve defect prediction models?

Considering collaboration information for the identification of defect-prone locations is based on the following intuition. For example, imagine a large module X that has been implemented and maintained by a single developer Kim in the past. Now, consider that there is a change to X by Kim. Because Kim knows X so well, the likelihood of a defect is lower. Now imagine that another developer Sandy changes X. Since Sandy has not worked in the past on X, the likelihood of a defect is increased, as Sandy may not know all side effects of the change. However, if Sandy has worked on a lot of other modules together with Kim, Sandy may also know X quite well or may know which aspects of it to pay attention to, since Sandy knows the programming style of Kim. This would in turn decrease the likelihood of a defect again. As this example shows, the social network between developers can have a big impact on how changes are considered from a software quality perspective.

To demonstrate how defect predictions can be improved through the use of collaboration aspects, we give a practical example. We build two defect prediction models for the project K3b (www.k3b.org): one that only uses source code and change metrics and a second one that also uses collaboration aspects.

We collected various software metrics to describe changes of artifacts. Regarding the change itself, we considered three things: (1) the state of the artifact before the change, (2) the state of the artifact after the change, and (3) the difference between the artifact states before and after the change. To describe the artifact state, we use software metrics that measure the size (lines of code, number of methods, number of attributes, etc.), dependencies to other artifacts (number of child classes, depth of the inheritance tree, etc.), and the number of defects that was already introduced by the artifact. Moreover, for each of the changes, we also had information available on whether it contained a defect or not. These metrics are the foundation for our first defect prediction model.

For the second model, we extended this metric set with the collaboration information described earlier, that is, ACC, REXP, and DCLA. Through these metrics, information about the relationship between changed artifact and the developer who performed the change is incorporated.

For both the models, we create a model called Ripper (Cohen, 1995). Ripper is created through a machine learning approach and learns the structure of defects by considering the metric data. We train the rules based on first two-thirds of the commits of K3b and test the performance on the other third. For the evaluation, we use the metrics recall and precision. The recall is the percentage of how many of the actually defective changes were predicted by the rules as defective. The precision is the percentage of how many of the changes predicted as defective are actually defective. The following table shows the results we achieved with and without the collaboration metrics:

	Recall	Precision
No collaboration	48.5%	47.3%
Collaboration	56.4%	54.3%

As shown in the table, the recall is increased by 11.9% and the precision by 7% through the additional information about the social aspects of the software development. Additional information, such as concrete graph structures and change coupling, may further improve the prediction performance.

15.5.2 Simulation Parameter Estimation

Simulation of software processes is an interesting approach to support project managers in software development planning. Derived knowledge about collaboration aspects in software development can be helpful to improve the simulation of software processes, for example, by refining simulation parameters. Considering software processes and their evolution as humans struggling with the changing requirements of the outside world and the complexity of the system from the inside, it is a valuable approach to model software evolution from the starting point of human behavior. For this purpose, we use agent-based simulation. The agents expose an individual behavior derived from observations of real-world behavior (e.g., Macal, 2010). The agents may represent developers, testers, and users, who are autonomous and proactive individuals. Developers function as active agents working on the artifacts, which in turn are the passive agents in the agent-based simulation model. For the agent-based modeling and implementation, we use *Repast Simphony* (North et al., 2013). To model the agent's behavior, observations of how developers, users, and testers communicate and interact with each other in the real world are needed. This information can be retrieved from VCSs, ITSs, MLs, and UFs by means of the mining infrastructure described earlier.

Agent-based simulation can then be applied to further examine the contribution behavior of different developer types. A direct result of this behavior is the growth of the software system under simulation. The different developer types are identified based on data mined from K3b. For each individual type, we compute an average update behavior that determines the contribution frequency of this developer to the simulated project. Based on the collected data, we distinguish between the following developer types: core developer, maintainer, major developer, and minor developer.

Core developers are the initial contributors and usually include the project leader. Many artifacts are known by them and they contribute by far the most. Major developers know specific areas of the project and fix most of the bugs assigned to artifacts known by them. A developer that contributes less commits and fixes fewer bugs is referred to as a minor developer. They may be specialized in one specific task or feature. A developer that primarily does maintenance work is referred to as a maintainer.

The simulation of artifact creation and deletion, which are responsible for the system growth, depends on the number of developers of each type, their corresponding average working days per month, the system size, and the simulation time. These parameters are set to values obtained from mining K3b. We assume that the number of artifacts created and deleted per commit follows a geometric distribution, using that version of the distribution where the number of failed attempts before the first success is counted. From a developer's point of view, success means that no files have to be created or deleted. The probabilities of this distribution are inferred from the update behavior of developers observed through the mining process. Comparing the resulting growth produced by simulation using this distribution depicted in Figure 15.4 with the real growth of K3b displayed in Figure 15.5 reveals that both are similar (Honsel et al., 2014).

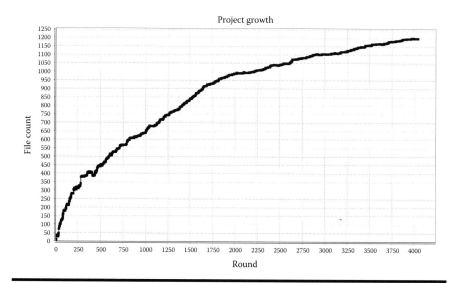

Figure 15.4   Simulated system growth.

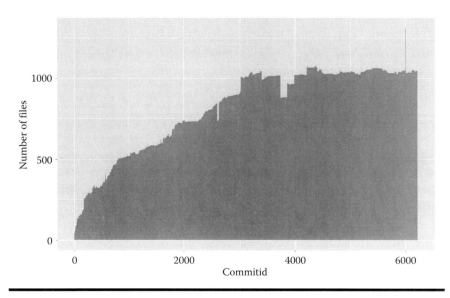

Figure 15.5   Empirical system growth.

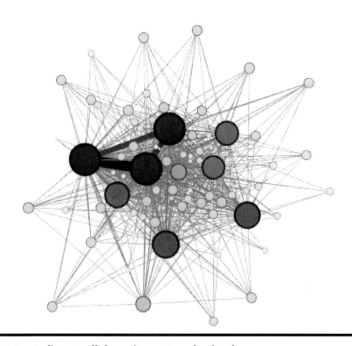

Figure 15.6   Indirect collaboration network of K3b.

Since collaboration is important for software development, it is promising to refine the simulation by adding collaboration parameters.

Figure 15.6 shows the *indirect collaboration network* of K3b. In this network, each developer is represented as a node. An edge is created between two nodes if they present two developers that worked on the same artifact *a* at different points in time. The node size corresponds to the number of other developers a developer has worked with, that is, the degree. The edge size corresponds to the number of indirect collaborations between the developers represented by the corresponding nodes, that is, its weight.

On the resulting visualization, we observed that there are three main contributors, five major contributors, and several minor contributors. Based on the edge sizes, it can be observed that the main contributors have a huge number of artifacts in common.

We reconstructed the same network resulting from the application of agent-based simulation, which is shown in Figure 15.7, where the same layout is used.

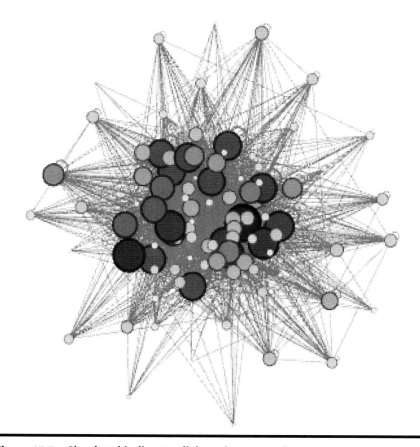

Figure 15.7   Simulated indirect collaboration network.

There we observed that the work is more distributed than in the real project and that strong collaborations do not exist.

We note that in both networks the diameter is three, which means that for every developer there is at most one person in between, so the collaboration distances remain quite small.

In order to refine the simulation and obtain results that are closer to the real observed development, we consider adding a probabilistic choice of the next artifact to work on for each developer, which has an impact on the collaboration. This choice is based on data mined from the VCSs, including the collaboration attributes described earlier. Specifically, we make use of REXP indicating the relative experience of the last developer that worked on an artifact with respect to all other developers that have worked on that artifact and AR providing an overview of the work distribution. The observed REXP for the five most frequently changed artifacts in K3b is visualized in Figure 15.8. There, some patterns for different developers can be identified, for example, every time a rise is visible, the artifact gets changed consecutively by the same developer and thereby increases its REXP.

By modeling these patterns, we can refine and steer the choice of artifacts on which agents in the simulation will work on, which results in simulations that are closer to reality.

The observed AR for the core developer, the maintainer, a major contributor, and a minor contributor of K3b over the time is visualized in Figure 15.9. There

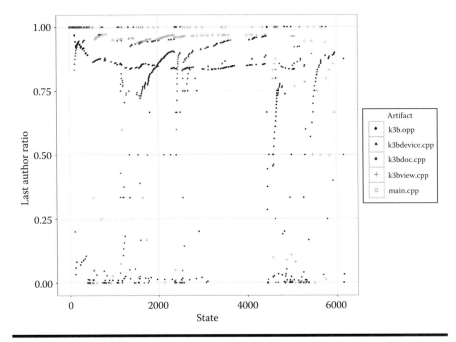

Figure 15.8 *Last author ratio* **for the five main files of K3b.**

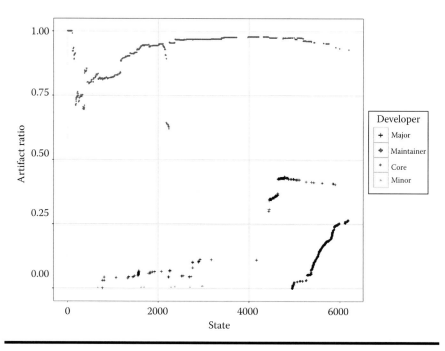

Figure 15.9 *AR* **for different developer types of K3b.**

we identified patterns for the activities of the different kinds of developers. For example, the core developer (the upper line) worked on almost all artifacts during all the development period, whereas the maintainer starts late in the project but gets to work on 25% of the artifacts in a rather short time.

By using this knowledge, we can refine the behavior models for the different developer types in the simulation model. Based on the observations from Figures 15.8 and 15.9, it is possible to improve the strategy for the selection of the next artifacts to work on for the different types of agents, improving the overall simulation outcomes by making them closer to reality.

15.6 Conclusion

In this chapter, we presented a multifaceted and interdisciplinary approach to aiding evidence-based decisions in software development based on mining, analyzing, and simulating collaboration aspects in the domain. We outlined a generic infrastructure for extracting facts related to software development as a whole and to collaboration in particular from software repositories. Then, we presented defect prediction as using the extracted facts as a typical analysis task to gain an insight into potential causes for problems in software development. We demonstrated how the defect prediction was improved through the consideration of social aspects of the software development. In our analysis, we used multiple social metrics at once. Future work in this direction is, for example, the detailed analysis of how influential each social factor is for defect predication. Hence, we will perform correlation analysis between the social metrics and the defects as well as the significance of the usage of these metrics within defect prediction models. Finally, we also showcased the use of the extracted facts for calibrating refining agent-based simulation of software development processes that can help in exploring the outcomes of different decisions. In future work, we plan to evaluate this by comparing empirical networks with simulated networks by using exponential random graph models (Hunter, 2008).

Further applications for the mined data include additional analyses and simulations for effort estimation and different kinds of visualizations in order to present complex relationships and vast amounts of data in an understandable manner.

In addition to further applications, additional sources of information and characteristics based on them and on the existing sources can be extracted and used in the various applications in order to improve their results or extend their scope. Future work also includes improving the scalability of the presented approaches by deploying the whole mining and analysis infrastructure in the cloud.

References

Bell, R.M., T.J. Ostrand, and E.J. Weyuker. 2006. Looking for bugs in all the right places. *Proceedings of the 2006 International Symposium on Software Testing and Analysis (ISSTA)*. ACM, Portland, ME.

Bicer, S., A.B. Bener, and B. Caglayan. 2011. Defect prediction using social network analysis on issue repositories. *Proceedings of the 2011 International Conference on Software and Systems Process (ICSSP)*. ACM, Honolulu, HI.

Bird, C., N. Nagappan, H. Gall, B. Murphy, and P. Devanbu. 2009. Putting it all together: Using socio-technical networks to predict failures. *Proceedings of the 20th IEEE International Conference on Software Reliability Engineering (ISSRE'09)*. IEEE Press, Mysore, India.

Catal, C. and B. Diri. 2009. A systematic review of software fault prediction studies. *Expert Systems with Applications* 36(4): 7346–7354.

Celik, N., H. Xi, D. Xu, and Y.-J. Son. 2010. Simulation-based workforce assignment considering position in a social network. *Proceedings of the Winter Simulation Conference (WSC)*, Baltimore, MD.

Cohen, W.W. 1995. Fast effective rule induction. *Proceedings of the 12th International Conference on Machine Learning*. Morgan Kaufmann, Tahoe City, CA.

D'Ambros, M., M. Lanza, and H. Gall. 2005. Fractal figures: Visualizing development effort for CVS entities. *Proceedings of the Third IEEE International Workshop on Visualizing Software for Understanding and Analysis (VISSOFT 2005)*. IEEE Press, Budapest, Hungary.

de Souza, C., J. Froehlich, and P. Dourish. 2005. Seeking the source: Software source code as a social and technical artifact. *Proceedings of the 2005 International ACM SIGGROUP Conference on Supporting Group Work.* ACM, Sanibel Island, FL.

Gao Y. and G. Madey. 2007. Towards understanding: A study of the SourceForge.Net community using modeling and simulation. *Proceedings of the 2007 Spring Simulation Multiconference.* Society for Computer Simulation International, San Diego, CA.

Hall, T., S. Beecham, D. Bowes, D. Gray, and S. Counsell. 2012. A systematic literature review on fault prediction performance in software engineering. *IEEE Transactions on Software Engineering* 38(6): 1276–1304.

Herbold, S. 2013. Training data selection for cross-project defect prediction. *Proceedings of the 9th International Conference on Predictive Models in Software Engineering (PROMISE).* ACM, Baltimore, MD.

Honsel, V., D. Honsel, and J. Grabowski. 2014. Software process simulation based on mining software repositories. *Proceedings of the Third International Workshop on Software Mining (SoftMine).* IEEE, Shenzhen, China.

Hu, W. and K. Wong. 2013. Using citation influence to predict software defects. *Proceedings of the 10th Working Conference on Mining Software Repositories (MSR).* IEEE Press, San Francisco, CA.

Hunter, D.R., S.M. Goodreau, and M.S. Handcock. 2008. Goodness of fit of social network models. *Journal of the American Statistical Association* 103: 481, 248–258.

Ibrahim, W.M., N. Bettenburg, E. Shihab, B. Adams, and A.E. Hassan. 2010. Should I contribute to this discussion? *Proceedings of the Seventh Working Conference on Mining Software Repositories (MSR).* IEEE Press, Cape Town, South Africa.

Macal, C.M. and M.J. North. 2010. Tutorial on agent-based modelling and simulation. *Journal of Simulation* 4(3): 151–162.

Meneely, A., L. Williams, W. Snipes, and J. Osborne. 2008. Predicting failures with developer networks and social network analysis. *Proceedings of the 16th ACM SIGSOFT International Symposium on Foundations of Software Engineering (SIGSOFT'08/ FSE-16).* ACM.

Menzies, T., J. Greenwald, and A. Frank. 2007. Data mining static code attributes to learn defect predictors. *IEEE Transactions on Software Engineering,* 33(1): 2–13, 2007.

Miranskyy, A., B. Caglayan, A.B. Bener, and E. Cialini. 2014. Effect of temporal collaboration network, maintenance activity, and experience on defect exposure. *Proceedings of the 8th ACM/IEEE International Symposium on Empirical Software Engineering and Measurement (ESEM).* ACM, Turin, Italy.

North, M.J., N.T. Collier, J. Ozik, E. Tatara, M. Altaweel, C.M. Macal, M. Bragen, and P. Sydelko. 2013. *Complex Adaptive Systems Modeling with Repast Simphony.* Complex Adaptive Systems Modeling, Springer, Heidelberg, FRG.

Pinzger, M., N. Nagappan, and B. Murphy. 2008. Can developer-module networks predict failures? *Proceedings of the 16th ACM SIGSOFT International Symposium on Foundations of Software Engineering (SIGSOFT'08/FSE-16).* ACM, New York.

Radjenović, D., M. Heričko, R. Torkar, and A. Živkovič. 2013. Software fault prediction metrics. *Information and Software Technology* 55(8): 1397–1418.

Rahman, F. and P. Devanbu. 2011. Ownership, experience and defects: A fine-grained study of authorship. *Proceedings of the 33rd International Conference on Software Engineering (ICSE).* ACM, Honolulu, HI.

Shihab, E., A.E. Hassan, B. Adams, and Z.M. Jiang. 2012. An industrial study on the risk of software changes. *Proceedings of the ACM SIGSOFT 20th International Symposium on the Foundations of Software Engineering (FSE'12)*. ACM, Cary, NC.

Tymchuk, Y., A. Mocci, and M. Lanza. 2014. Collaboration in open-source projects: Myth or reality? *Proceedings of the 11th Working Conference on Mining Software Repositories (MSR)*. ACM, Hyderabad, India.

Wiese, I.S., F.R. Côgo, R. Ré, I. Steinmacher, and M.A. Gerosa. 2014. Social metrics included in prediction models on software engineering: A mapping study. *Proceedings of the 10th International Conference on Predictive Models in Software Engineering (PROMISE)*. ACM, Turin, Italy.

Index